ESSENTIAL STRATEGIES

ESSENTIAL

STRATEGIES

Integrating Reading and Writing

DANA C. ELDER
MARK LESTER

Eastern Washington University

MACMILLAN PUBLISHING COMPANY
New York

MAXWELL MACMILLAN CANADA
Toronto

MAXWELL MACMILLAN INTERNATIONAL
New York   Oxford   Singapore   Sydney

Editors: Barbara A. Heinssen and Tim Julet
Production Supervisors: Sharon Lee and Jeffrey H. Chen
Production Manager: Lynn Pearlman
Text Designer: Angela Foote
Cover Designer: Robert Freese
Cover photo: © John Marshall/AllStock

This book was set in Goudy by Americomp
and was printed and bound by Arcata Fairfield.
The cover was printed by New England Book Components, Inc.

Macmillan Publishing Company
866 Third Avenue, New York, New York 10022

Macmillan Publishing Company is part of
the Maxwell Communication Group of Companies.

Maxwell Macmillan Canada, Inc.
1200 Eglinton Avenue East
Suite 200
Don Mills, Ontario M3C 3N1

Library of Congress Cataloging-in-Publication Data

Elder, Dana C.
      Essential strategies : integrating reading and writing / Dana C.
Elder, Mark Lester.
        p.   cm.
      Includes index.
      ISBN 0-02-332220-9 (paper)
      1. English language—Rhetoric.   2. Reading (Higher education)
I. Lester, Mark.   II. Title.
PE1404.E43   1994
808'.042—dc20   93-1432
                                                                CIP

Printing: 1 2 3 4 5 6 7   Year: 4 5 6 7 8 9 0

In memory of Mina P. Shaughnessy (1925–1978), who opened the door to integrated language arts instruction and learning for us and for all students.

TO THE INSTRUCTOR

Why Use This Book?

With several hundred new composition textbooks and new editions of successful texts appearing each year, why should you choose this one?

▲ *Essential Strategies* is student-centered. Students participated in every aspect of this book's creation. Chapter themes were chosen with their interests in mind. Exercises and activities were shaped by student feedback. There is an unusually high number of actual student essays used with the permission of the student authors. These student essays provide models and low-risk learning experiences for other students. The "Final Editing" section of each chapter deals with the kinds of grammar and usage errors actually made by beginning student writers.

▲ *Essential Strategies* integrates all aspects of writing—reading, drafting, revising, vocabulary building, and grammar and usage—more than any other book on the market.

▲ *Essential Strategies* treats in each chapter a single writing technique and a single usage strategy in much greater depth than is found in any other book. Each chapter helps students achieve a high level of mastery that is both rewarding and motivating.

▲ *Essential Strategies* contains a wealth of language-rich activities and exercises that allow instructors to customize the material to meet the needs of their own classes.

▲ *Essential Strategies* is user-friendly. Every writing assignment is supported by model student essays that help the writer see what makes a good performance for this particular assignment. In the area of grammar and usage, Chapter 1 contains "A Survival Guide to Grammar Terms" that gives simple, practical definitions of basic grammar terms so that students and teachers share a common vocabulary for talking about grammar and usage problems. There is also a glossary at the end of the book that defines and illustrates every grammatical and usage term used in the book.

▲ *Essential Strategies* is instructor-friendly, too. Exercises appear in full-size format, and the pages on which they appear are perforated so that they can be removed and shared with the teacher and other students (tbus saving reproduction costs). The book is also supported by a detailed Teacher's Manual and a grammar and usage Test Packet that provide assessment tools and additional activities in support of the material covered in each chapter.

Chapter Organization

While the chapters are roughly sequenced in the order of difficulty, each chapter is a self-contained unit that can be taught independently of the other chapters—except that Chapter 1 should be taught first and Chapter 12 last. Most chapters have the following four sections:

Section 1: Reading

The reading in each chapter plays three roles: (1) it is an interesting sample of good writing in its own right, (2) it serves as a model of nonfiction writing, and (3) it provides background and/or a point of departure for the students' own writing in the Drafting and Revising sections.

The reading process is supported by pre- and post-reading discussion questions that employ both individual and peer group activities. These activities also serve as prewriting for the Drafting and Revising sections. Following each essay is a small, self-contained unit on vocabulary building that focuses on word families, prefixes, and suffixes—all using words taken from the reading.

Section 2: Drafting

Each of these sections includes pre-writing activities and a writing prompt. Each prompt elicits a kind of writing students will be called on to produce both in school and out, and each chapter's prompt has three parts: (1) the assignment itself, (2) samples of what other students have written in response to the assignment, and (3) suggestions on organizing that type of written discourse (usually in outline form).

Section 3: Revising

Each of these sections focuses on a single revision strategy. Each discusses a particular problem of style, organization, or audience, using actual students' essays to illustrate the problem. Next, the chapter gives the students a specific revision strategy for dealing with that problem. Finally, the students become proficient in that strategy by using it to revise additional student drafts before revising their own.

Section 4: Final Editing

This section concentrates on a single error of punctuation, mechanics, or usage. All the grammatical terms or concepts that are necessary to show students how to recognize and correct this type of error are included within the chapter. Thus each chapter stands alone and can be taught without reference to any other chapter. The pedagogical material in each chapter is based on an analysis of the actual causes of that error and provides students with specific, hands-on techniques that they can use to monitor and correct the same kind of error in their own writing. Students become proficient in using these techniques by editing other students' drafts before editing their own writing.

Acknowledgments

Our gratitude goes first of all to the many students who graciously contributed their ideas and their writing to this book. We also wish to thank Debbie Louie and Christy Friend for their original essays and Lynn Harty for her suggestions for students' use of dictionaries. Important production work was also contributed by Diane Weber and Lynn Harty, and our appreciation goes to them. Thanks also go to the following reviewers who offered many helpful suggestions during the manuscript stage: Donna Alden, New Mexico State University; Louise Baker, Augusta College; Sara M. Blake, El Camino College; Robyn Browder, Tidewater Community College; Michael Burke, East Field College; Santi Buscemi, Middlesex Community College; Jim Creel, Alvin Community College; Debra Journet, University of Louisville; Gilda Kelsey, University of Delaware; Ellen Andrews

Knodt, Pennsylvania State University; Diane Martin, Eastfield College; Maureen O'Brien, Springfield Technical Community College; Joyce Parris, Asheville-Buncombe Technical Community College; William Pierce, Prince Georges College; Fred Reynolds, Old Dominion University; William Sheidly, University of Connecticut; Juanita Stockwood, Haywood Community College; Howard B. Tinberg, Bristol Community College; and Carol Wershoven, Palm Beach Community College.

CONTENTS

CHAPTER 1 **COLLEGE LANGUAGE SKILLS**   2

What You Will Be Asked to Do   4
Language Skills Self-Assessments   8
Getting Started   13
Final Editing Diagnostics   17
A Survival Guide to Grammar Terms   19

CHAPTER 2 **TRAFFIC INCIDENTS**   36

SECTION 1 **READING ABOUT DETAILS OF PLACE**   38

A: Pre-Reading   38
    Discussion   38
    Reading Suggestions   41
    Vocabulary Preview   41

B: "Collision on a Country Road" by Edward Ziegler   42

C: Post-Reading   46

D: Vocabulary Building   47

    1. Different Uses of *post-*   47

    2. Different Uses of *trans-*   48

    3. Word Connotations   49

SECTION 2: DRAFTING WITH SPECIFIC DETAILS   50

A: Pre-Writing   50

B: Writing a First Draft   57

SECTION 3: REVISING FOR DETAILS OF PLACE   57

A: Details of Place   57

B: Revising Drafts of Student Traffic Narratives   58

C: Revising Your Draft   65

D: Helping Others to Revise Their Drafts   65

SECTION 4: FINAL EDITING FOR SENTENCE FRAGMENTS   66

A: Fragment Category One: Emphatic Adverbs   71

B: Fragment Category Two: *-ing* Words   74

C: Fragment Category Three: Noun Renamers   76

CHAPTER 3   CONSUMER LETTERS   80

SECTION 1: READING ABOUT CONSUMER COMMUNICATIONS   82

A: Pre-Reading   82

    Sample Consumer Letter 1   83

    Discussion   84

    Sample Consumer Letter 2   84

    Discussion   85

Reading Suggestions   86
Vocabulary Preview   86

B: "Consumer Communication" by D. C. Elder   87
C: Post-Reading   90
D: Vocabulary Building   91
    1. Two Meanings of Words Related to *note*   91
    2. *-ive* Adjectives Formed from Verbs   92
    3. Different Forms of *in-*   92

SECTION 2: **DRAFTING CONSUMER LETTERS   94**

A: Pre-writing: Sample Consumer Letters   94
B: Writing a First or Initial Draft: Consumer Letter Prompt   101

SECTION 3: **REVISING CONSUMER LETTERS FOR SPECIFICITY, CLARITY OF PURPOSE, AND FORM   103**

A: Specificity, Clarity of Purpose, and Form   103
B: Revising Drafts of Student Consumer Letters   103
C: Revising Your Consumer Letter   106
D: Helping Others to Revise Their Consumer Letters   107

SECTION 4: **FINAL EDITING FOR RUN-ON SENTENCES   107**

A: Generalization/Example Run-on Errors   111
B: Contrastive Run-on Errors   114
C: Commentary Run-on Errors   116

CHAPTER **4**   **APHORISMS   122**

SECTION 1: **READING FOR DETAILS OF EMOTION   124**

A: Pre-Reading   124
    Discussion   124
    Reading Suggestions   125
    Vocabulary Preview   126

B: "The World According to Claude" by Anthony Walton   126

C: Post-Reading   129

D: Vocabulary Building   130

    1. Words Related to *faith*   130

    2. Words Related to *cross*   131

    3. Words Related to *traction*   132

SECTION 2: **DRAFTING FOR DETAILS OF EMOTION   134**

A: Pre-Writing: Aphorisms and Details of Emotion   134

B: Writing a First or Initial Draft   138

SECTION 3: **REVISING FOR DETAILS OF EMOTION   138**

A: Details of Emotion   138

B: Revising Drafts of Student Essays   139

C: Revising Your Draft   147

D: Helping Others to Revise Their Drafts   148

SECTION 4: **FINAL EDITING FOR COMMAS AND COORDINATING CONJUNCTIONS   148**

A: Omitting Commas with Coordinating Conjunctions   149

B: Incorrectly Adding Commas with Coordinating Conjunctions   155

CHAPTER
5

THE SECOND SHIFT

Problems and Solutions in Two-Income Households   160

SECTION 1: **READING ABOUT TWO-INCOME FAMILIES   162**

A: Pre-Reading   162

    Discussion   163

    Reading Suggestions   163

    Vocabulary Preview   163

B: "The Second Shift: A Candid Look at the Revolution at Home" by Rebecca Allen   164

C: Post-Reading   167

D: Vocabulary Building   168

    1. Words Related to *tri-*   168

    2. Words Using Latin Numbers   168

    3. Using *-ify* and *-ication*   170

E.1: Additional Reading: "I Want a Wife" by Judy Syfers   171

E.2: Additional Reading: "Invest in Your Children's Future"   173

**SECTION 2: DRAFTING TO IDENTIFY A PROBLEM
AND SUGGEST A SOLUTION   174**

A: Pre-Writing   174

B: Writing a First or Initial Draft   178

SECTION 3: REVISING TO ADD QUALIFIERS   184

A: Categorical Statements and Qualifiers   184

B: Revising Drafts of Student Essays   185

C: Revising Your Draft   191

D: Helping Others to Revise Their Drafts   191

E: Optional Revision   191

**SECTION 4: FINAL EDITING FOR PUNCTUATING SUBORDINATING
CONJUNCTIONS AND CONJUNCTIVE ADVERBS   192**

A: Punctuating Subordinating Conjunctions   192

B: Punctuating Conjunctive Adverbs   197

C: Testing for Subordinating Conjunctions and Conjunctive Adverbs   204

CHAPTER 6   SERVICE INDUSTRY JOBS   210

**SECTION 1: READING FOR EXAMPLES THAT SUPPORT
GENERALIZATIONS   212**

A: Pre-Reading   212

    Discussion   213

    Reading Suggestions   213

    Vocabulary Preview   213

B: "Inside the Golden Arches" by Marcus Mabry   214

C: Post-Reading   217

D: Vocabulary Building   217

    1. Latin Phrases Used in Writing   217

    2. *-ee* and *-or* Pairs   219

SECTION 2: DRAFTING WITH SUPPORTING EXAMPLES   220

A: Pre-Writing   220

B: Writing a First or Initial Draft   225

SECTION 3: REVISING FOR SUPPORTING EXAMPLES   230

A: Adding Examples   230

B: Revising Drafts of Student Essays   231

C: Revising Your Draft   239

D: Helping Others to Revise Their Drafts   240

E: Optional Revision   240

SECTION 4: FINAL EDITING FOR WRONG CHOICE OF VERB TENSE   240

A: Past and Present Tense Shifting Errors   241

B: Failure to Use the Perfect Tenses   251

C: Failure to Shift Tense in Indirect Quotation   259

CHAPTER 7   CAREER TRAINING OPTIONS   266

SECTION 1: READING ABOUT CAREER TRAINING OPTIONS   268

A: Pre-Reading   268

    Discussion   268

    Reading Suggestions   269

    Vocabulary Preview   269

B: "Careers 101: Occupational Education In Community Colleges" by Neale Baxter   270

C: Post-Reading   278

D: Vocabulary Building   279

    1. Occupational terms in -*er,* *ist,* and -*ian*   279

    2. Noun/Verb Stress Shifts   280

    3. Changing *d* in Verbs to *s* in Nouns   282

SECTION 2: DRAFTING FOR CLARITY AND COMPLETENESS OF INFORMATION   283

A: Pre-Writing   283

B: Writing a First or Initial Draft   288

SECTION 3: REVISING FOR CLARITY AND COMPLETENESS OF INFORMATION   288

A: Clarity and Completeness of Information in Career Option Letters   288

B: Revising Drafts of Student Career Option Letters   289

C: Revising Your Letter About a Career Training Option   295

D: Optional Revision   295

SECTION 4: FINAL EDITING FOR SUBJECT-VERB AGREEMENT   295

A: "Lost Subject" Error   297

B: "All of the Above" Error   303

C: *There Is/There Was* Error   309

CHAPTER 8   CULTURAL DIFFERENCES   314

SECTION 1: READING ABOUT CULTURAL DIFFERENCES   316

A: Pre-Reading   316

    Discussion   317

    Reading Suggestions   317

    Vocabulary Preview   318

B.1: Four Guns' Speech   318

B.2: "Time Peace" by Debbie Louie   320

C: Post-Reading   323

D: Vocabulary Building   324

1. Words Relating to *dormus*, "house"   324

2. Different Meanings of the Prefix *dis-*   325

3. Words Derived from *prior/primus*, "first"   326

SECTION 2: DRAFTING WITH DETAILS AND EXAMPLES OF POSITIVE CULTURAL OR FAMILIAL DIFFERENCES   328

A: Pre-Writing: Comparing and Contrasting   328

B: Writing a First or Initial Draft   336

SECTION 3: REVISING BY ADDING TRANSITIONS   336

A: Adding Transitions   336

B: Revising Drafts of Student Essays   337

C: Revising Your Draft   345

D: Helping Others to Revise Their Drafts   346

E: Optional Revision   346

SECTION 4: FINAL EDITING FOR PRONOUN PROBLEMS   346

A: Wrong Pronoun Form in Noun Compounds   346

B: Unclear Pronoun Reference   351

C: Using Indefinite *You*   357

D: Using *They* to Refer to a Singular Antecedent   359

CHAPTER 9   ESSAY EXAMS   366

SECTION 1: READING ABOUT ESSAY EXAMS   368

A: Pre-Reading   368

Discussion   368

Reading Suggestions   369

Vocabulary Preview   369

B: "Learning to Succeed Under Pressure: Essay Exam Strategies" by Christy Friend   370

C: Post-Reading   377

D: Vocabulary Building   379

    1. Two Different Meanings of *re-*   379

    2. Changing Nouns to Adjectives by Adding *-ic*   380

SECTION 2: **UNDERSTANDING ESSAY EXAM PROMPTS AND ORGANIZING YOUR RESPONSE   382**

SECTION 3: **STUDYING FOR AND WRITING AN ESSAY EXAM   384**

"Packages" by Anthony Prakanis and Elliot Aronson 385

SECTION 4: **FINAL EDITING FOR RELATIVE CLAUSES   393**

A: Punctuating Restrictive and Nonrestrictive Clauses   393

B: Choosing Between *That* and *Which*   398

C: Choosing Between *Who* and *Whom*   400

CHAPTER 10   STRESS MANAGEMENT   408

SECTION 1: **READING FOR STRESS MANAGEMENT STRATEGIES   410**

A: Pre-Reading   410

    Discussion   410

    Reading Suggestions   411

    Vocabulary Preview   411

B: "Tips for Reducing Stress"   412

C: Post-Reading   413

D: Vocabulary Building   414

    1. Causative/Noncausative Verb Pairs: *lay/lie; set/sit; raise/rise*   414

E: Additional Reading: "A View from the Plateau" by George Leonard   418

SECTION 2: **RESEARCHING AND WRITING ABOUT A STRESS MANAGEMENT STRATEGY   420**

A: Pre-Writing   420

Finding Articles in the Library   420

Following Guidelines for Responsible Use of Sources   422

B: Writing a First or Initial Draft   423

SECTION 3: **REVISING TO MAKE RESPONSIBLE USE OF SOURCES   425**

A: Responsible Use of Sources   425

B: A Student Essay in Which the Writer Makes Responsible Use of Sources   428

C: Revising Student Drafts for Responsible Use of Sources   430

D: Revising Your Essay to Make Responsible Use of Sources   440

E: Optional Revision   441

SECTION 4: **FINAL EDITING FOR APOSTROPHE ERRORS   441**

A: Apostrophes in Contractions   441

B: Possessive Apostrophes   444

C: Apostrophes in Time Expressions   455

CHAPTER 11   BEING EDUCATED   460

SECTION 1: **READING OPINIONS ON WHAT IT MEANS TO BE EDUCATED   462**

A: Pre-Reading   462

Discussion   463

Reading Suggestions   463

B.1: "Living Education" by Michele Cooke   464

B.2: "Learning on the Farm" by Randall Trinkle   466

C: Post-Reading   467

D: Vocabulary Building   468

    1. Building Words with *en-* and *ment-*   468

    2. Words Related to *form*   470

    3. Words Derived from *specere*   471

SECTION 2: **DRAFTING TO PRESENT YOUR OPINION AND ACKNOWLEDGE OTHER PERSPECTIVES ON THE ISSUE   472**

A: Pre-Writing   472

B: Writing a First or Initial Draft   478

SECTION 3: **REVISING TO ACKNOWLEDGE OTHER PERSPECTIVES ON THE ISSUE   478**

A: Other Aspects of an Issue or Idea   478

B: Revising Drafts of Student Essays   479

C: Revising Your Draft   493

D: Helping Others to Revise Their Drafts   494

E: Optional Revision   494

SECTION 4: **FINAL EDITING FOR FAULTY PARALLELISM   494**

A: Elements That Are Different Parts of Speech   499

B: Faulty Verb Form Parallelism   504

CHAPTER 12   **USING COLLEGE LANGUAGE SKILLS   512**

Revising Your Best Paper   514

Final Editing Strategies   520

Afterword 526

APPENDIX I: GLOSSARY OF GRAMMAR TERMS   527

APPENDIX II: "USING A DICTIONARY" BY LYNN HARTY   538

APPENDIX III: EASILY CONFUSED WORDS   543

INDEX   548

ESSENTIAL STRATEGIES

CHAPTER
◄►
1

COLLEGE
LANGUAGE
SKILLS

This book is an opportunity for you to share, practice, and enjoy language skills as tools for private thinking, communication with others, and educational and career advancement. This is a language skills book. It offers lessons and practice in talking, listening, reading, writing, and revising papers you have written. It includes instruction and practice in correcting grammar errors in your writing (editing), and there are also lessons and exercises designed to help you increase your vocabulary.

In this first chapter we, the authors, will offer some ideas on the kinds of things you will be asked to do and why you will be asked to do them. Our ideas are only part of this process. Because the whole purpose here is to help you to gain more and more language skills, you will be asked to contribute to this introductory chapter. Even here you will need to read, speak, listen, write, and edit.

What You Will Be Asked to Do

Because most people like to know what is coming and what they will be asked to do, the following few pages describe the way this book is organized. Some reasons why people would do all these activities are also included in these pages.

Each chapter of this book, except the first, the ninth, and the last, is organized in the following pattern:

Section 1: Reading
    A. Pre-Reading
    B. Reading
    C. Post-Reading
    D. Vocabulary

Section 2: Drafting
    A. Pre-Writing
    B. Writing a First Draft

Section 3: Revising
    A. Learning a Revision Strategy
    B. Revising Drafts of Student Essays
    C. Revising Your Draft
    D. Revising Someone Else's Draft

Section 4: Final Editing

Section 1: Reading

Reading is one of the best ways to learn about things and about language. Therefore each chapter contains one or more readings. Before reading, you will be asked to do some activities. These **Pre-Reading** activities involve talking with and listening to others and thinking about the subject of each reading before you read it. In addition, before each reading you will find questions that suggest what you might look for in the reading.

You are asked to do pre-reading activities for several reasons. First, pre-reading discussions help you to remember and think about what you already know about the subject of the reading. Second, hearing what others say about a subject, their experiences and their opinions, provides you with even more ideas. Third, talking with others is an excellent way to practice your communication skills.

There are two things you should remember to do while sharing ideas with others:

1. Listen carefully to others. When you don't understand what is being said, ask politely for an explanation or an example. Communicating with others is not arguing with them. Every person has a right to his or her own ideas and opinions.

2. Every person should contribute. You need to share your ideas, and you need to encourage others to share theirs.

Every chapter contains one or more **Readings**. These are essays. Essays are a major type of written communication. In essays writers present ideas and opinions and include facts, details, examples, and reasons to make those ideas and opinions clear to the person who reads the essay. An essay always has a purpose. The purpose could be to share information, to suggest ways to solve a problem, or to change how the reader thinks about something.

Some of the essays in this book were written by professional writers, and some were written by students. Some are more difficult to read than others. Before some of the readings are **Vocabulary Previews**. These include brief definitions of words found in the readings. Normally, reading an essay twice is a good idea. Rereading is an important learning strategy. The second time you read an essay, you get more out of it.

Following most of the readings are **Post-Reading** discussion questions/suggestions. These offer you additional opportunities to review the contents of the readings and to develop your own thoughts about the readings' contents.

There are three kinds of post-reading questions/suggestions in each chapter—Remembering, Analyzing, and Discovering:

Remembering: These questions/suggestions ask that you remember the contents of what you have read. Recalling facts and details is a key studying and learning skill.

Analyzing: These questions/suggestions ask about the writer's purpose, the kinds of facts, details, and examples the writer uses, how the writing is organized, and the writer's audience. They ask not just what the author wrote but why he or she wrote it that way.

Discovering: These questions/suggestions ask you to think and talk about your own experiences and opinions as they relate to the contents and topics of the readings. They ask you to make connections between what you read and your own life.

Vocabulary lessons and exercises appear in each chapter. Basically, the more words you know and use, the better. This book emphasizes words that come from Latin into English. Latin, the language of ancient Rome, is one of the foundations of modern English. While learning and working with these English words based on Latin words, pay attention to how the words are made. This will help you to understand still other words that are made in the same ways. Also, learning new words can be fun. You can use your new words both in and out of class. Better still, you can use these words in your own writing.

Section 2: Drafting

Good writers use a writing process. They get ready to write (pre-write), write first or initial drafts of their essays, and then rewrite (revise) them to make them even better.

Each chapter contains **Pre-Writing** activities. These activities are designed to help you to discover, remember, and organize the material you will put into your own writing. Good writers don't just write. They think about and plan their writing before they write. Since different kinds of writing call for different kinds of pre-writing, the more pre-writing strategies you know, the better.

Also in Section 2 of each chapter is a prompt. A **prompt** tells you what you are supposed to write about. Following the prompts in some chapters are suggested outlines for organizing your writing. You may or may not use these outlines—it is your choice. Sometimes, however, having an outline makes it easier to organize and write about your ideas.

Section 3: Revising

After you have written a first or initial draft of a letter or an essay, it is time to *revise* it to make it even better. Each chapter contains one **Revision** strategy. Just as knowing many ways to pre-write helps a writer, knowing many ways to revise is also beneficial. Revising is not correcting grammar, punctuation, and spelling errors. Revising is changing what you have written to make your ideas clearer and more attractive to your readers.

Because practice is one of the best ways to learn anything, the Section 3 in each chapter presents a revision strategy, invites you to practice the strategy on other students' writing, and then asks you to use the revision strategy on your own writing and on the writing of the people with whom you are working.

Section 4: Final Editing

The very last step in the process of writing is **Editing**. Editing is checking your revised draft for spelling, typographical, punctuation, and grammar errors. Once found, these errors should be corrected.

Beginning to Work with Others

In groups of four, five, or six students, introduce yourself to the people in your group, and then tell them about something you do really well. Then share ideas with these people about (1) your favorite kinds of reading, (2) your favorite kinds of writing, and (3) one word that you know and use that not everybody knows and uses.

Getting Started

By the time you read this, you will have read, spoken, heard, and written about language skills. You will have thought about them. You will have answered questions about your own language habits and skills. All of these activities can be considered pre-writing for the paper you are about to write.

The purpose of this first paper is for you to show your instructor your writing skills. Your paper will not be graded, but still you should do your very best.

✓ Prompt:

Using specific details and examples to support your opinion, write a paper in response to this question: "What is the purpose (or purposes) of a college education?"

The following papers were written by students in response to this prompt. Read them. Then write your own paper answering the question, "What is the purpose (purposes) of a college education?" Write what you believe rather than what you think the instructor wants you to write.

Student Paper 1

There are many purposes of a college education.

First of all, meeting new friends, friends that you will have for probably the rest of your life, because if you don't have friends, your life will be boring and uneventful.

Moving out of the house is a great purpose for going to college. It gives you a chance to be on your own for the first time and teaches you how to live on your own.

Another purpose of a college education is spending your parents' money. What other better investment is there? When they retire and need money, you know who they're going to turn to.

The most important purpose of a college education probably would be to learn the most you could possibly learn about the profession you would like to spend the rest of your life doing. College provides so many different opportunities for you to explore to see if you would be interested in them as professions. If you try different opportunities you are bound to find the right one, which you could spend the rest of your working life doing. If you don't go to college, the chances of you finding a job that pays good and that you enjoy doing are slim. Having a college education almost promises a good paying job that you like.

The final and most important purpose of a college education is that when you graduate from college you will know how to play quarters and tap a keg. (Just kidding)

Jeff M.

Student Paper 2

The purpose of a college education has increased greatly in the last few years.

With all the increase in computer knowledge and high tech machinery, a higher education is needed to compete in today's world.

A job that took twenty people to do in the 60's and 70's, now only takes a few people with the help of our modern day equipment. Therefore there are that many more people out looking for the better jobs. Common sense tells us that the ones with more education will most likely get the job. Sure, McDonalds, Burger King, and Wendys can always use hamburger flippers. And, sure, Safeway, Albertson, and Excell can always use more box boys. I'm sure you could even get on with one of the many gas stations around your town. But is that where you want to spend the rest of your days? The last I heard, Shell doesn't have a great retirement program.

Another great reason is the fact that the majority of your friends quit after high school, and you've got the guts to go for more.

Being a graduate from high school is no longer a factor in today's world. Before our grandparents were kids, if someone had gone to school for a few years they were well off. Then for my grandparents, finishing grade school was the main focus. When my parents were in school, a high school diploma was what you needed to do well in the world. Now bosses want even more education from their employees.

College also offers a much higher level of education than one can get in high school. People can learn and specialize in a field that they enjoy.

A person who attends college has the chance to meet many other students and can build many friendships.

There are some major reasons that college education is important. There are many others that could have been touched upon.

David F.

Student Paper 3

My purpose (or purposes) of a college education is that the more knowledge you gain, the better off in life you will be. I mean you will or could have a better job (which means more money), better benefits, nicer house, car, clothes, and most of all just a more successful lifestyle.

Another purpose of mine for a college education is that a lot of people after graduating just hang around doing nothing. They might have graduated three or four years ago and still come to the high school's parties. I definitely don't want to be one of them.

A third reason for me is to make others happy with me, like my mother, father, brother, sister, and just my family in general. Also my girlfriend's mom, who is going back to school now at UPS in Tacoma, also is very proud of me. I like it when people are proud of me.

A fourth reason is, among all of my friends, after graduation college is the next step. It's kind of like the thing to do. When we talk at parties or large gatherings back at home, that's what everyone talks about. If you're not in college or if I weren't here, I'd probably have nothing to talk about and feel out of place.

Next, a really good purpose (for me at least) is for sports. I love sports, and I wouldn't have a chance to compete in them if I wasn't here. I really enjoy the challenge of making myself better or the best I can be. Also everybody always says that college is the best part of your life, and I want to enjoy the best part of my life. Plus I always wanted to find out if this is true or not, and what better way to find out than to experience it.

In closing, I would like to restate that to me the most important reason or purpose of my being here is to learn so I will be successful in life and provide the better things in life for not only myself but my family and others around me, including the community.

Terry R.

Now write your paper responding to the question, "What is the purpose (or purposes) of a college education?"

Self-Test 5: The pronoun substitution test for noun phrases.

Underline the noun phrases that follow the verb. Show that your answer is correct by rewriting the sentence in the space provided, substituting a pronoun for the underlined noun phrase. The first question is done as an example.

1. The doctors discovered the cause of the infection eventually.
*Answer: The doctors discovered **the cause of the infection** eventually.*
             *The doctors discovered   **it**   eventually.*

2. Dust covered the entire surface of the table.

_____

3. I completed the lengthy questionnaires promptly.

_____

4. The students performed the difficult choral work by Brahms beautifully.

_____

5. The reviewers criticized the remake of *The Maltese Falcon* without mercy.

_____

6. The government took all the suppliers of the defective parts to court.

_____

VERB PHRASES: A verb phrase consists of a **verb**, the head of the verb phrase, and any number of optional adverbs and prepositional phrases that modify the verb. Most verbs also require a **complement** in order to be grammatical. For example, the verb *fix* requires a noun phrase as a complement; that is, when we engage in the act of fixing, we must fix *something*:

The carpenter <u>fixed the broken railing</u>.
         Verb   Complement
              Verb Phrase

We cannot use the verb *fix* without a complement: **The carpenter fixed.* The verb *sneeze*, however, is one of a group of verbs that does not require a complement:

The carpenter <u>**sneezed**</u>.

The relationship between verbs and their complements is extraordinarily complex and subtle. A good deal of what it means to "know" English resides in our knowing the possible relationships between verbs and all of their various complements.

Verb phrases are also called **predicates**.

✓ Helpful Hint:

Most verb phrases can be identified by asking a "what do" question. For example, the "what do" question for the sentence *The carpenter fixed the broken railing* is *What did the carpenter do?* The answer, *fixed the broken railing*, is the verb phrase. The "what do" question for the sentence *The carpenter sneezed* is *What did the carpenter do?* The answer is the one word verb phrase *sneezed*.

Self-Test 6: The "what do" test for verb phrases

For each of the following sentences, ask the "what do" question to get back the verb phrase as the answer. The first two questions are done as examples.

1. Ralph called the reporter.
"What do" question: *What did Ralph do?*
Answer: *Called the reporter*

2. Our unit administers all the new programs.
"What do" question: *What does our unit do?*
Answer: *Administers all the new programs*

3. The new owners repainted the room.
"What do" question: _____
Answer: _____

4. The students made some good suggestions.
"What do" question: _____
Answer: _____

5. The manager wrote down the applicant's name and address.
"What do" question: _____
Answer: _____

6. Sam deliberately ignored the fat man's demand to produce the statue.
"What do" question: _____
Answer: _____

7. All this grammar gives me a headache.
"What do" question: _____
Answer: _____

PREPOSITIONAL PHRASES: Prepositional phrases are made up of two pieces: a **preposition** that serves as the head of the phrase plus a noun phrase that is called the **object of the preposition.** Prepositions are words such as *across, after, at, before, by, during, in, of,* and *with.* Prepositions together with their following object noun phrase make up prepositional phrases, such as the following examples:

Prepositional phrase	=	Preposition	+	Noun Phrase
across the river		across		the river
after it		after		it
during our lunch		during		our lunch
by Shakespeare		by		Shakespeare
in a minute		in		a minute
of mine		of		mine
with an old friend		with		an old friend

C: Clauses

Clauses consist of two phrases: (1) a **noun phrase** and (2) a **verb phrase.** For example, the sentence *The girl next door plays the piano* consists of these two phrases:

The **girl** next door   **plays** the piano.
  Noun Phrase   **Verb Phrase**

In a clause, the noun phrase and the verb phrase enter into a special relationship. The verb in the verb phrase must **agree** with the head noun in the noun phrase. In the preceding example, *plays* agrees with *girl*, the head of the noun phrase. This relationship is called **subject–verb agreement.** The head noun in this noun phrase is the **subject,** and the noun phrase the subject is in is called the **subject noun phrase.** If we change the subject noun from *girl* (singular) to *girls* (plural), the verb *plays* (singular) must also change to the plural form *play* in order to continue to agree with the new subject noun:

The **girls** next door   **play** the piano.
  Noun Phrase   **Verb Phrase**

✓ Helpful Hint:

A good way to identify subject noun phrases is to ask a "who" or "what" question. The answer will be the subject noun phrase. For example, the "who/what" question for the sentence *The girl next door plays the piano* is *Who plays the piano?* The answer, *The girl next door*, is the subject noun phrase.

Self-Test 7: The "who/what" test for subject noun phrases

For each of the following sentences, ask the "who/what" question, and then give the subject noun phrase (NP) answer. The first two questions are done as examples.

1. The earthquake last night cracked our living room window.
"Who/what" question: **What** *cracked our living room window?*
Subject NP answer: *The earthquake last night*

2. The children on the bus were making an unholy racket.
"Who/what" question: **Who** *were making an unholy racket?*
Subject NP answer: *The children on the bus*

3. Many of the reporters began leaving to file their stories.
"Who/what" question: _____
Subject NP answer: _____

4. A sinister-looking man in a black cape came to the door.
"Who/what" question: _____
Subject NP answer: _____

5. An apartment in our building is going to be rented.
"Who/what" question: _____
Subject NP answer: _____

6. Using a harsh detergent can eventually ruin your clothes.
"Who/what" question: _____
Subject NP answer: _____

There are two types of clauses: **independent clauses** and **dependent clauses**.

Independent clauses are **sentences**. Every sentence must contain at least one independent clause. The example sentence used earlier, *The girl next door plays the piano*, is an independent clause. It is possible to have more than one independent clause in a single sentence provided that the two independent clauses are either (1) joined by a comma and a coordinating conjunction, or (2) joined by a semicolon (;), as shown in these examples:

<u>This is an independent clause</u>, and <u>this is another one</u>,
    Independent Clause   **Independent Clause**

<u>This is an independent clause</u>; <u>this is another one</u>.
    Independent Clause   **Independent Clause**

Independent clauses are also called **main clauses**.

Dependent clauses can never be a sentence by themselves. Dependent clauses must always be attached to (and be "dependent" on) an independent clause. In the sentence *I hate doing dishes because we can never get enough hot water*, the independent clause is *I hate doing dishes*, and the dependent clause is *because we can never get enough hot water:*

I hate doing dishes because we can never get enough hot water.
Independent Clause   **Dependent Clause**

The independent clause can stand alone as a sentence by itself:

I hate doing dishes.

However, the dependent clause cannot stand alone as a sentence:

*Because we can never get enough hot water.

✓ Helpful Hint:

Independent clauses can always be turned into a question that can be answered "yes" or "no." Dependent clauses, phrases, or any other kind of grammatical unit that is not an independent clause cannot be turned into a "yes/no" question. For example, we can turn the independent clause *I hate doing dishes* into the "yes/no" question *Do I hate doing dishes?* However, we cannot turn the dependent clause *because we can never get enough hot water* into a "yes/no" question: *Because can we never get enough hot water?*

Self-Test 8: The "yes/no" test for identifying independent clauses

Below are a mixture of independent and dependent clauses punctuated with periods. Write **independent** underneath each independent clause. Confirm your answer by changing each independent clause into a "yes/no" question. The first question is done as an example.

1. I went home and took a shower.
Answer: *I went home and took a shower.*
            Independent
   Did I go home and take a shower?

2. Whatever you want.

_____

3. You wouldn't understand.

_____

4. After you called about the package from the mail room.

_____

5. He is going to take a nap.

_____

6. If it's okay with you.

_____

The final grammar term we will discuss is the **coordinating conjunction**. The coordinating conjunctions are *and, or, but, for, nor, so,* and *yet.* Coordinating conjunctions join two or more elements that play the same grammatical role. When two or more elements are joined by a coordinating conjunction, they are called a **compound.** Here are examples of various kinds of compounds, all joined with the coordinating conjunction *and*:

Compound subject:	<u>John and Mary</u> live in Chicago.
Compound complement:	Mary bought <u>a notebook and some pencils.</u>
Compound verb phrase:	John <u>lives in Chicago and drives to work.</u>
Compound sentence:	<u>Mary is learning Greek, and I am learning Italian.</u>

Self-Test 9: Identifying compound elements joined by a coordinating conjunction

In the following sentences, the coordinating conjunction *and* is in bold. Underline the elements joined by *and*. Underneath, write the name of the compound: compound subject, compound predicate, compound verb phrase, or compound sentence. The first question is done as an example.

1. The children rang the doorbell **and** then ran away.
Answer: *The children <u>rang the doorbell **and** then ran away.</u>*
Compound verb phrase

2. Ralph **and** Alice never agree on anything.

3. I packed some casual clothes **and** one dressy outfit.

4. In old movies the hero always defeated the bad guys **and** got the girl.

5. I washed the car, **and** my brother waxed it.

6. The receptionist answers the phone **and** takes messages.

Answers to Self-Tests

Self-Test 1: The *the* test for nouns

1. defend/defense <u>*the defend</u>   <u>the **defense**</u>
Noun

2. authority/authorize *the **authority**   *the authorize*
   <u>Noun</u>

3. lengthen/length **the lengthen   the **length***
   <u>Noun</u>

4. concession/concede *the **concession**   *the concede*
   <u>Noun</u>

5. discover/ discovery **the discover   the **discovery***
   <u>Noun</u>

6. performance/perform *the **performance**   *the perform*
   <u>Noun</u>

Self-Test 2: The *will* test for verbs

1. realization/realize **will realization   will **realize***
   <u>Verb</u>

2. enlarge/large *will **enlarge**   *will large*
   <u>Verb</u>

3. sale/sell **will sale   will **sell***
   <u>Verb</u>

4. authority/authorize **will authority   will **authorize***
   <u>Verb</u>

5. choose/choice *will **choose**   *will choice*
   <u>Verb</u>

6. publish/publication *will **publish**   *will publication*
   <u>Verb</u>

Self-Test 3: The *very* test for adjectives

1. widen/wide **very widen   very **wide***
   <u>Adj</u>

2. religious/religion *very **religious**   *very religion*
   <u>Adj</u>

3. profession/professional **very profession   very **professional***
   <u>Adj</u>

4. beautiful/beauty *very **beautiful**   *very beauty*
   <u>Adj</u>

5. likelihood/likely **very likelihood   very **likely***
   <u>Adj</u>

6. difficulty/difficult *very difficulty   very **difficult***
                                                    Adj

Self-Test 4: The movement test for adverbs that modify verbs

1. I **usually** work on Monday. *__Usually__ I work on Monday.*
                                        Adv

2. We walk in the park **often**. *__Often__ we walk in the park.*
                                        Adv

3. I hung up the phone **promptly**. *__Promptly__ I hung up the phone.*
                                            Adv

4. Harry is always **prompt**. *Can't move **prompt**. **Prompt** is not an adverb.*

5. The reaction was **quick**. *Can't move **quick**. **Quick** is not an adverb.*

6. It was all over **quickly**. *__Quickly__, it was all over.*
                                        Adv

Self-Test 5: The pronoun substitution test for noun phrases

1. The doctors discovered the cause of the infection eventually.
Answer: *The doctors discovered **the cause of the infection** eventually.*
              *The doctors discovered **it** eventually.*

2. *Dust covered **the entire surface of the table**.*
*Dust covered **it**.*

3. *I completed **the lengthy questionnaires** promptly.*
*I completed **them** promptly.*

4. *The students performed **the difficult choral work by Brahms** beautifully.*
*The students performed **it** beautifully.*

5. *The reviewers criticized **the remake of The Maltese Falcon** without mercy.*
*The reviewers criticized **it** without mercy.*

6. *The government took **all the suppliers of the defective parts** to court.*
*The government took **them** to court.*

Self-Test 6: The "what do" test for verb phrases

1. Ralph called the reporter.
   "What do" question: *What did Ralph do?*
   Answer: *Called the reporter*

2. Our unit administers all the new programs.
   "What do" question: *What does our unit do?*
   Answer: *Administers all the new programs*

3. The new owners repainted the room.
   "What do" question: *What did the new owners do?*
   Answer: *Repainted the room*

4. The students made some good suggestions.
   "What do" question: *What did the students do?*
   Answer: *Made some good suggestions*

5. The manager wrote down the applicant's name and address.
   "What do" question: *What did the manager do?*
   Answer: *Wrote down the applicant's name and address*

6. Sam deliberately ignored the fat man's demand to produce the statue.
   "What do" question: *What did Sam do?*
   Answer: *Deliberately ignored the fat man's demand to produce the statue*

7. All this grammar gives me a headache.
   "What do" question: *What does all this grammar do?*
   Answer: *Gives me a headache*

Self-Test 7: The "who/what" test for subject noun phrases.

1. The earthquake last night cracked our living room window.
   "Who/what" test: **What** *cracked our living room window?*
   Subject NP answer: *The earthquake last night*

2. The children on the bus were making an unholy racket.
   "Who/what" test: **Who** *were making an unholy racket?*
   Subject NP answer: *The children on the bus*

3. Many of the reporters began leaving to file their stories.
   "Who/what" question: *Who began leaving to file their stories?*
   Subject NP answer: *Many of the reporters*

4. A sinister-looking man in a black cape came to the door.
   "Who/what" question: *Who came to the door?*
   Subject NP answer: *A sinister-looking man in a black cape*

5. An apartment in our building is going to be rented.
   "Who/what" question: *What is going to be rented?*
   Subject NP answer: *An apartment in our building*

6. Using a harsh detergent can eventually ruin your clothes.
   "Who/what" question: *What can eventually ruin your clothes?*
   Subject NP answer: *Using a harsh detergent*

Self-Test 8: The "yes/no" test for identifying independent clauses

1. I went home and took a shower.
   Answer: <u>*I went home and took a shower*</u>.
   Independent
   Did I go home and take a shower?

2. *Whatever you want.*
   There is no "yes/no" question because it is not an independent clause.

3. <u>*You wouldn't understand.*</u>
   Independent
   Wouldn't you understand?

4. *After you called about the package from the mail room.*
   There is no "yes/no" question because it is not an independent clause.

5. <u>*He is going to take a nap*</u>.
   Independent
   Is he going to take a nap?

6. *If it's okay with you.*
   There is no "yes/no" question because it is not an independent clause.

Self-Test 9: Identifying compound elements joined by a coordinating conjunction

1. The children rang the doorbell **and** then ran away.
   Answer: *The children <u>rang the doorbell</u> **and** <u>then ran away</u>*
   Compound verb phrase

2. *Ralph* **and** *Alice never agree on anything.*
   **Compound
   subject**

3. I packed *some casual clothes* **and** *one dressy outfit.*
   Compound complement

4. *In old movies the hero* *always defeated the bad guys* **and** *got the girl.*
   Compound verb phrase

5. *I washed the car,* **and** *my brother waxed it.*
   Compound sentence

6. The receptionist answers the phone **and** takes messages.
   Compound verb phrase

TRAFFIC INCIDENTS

◀▶ Reading about Details of Place
1

A: Pre-Reading

Things happen to people, and people tell others about these happenings. Telling stories about events in our lives, large and small, satisfies several human needs.

First, when sharing the details of an experience with someone, we must select details from the experience and put them into an understandable order. This process of selecting and putting details in order actually helps us to understand the experience better. The more we understand an incident that has happened to us, the better we are able to see what that happening might mean. Are there lessons learned that might be useful in the future? In that situation, what did we do that helped, and what might we do differently if we face a similar situation in the future?

Second, telling someone about something that happened also satisfies the human need to share experience. We share our experiences in order to connect ourselves with others. The person listening to the story may have had a similar experience or may learn something from our story. The listener may even help us to understand our own experience better.

Details are the raw materials of stories, and details of place are especially important. Incidents happen in specific places. A person hearing or reading a story needs details of place to understand the events in the story. The person telling or writing the story needs to provide these details.

The title of the reading in this chapter, "Collision on a Country Road," contains a detail of place. From the title alone the reader can assume that this reading will be about something that happened, a traffic accident, and that this accident happened in a particular place.

Pre-Reading Activities

Discussion

1. Details of place work very well in stories when they require the listener or reader to think—when the listener or reader gets to figure out what the details mean. For

example, details about weather conditions in a story work better when the listener or reader has to add them up. Look at the two following sentences:

a.   It was a dark and stormy night.

b.   Through the steamy windshield, Anna could see the center line on the highway only in the instant after the wiper blade had shaved the rain from the glass. The car's headlights reached out a few feet and then were swallowed by the night.

The second sentence allows the reader to think, to add up the details and know it was "a dark and stormy" night.

Take five minutes and create some details of place for one of the following sentences, details that let the reader or listener add up what the details mean.

Now share the sentences you have created with others and talk a little about what the details in those sentences suggest to them. Feel free to change your details and to suggest ways others might make their details even better.

2.   Everyone knows that driving or riding in a motor vehicle can be dangerous. With others, discuss some driving conditions that may be dangerous.

a. It was a sunny summer day.

b. _____

_____

_____

_____

_____

_____

a. The old house looked haunted.

b. _____

_____

_____

_____

_____

_____

a. It was a lonely stretch of highway.

b. _____

_____

_____

_____

_____

_____

Reading Suggestions

(Keep these suggestions in mind as you read "Collision on a Country Road.")

1. Some people think that the most important question about a traffic accident is "Whose fault was it?" What does the author of "Collision on a Country Road" think is the most important question?

2. Underline, highlight, or copy details that the author uses that help you to get a sense of place while reading.

3. What is the author's purpose? What does he want the reader to think, feel, or do as a result of reading what he has written?

Vocabulary Preview

deceleration: slowing down. (The car <u>decelerated</u> as it approached the stop sign.)

inconceivable: unthinkable. (That people would vote to increase taxes is <u>inconceivable</u>.)

meticulously: with close attention to detail. (The banker reviewed the loan application <u>meticulously</u>.)

profusely: abundantly. (The president praised the company's workers <u>profusely</u>.)

trauma: damage caused by sudden injury. (In addition to a broken leg, the victim suffered emotional <u>trauma</u>.)

triage: sorting. (The medics completed <u>triage</u> and put the most seriously injured accident victim in the first ambulance to arrive on the scene.)

velocity: speed. (The <u>velocity</u> of a motor vehicle is normally measured in miles per hour.)

B: Reading

"Collision on a Country Road"

BY EDWARD ZIEGLER

Priscilla Van Steelant, 39, finished shopping just before 12:30 P.M. and headed north on Madison Road in Culpeper, Va. It was an unseasonably warm day for March but not warm enough to put down the top of her dark-red '89 convertible. She took Route 229 toward the turnoff onto County Route 640, which led to her home in Jeffersonton.

Meanwhile, Ron Woody, a 22-year-old carpenter, finished hammering nails into two-by-four studs in a house he was helping build. He glanced at his watch. He would have to hurry if he was going to be on time to pick up his wife in town.

When he wheeled out of the driveway in his bright-red '89 sedan, it was nearly 12:40 P.M. He made a left turn on County Route 640 and slipped a borrowed cassette into the tape deck.

Van Steelant had already turned off the main road. She was heading east along the same quiet, rural Route 640. The road winds through rolling green fields and forests just east of the Blue Ridge Mountains.

Monica Stover, 21, was in her grandmother's house when she heard screeching tires and a thud that shook the house. She rushed outside and down the driveway. Two cars were smashed so horribly that she began to tremble. She hurried back inside and dialed 911.

Neighbor Ruth Gillespie jumped up from her desk when she heard the tremendous crash. Running outside, she saw that two cars had met head-on in front of her house. No one was moving. Certain that people were dying, Gillespie ran back inside to phone for help.

Seconds later, pagers all over town began to emit their signals, summoning emergency-services volunteers. Rescue Squad 2nd Lt. Chick Lauffer and two crew members were parked in a convenience-store lot a few miles south of the site when they heard the call over the ambulance radio: "Auto accident—two vehicles—personal injury. Route 640 about one mile east of Route 220." Knowing 640 as a narrow and straight road, Lauffer immediately suspected a head-on collision. He turned on the siren and moved at high speed toward the scene.

Grim Expectations. A burly rescue-squad veteran, Lauffer was well acquainted with death. In his 27 years' experience, he had served as a shock-trauma technician in nearly a thousand car accidents, heart attacks, fires and drownings.

He knew all too well that most head-on collisions mean grisly death or terrible personal injury. Drivers are generally found unconscious, bleeding profusely, imprisoned in twisted metal and breathing in rales and whistles—the burbling sounds of air trying to move through fluid. That's what Lauffer and his crewmates, Steve Miller and Kenneth Mills, fully expected to find.

Approaching a rise on Route 640, Lauffer saw Gillespie waving a red flag at him. Two wrecks lay before him with no sign of either driver. He radioed his assessment of the crash to the approaching police and fire squads.

As he walked to the cars, Lauffer had to make a series of fast triage judgments. Who needs help most? Who is most likely to survive? A bright-red Chrysler Le Baron lay crushed, its hood and roof panel buckled upward, its windshield smashed and partially torn from its frame. The left door had been severely crumpled, the engine rammed into the fire wall. Lauffer couldn't see a body inside the car or anywhere around it.

Twenty feet away was another Le Baron, its rear end tossed into a ditch. The convertible's hood had been smashed back, the canvas top had popped open and the left front wheel, its tire flattened, lay at a wildly canted angle. The whole automobile had been bent into a bowed shape.

Lauffer approached the convertible. There was a woman seated on the passenger's side. "Were you in this collision?" he asked.

"Yes."

"You all right?"

"Yes, I'm all right," Van Steelant responded.

"Is the driver around?"

"I am the driver."

"*You're* the driver?"

It was inconceivable. Surveying the inside of the vehicle, Lauffer saw the left side, the dashboard and floorboard all collapsed inward toward the driver's seat.

Lauffer asked her what day it was. "March 12," she answered. He asked her who the President was. "George Bush," came the reply.

Convinced that she was oriented as to time and place, he directed Miller to complete a secondary examination.

Next Lauffer asked Mills to help him find the driver of the other car. After peering under the sedan and seeing no one, they started searching up on the bank and back into the woods. Lauffer had seen wrecks where the driver had been thrown out of sight. Then Lauffer looked up to see a tall young man limping along the road toward them.

Scraps of Fabric. A few minutes before, Gillespie had seen Ron Woody, seeming dazed, climb out of his smashed car. After assuring her that he was all right, he told her he had to make a call. She showed him the way to her phone.

"Honey," she heard him say, "I just had a wreck and won't be able to pick you up. . . . Probably totaled."

When Lauffer spied him back at the accident scene, he asked, "You the driver of that car?"

"Yes, sir."

Again Lauffer was skeptical. He studied the twisted metal hulk, then the six-foot-two-inch young man. Nothing in his long experience had prepared him for the bizarre contradiction between the demolished wreck and its uninjured driver.

As Woody complained of an aching shin, Mills suggested that he sit down on the transom of the ambulance. Mills slit Woody's blue jeans with a pair of bandage scissors to examine his leg. "All I saw was 'road rash,' " he later said. "His leg was bruised and discolored. His arm had a scratch on it, but it had stopped bleeding."

Meanwhile, Van Steelant complained of aching legs and feet. Lauffer recommended that both drivers be transported to the hospital for further observation, but neither wanted to go.

It was only then that Lauffer re-examined the two ruined automobiles. Atop each steering wheel was the flimsy remnant of nylon that minutes before had been an inflated air bag. "My God," he said aloud, as the realization came to him. These scraps of fabric had made it possible for the two drivers to cheat both death and serious injury.

When Virginia State Police Trooper Gary Dawson arrived, he seated both drivers in his patrol car and made out his report. He measured distances, skid marks and other indications of the angles and velocities of the crash.

Two hours later, two large flatbed trucks came to haul the untowable wrecks away. Woody's wife, Kim, showed up and drove him home. Trooper Dawson took Van Steelant to her house.

Ron Woody later decided he wanted to retrieve one thing from his car—the tape he borrowed. The next day Kim drove him down to Corbin's Shell Station, where his crushed car had been taken. He could not free the cassette from the tape deck, so badly warped was the metal by the impact. He realized more vividly than ever that he owed his life to the air bag.

Blink of an Eye. In the weeks that followed, this would become one of the most intensively analyzed auto crashes ever. The Insurance Institute for Highway Safety, a research organization backed by 325 insurance companies, bought the wrecks and assembled a team of automotive engineers and scientists to examine them meticulously.

The investigation revealed exactly what had happened. Ron Woody had seen a car heading toward him on his side of the two-lane road and had virtually stood on his brakes. Then he was aware that his face was being buried in a balloon-like pillow. Van Steelant remembers her bag suddenly billowing in front of her nose. "It was a jolt, but not a hard jolt. Like when you were a kid and jumped on a mattress."

The Insurance Institute team established that the crash was the equivalent of each of them hitting a stationary object at 68 M.P.H. As the cars slammed together, each driver's head was thrown forward with 1700 pounds of force.

At the instant the bumpers collided, small coiled sensors mounted behind each bumper sprang into action. In a catastrophic deceleration, these sensors uncoil, make contact with a nearby terminal and trigger a jolt of electricity that runs along a wire leading to the steering wheel.

In the hollowed-out center of the steering wheel is a small device resembling a miniature stack of records, metallic gray in color. This is a powerful propellant, sodium azide, which responds swiftly to an electrical charge by bursting into almost instantaneous flame and spewing out nitrogen gas. As the gas belches into the woven nylon bag that surrounds the discs, the bag inflates in 1/25 of a second—no longer than it takes to blink your eye.

Ripping Metal. By the time the hood of each car began to crumple, both bags were fully inflated and positioned directly in line with the head and torso of each driver. As their heads slammed forward, the folds of the air bag softened the impact, like a big balloon. At maximum inflation, the bags began to vent nitrogen gas to ensure the gentlest impact possible.

Within seconds the cars had bounced apart and come to rest. Each air bag emitted almost all of its nitrogen and became limp again, freeing the driver from the momentary restraint it had exerted.

As engineers probed deeper into the physical evidence, they made a series of chilling discoveries. The woven nylon of Van Steelant's seat belt, which she was wearing at the time, reached melting temperature from the friction caused on the seatbelt mounting as it restrained her forward movement in the instant before the air bag stopped her.

Ron Woody was not wearing his seat belt. The engineers had no doubt that he would have been killed had it not been for his air bag.

Though both drivers had refused treatment beyond the first aid on the scene, each had severe bruises and aches that got much worse the next day.

"I didn't go to work for four days," Woody says. "I felt like I used to after playing linebacker in high school." His visible injuries included a cut on his left elbow and a bruised left knee.

Van Steelant fared worse. She had multiple bruises and had bitten through her lip. Her legs and feet were particularly sore because the force of the crash had sent a wave of rippling metal through the floor of her car, sharply stinging them. An hour after she got home, her husband took her to the emergency room. X rays were taken of her legs and feet, but no broken bones were then found. Weeks later, a small fracture in one foot was discovered.

A feeling of profound wonderment remains among both principals and witnesses that death was defied that day on Route 640. For those who carefully combed through the evidence, there is an enduring satisfaction that the post-mortems conducted were of automobiles, not people. The two fragments of fabric that Chick Lauffer discovered draped over the steering wheels can take the credit for that. ■

Ziegler, Edward. "Collision on a Country Road." *Reader's Digest* September 1990: 49–53. Reprinted with permission from the September 1990 *Reader's Digest*. Copyright © 1990 by The Reader's Digest Association, Inc.

C: Post-Reading

Discussion Suggestions/Questions

Remembering

1. When their cars crashed into each other, were Priscilla Van Steelant and Ron Woody wearing seat belts?

2. What research organization bought the two wrecked cars and why?

Analyzing

1. Edward Ziegler, author of "Collision on a Country Road," does not tell the reader whose fault the collision was. Why do you suppose he chooses not to?

2. Share the details of place you underlined, highlighted, or copied on a sheet of paper while reading "Collision on a Country Road." Discuss with others what these details mean to you and why Edward Ziegler might have created and used these details.

Discovering

1. Often what the reader thinks of while reading is more important than what the author of the reading writes. There are ideas you had while reading this selection. Discuss these with your peers.

2.   A state patroller once said that accidents don't happen at miles per hour; they happen in inches per second. What did this person mean? Can you think of incidents from your experience that can serve as examples to support this idea?

D: Vocabulary Building

1. Different uses of *post-*

Post-Mortem: ". . . there is an enduring satisfaction that the **post-mortems** conducted were of automobiles, not people."

Ziegler: "Collision on a Country Road"

Literally, *post-mortem* means an autopsy, a physical examination of a person's body after death. However, often (as in the reading passage), post-mortem is used more broadly to mean any kind of after-the-fact examination. The word post-mortem comes from two Latin words: *post*, or "after," and *mortem*, a form of *mors*, "death."

Post is usually used in combination with other words. Examples are *postgraduate* ("after graduation"), *postwar* ("after the war"), and *postoperative* ("after an operation"). However, its most frequent use is in telling time, although you may not have recognized it because it usually appears as part of an abbreviation: P.M. This form is an abbreviation of the Latin word *postmeridianus*, a phrase that refers to the position of the sun just after (*post*) it has reached its highest point in the sky (i.e., noon).

Many English words come from *mors*, the Latin word for death. From *mors* we get *morgue*, the place where the dead are kept, and the adjective *morbid*, which originally meant diseased, but now means unhealthy or unnatural (for example, "a *morbid* fear of the dark"). Words related to *morbid* are *morbidity*, which refers to the state of being morbid, as in "his *morbidity* drove away his friends," and *moribund*, which literally means "at the point of death," although it is more often used to mean that something is hopelessly out of date or obsolete, as in "a *moribund* philosophy."

Vocabulary Building Activity 1: Different uses of *post-*

In the left column are different words that use the prefix *post-*. Match these words with their dictionary definitions in the column on the right. Some of the words you may not know, but you might guess what they mean by thinking about their parts.

Words	Dictionary Definitions
1. postglacial	a. ____ occurring immediately after birth
2. postnasal	b. ____ a message added at the end of a letter after the writer's signature
3. postnatal	
4. postnuptial	c. ____ behind the nose
5. postscript	d. ____ the time following a glacial period
	e. ____ happening after the marriage

2. Different uses of *trans-*

> <u>Transom:</u> ". . . Mills suggested that he sit down on the **transom** of the ambulance."
>
> *Ziegler: "Collision on a Country Road"*

The basic meaning of *transom* is a crosspiece in a structure. In a building, a *transom* is a beam that goes across the top of a door or a window. In the reading passage, the word *transom* refers to the metal platform that goes across the back of the ambulance. The word *transom* comes from the Latin word *transtrum,* "something that goes across." The first part of *transtrum* is the prefix *trans-*, "across," which appears in more than one hundred English words that come from Latin. In most of these words *trans-* has the basic meaning of spanning across something or causing something to move from one side to another. A good word to help you remember this meaning is *transit*, as in *Rapid Transit. Transit* means the act of going from one place to another.

Sometimes the idea of going across from one thing to another is only metaphorical. For example, in grammar a *transitive* verb is a verb that requires an object. In other words, the meaning of the verb "goes across" to its object. A verb that does not require an object is an *intransitive* verb. Its meaning does not "go across" to an object. For example, the verb "kill" is transitive because it must "go across" to an object. When someone kills, he or she must kill something (for example, "The farmer killed the duckling."). On the other hand, the verb "die" is intransitive because it cannot "go across" to an object. For example, we cannot say "The farmer died the duckling." We can only use the verb "die" as an intransitive, a verb without an object (for example, "The duckling died.").

Vocabulary Building Activity 2: Different uses of *trans-*

In the left column are different words that use the prefix *trans-*. Match these words with their dictionary definitions in the column on the right. Some of the words you may not know, but you might guess what they mean by thinking about their parts.

Words	Dictionary Definitions
1. transact	a. ____ to reverse or change the order or place of things
2. transcend	b. ____ a copy (of a record or document)
3. transcript	c. ____ to pass beyond (a limit); to surpass
4. transfusion	d. ____ the transfer of liquid; the injection of blood or plasma into the bloodstream
5. transpose	e. ____ to do; to carry out (business or affairs)

3. Word connotations

Sensor: "At the instant the bumpers collided, small coiled **sensors** mounted behind each bumper sprang into action."

Ziegler: "Collision on a Country Road"

A *sensor* is a device that senses and responds to a signal or stimulus. The word *sensor* is derived from the Latin word *sensus*, "sense," as in the sense of sight or sense of hearing. Many of the English words derived from *sensus* can have either positive or negative connotations, depending on the way they are used. The term "connotation" means the associations we have about the word that go beyond its factual, literal meaning. When we say that a word is "loaded," we are talking about its connotations. For example, to say that a person is **sensitive** can be either a positive or a negative comment. On the positive side, it can mean that the person is very aware of and sympathetic to other people. On the negative side, it can mean that the person is touchy and takes offense too easily.

Vocabulary Building Activity 3: Connotations

The following words on the left are all verbs whose basic meaning is to "walk." However, each of these words has a very different set of connotations. Match the words on the left with the person on the right who would be most likely to enter a room in this manner.

Words	Person
1. **crept** into the room	a. ____ Your bad-tempered uncle Ralph, who always seems to be angry about something
2. **swaggered** into the room	b. ____ Your mousy cousin Alfred, who seems to be afraid of his own shadow
3. **tripped** into the room	c. ____ Captain Hook, the villain in <u>Peter Pan</u>
4. **stomped** into the room	d. ____ Grand Dutchess Gertrude, the bluest of the bluebloods
5. **swept** into the room	e. ____ Your dopey cousin Sally, who never pays attention to what she is doing

SECTION

◄►

2

Drafting with Specific Details

A: Pre-Writing

People prepare themselves to write in many ways. Reading, thinking, and talking to others are good ways to prepare to write. People can also prepare themselves to write using other preparation or pre-writing strategies, and using strategies that fit the writer's issue and purpose is especially helpful. Since "Collision on a Country Road" by Edward Ziegler is about a particular traffic accident and what it might mean, he chose to include several details of place. He chose to make most of his article a story so that the reader could understand the events he presents in a context. County Route 640 is a real road. The events he describes actually happened.

To prepare himself to write, Mr. Ziegler may have visited the spot on County Route 640 where this collision took place. He must have read the reports written by the rescue squad and traffic police personnel who responded to Ruth Gillespie's emergency phone call. He may have spoken to each of the people he mentions in the article. All of these activities are pre-writing strategies, ways writers prepare themselves to write.

You will soon be writing about an experience you have had or you know about concerning traffic problems or traffic safety. Most people have driven or ridden in motor vehicles. Many people have been in accidents or had close calls while riding in motor vehicles. Perhaps you have already thought of some of your traffic experiences while reading, thinking, and talking about "Collision on a Country Road."

Pre-Writing Activity 1: Choosing A Traffic Incident

a. The first kind of pre-writing here is to tell others in your class about a traffic incident you were in or you know about. Your story does not have to be dramatic, does not need to include death and destruction. It could be something as simple as the time you ran over the neighbor's mailbox. You could tell about the time you made a narrow escape from danger or the time you were glad you were wearing a seat belt. Incidents that helped you to learn something about driving or driving safety tend to make for better stories. With others, then, share a traffic incident from your experience. To help your listeners understand what happened, include as many details of place as you can remember. If you don't remember many details, make some up. Being creative in this way is sometimes a necessary part of preparing to write.

b. After you have chosen and told a traffic story to others, sit down and write for ten to fifteen minutes about why you remember this incident. Do not worry about spelling or punctuation. Try to get as many words, details, and ideas on paper as possible. **Do not write the story; write about what the incident means to you.**

Pre-Writing Activity 2: Describing the Setting

Traffic incidents happen at specific times of the year, in particular weather conditions, on specific road surfaces, and with different kinds and quantities of other vehicles present. They always involve particular vehicles. Here you are asked to write two details for each of these elements in your traffic incident.

DRAFTING

a. Details of time of year (season)

Sample detail: The wheat growing on both sides of the gravel road was green and about twelve inches tall (spring).

1. _____

_____

_____

_____

_____

_____

_____

_____

_____

2. _____

_____

_____

_____

_____

_____

_____

_____

_____

_____

b. Details of weather

Sample detail: With the breeze blowing through the open window, it didn't seem quite so hot.

1. _____

_____

_____

_____

_____

_____

_____

_____

_____

2. _____

_____

_____

_____

_____

_____

_____

_____

_____

DRAFTING

DRAFTING

c. Details of road conditions

Sample detail: On the tighter corners and forty yards before every stop sign or intersection, the road was badly washboarded.

1. _____

_____

_____

_____

_____

_____

_____

_____

2. _____

_____

_____

_____

_____

_____

_____

_____

_____

d. Details of other traffic present

Sample detail: In the next four miles, two pickup trucks and one tractor passed me going the other direction.

1. _____

_____

_____

_____

_____

_____

_____

_____

2. _____

_____

_____

_____

_____

_____

_____

_____

_____

DRAFTING

DRAFTING

e. Details of the vehicle

Sample detail: My 1978 Ford Courier pickup was white—except for the long stripes of rust on the front quarter-panels in front of both doors.

1. _____

_____

_____

_____

_____

_____

_____

_____

2. _____

_____

_____

_____

_____

_____

_____

_____

B. Writing a First Draft

After you have completed the two kinds of pre-writing suggested, look back over this work. Try to recreate your incident in your mind, and then start writing your traffic incident. Your paper does not have to be just a story. It might start with a story and then include some of your ideas on what the incident means. It might be all story, leaving the reader to think about what the story means.

While writing, do not worry about spelling, punctuation, or grammar. Try to write the whole paper at once. Some people run out of things to write while writing; they get "stuck." If you get stuck, copy one of the details you wrote while pre-writing into your draft. You do not need to use all of the details in your paper that you pre-wrote. You may use them all and add some more if you like. You may use only a few of them. It is your paper.

You will probably work more on this paper after you have written it. For now, try to include plenty of details of place so that a reader can really understand what happened.

SECTION

3

Revising for Details of Place

REVISING

A: Details of Place

Experience is perhaps the best teacher. We store the details of things that happen to us and our thoughts about those events in our memories. Later, when we face events similar to those we have already experienced, we draw upon our storehouse of memories to make new decisions. We often decide what to do in a present situation based on what we learned from a similar situation in the past.

We also learn from other people's experiences. Part of the magic of language—both hearing it and reading it—is the fact that it allows us to share and learn from experiences that are not our own. This is called vicarious experience and can be just as important as first-hand experience. For example, none of us was there when the events Edward Ziegler presents in "Collision on a Country Road" happened, yet we can experience those events vicariously by reading what he wrote about them.

A central part of sharing experience is providing enough of the details of that experience that the person we are communicating with can, in a sense, participate in the event. A method for doing just that is to include details of place.

When we talk with friends we normally use a kind of shorthand for details of place. To someone who knows the street on which you live, for example, you might say an event took place in the street in front of your house. On the other hand, when telling the same story to someone who does not know that street, you might add some details describing that street—the pothole that is six inches deep and eighteen inches wide and the twenty-eight foot mobile home that your neighbor leaves parked on that street eleven months out of every year. These details not only make the story clearer to the listener but also make it more interesting. The details help the listener to picture the place in his or her mind.

Details of place are just as important when you write rather than tell a story. Look at the following pairs of examples.

Example One

Shorthand: "I took the road to Peter's house."

Including details of place: "I took old Highway 95, two lanes of patched asphalt that snake southward through rolling hills covered with wheat stubble."

Example Two

Shorthand: "It was snowing."

Including details of place: "Snowflakes drifted down from the windless sky, disappearing just as they touched the wet, black pavement."

The details of place provide more information, letting readers make connections between the details and their own experiences. The details help readers to share in the experiences vicariously.

B: Revising Drafts of Student Traffic Narratives

The following are drafts of three different students' stories about traffic incidents. Read the first one, "Car Accident." While reading, look for places where the writer uses "shorthand" rather than including details of place.

Student Draft: "Car Accident"

CAR ACCIDENT

On a spring day I jumped into my car to head up to get my hair cut. Being spring, it was a normal rainy day on the west side of Washington.

I screamed up to the center where I usually got my hair cut. As I approached the stoplight at the intersection, I thought to myself; boy is the traffic heavy, and it is raining like crazy.

The light turned green, and I flew off the line. I noticed these people on the side of the street and thought I recognized them. I looked up back onto the street, and there was a brown Toyota Celica right in front of my bumper. I hit the brakes hard and swerved to avoid the stopped Toyota. I slid because of the wet, slick street. Then impact occurred, and I hit the car's back bumper with the left bumper of my yellow Capri.

The lady slowly got out of her car, and I looked at my car with shame. The Toyota didn't even hardly have a scratch. My car was crushed; the front left fender was pushed way in and wiped out.

We exchanged insurance companies' names, and I called my parents. When my mom showed up, she became very mad. I had never seen my mom burn out in her car, but she got so angry that she peeled out.

My car had to be repaired, and for some unknown reason we had to pay five hundred dollars for repairs on the lady's undamaged car. It took five months to get the parts and time to finally fix my poor yellow Capri. Unfortunately, the colors do not match, so my car will never be the same.

As for the way I drive now, I am more cautious and do not drive as close to the car in front of me as I used to.

Curt K.

REVISING

Now look again at the same piece of writing. In this version, words that are shorthand for details of place have been <u>underlined</u>. Language that describes these shorthand details of place has been added *in italics*.

CAR ACCIDENT

On a spring day I jumped into my car to head up to get my hair cut. Being spring, it was a *normal rainy day* on the west side of Washington. *The sky was a low gray-white blanket of cloud and exhaust fumes, and the rain came down in huge drops that joined together to make the road surface a kind of shallow lake.*

I screamed up to *the center* where I usually got my hair cut. *The center was like most small shopping centers, a large parking area with yellow lines painted on it to mark the spaces, surrounded by many one-story shops all connected to one another. There was a pet store, a supermarket, an auto parts franchise, a styling salon, a pizza place, and a fast-food burger joint.* As I approached the stoplight at the intersection, I thought to myself; boy is *the traffic heavy*, and it is raining like crazy. *It was late in the afternoon, and the delivery trucks were everywhere, joined by all the people trying to get home before the real commuter traffic jam got started. Station wagons, compacts, pickup trucks, and those delivery trucks, all with stoplights and turn signals blinking back and forth, were stopping, changing lanes, turning, and speeding up and slowing down all at once.*

The light turned green, and I flew off the line. I noticed these people on the side of the street and thought I recognized them. I looked up back onto the street, and there was a brown Toyota Celica right in front of my bumper. I hit the brakes hard and swerved to avoid the stopped Toyota. I slid because of the wet, slick street. Then impact occurred, and I hit the car's back bumper with the left bumper of my yellow Capri.

The lady slowly got out of her car, and I looked at my car with shame. The Toyota didn't even hardly have a scratch. My car was crushed; the front left fender was pushed way in and wiped out.

We exchanged insurance companies' names, and I called my parents. *There were the two cars, my Capri and that Toyota, stuck right there on the edge of the intersection. By then the traffic was really backing up, and people were honking and shouting at one another. Some people were getting out of their cars to see what had happened. This just made it worse.* When my mom showed up, she became very

> mad. I had never seen my mom burn out in her car, but she
> got so angry that she peeled out.
>   My car had to be repaired, and for some unknown reason
> we had to pay five hundred dollars for repairs on the
> lady's undamaged car. It took five months to get the parts
> and time to finally fix my poor yellow Capri. Unfortunately,
> the colors do not match, so my car will never be the same.
>   As for the way I drive now, I am more cautious and do
> not drive as close to the car in front of me as I used to.
>
>   Curt K.

Practicing Revising for Details of Place

Following are two more drafts of narratives written by students about traffic incidents.

Revising Activity 1: "The Dark Corner"

Working with others or alone, revise the student draft "The Dark Corner" by adding details of place in the spaces provided. You will need to make up these details, so use your imagination.

REVISING

Student Draft: "The Dark Corner"

REVISING

THE DARK CORNER

   The incident that I remember most of all was the wreck that involved four of my good friends. The wreck occurred on a warm August morning; the time was about 2:00 A.M. The guys recalled the moon being very bright and the wind blowing at high speeds. The boys were on their way back to the Spokane Reservation on the Davenport-Fruitland highway. This highway has only a couple of real sharp corners, but <u>one corner</u> is very sharp.

_____

_____

_____

The accident occurred twenty miles out of Davenport on the road's sharpest corner. The driver was feeling tired, so he asked the other three boys if any one of them wanted to drive. He recalls looking over at the front passenger. He was fast asleep. With no answer from them, he pressed on. He recalls catching himself dozing off, then shaking his head trying to stay awake. As he rounded the corner he fell asleep, and the car became airborne for eighty feet. The impact was tremendously hard. The car landed in <u>a field of high wheat</u>, making it hard to see from the highway.

_____

_____

_____

The driver was knocked unconscious, and the other three boys were conscious, but all hurt. The front passenger was not wearing his seat belt; therefore, he was slammed into the windshield. He suffered a bruised head and a couple of stitches. The other two boys in the back were both badly injured. The guy on the passenger's side was slammed into the front seat; he suffered a dislocated shoulder, a few stitches and a lot of bruises. He also was not wearing a seat belt. The other passenger was injured the most seriously of all. He was wearing a seat belt. The impact of the crash was so great that the seat belt broke, after causing some serious damage to his intestines. He was in need of some help immediately. At 2:00 a.m. in the morning there was no traffic on the road. The nearest house was miles away. They began to fall into the state of shock. The front passenger and the rear passenger were panicking, due to the cry for help coming from the badly hurt guy that was suffering from internal bleeding. Hurt as they were, they began to run to the <u>nearest house</u>.

_____

_____

_____

As the two reached the house, dogs began to bark, scaring them. They ran past the dogs in hope of not getting bit, they reached the house's front door, and they began pounding on it. A woman answered the door and screamed in fear as she saw the two boys' bloody faces and clothing. Soon the ambulance arrived and took the four to the hospital. Three of them were released that day. The other one was in serious condition though; he underwent many surgeries before being spared his life. He had to have eighteen feet of his intestines removed, and he suffered a broken back as well.

The reason I recall this wreck so well is because these four guys were my good friends. Another reason is that they were all four on the basketball team. We were getting ready to play a big play-off game with Selkirk for league champions. The game was postponed due to the concern for the guy who was undergoing the operations.

Loren K.

REVISING

Revising Activity 2: "Windshield Fear"

Working alone or with others, revise the student draft "Windshield Fear" in the following way:

a. Underline or highlight the shorthand details of place in the draft.

b. In two or three sentences, fill in some details of place to help the reader share in the experience. You will need to imagine or invent these details.

Student Draft: "Windshield Fear"

WINDSHIELD FEAR

Two vehicles, one a small, light-brown, compact car and the other a jacked-up, full-size Chevy pick-up truck, were traveling in the same direction. It was a warm day in June just before the local high school's graduation day.

Road conditions were prime for driving; roads dry and air warm which contributes to a more laid-back commute compared to the usual hectic rush-hour traffic.

As we drove along with the windows down and the music moderately high, we both contributed in a light conversation. There were a lot of other cars around; all of them seemed to be spaced safely two and a half seconds away from each other as taught in drivers' education.

In the wink of an eye it happened. The little light-brown compact car smacked right into the bumper of the huge truck that was stopped at the red light that now seemed to be burning to the eye but yet wasn't seen just seconds before.

In these few seconds, many things all happened. The driver's name was yelled, and the gruesome picture of a mangled face flashed through my mind as it crashed through a thick glass windshield. This picture made me act on an automatic response because I realized for the first time in my life I wasn't wearing a seat belt. I threw myself onto the floor-board of the car and crammed my face deeply into the leather of the seat to keep my face as far away from the windshield as possible. I just held on tight, waited for the impact, and hoped it wouldn't be too severe. Also, in the seconds of the accident, I slammed onto the floor board and then back into the seat, where I sat upright when the car finally stopped.

After listening to Rob yell, "My mom's gonna kill me!" about a million times, I finally pried my eyes open to see nothing but brown all in the windshield, and I felt my ankle throb faster and faster. I tilted my whiplashed head forward to see my black and blue, extremely swollen foot. At this point, I was in such shock that I began laughing hysterically.

The next thing I saw was the truck that was in front of us, the truck we had smashed into. The bumper was merely tilted about a half an inch upwards.

There were two court dates on which we both had to appear. Other than these, the incident is rarely discussed without laughing. Ever since this accident, when riding with Rob, I am very outspoken as a backseat driver and tend to imagine I have my own set of brakes. Because Rob is extremely embarrassed about the situation, there is always a bit of friendly harassment as we pass our accident's location.

Christie B.

C: Revising Your Draft

Working with others or alone, revise the draft about a traffic incident you have written in the following ways. These are revision strategies you have already used in this chapter.

a. Underline or highlight the shorthand details of place.

b. In two or three sentences for each highlighted shorthand detail, add details of place to make your story more clear and more interesting to a reader.

D: Helping Others to Revise Their Drafts

Exchange drafts of traffic incident papers with another writer. Then do activities C.a and C.b on each other's drafts. Here you will need to make up details of place. Have fun doing this. Writing that is fun to do tends to be fun to read.

REVISING

SECTION 4

Final Editing for Sentence Fragments

[Reminder: Appendix I contains definitions and examples of all grammar terms.]

A **sentence fragment** is a piece of a sentence separated from the rest of its sentence and punctuated as though the piece were a complete, self-contained sentence in its own right. Here are some examples of sentences with the fragment portion in bold. [The * reminds us that the written sentence is ungrammatical or punctuated incorrectly.]

1.   There is always something to be done. ***The dishes. Homework. Housework.**

2.   College makes you a better person. ***By forcing you to find out who you are.**

3.   It was a terrible day. ***Cloudy, windy, and a fifty percent chance of snow.**

4.   He was really dressed up for the interview. ***Which would take place in the president's office.**

5.   There are many people one will meet in the years one spends in college. ***Not to mention all the great social happenings.**

Fragments are hard to deal with in writing because we use fragments as a normal and accepted part of everyday speaking. If someone were to read the five example sentences out loud to you, you would not notice any fragments because the person reading the sentences would use the intonation of his or her voice to connect the fragment to the preceding main clause. In addition, fragments play an important role in speaking that they do not play in writing. In the quick give and take of conversation, we do not have time to plan what we say very far ahead of time. Sentence fragments are a way of clarifying what we have just said without having to stop and then start our sentences all over again. Sentence fragments are an easily understood form of mid-course correction. They are a way of looping back on a sentence without breaking our train of thought or confusing the listener. They allow us to comment on, emphasize, explain, elaborate or give examples of our topics.

However, in formal writing, sentence fragments are inappropriate. We expect formal writing to be carefully planned. In this kind of writing, sentence fragments should not be needed to clarify an idea because it is the writer's obligation to make the idea clear from the start. Using sentence fragments for clarification is a sign of poorly planned writing—a sign of a writer who has lost control.

A good way to tell if something is a fragment is to see if you can turn it into a question that can be answered by a "yes" or "no" answer. Sentences can be turned into questions, but fragments cannot be. To demonstrate how the question test works, here is the first example fragment sentence:

1.   There is always something to be done. *The dishes. Homework. Housework.**

When we apply the question test to the sentence in the example, we get a grammatical question: *Is there always something to be done?* When we try to apply the question test to the three fragments (*The dishes. Homework. Housework.*) we cannot make questions. What is the question form of *The dishes?* There isn't any. Therefore, *The dishes* is a fragment.

Editing Activity 1: Using the Question Test to Identify Sentence Fragments

Apply the question test to the four remaining example fragment sentences by turning the complete sentences into questions:

---

1. College makes you a better person. *By forcing you to find out who you are.**
   Question test_____

2. It was a terrible day. *Cloudy, windy, and a fifty percent chance of snow.**
   Question test_____

3. He was really dressed up for the interview. *Which would take place in the president's office.**
   Question test_____

4. There are many people one will meet in the years one spends in college. *Not to mention all the great social happenings.**
   Question test_____

There are three ways to correct a fragment:

(a)   Attach the fragment to the preceding complete sentence.

(b)   Expand the fragment into a complete sentence.

(c)   Rewrite both the preceding complete sentence and the fragment to make them into a single combined sentence.

We will discuss each of these alternatives in turn.

(a)   **Attach the fragment to the preceding complete sentence.**

This is the most common way to eliminate a fragment, and depending on the type of fragment, it is usually (but not always) the simplest and best way, provided that the correct punctuation is used. The example fragment sentences can be corrected in this way:

1a.   There is always something to be done—the dishes, the homework, and the housework.

2a.   College makes you a better person by forcing you to find out who you are.

3a.   It was a terrible day—cloudy, windy, and a fifty percent chance of snow.

4a.   He was really dressed up for the interview, which would take place in the president's office.

5a.   There are many people one will meet in the years he or she spends in college—not to mention all the great social happenings.

Notice the different punctuation used in joining the fragment to the preceding complete sentence. Sentences 1a, 3a, and 5a use dashes to join lists onto the preceding complete sentence. Sentence 2a does not need any punctuation to join the fragment onto the preceding complete sentence. Sentence 4a uses a comma to join a nonrestrictive clause beginning with *which* onto the noun it modifies in the preceding complete sentence.

(b)   Expand the fragment into a complete sentence.

This option is very useful when you want to emphasize the importance of the idea contained in the original fragment or if you want to write more about the idea contained in the original fragment.

1b.   There is always something to be done. The dirty dishes piled in the sink are attracting flies, you are two days behind in your homework, and the housework doesn't even bear thinking about.

2b.   College makes you a better person. It forces you to find out who you are.

3b.   It was a terrible day. It was cloudy and windy, and there was a fifty percent chance of snow.

4b.   He was really dressed up for the interview. The interview would take place in the president's office.

(c)   Rewrite both the preceding complete sentence and the fragment to make them into a single combined sentence.

This alternative is probably the best one for example 5. Here is the original example again:

5.   There are many people one will meet in the years one spends in college. *Not to mention all the great social happenings.**

In the essay from which 5 was taken, the writer lists the benefits of going to college. After completing the first sentence in the example, which mentions the benefit of meeting people, the writer then thought of a second benefit—*all the great social happenings*—and tacked it on as a sentence fragment.

The best alternative would be to rewrite the two benefits of going to college as equal ideas:

5a.   There are many people one will meet in the years one spends in college and many great social happenings one can attend.

Notice how much better 5a is than just sticking the fragment onto the end of the preceding complete sentence:

5b.   There are many people one will meet in the years he or she spends in college— not to mention all the great social happenings.

Although the solution in 5b is grammatically correct in eliminating the fragment error, it is not a very good solution because what follows the dash still seems to be added on as an afterthought.

Editing Activity 2: Identifying and Correcting Sentence Fragments

The following student essay contains numerous fragments, all of them in bold type. Correct each fragment in the manner that you think works best for this essay. Explore all three ways of correcting fragments: joining the fragment with the preceding complete sentence, making the fragment a complete sentence, and rewriting both the fragment and the preceding sentence as a new combined sentence.

Student Draft: "Just Another Summer Day"

Kyle S.
English Writing, Sec 6
April 15, 1993

JUST ANOTHER SUMMER DAY

I had a car full of friends, and we just needed to pick up one last person before we headed off to our baseball game. **The biggest game of the year.** It was a very hot day, and all the windows were down in my 60 Volkswagen bug. We all had our shirts off, and the sweat was dripping down our backs. **Making us stick to the hot black vinyl seats.** We cruised along laughing and goofing around. Since it was our last and most important game, we were just trying to stay loose and keep a positive outlook for the game. Out of the murmur in the back seat someone shouted, "Don't forget to pick up Anthony," so I quickly made a right turn on 21st street and went down a suburban street. **Which had cars parked on both sides.**

I was now following a blue and silver truck. **The biggest Ford made.** After a few blocks it veered off to the left side of the street. Since it was a residential street, I assumed that the truck was about to park or was going to pull into a driveway on the left side of the street, but in reality the driver was making a wide swing to the left. **So he could turn into his driveway on the right.** I turned around to the back seat to ask who was pitching for Shadle Park that day, but before I got an answer someone yelled, "Kyle, look out!" When I turned back around, all I saw was the side of that gigantic blue and silver truck. **Right in front of me.** I quickly jammed on my brakes, but I wasn't in time. My little car seemed to be in slow motion as I slammed into the right side of the truck. **Just behind the passenger's door.**

The few seconds of utter silence after the crash seemed to last for an eternity. Now I had to deal with the aftermath. I looked around and asked if everyone was all right. The response was positive. In a state of shock, I knew I had to get out of my car and see the damage. **Reaching for the door handle.** Hoping for no serious damage, I stepped out onto the pavement and into the

> shadow of the driver of the truck, a huge, lumberjack-like man. **Who asked me what I thought I was doing.** I said I was sorry in the most pathetic voice imaginable. The man was actually quite polite and considerate. He discussed what had happened in a civilized manner. **Without once raising his voice.** We worked out the details of reporting the accident. **To my surprise, smoothly and fairly.** All I had to do then was to face my parents. **And break the news.**

Once a writer has identified a sentence fragment, it is relatively easy to eliminate the fragment by incorporating the fragment into the preceding complete sentence or promoting the fragment to the status of a complete sentence. The trick, of course, is learning how to spot the sentence fragment initially. Some writers find it hard to find their own sentence fragments because they are hearing (rather than seeing) what they write. Many beginning writers write by ear and not by eye. That is, when they write, they are dictating spoken language to themselves. When these writers hear a sentence fragment in their writing, the fragment sounds fine because fragments are a normal part of the spoken language. These writers can only begin to spot sentence fragments when they *see* their writing as well as hear it.

A very useful trick for finding sentence fragments is to read through each paragraph backwards, sentence by sentence. This trick works because a sentence fragment is really a part of the preceding sentence, which the fragment clarifies or elaborates in some way. If you read the fragment before you read the preceding sentence, the incompleteness of the fragment sticks out because you haven't yet seen the sentence it attaches to. For example, reading backwards, the fragment "Not to mention all the great social happenings" sticks out because it is cut off from the preceding sentence. Without that preceding sentence, the fragment doesn't make any sense. Any time you suspect that what is punctuated as a sentence might be a fragment, check it out with the "yes/no" question test.

Sentence fragments do not have some random, unpredictable defect that makes them incomplete. Most sentence fragments fall into one of three definite categories, depending on the way they complete or relate to the preceding sentence. Most fragments are either **emphatic adverbs, -ing words,** or **noun renamers.** By knowing what the most likely types of fragments are, you will be better able to spot them in your own writing.

A: Fragment Category One: Emphatic Adverbs

In this category are various kinds of adverb expressions that tell when, where, or why something happened. Since these fragments are merely adverb expressions detached from the preceding complete sentence, it is easy to correct this type of error by reattaching the adverb expression to the preceding complete sentence. Usually no punctuation is required. Here are some examples from student essays. The fragments appear in bold type. Following each fragment sentence is a corrected form of the sentence:

6. He got a speeding ticket. *On the way home from the party.

6a. He got a speeding ticket on the way home from the party.

7. I switched off the computer. *Without saving my paper first.

7a. I switched off the computer without saving my paper first.

8. A degree in engineering seemed like it would be a good major. *Because there would be plenty of jobs in that field.

8a. A degree in engineering seemed like it would be a good major because there would be plenty of jobs in that field.

9. I did my paper over and over again. *Until I was sure it was right.

9a. I did my paper over and over again until I was sure it was right.

10. Life seems tough for them. *Especially when they look ahead and are uncertain of what is going to happen when they finally make it through college.

10a. Life seems tough for them, especially when they look ahead and are uncertain of what is going to happen when they finally make it through college.

Editing Activity 3: Identifying and Correcting Emphatic Adverb Fragments

The following student essay contains emphatic adverb fragments. The number of fragments in each paragraph is given in parenthesis at the end of the paragraph. Underline all the fragments, and then correct them in the way that you think works best for this essay.

Student Draft: "Accident on Crystal Mountain Road"

```
                                        Dennis S.
                          English Writing, Sec 6
                                   March 12, 1993

          ACCIDENT ON CRYSTAL MOUNTAIN ROAD

    On a cold winter evening in January, six of my friends
and I decided to skip school on Monday and go skiing at
Crystal Mountain. Because we could go skiing all day on
Mondays for only eight dollars. On Sunday evening we
packed up all the skies, boots, poles, snow suits and the
other gear. Along with money and food for lunch, of
course. (2)
```

We went in two different cars. I and three of my friends went in a 1987 Toyota 4Runner; the remaining three people went in an old three door Honda Accord. We left home about seven on Monday morning. We drove south on I-5 for about an hour and then took exit 93 to Auburn. Once we got to Auburn, we took exit 72 to Crystal Mountain Road, which is a windy, steep, one-lane road. Without guard rails. The weather was getting bad: the wind started to pick up, and it was beginning to snow. (1)

About 20 or so miles from the ski area, the Honda hit a patch of ice the size of a baseball infield. It started to spin out of control, and then it went down a 200-foot slope. The car tumbled, turned, flipped, and bounced around like a pinball for about 70 feet. Until it finally hit a tree the size of the Space Needle. The Honda was upside down. With the passenger door pinned up against the tree. (2)

By the time we had run down to the car, I thought everyone would be dead; then I heard some screaming and yelling for help. It sounded like they were dying. The wind started blowing in gusts, and the snow was coming down heavily. Like a blizzard in Antarctica. The car was a mess. It looked like it belonged in a junkyard. When we tried to open the driver's door, it was jammed. So we looked for another way to get into the car. The back window had been blown out. So we thought there would be a chance to get them out through it. I crawled through the window and grabbed the passenger in the back seat and dragged him out. He was cut on the face from the broken glass and was in a daze. The passenger in the front seat, who was just shaken up, was able to crawl out on his own. However, the driver was trapped behind the wheel. So two of us climbed back into the car and were able to get him out. Through the back window. He had a broken leg and was bleeding badly from head wounds. So we carried him up the hill. As fast as we could. I drove him to the nearest hospital, which was about 30 miles away in Auburn. I never drove so fast and so carefully in all my life. (7)

B: Fragment Category Two: *-Ing* Words

A number of fragments begin with an *-ing* word. These *-ing* fragments play two basic roles: (a) as adjectives that modify a noun in the preceding complete sentence or (b) as adverbs that explain why or how something was done in the preceding complete sentence. Often an *-ing* fragment can be interpreted as playing either role, so we have a number of alternative ways in which we can correct the fragment error depending on which meaning we choose to emphasize. Here are some examples of *-ing* fragments from student essays, each followed by several possible corrections:

11. Some freshmen goof off for the whole year. *Believing that the first year doesn't really count.

11a. Adjective: Some freshmen, who believe that the first year doesn't really count, goof off for the whole year.

11b. Adjective: Some freshmen, believing that the first year doesn't really count, goof off for the whole year.

11c. Adverb: Some freshmen goof off for the whole year because they believe that the first year doesn't really count.

12. I decided to go to college. *Increasing my chances for a better job in the future.

12a. Adjective: I decided to go to college, increasing my chances for a better job in the future.

12b. Adverb: I decided to go to college because that would increase my chances for a better job in the future.

13. College gives you a whole new perspective. *Opening your eyes and mind to the world.

13a. Adjective: College, opening your eyes and mind to the world, gives you a whole new perspective.

13b. Adverb: College gives you a whole new perspective because it opens your eyes and mind to the world.

Editing Activity 4: Identifying and Correcting *-ing* Fragments

The following student essay contains a number of *-ing* sentence fragments (and a few emphatic adverb fragments to keep you in practice). Underline the fragments, and then correct them in the way that you think works best for this essay. The number of fragments in each paragraph is given in parentheses at the end of the paragraph.

Student Draft: "The Pizza Parlor Accident"

```
                                        Joel B.
                            English Writing, Sec 6
                            February 26, 1993

              THE PIZZA PARLOR ACCIDENT
    The phrase that pops into my mind when someone says
"accident" would have to be what my dad told me. Before
I was involved in my first wreck. He said that I shouldn't
try to come home for lunch because I didn't have enough
time to make it back for my first afternoon class. Well,
I paid no attention to what my father told me. Being an
independent young person. (2)
    My accident occurred about five days after I got my
license. Diagonally across the intersection from my
school is a pizza parlor hang-out for anyone. Wanting
cheap food and fast service. They sold pizza for 50 cents
a slice and pop for the same price, so naturally this
place was always packed with students. There were so many
people in this dorm-sized restaurant that people stood
outside. Waiting to get in even in the cold and rain.
Students crossed the street at any time. Running back and
forth without looking. (3)
    On the day of the accident I entered the intersection
across from the hang-out. I was in the left lane of a
four-lane road. Waiting to make a left-hand turn. Coming
the opposite direction, was a small blue Chevy S-10 pickup
that also wanted to make a left-hand turn in front of me.
I was really getting anxious to get out of the intersec-
tion before the light turned red, so I began edging
further and further into the turn. Leaving myself more
vulnerable as I moved forward. Since there were no other
on-coming cars, I proceeded to turn left. Glancing up at
the light, which turned yellow just then. Everything
seemed to move slowly as if my mind were warning me. Even
the radio seemed to change into a whisper. I looked to my
right and saw the driver of the pickup bracing himself for
an impact. My guess was that he had sped up a lot. Trying
to make the light before it turned red. The pickup hit me
with such force that it made my head strike the window on
the driver's side. Shattering it into a million pieces.
(5)
```

After I came to, I got out of the car to take a look at the damage done to the right side of my car. My eyes popped open to the size of ping-pong balls, and my mouth dropped: my right quarter panel was all dented up, but there was not a scratch on the pickup truck except for a small ding in his bumper. Suddenly my vision blurred over. From drops of blood coming from a deep cut above my eyelid. As I was wiping the blood out of my eyes, I had a vision of my father. Standing over me saying, "I warned you not to try to come home for lunch." I then thought of what my dad would do to me when I got home. I started yelling at the other driver as loudly as possible for a person in pain. Using every word not allowed in the dictionary. This only made matters worse because then we were both yelling at each other. Not getting anywhere with our predicament. Finally I got into my car and moved it out of the way before someone else came along and hit me. Sitting on the broken glass from the shattered window. (5)

The most embarrassing part of the whole accident was that about fifty students outside the pizza place were just standing there. Watching the whole thing. Within an hour the whole school knew about the accident. It took months for them to quit teasing me about the accident and my standing there with blood running down my face. Screaming at the other driver. Now whenever my father tells me something, I at least take notice of what he is saying. (2)

C: Fragment Category Three: Noun Renamers

A common type of fragment renames a noun in the main sentence. Usually we can correct these renaming fragments by merely attaching the fragment to the noun in the preceding complete sentence with a comma, colon, or dash. Here are some examples from student essays with fragments of this type in bold, each followed by a corrected sentence that has joined the fragment to the preceding sentence.

14.   The student union attracts many different kinds of people. *Jocks, nerds, and even professors.

14a.   The student union attracts many different kinds of people: jocks, nerds, and even professors.

EDITING

15.   One also develops many wonderful friendships at college. *Friendships so close that they will continue for the rest of our lives.**

15a.   One also develops many wonderful friendships at college—friendships so close that they will continue for the rest of our lives.

16.   Real education in college comes from the experiences we have while we are in school. *Experiences that we would never have had if we hadn't gone to college.**

16a.   Real education in college comes from the experiences we have while we are in school, experiences that we would never have had if we hadn't gone to college.

Often renaming fragments are used as examples. Typically, these fragments begin with such words as *that is*, *namely*, *for instance*, *like*, and (most commonly) *for example*. Here is such a fragment sentence, followed by its corrected form:

17.   I would like to have a great job waiting for me when I finish college. *For example, a job in a computer company.**

17a.   I would like to have a great job waiting for me when I finish college—for example, a job in a computer company.

Editing Activity 5: Final Editing of a Student Essay

The following student essay contains a number of fragments. Underline the fragments, and correct them in the way you think works best for this essay. The number of fragments in each paragraph is given in parentheses at the end of the paragraph.

EDITING

Student Draft: "Accident in Hawaii"

Jason H.
English Writing, Sec 6
March 4, 1993

ACCIDENT IN HAWAII

I remember when both my brother and sister were in a car accident in January 1986. They were going to Hawaii Preparatory Academy (HPA). A school on the other side of the island. They were going to school in my brother's truck. Which was a black, two-door, four-wheel drive Nissan King cab. Inside our truck there were four seats. Two in the front and two in the back. They were coming down a steep hill followed by a big red truck with a Love's bakery sign on it. The truck was delivering bread to a Sure Save store. Which is next to HPA. Both trucks were going about forty to forty-five miles an hour. There were road construction signs everywhere, and you could see workers in their machines. Moving along the road. Up ahead, a construction machine crossed the road, causing the whole line of traffic to stop. However, the old man driving the Love's truck didn't see everyone stopping because he had been drinking beer for an hour before the accident. (5)

The old man hit my brother's truck. Smashing it like an aluminum can. Neither my brother nor my sister were wearing seat belts. My sister hit her head against the windshield. Which shattered from the impact. My brother was luckier; he escaped with only bruises and scrapes. The crash pushed my brother's truck forward into the back of a blue 1984 Mazda car. Which was in front of them. The truck hit the Mazda hard. Destroying the whole back of the car. (4)

My brother then looked at Debbie, my sister, to see if she was all right, but she wasn't. She was unconscious, and her head was against the window. With pieces of glass in her hair and body. Half an hour later the ambulance came. A few minutes later my sister woke up with a headache. The size of a mountain. The rescue squad men put her and my brother into the ambulance and took them to Hilo. Which is where the nearest hospital is. (3)

Our Nissan truck had to be towed away to the junkyard. The crash actually had made the truck about four feet shorter, making it impossible to repair it. The crash ruined the Mazda's back end. Which had to be completely rebuilt. The Love's bread truck only had to have its bumper replaced and was shortly out on the road. Delivering bread again. The driver of the bread truck was convicted of drunk driving. He then lost his driver's license. Which also caused him to lose his job. (3)

CHAPTER 3

CONSUMER LETTERS

SECTION

1

Reading About Consumer Communications

A: Pre-Reading

Writing is a resource for communication. Different types of writing have developed through time to accomplish different kinds of communication. A major form of written communication is the letter, and there are two major types of letters. One is the **personal letter**. Most people have written many of these. Before the widespread use of the telephone, people stayed in touch with family and friends by writing personal letters. In these letters they shared the events of their lives—births and deaths, weddings and graduations, news of other friends and relatives, and opinions on things that mattered to them. Prior to the telephone, writing personal letters—several every week—was a normal part of most people's lives.

Writing and sending personal letters is still an excellent way to communicate. Stamps are cheaper than long distance telephone charges, and sometimes a person can write things in a letter that would be inappropriate or awkward to say over the telephone. With writing, too, a person can think about what he or she wants to say and rewrite a letter so that it communicates just what that person intends.

Most writing teachers believe that writing personal letters regularly helps people to become better and better writers. This chapter is not about writing personal letters, even though all people should do this kind of writing. This chapter is about the other major kind of letters—**business letters**. Business letters come in many shapes and sizes, including consumer letters of various kinds.

Consumer letters are those in which a consumer of products or services communicates with a business that provides those products or services. There are at least four kinds of consumer letters, and each kind has a different purpose.

1. Consumer complaint. Perhaps the most common type of consumer writing is the consumer complaint. The purpose here is to solve the problem. Say, for example, a person buys a toaster on sale and then finds that the toaster always burns the toast. This person takes the toaster back to the discount store where he or she bought it and is told by an employee of the store that the store will neither repair nor replace the toaster. The person with the toaster might then write a consumer complaint letter, either to the discount

store manager or to the manufacturer of the toaster, describing the problem and asking for a solution. Businesses normally respond to this kind of writing.

2. Consumer suggestion. Another kind of consumer letter is the one that contains a suggestion for how a business or a product can be improved. The purpose here is to help the business better serve its customers. The United States Post Office invites people to make such suggestions. These letters are taken seriously and sometimes result in changes of services or procedures.

3. Consumer request. People sometimes write to businesses to request information. The purpose here is to get information otherwise unavailable. They might ask a manufacturer for a current catalogue of products and a price list. They might write to a business located in another part of the country or overseas for a product unavailable in their home town. They might write requesting information on how to obtain a replacement part for a piece of equipment they already own. Businesses normally respond helpfully to these letters. Even when they cannot help the writers, they might know of someone who can.

4. Consumer praise. Consumer praise letters are rarer than they should be. Most consumer letters a business receives are consumer complaint letters. The purpose of consumer praise letters is to let people know they are appreciated. These letters are a more formal way of saying "thank you." In a consumer praise letter the writer tells a business or a manufacturer about something that the organization or one of its employees has done well. For example, a consumer praise letter could be written to a bank manager telling him or her how helpful and courteous a particular employee of the bank was when the consumer was getting a loan to finance a new car. A person could also write to a manufacturer telling the officers of that company how happy that person has been with the products of that company. Businesses normally respond to consumer praise letters. Frequently a supervisor will share such letters with other employees of the company.

Consumer letter writing provides an excellent opportunity to practice tailoring what you write to your audience. In writing one gets to think about the audience ahead of time. Keeping an audience in mind is always wise, but it is especially important in consumer writing. In fact, consumer letter writing has the advantage that the writer is communicating with a real audience. Someone, other than a teacher or other students, will read what the writer writes.

Pre-Reading Activities

Sample Consumer Letter 1

Imagine that you are the manager of a business called American Car Stereo and that you have just received the following consumer complaint letter.

READING

N.E. 218 Standard
Lodestone, Wisconsin 53735
June 6, 1993

Manager
American Car Stereo
West 112 Main Street
Lodestone, Wisconsin 53735

Dear Leader of the Pack:

You stupid people have done it again. When I bought that car stereo the salesperson said it was guaranteed. It never did work. Three times I've brought it in to your overpriced and understaffed store, and each time I waited at least ten days to get it back. I have the stereo now, and it still doesn't work.

What do I have to do? Maybe I should throw this stereo through your front window. The breaking glass sound would be the only music it ever made. It would be music to my ears.

Unhappily yours,

D. Bell

Discussion

Since consumer writing is writing that hopes to get something done, think about what you would do in response to this letter.

Then, with others, discuss the letter:

1. Who is the writer?

2. What is he or she like?

3. What is the writer's purpose?

4. What would you, as audience for the letter, do in response to it?

5. Why would you respond in that way?

Sample Consumer Letter 2

Imagine that you are R. Winters and that you have just received the following consumer praise letter. You have been the project coordinator for eight years, and you have never received a consumer praise letter in all that time.

```
E. 111 19th Avenue
Twin Rivers, ID 83301
November 17, 1993

R. Winters, Project Coordinator
Regional Solid Waste Disposal Project
W. 808 River Blvd.
Twin Rivers, ID 83301

Dear Project Coordinator Winters:

I am writing to commend the work of your subordinate,
Kathy Pearson. I first contacted her on October 24 of this
year concerning my neighbor's inability to control his
garbage. I had spoken with this neighbor about the problem
several times before this day, and he had not taken any
steps to remedy it. I spoke with Ms. Pearson again on
November 7. She was polite and candid, and she promised
to address the problem. On November 14, I noticed that my
neighbor had new garbage cans with functional lids. These
cans end an annoyance my wife and I have experienced for
more than two years.

Specifically, I commend Ms. Pearson's communication skills
and her efficiency. Given the many responsibilities I am
sure she has, for her to attend to my difficulty and solve
the problem in thirty days is very impressive.

I thank her, and I thank you.

Sincerely,

Michael B.
```

Discussion

1. Talk about the person who wrote this letter:

    a. What is this person like? What does the letter reveal about him?

    b. What is the writer's purpose?

2. Talk about how you, if you were Project Coordinator Winters, would respond to this letter.

    a. Would you write a letter to Michael B.? What would you say?

    b. What might you say to Kathy Pearson?

READING

Reading Suggestions

(Keep these suggestions in mind as you read "Consumer Communication.")

1. The introduction to this chapter discusses consumer writing, but consumer speaking is also an issue. The following reading is about consumer speaking, about dealing with a salesperson and buying a product. An important part of consumer speaking is keeping in mind the goals of the audience, the salesperson. Communication takes at least two communicators. Think about the communication described in this reading from the salesperson's perspective.

2. The reading is about the process of buying something. How is this process like the writing process?

3. While reading, you will probably think of experiences you have had that were like the one the writer describes. Make little notes to yourself so you can remember and share these experiences with others later.

Vocabulary Preview

capacity: the amount something will contain. (The gas tank has a twelve gallon capacity.)

combative: angry, combat-like. (When you ask someone for a favor, it is best not to be combative.)

incentive: extra benefit. (The gas station offered free coffee as an incentive to customers.)

negotiate: trying to reach a decision acceptable to two people who do not agree on something. (The owner and the buyer negotiate the price of the used car.)

rhetoric: This word has at least two very different meanings.

a. empty talk. (The politician used a lot of rhetoric but did not answer the question.)

b. thinking about what you will communicate before you communicate it. (Thanking a friend for a past favor before asking for another one is good rhetoric.)

B: Reading

"Consumer Communication"

BY D. C. ELDER

When my wife Robin and I bought our home five years ago, we ended up spending most of the money we had just buying the house. In addition to the down payment, we had to pay what are called "closing costs." These included things like loan fees, mortgage insurance, credit checks, and lawyer fees. Anyway, it turned out that buying an inexpensive home was more expensive than we had thought it would be.

Having lived in an apartment for many years we owned no appliances, so we needed a refrigerator, a washer, and a dryer. An old stove came with the house. Robin and I were tired of doing our laundry at the laundromat, and because we had little choice we went to Saint Vincent De Paul's discount store and bought used appliances. We bought a large refrigerator that worked pretty well but sounded, when it switched on, like a Boeing 747. We bought an old washer and dryer set. The dryer we still have, but the washer, after about a year, got into the habit of "walking" away from the basement wall and out into the room whenever we ran it. We put up with this washing machine's bad habit for several years, but then it learned a new trick. In addition to "walking," it learned to turn itself on and off whenever it liked. So instead of taking thirty-five to forty minutes to go through the wash cycle, it started taking four to five hours to wash a load of clothes.

We decided to buy a new washing machine. Then we read various consumer guide magazines and decided which features—size of motor, number of wash cycles, load capacity—and which manufacturers and models would be best for us considering how much money we were willing to spend. We took notes on our reading and on our discussions.

Next, with notes in hand, we drove around and looked at washing machines. We stopped at five different stores, looked at about a hundred machines, and talked to a half a dozen salespersons. During this process, we took even more notes to remind us who had which machines and at what price.

Looking at our notes later, it turned out that one national retail store and one locally owned business had the washing machine we wanted to buy. We had bought appliances from the local business before, and the people there had provided good prices and good service, but the national retail store had the machine we wanted on sale and, therefore, had a lower price. The time had come for us to use our consumer communication skills.

Communication between consumers and salespeople need not be combative. Both parties can feel good about the interaction; both parties can feel like winners. The key is thinking about the factors in a communication situation ahead of time. The factors, fortunately, remain basically the same in many communication situations. Effective communicators think about the subject, audience, purpose, and how they want the audience to perceive them.

What does this have to do with washing machines? Well, to prepare to communicate, my wife and I had read and talked about washing machines (subject). Our goal (purpose) was clear: we wanted to buy a reliable washing machine that fit our laundry washing needs, and we wanted to pay the lowest possible price for it.

Next we considered audience. We wanted to buy from the locally owned business. We had met the salesperson there, a man named Paul. We believed that Paul wanted to sell us a washing machine. He would make money for himself and for his company by doing so. Finally, we thought about how we wanted Paul (the audience) to perceive us—what could we say that would make him want to help us get the best possible deal on a washing machine?

To help ourselves to think through this communication situation ahead of time, we made a communication triangle:

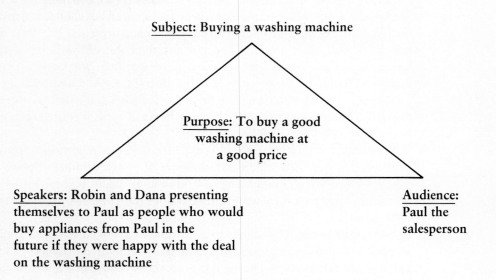

Subject: Buying a washing machine

Purpose: To buy a good washing machine at a good price

Speakers: Robin and Dana presenting themselves to Paul as people who would buy appliances from Paul in the future if they were happy with the deal on the washing machine

Audience: Paul the salesperson

Once we were ready, Robin and I called ahead to be sure Paul was working, and then we drove to the locally owned appliance store. Paul remembered us from our previous visit and walked right to us when he saw us. After exchanging pleasant greetings, the conversation (communication) went something like this:

I said, "We're pretty interested in the Whirlpool you showed us last week, the one with the extra-large capacity and the automatic extra rinse cycle."

Paul, being a good salesperson and knowing that people like to look at what they are thinking about buying, escorted Robin and me over to the machine we were talking about. "This is a very good washing machine," he said. "Aren't you the guys who told me it was listed as a 'best buy' in one of the consumer magazines?"

"Yes," I replied.

"Well," he said, "I've sold several of these, and people have been happy with them. We haven't heard a single complaint."

"We have a few questions, though," said Robin.

"That's what I'm here for," replied Paul.

"Well," said Robin, "we found the same machine at another store (she named the store), and they've got it on sale for fifty dollars less than your price."

I quickly added, "But we've done business with you people before. We bought our refrigerator here last year (we'd gotten tired of listening to the Boeing 747, and it had begun to leak water into the vegetable bin), and we were very happy with the service, the refrigerator, and the price. We'd rather do business with you," I said.

"Well," said Paul, "I could match the other store's price, but I'd need verification."

Robin shuffled through our notes for a minute and produced a copy of the advertisement the other store had put in the local newspaper. Handing it to Paul she asked, "Will this do?"

Paul looked at it for a few seconds and said, "Yes, this is fine. Would you two excuse me for just a minute?"

"Of course," we said.

Paul took the advertisement and walked across the showroom full of washers, dryers, microwave ovens, stoves, and refrigerators to a door marked "Office." He went through the door and closed it behind him.

Robin and I stood admiring the washing machine and negotiating which of us would be able to be home to accept delivery of it.

Paul returned about two minutes later. "I'll match the price," he said.

"Another question I've got," Robin said, "is about delivery charges. I appreciate your matching the price, but I feel like we need an incentive to buy your machine rather than spend the money at the other store."

"What are you saying?" asked Paul. But he was smiling, so we knew he knew what was coming.

"Well," Robin said, "if you'll throw in free delivery, that would make it twenty-five dollars cheaper for us to buy this washing machine from you right now."

"If I do that," asked Paul, "do we have a deal?"

"Yes," Robin said.

"Then we have a deal," stated Paul, and he reached out and shook Robin's hand.

The story of the washing machine is really a story of consumer communication. Basically, we did our homework, and we did our "pre-writing." We gathered information and thought about the subject (washing machines), the audience (Paul the salesperson), the purpose (getting a good deal on the right washing machine), and what to say when the communication happened (how to present ourselves). We were *prepared* to communicate, and then we made a deal.

The point is that we used "consumer rhetoric." Another point, of course, is that we have been using that washing machine nearly every day for about a year, and it works really well. Robin and I may be talking to Paul the salesperson again soon—about a new dryer. ■

C: Post-Reading

Discussion Suggestions/Questions

Remembering

1. What are "closing costs?"

2. What did Robin and Dana negotiate?

3. What did Robin and Dana use to verify that the other store had the same washing machine on sale?

Analyzing

1. When communicating with an employee of a business, it is wise to keep in mind what might be important to that person. With others, discuss what sorts of things are important to people who work for businesses. To start, you might discuss Paul's motive for making the deal on the washing machine. Then list three things that are important to any business that works with the public.

2. The person who wrote "Consumer Communication" and his wife went through a process to buy a washing machine. Discuss with others the steps of this process. Then list those steps.

3. Some people think that using bargaining or making a deal is a type of lying, a way to trick people. Did the husband and wife who bought the washing machine in the reading trick or lie to Paul the salesperson? From your point of view, is

preparing for a communication situation a form of dishonesty? Discuss your thoughts on this issue with others.

Discovering

1. You may have thought of times when you have done some successful bargaining. Share these examples with your peers. Make the communication situation clear by including specific details in your story.

2. Using "rhetoric" in the sense of thinking about what you will say before you say it is something everybody does. For example, a person who wanted to ask his or her employer for a day off would think about what to say before saying it to the employer. In what kinds of situations do you use rhetoric?

D: Vocabulary Building

1. Two meanings of words related to *note*

<u>Notes:</u> "We took notes on our reading and on our discussions."

Elder: "Consumer Communication"

The word **note** comes from the Latin word *nota*, which originally meant a distinctive mark or brand by which something could be identified, like a brand on a calf. In later Latin *nota* also came to mean marks on paper, that is, written letters. Thus, in Latin two related but different meanings of *nota* evolved: (1) meanings having to do with recognizing or identifying something and (2) meanings having to do with writing.

In English there are a number of words related to **note** used in the first meaning of recognizing or identifying something. A good example is the verb **notice**, which means to recognize or pay attention to something. Something that we notice is **notable** or **noticeable**. *Note* itself can also be used in this sense as in "the TV reporters **noted** the President's speech." We call something **noteworthy** when it is worth paying attention to. To give someone **notice** is to **notify** him or her. When someone attracts positive attention, we refer to him or her as a **noted** person, but if a person attracts negative attention, we say that he or she is **notorious**.

There are also a number of words related to *note* used in reference to writing. The word *note* can refer to a short letter. A **notice** can also be a formal written announcement, like a **notice of sale**. The word *note* can refer to **notation**, the way something is written. We extend the meaning of *note* to include things that are represented by notes or marks on paper, such as a **musical note**. Someone who writes things down is a **notary**, as in the phrase **notary public**, a public officer authorized to certify documents and take oaths. We write on **note paper** and keep what we write in a **notebook**.

Vocabulary Building Activity 1: The Two Meanings of Words Related to *Note*

There are two basic meanings associated with the word *note:* (a) one group of meanings related to recognizing or noticing something and (b) a second group of meanings related to writing. After each sentence in the right column, write the letter (a) or (b) that corresponds to the meaning of the word in bold.

a. refers to recognizing or noticing something

b. refers to writing

1. Ms. Smith was a *noted* explorer._____

2. If we take out a loan, we must sign a *promissory note* that acknowledges our responsibility to repay the loan._____

3. I'm sorry; I didn't *notice* you standing there._____

4. A *footnote* is something written at the foot of the page._____

5. The sheriff posted the *notice* on every telegraph pole in the country._____

6. In his Gettysburg Address Lincoln said, "The world will little *note*, nor long remember, what we say here."_____

2. *-ive* adjectives formed from verbs

3. Different forms of *in-*

Inexpensive: "Anyway it turned out that buying an *inexpensive* home was more expensive than we had thought it would be."

Elder: "Consumer Communication"

Inexpensive is the negative form of the adjective **expensive**. *Expensive* and the noun **expense** both come from the verb to **expend**, as in "to expend effort." *Expend* comes from a Latin verb *expendere*, which meant "to weigh out money." Since the value of gold and silver coins was determined by weight, people used to determine the correct number of coins to use in buying something by weighing them out rather than by counting them out. The Latin verb *expendere* came into English twice. Our verb *expend* first came into English in the fifteenth century. However, *expendere* had also come into Old English in the eleventh century. That word evolved into the word we now know as the verb **spend**.

The ending *-ive* is used in many words derived from Latin to change a verb into an adjective, such as **attract/attractive; possess/possessive; effect/effective**. Notice that in changing the verb *expend* to the adjective *expensive*, the *d* disappears. In Latin grammar, adjectives that came from verbs often had quite irregular forms. Another example that follows this same pattern is the adjective verb **explode** and its corresponding *-ive* adjective form **explosive**.

Vocabulary Building Activity 2: *-ive* Adjectives Formed from Verbs

In the left column are *-ive* adjectives formed from verbs. In the space provided in the right column, write in the verb that the adjective comes from. The first question is done as an example.

-ive Adjective	Verb
1. decisive	*decide*
2. active	_____
3. expansive	_____
4. deceptive	_____
5. productive	_____
6. decorative	_____
7. offensive	_____
8. absorptive	_____
9. corrosive	_____
10. attentive	_____

The Latin prefix *in-*, meaning "not," is used only with adjectives. The related negative prefix in English is *un-*. We tend to use *in-* with words derived from Latin, although we use *un-* with both English words and a few words derived from Latin. For example, we say **infirm** (a Latin word) but **unwell** (an English word). The prefix *in-* was one of the most common prefixes in Latin. It also appears in hundreds of English words of Latin origin. Like the related English prefix *un-*, the main function of *in-* is to make adjectives negative. An unusual feature of *in-* is that it changes form. Depending on the first letter of the adjective that *in-* is attached to, *in-* can change to *il-*, *im-*, or *ir-*. The following exercise will give you enough examples of this change to figure out the rule that determines the form of *in-*.

Vocabulary Building Activity 3: Different Forms of *In-*

In the left column are adjectives derived from Latin words. In the appropriate column on the right, write in the negative form of the adjective, using the correct form of the negative prefix *in-*. When you have finished, see if you can state a rule that predicates which form of *in-* is used. The first two questions are done as examples.

Adjectives	in-	il-	im-	ir-
1. logical		*illogical*		
2. perfect			*imperfect*	
3. accurate				
4. replaceable				
5. coherent				
6. literate				
7. mature				
8. dependent				
9. regular				
10. legal				

SECTION
◄►
2

Drafting Consumer Letters

A: Pre-Writing: Sample Consumer Letters

Four kinds of consumer letters are mentioned in the introduction to this chapter: (1) consumer complaint, (2) consumer suggestion, (3) consumer request, and (4) consumer praise. Although all four types of consumer letters are useful, perhaps the most satisfying to write are consumer complaint and consumer praise letters.

Since all people are consumers, most people can easily think of consumer experiences to complain about or praise somebody for. Many people find that it is easier and more enjoyable to write consumer praise letters.

Pre-Writing Activity 1: Thinking and Talking about Consumer Letters

Look at the following drafts of consumer letters written by students. One of the most important parts of consumer writing is the specific details. By including names, dates, brand names, and model numbers of products, consumer writers communicate more clearly and powerfully. Think about or talk with others about what makes each of these letters effective or less effective.

Consumer Praise Letter

```
P.O. Box 1128
Tampa, FL 33602
November 25, 1993


PATAGONIA
1609 W. Babcock St.
P.O. Box 8900
Bozeman, MT 59715

Dear Patagonia Repair Persons:

I received my Patagonia Trailblazer jacket back from your
company; I had sent it to your company for repairs. The
plastic snaps on the jacket had broken off while I was
skiing. At first I was hesitant about getting plastic snaps
reattached to my jacket, but I have had my jacket back for
about six months now, and no more problems have arisen
with the snaps. I mainly want to thank you for the
efficiency of your staff. I didn't just receive my jacket
promptly but was amazed that my coat was cleaned.

Thank you for getting the grease stains out and the quick
return of my jacket with satisfactory snaps.

Sincerely,


Syrece S.
```

Consumer Complaint Letter

171 E. Pole Road
Lynden, VA 25918
December 4, 1993

Geoffrey Engstrom, Quality Control Inspector
Panasonic Products, Incorporated
6295 High Drive Blvd.
Los Angeles, CA 92006-5813

Dear Mr. Engstrom:

Your name was mentioned to me by the Aspen Sound Company in Los Angeles, California, as they were unable to deal with my problem. Recently, I purchased a Panasonic Portable Stereo Component System (Tx-CW43 model). The stereo system has a nice quality auto reverse relay system. The problem is when I purchased the system two months ago on October 4, the auto reverse, side two, tape cassette was dysfunctional. I ruined three of my tapes and it still hasn't been able to be repaired.

I took it back and asked for a refund. They replaced it with the same model, and the same problem happened again. I'm not satisfied, so I'm taking this system back and asking you for a full refund. I have enclosed the receipt and the request form they have given me. The time it has taken me to get something accomplished with this situation has upset me greatly. I hope you can take care of this problem immediately.

Sincerely unsatisfied,

Lorilyn M.

Consumer Praise Letter

---

424 Morrison
Cheney, WA 99004
November 21, 1993

Manager
Al's Auto Supply
N. 8117 Division
Spokane, WA 99207

Dear Manager:

I have been buying products at your store for a couple of years now, and I am really impressed with your competitive prices and all of your friendly employees who go out of their way to help customers. I brought an alternator into your store on October 18, and I wasn't sure if the alternator was still good or not. John, one of your employees, was more than happy to test it, and without asking, he gave me a price on a new one.

Keep up the good work.

Sincerely,

Jeff M.

Consumer Praise Letter

Streeter Hall RM #509
College Town, Alaska 99697
December 4, 1993

Susan Mackey, Director
Financial Aid and Scholarship Office
Eastern University, MS-145
College Town, Alaska 99697

I just wanted to thank your office personnel, and especially Barbara O'Neill, for all the help I have received
this year with my Financial Aid forms. Barbara is a
wonderful person, to me, and it might be her job, but she
sure does it well; she helped me to understand what to do,
how to do it, and why it needed to be done. For example,
I turned some papers in late, and I didn't know what was
going on. I went up to the Financial Aid Office and asked
for an appointment of some sort. They were very busy and
couldn't get me in for some time, but Barbara happened to
walk out and hear what was going on. Her ten o'clock
appointment was late, so she took me back to her office and
explained to me what I needed to do and what to wait for.

Also, whenever I call the office, if Barbara is not in
because of lunch or if she's on another line, she gets
back to me promptly. In your office, I'm sure there are a
lot of people like Barbara, and I'm very thankful.

Thanks again for all the help and for taking the time to
read this letter because I know how busy you people are.
I'm also glad to have people like Barbara in Eastern
University's Financial Aid and Scholarship Office.

Sincerely,

Terry D.

Pre-Writing Activity 2: Talking about Consumer Experiences

With others, talk about recent consumer experiences you have had. Has an employee
of a bank or a gas station or a grocery store been more pleasant and helpful than usual?

Is there something you have bought recently that you are not happy with? As a student, you are a consumer of education. Has somebody who works for the school you attend been especially helpful to you? You will be writing a consumer letter. You might as well write to a real person about a real situation.

An important kind of pre-writing is thinking about the communication situation. Choose one of the situations you have shared with others and brainstorm some ideas about the features of the communication situation on the worksheet that follows. Remember that all of these features are related to one another. You may consider the features in any order. Start with the feature (1, 2, 3, or 4) about which you have the most ideas.

1. Subject. What are the facts? Consumer writing works best when the writer includes names, dates, and model numbers for the products discussed.

2. Reader or audience. Think about the person to whom you will write. First, who should it be? For example, when praising an employee it is customary to write to that person's supervisor. When writing a consumer complaint it is best to write to a person who can do something about your situation. For example, you wouldn't write to a meter-checker to complain about a parking ticket. In the following space, make some notes about the person to whom you will write. Who is the person, and what is important to him or her?

3. Writer or consumer. How do you want to present yourself? Do you want to sound angry or polite? How much information about yourself do you want to include in your letter?

4. Purpose. What do you want to happen as a result of your letter?

Optional: Share and discuss with others your ideas on the pre-writing activity.

Consumer letters are most effective when they are addressed to a particular person. You need to get the name of the person who has the power to help you. Probably you can call the business to which you will write and get that name. You also need an address, which you can probably get from the phone book. This pre-writing activity is to get the information you need.

Name: _____ Title:_____

Address: _____

B: Writing a First or Initial Draft: Consumer Letter Prompt

After you have completed the pre-writing, look back over this work. Then write your letter. Since consumer letters are business letters, use the following business letter format. Using this format is wise. It makes the writer look good. There are other business letter formats, but this one is perfectly acceptable.

DRAFTING

DRAFTING

YOUR STREET ADDRESS

CITY, STATE ZIP CODE

DATE

Name of audience, title of that person
Name of business
Street address
City, state zip code

Dear [name of audience]:

Message (What is the situation, and what do you want to communicate about it?)

_____

_____

_____

_____

_____

Closing remark (This is usually a brief thank you for the audience's having read your letter.)

_____

_____

_____

_____

Sincerely,

Your signature

Your typed name

Revising Consumer Letters for Specificity, Clarity of Purpose, and Form

A: Specificity, Clarity of Purpose, and Form

Three features of consumer letter writing are particularly important.

1. Specificity. The person who receives a consumer letter appreciates specific details. Dates, brand names, and model numbers or names of products are needed. Names and addresses of both the business and the consumer are important.

2. Clarity of purpose. A consumer letter should be very clear about what the consumer expects the business to do in response to the letter.

3. Form. Two levels of form are important in this kind of writing. First, the letter should conform to the business letter format—it should look like a business letter. Second, the spelling, grammar, and punctuation in a consumer letter must be correct. Grammar, punctuation, or spelling errors interfere with communication. Also, accuracy in such matters invites a professional response.

B: Revising Drafts of Student Consumer Letters

Read the following three consumer letters written by students. While reading them, pay special attention to (1) specificity, (2) purpose, and (3) form. What suggestions would you make to the writers of these letters? Share your suggestions with others.

REVISING

Student Letter: Consumer Complaint

P.O. Box 743
Ephrata,WA 99209
November 25, 1993

Manager
Ephrata Florists
825 Basin SW
Ephrata, WA 99203

Dear Manager:

On Oct. 28, 1993, I ordered a boutonniere for Homecoming which was on the evening of Nov. 2, 1993. I was very disappointed in the quality of the boutonniere. It was supposed to be a white rose tipped in blue. I specifically told the clerk, Karen, not to put any baby's breath or ribbons on it.

To my surprise, on Saturday afternoon when I picked it up, the boutonniere had transparent ribbon and black baby's breath. In addition the rose was already turning brown. With only two hours until I was supposed to be picked up by my date, I proceeded to remove the ribbon and baby's breath at home. During the course of the evening, I noticed the white rose looked like it had died and gone to heaven.

I am not writing this for a refund, but just to let you know so you can take care of this kind of inconvenience in the future. Do not worry. I will continue to give you my business as in the past.

Sincerely,

Tracey L.

Student Letter: Consumer Complaint

P.O. Box 18632
Sunview, CA 94720
November 25, 1993

Manager
Hershey's Chocolate Co.
S. 3625 8th Avenue
Chicago, Illinois 95768

Dear Mr. Candy Man:

A couple of days ago I bought a candy bar made by your company from a Safeway grocery store near my house. The candy bar I bought was a Hershey's chocolate bar, which is usually one of my favorite kinds of candy. This particular candy bar had a real bitter taste and gave me an upset stomach. I went back to the store the next day and bought another one, and the same thing happened again. I just thought I would write you and tell you that you have a bad batch of candy out on the shelves, and you probably should have them taken off the shelves and replaced with new ones before you start getting a lot of complaints about people getting sick off your candy bars.

Concerned,

Kevin C.

REVISING

Student Letter: Consumer Praise

```
Route 6, Box 1
Manson, AL 21340
November 25, 1993


P. Tait, Manager
Lake Reclamation District
145 Roses Ave.
Manson, AL 21349

Dear Manager Tait:

I am writing to express my gratitude toward your employ-
ees. On October 25, at about 11:00 P.M. as I was about to
go to bed, I heard a loud snap and then a sudden woosh.
I ran outside to see what the noise was and made the
discovery that it was a large irrigation pipe. I phoned
one of your employees at that second. They arrived in the
following three minutes and shut off the gushing water.
500 gallons per second had been running out of the pipe
for about the last four minutes. They worked long and hard
through the night trying to fix the broken 32" pipe. The
pipe was fixed and many of my trees were saved. The damage
to my property was less significant than to the county
road. The water gushing out of the pipe washed numerous
amounts of gravel into my orchard, but it was the volume
of water that washed out many of my sprinklers and trees.
I am grateful for the fast response of your employees and
the amount of damage they minimized by shutting off the
water.

Thankfully yours,


David L.
```

C: Revising Your Consumer Letter

Using the strategies you have practiced, revise your own consumer letter for (1) specificity, (2) clarity, and (3) form.

D: Helping Others to Revise Their Consumer Letters

Exchange consumer letters with other students in your class. Then read the letters and suggest improvements in (1) specificity, (2) clarity of purpose, and (3) form. Basically, you are helping one another to make these letters as good as they can be.

SECTION
◀▶
4

Final Editing for Run-on Sentences

A **run-on sentence** consists of two or more **independent clauses** that have been joined together without the required punctuation. (An independent clause is a clause that can stand alone as a complete sentence. Every sentence must contain at least one independent clause.) Incorrectly joining the two independent clauses together with only a comma is called a **comma splice**. Incorrectly joining the two independent clauses together with no punctuation at all is called a **fused sentence**. Here are some examples of each type of run-on sentence from student essays with both independent clauses underlined: (The *
reminds us that the sentence is ungrammatical or incorrectly punctuated.)

Comma Splice:

1. *Education opens up your world, it creates an awareness of the world around you.

2. *The high cost of college can be overcome, many companies looking for employees will pay tuition if they hire you.

3. *Learning is enjoyable to most everyone, I believe that it is a way of discovering oneself and the society we live in.

Fused Sentence:

4. *I like for people to be close it is like being in a big, happy family.

5. *I love to play football it has been fun for me for many years.

For the most part, run-on sentences are errors of punctuation, not of grammar or thinking. In most run-on sentences, the ideas that the two independent clauses express are very closely related—so closely related, in fact, that the writer does not want to separate these two ideas by putting them into different sentences. So the problem of run-ons is not in changing what the writer is trying to do; the problem is learning the right punctuation.

As you can tell from these examples, there is no real difference in the way that comma splices and fused sentences are used. Not surprisingly, then, it also turns out that there is no difference in the way that we correct comma splice errors and fused sentence errors. Accordingly, we will lump both comma splice and fused sentence errors together as run-on errors.

The Yes/No Question Test for Run-On Sentence Errors

The first step in dealing with run-on errors is learning to see them in your own writing. A simple test for finding run-on errors is to turn the sentence into two (or more) yes/no questions—questions that can be answered with either yes or no. The idea of the yes/no question test is that every independent clause can be changed into a yes or no question. For example, see the following independent clause:

6.   This is an independent clause.

It can be changed into the following yes/no question:

6a.   Is this an independent clause?

We can tell when a sentence contains two independent clauses because each independent clause will produce its own yes/no question when we apply the yes/no test. If the two independent clauses are not punctuated correctly—that is, if they are separated by only a comma or are not separated by any punctuation at all—then the sentence is a run-on sentence. Here is how the yes/no question test works for the following five run-on sentences:

1.   *Education opens up your world, it creates an awareness of the world around you.
       Yes/no test 1: Does education open up your world?
       Yes/no test 2: Does it create an awareness of the world around you?

2.   *The high cost of college can be overcome, many companies looking for employees will pay tuition if they hire you.
       Yes/no test 1: Can the high cost of college be overcome?
       Yes/no test 2: Will many companies looking for employees pay tuition if they hire you?

3.   *Learning is enjoyable to most everyone, I believe that it is a way of discovering oneself and the society we live in.
    Yes/no test 1: Is learning enjoyable to most everyone?
    Yes/no test 2: Do I believe that it is a way of discovering oneself and the society we live in?

4.   *I like for people to be close it is like being in a big, happy family.
    Yes/no test 1: Do I like for people to be close?
    Yes/no test 2: Is it like being in a big, happy family?

5.   *I love to play football it has been fun for me for many years.
    Yes/no test 1: Do I love to play football?
    Yes/no test 2: Has it been fun for me for many years?

The *yes/no* test shows that all of the five sentences contain two independent clauses. Since these independent clauses are incorrectly joined with either a comma or with no punctuation at all, all five sentences are run-ons.

Editing Activity 1: Using the Yes/No Test to Identify Run-On Sentences

Use the *yes/no* test on the following sentences. If the *yes/no* test shows that the sentence contains two independent clauses, and if the independent clauses are joined with either a comma or with no punctuation at all, write *run-on*. If the *yes/no* test shows that the sentence contains only a single independent clause, write *okay*. The first question is done as an example.

1. College is something of a privilege it almost always promises a job.
   Answer:
   Is college something of a privilege?
   Does it almost always promise a job?
   Run-on

2. It was the career that I wanted, it was a chance at a real future for me.

3. I signed up for three years, I was told that I was going to airborne school.

4. We can better our education in college we will learn about who we are.

5. My roommate tries to leave me alone when I have a lot of work to do.

6. My oldest brother made a mistake he ended up going to school an extra year.

7. You should have studied more for that big test in chemistry.

8. You will also learn to deal with other people you will gain people skills that help with everyday life.

9. Going to school is necessary in our technological society we need the tools to compete in today's world.

10. Learning to use your mind is an important aspect of getting an education a mind becomes dormant without stimulation.

_____

_____

_____

11. She said that she was sorry that I was leaving and that she would give me a call.

_____

_____

_____

Three Types of Run-On Errors

Nearly all run-on errors fall into one of three categories, depending on the relationship of the two independent clauses to each other. Knowing about these categories is important for two reasons: (1) knowing the typical profile of run-ons will help you recognize them in your own writing, and (2) the three different types of run-on errors are corrected in different ways. The three types of run-on errors are the following:

1. The first independent clause is a generalization that the second independent clause elaborates or explains or illustrates. We will call this type the **generalization/example** run-on error.

2. The first and second independent clauses deliberately contrast with each other. We will call this type the **contrastive** run-on error.

3. The second independent clause is a comment on or reaction to what was said in the first independent clause. We will call this type the **commentary** run-on error.

A: Generalization/Example Run-on Errors

This is by far the most common type of run-on error. Roughly half of all run-on errors belong to this category. Here are two typical run-on errors of this type taken from student essays, with a brief commentary on each:

7.   *Money is not happiness, it can't buy love or trust.

In the second independent clause of (7), the author supports the generalization that money can't buy happiness by naming two important things that money cannot buy.

8.   *People learn to accept others for what they are, they don't try to change them.

In the second independent clause of (8), the author gives an example of what acceptance of others means—people don't try to change others.

The generalization/example type of run-on error is relatively easy to correct because the ideas in the two independent clauses are naturally related. In most cases of this type of run-on error, the solution is simple. Keep the ideas together in the same sentence by using a semicolon (;) to join the two independent clauses. The two run-on sentences at the beginning of this section could be corrected by using semicolons:

7a.   Money is not happiness; it can't buy love or trust.

8a.   People learn to accept others for what they are; they don't try to change them.

Sometimes a good alternative to the semicolon is to change the second independent clause to a subordinate clause by using words such as *because* or *since*. This is a particularly effective alternative for sentence (7):

7b.   Money is not happiness **because** it can't buy love or trust.

A common mistake with run-on sentences of the generalization/example type is to join the two independent clauses with a comma and the expression *for example*:

8b.   *People learn to accept others for what they are, **for example**, they don't try to change them.

Sentence (8b) is still a run-on. Using *for example* doesn't change anything because the two independent clauses are still joined only with a comma. Again, the simplest solution is to use a semicolon:

8c.   People learn to accept others for what they are; **for example**, they don't try to change them.

Editing Activity 2: Identifying and Correcting Generalization/Example Type Run-ons

The following letter contains a number of generalization/example type run-on errors. Using the yes/no question test, find and underline all the run-on sentences, and then correct them in the way that you think works best for this letter. The number of run-on sentences in each paragraph is given in parentheses at the end of the paragraph.

313 N. Elm St.
Los Angeles, CA 93854
February 12, 1993

Howard Johnson, Manager
SuperVac Warehouse Distributor
2001 1st St.
New York, New York 10022

Dear Mr. Johnson:

I recently bought the SuperVac 150 Deluxe model from your north-west distributors. It did not work properly, it wouldn't pick up any dirt at all. I returned the vacuum cleaner to your distributor, and one of your employees, Dan Ackerman, put the hose attachment on the vacuum cleaner to make sure it worked correctly. Mr. Ackerman was very polite and helpful, for example he took time to make sure I knew how to attach the hose myself. (2)

When I got home, the vacuum cleaner worked fine on the carpets, it picked up everything without any strain. But when I attached the hose and tried to dust, it broke down. The suction noise got louder and louder, it sounded like the vacuum cleaner was tearing itself apart. Finally the vacuum bag popped open. It made a big mess in my living room my white carpet got dirt and grease all over it. (3)

I returned the vacuum cleaner to your distributor and explained the situation. They said that I must have sucked something up in the vacuum cleaner and blocked it, but when they looked inside, they couldn't find anything. They said they could fix the carpet cleaner but not the hose attachment. I need a general-purpose vacuum cleaner, I must be able to dust as well as vacuum. When I asked for a refund, they refused to give me one. (1)

Enclosed is a copy of my receipt of purchase and the warranty. As you can see, the vacuum cleaner is brand-new, I bought it less than a month ago. My family has had a SuperVac for years. It worked perfectly we never had to have it fixed even once. I would like to continue using your products, but if I don't receive a full refund, I will take my business to someone else. (2)

Sincerely,

Tina P.

EDITING

B: Contrastive Run-on Errors

In this type of run-on error, the two independent clauses are designed to contrast with each other. Often sentences of this type have a kind of one-two punch in which the first independent clause sets up a contrasting statement in the second independent clause. For example, here is a contrastive run-on sentence from a student essay:

9.   *Knowledge can't hurt you, it's the lack of knowledge that will.

The first independent clause, *Knowledge can't hurt you*, sets up the contrasting statement that what will hurt you is the lack of knowledge. The second independent clause is like the punch line of a joke that the first independent clause sets up. Here are more examples from student essays:

10.   *Their college education was great, the problem was the way they used it.

11.   *These aren't like the people you knew from high school, these are people just like yourself.

12.   *I'm not a 4.0 student, I'm just a 2.9 student.

All four of these sentences could be corrected merely by joining the two independent clauses with a semicolon:

9a.   Knowledge can't hurt you; it's the lack of knowledge that will hurt you.

10a.   Their college education was great; the problem was the way they used it.

11a.   These aren't like the people you knew from high school; these are people just like yourself.

12a.   I'm not a 4.0 student; I'm just a 2.9 student.

However, there are other punctuation options that you should also consider. One option is to emphasize the difference in ideas between the independent clauses by separating them with a dash (two hyphens on a typewriter or computer) or even by putting them in separate sentences. These options would work especially well with sentence (12):

12b.   I'm not a 4.0 student—I'm just a 2.9 student.

12c.   I'm not a 4.0 student. I'm just a 2.9 student.

Editing Activity 3: Identifying and Correcting Contrastive and Generalization/Example Type Run-on Errors

The following letter contains a number of both contrastive and generalization/example type run-on errors. Using the yes/no question test to help you, find and then underline all

EDITING

the run-on sentences. Then correct them in the way that you think works best for this letter. The number of run-on sentences in each paragraph is given in parentheses at the end of the paragraph.

```
1456 S. Easy St.
Sunnyside, WA 98945
May 10, 1993


Earnest Tappit, Manager
Sus Pect Motors
313 Main St.
Sunnyside, WA 98944

Dear Mr. Tappit:

I am writing this letter in regard to our 1991 Chevrolet
Beretta GT. This car is less than a year old, we purchased
it new from you on June 1, 1992. The car itself has run
fine, the problem is the paint job. Two months ago we
noticed that the paint on the hood was cracking. Now the
paint is actually chipping off, it looks like the car is
molting. When we first bought the car, we got a special wax
from your body shop at the suggestion of the salesman. I
have kept a heavy coat of wax on the car at all times to
protect it from the salt on the winter roads and the dust
in summer time. The car has always been protected from the
elements, it is always kept in a garage when it is not
being driven. (4)

When I saw that the paint was cracking and chipping off,
I took the car back to you to get the car repainted. The
man we talked to said that you wouldn't do anything unless
we paid for all of it. He refused to repaint the car, he
even refused to repair the damage. He claimed the paint
had been damaged by gravel from driving on unpaved roads,
then he claimed that we hadn't taken care of the car. I
know that both these claims are untrue, I have taken very
good care of the car. I didn't buy a car from you just to
get a good price, I expect reasonable service as well. (4)
```

```
Finally, we talked to the service manager. He was not very
helpful, in fact, he was even worse. After he looked the
car over, he said that the reason the paint was cracking
and chipping was that the car had been in a wreck, it had
been repainted, and whoever had done the job had not put
the bonding on correctly so that the paint was now coming
off. I am the only person who drives this car, nobody else
has ever used it. This car has never been in a wreck, it
has never been in an accident of any kind. If this car has
ever been damaged by being in an accident, the accident
took place before I bought the car from you. I don't want
any more evasions, I want an answer. Did you sell us a
once-wrecked vehicle as a new car? (5)

Sincerely,

Melinda H.
```

C: Commentary Run-on Errors

The final type of run-on error is created when the second independent clause is a comment on or a reaction to the idea expressed in the first independent clause. The second independent clause is often like an aside—a line that an actor turns and delivers directly to the audience. In the case of writing, it is like the writer directly addressing the reader. Here are two examples from student essays of this type of run-on error:

13. *You come out of the exam with 95% or even 100%, now that is rewarding.

14. *Everything I put into school will be worthwhile if I get this job, if I don't get it, well, I'll have to live with it.

In essays based on personal experience, commentaries on what you have just written can be very effective. Since a commentary is not a continuation of the idea expressed in the first independent clause, a semicolon is not a good way to join the two independent clauses. A better solution is to emphasize the contrast between the idea in the first independent clause and the commentary on it in the second independent clause by a dash or by a period. Here are both of these solutions applied to example run-on sentences 13 and 14:

13a. Dash: You come out of the exam with 95% or even 100%—now that is rewarding.
Period: You come out of the exam with 95% or even 100%. Now that is rewarding.

14a. Dash: Everything I put into school will be worthwhile if I get this job—if I don't get it, well, I'll have to live with it.

Period: Everything I put into school will be worthwhile if I get this job. If I don't get it, well, I'll have to live with it.

In more formal papers, contrastive sentences (even when punctuated correctly) should not be used very often. Like exclamation points or words underlined for emphasis, contrastive sentences quickly become tiresome if used too often.

Editing Activity 4: Editing for Run-on Errors

The following sentences came from student essays. Using the *yes/no* question test to help you, find and then correct the run-on errors in the way that you think works best. If a sentence does not contain a run-on error, write *okay*. The first question is done as an example.

1. I am here because I love school it is fun learning new things.
   I am here because I love school; it is fun learning new things.

2. College offers more to students than jobs, an education helps make the student a well-rounded person.

3. A person can go into business for oneself, if the business were to fail, one could always apply those business skills to a job working for someone else.

4. I don't think about how college will get me a job in the future, I think about how college is affecting my personal and mental life now.

5. Finding a job with so much competition in our society is tough, that's why I'm staying in school.

6. The army recruiter told about all the things I could learn while they were paying me to learn them, well, it sounded good at the time.

7. The class wasn't hard, it was impossible!

8. I like for people to be close because it is kind of like being in one big, happy family.

9. Another reason to justify all this work we do now is the involvement with other students, for example, you might discover who you are.

10. It used to be that most young people wouldn't go to college because they would get married and go to work.

11. It doesn't stop after one year either, it keeps adding up year after year.

Editing Activity 5: Editing for Run-On Errors in an Essay

The following letter contains a number of run-on errors of all types. Underline all the run-on sentences, and then correct them in the way that you think works best for this letter. The number of run-on sentences in each paragraph is given in parentheses at the end of the paragraph.

23917 Sinto Ave.
Spokane, WA 99687
November 27, 1993

T. Hopton, Ski Patrol Director
Whistler Mountain Ski Area
213 N. 3rd St.
Whistler, British Columbia

Dear Mr. Hopton:

I am writing this letter to thank you and your patrol for your help. Last week when I was skiing at Whistler Mountain, I had a bad spill under chair nine, it was a real wipe-out. I could not move my left leg or find my new skis. I was afraid that I would be there for hours before people going up the chair lift could get to the top, call the ski patrol, and have someone work his or her way up to me. I knew I wasn't in real danger of freezing, but I was getting worried, you never know when you might go into shock. One of your patrol members, Karen Rivers, saw me lying on the slope, how she spotted me in the blowing snow, I'll never know. (3)

Karen was very professional, she knew exactly what to do. Somehow she managed to roll me onto the sled without hurting my knee, this was no easy trick because I really couldn't help very much. After I was wrapped up in a blanket, she searched around and found my new skis, I was really afraid that they were gone for good. She stayed with me until we were back in the lodge and I was comfortable in the warming room, she even got me some coffee and a magazine while we were waiting for the doctor to come. When the doctor came, he examined me and found that I had dislocated my knee. When he took hold of my leg, I nearly fainted, just ask Karen how I turned as white as a ghost. Then he popped the knee-cap back into place it went in with a little click and stopped hurting almost instantly. My leg is absolutely normal now, it is hard to believe that it even happened, except when I remember the doctor taking hold of it. (7)

I would like to thank Karen for all of her help, she was terrific. You certainly have a well-trained ski patrol, her rescue techniques were right out of the textbook. I know that rescue work is her job, she does this kind of thing every day. Nevertheless, without her help I might have been in real trouble on that mountain, for example I might have had more trouble with my leg and might even have had to buy a new pair of skis. (4)

Sincerely,

Tim O.

APHORISMS

Reading for Details of Emotion

A: Pre-Reading

Aphorisms are short sayings that seem to point to truths about life. For example, you have probably heard the saying "What goes around, comes around." This is an aphorism. Part of what it means is that if you are rude to someone, someone else will be rude to you. On the other hand, if you are responsible and honest, others will also tend to be responsible and honest with you.

These short sayings present values. They can be very useful resources for thinking about how you should behave. Another personal example comes from a student. Her father used to say to her, "You'd complain if you were hung with a new rope." As a child, this confused her. If she were hanged, what difference would the age or condition of the rope have on the outcome? Later, she realized that part of what her father meant was that her usual response to many things was to complain about them. Whenever she was asked to do something like mow the lawn, her response was usually "But I was going to meet my friend," or "But it's my brother's turn to cut the grass."

This aphorism pointed to a larger principle: people don't enjoy hearing excuses and complaints. Everybody complains sometimes—and with good reason—but if a person's response to everything is to complain, that person is out of balance. This student's father actually taught her a truth about living. It was good advice for all of us.

Pre-Reading Activities

Discussion

1. With the whole class or in small groups, discuss possible meanings of some of the following aphorisms. One useful way to do this is to imagine a situation in which one person would give this advice to another person.

   a. When in doubt, ask.

   b. Moderation in all things.

    c. What's good for the goose is good for the gander.

    d. When the going gets tough, the tough get going.

    e. Never count your chickens before they hatch.

    f. Practice makes perfect.

    g. If you can't say anything nice, don't say anything at all.

    h. Never judge a book by its cover.

    i. That's the way the ball bounces.

    j. What goes around, comes around.

    k. Don't look a gift horse in the mouth.

    l. If at first you don't succeed, try, try again.

    m. Anything worth doing is worth doing right.

2. Think of aphorisms that you like and have found useful. With others, take turns sharing them and discussing what they might mean. Try to think of sayings that have meaning for you. This is easier than it sounds. One way to come up with aphorisms is to recall those expressions your father, mother, or one of your teachers repeated until you were sick of them. Remember that not all aphorisms are true for all people.

Reading Suggestions

(Keep these suggestions in mind as you read "The World According to Claude" by Anthony Walton.)

1. Some people think that education gives a person intelligence. What opinion does the author of the "The World According to Claude" seem to have on this issue?

2. Underline, highlight, or write on a piece of paper any sayings included in the reading that <u>you</u> think identify a truth about life and any which <u>you</u> think are not true.

3. Are aphorisms nuggets of wisdom or annoying repetitions of mindless sayings? What does the author of "The World According to Claude" think about aphorisms?

4. What is Anthony Walton's purpose? What does he want the reader to think, feel, or do as a result of reading what he has written?

Vocabulary Preview

contemplate: think about. (Many people <u>contemplate</u> the meaning of life.)

excruciating: very painful. (My friend's death was <u>excruciating</u>.)

fidelity: loyalty. (She showed <u>fidelity</u> to her parents by visiting them every week.)

frugality: being careful about spending. ("A penny saved is a penny earned" is an aphorism about <u>frugality</u>.)

intractability: being unchangeable, immovable. (He showed his <u>intractability</u> by not even listening when I tried to change his mind.)

ruptured: broken. (The radiator was <u>ruptured</u> in the accident.)

unrelenting: never changing, never giving up. (He was <u>unrelenting</u> in his search for a better job.)

B: Reading

"The World According to Claude"

BY ANTHONY WALTON

"You can get by, but you can't get away." I kept hearing my father's voice, and it was annoying. Here I was, spending a beautiful Saturday morning in a Santa Monica hardware store instead of driving up the California coast or sleeping in.

I was sorting through aisles of plastic pipe connectors, all because someone had tried to get away with building a sprinkler system on the cheap. The system had ruptured, flooding my friend's yard and sidewalk. To avoid a hefty plumber's fee, we had to do the repairs ourselves. I couldn't help hearing my father again: "Do it right the first time."

I've grown accustomed to hearing Claude's voice. As I've gotten older, I hear him almost every day. "You're penny-wise and dollar-foolish." "You got champagne tastes but a water pocket." "Don't believe everything you hear." As my friends and I run into brick walls working our way into adulthood, I am increasingly amazed at the sometimes brutal truth that my father has imparted in his seemingly offhand way.

One Christmas Eve, he and I were working on the furnace of a rental house he owns. It was about 20 below outside and, I thought, colder inside. Tormented by visions of a family-room fire, cocoa and pampering by my mother (I was home from college), I wanted my father to call it a day and get on with the festivities. After all, it was Christmas.

"We can't," said my father. "This is these people's home. They should be home on Christmas." He continued wrenching and whanging on a pipe.

I saw an opening. "Exactly. We should be home on Christmas."

He shook his head. "It ain't that simple."

"It'd be simple to call somebody."

"You got a thousand dollars?"

"No. But you do."

"The reason I got it is, I don't give it away on things I can do myself."

A couple of hours later, when we had finished and were loading our tools into the car, he looked at me. "See? That wasn't so hard. But nobody can tell you anything. That thousand dollars will come in handy. In fact, I'll probably have to send it to you." He shook his head, closed the trunk and said, "Boy, just keep on living."

"Just keep on living." I often thought it sounded like a threat, but now I see that he was challenging me to see the world as it is and to live in it responsibly. I was like a lot of kids I knew, middle-class, happy, successful at most of what I attempted—but largely at the expense (literally) of my father and world he created. Now as I contemplate creating a world for his grandchildren, I gain more respect for such an accomplishment and the unblinking steadiness it takes.

My father is the kind of man overlooked or ridiculed by the media. His values— fidelity, simplicity and frugality—are spurned by younger people, but I am beginning to see that these are the very values that keep a society functioning.

"Boy, you got to get a routine." He has gone to a job he does not like, in a steel factory, for 36 years. One day I asked him why, and he looked at me as if I had rocks in my head: "That's where the money is." And he has been married to the same woman for 31 years. "Marriage gives you a reason to do things."

As I gain more experience in a world where, it seems, virtually everything is disposable, I begin to appreciate the unsurpassed values of steadiness and limited objectives. I'm reminded of the television family "All in the Family" and how much of the humor was directed at the willfully uninformed, purposely contrary Archie Bunker. It occurs to me, as I contemplate buying my first house, that everyone else, including his son-in-law, Meathead, who gloried in putting Archie down, was sleeping in Archie's house and eating Archie's grub. I'm increasingly aware of how much security my father has brought to my adventures.

They were adventures he rarely understood. My father was born into excruciating poverty in rural Mississippi during the Depression. He had very little formal education, leaving school early to support his brothers and sisters, and bounced from Holly

Springs, Miss., to Memphis to Chicago to the Air Force. But along the way he acquired a world view as logical as Newton's.

The first and most important law of the world according to Claude is "Have the facts." God is the only thing he takes on faith. Recently, searching for a new lawn tractor, he went to three different dealers and got three different prices for the same machine. "I'm from just outside Missouri; you got to show me." He then went to a fourth dealer and purchased a larger tractor for less money.

I used to laugh at one of his hobbies, analyzing financial tables. He would look up from half an hour of calculating and announce: "Did you know if you put five cents in the bank when Columbus came to America, at 5¼ interest compounded daily, today you'd have $1,000,565,162 (or some such figure)?" Now I phone him for advice about financing a house or car, and I'm beginning to understand how he can own real estate and several cars, educate his kids and regularly bail those kids out of jams. "Boy, a nickel only goes so many ways. But nobody can tell you nothing. Just keep on living."

And I've kept on living and surrendered a lot of illusions, one by one. Claude says, "You reap what you sow." I call this idea karma, that what goes around comes around. Claude cautioned me one night as I went out to break off with a girlfriend, "Remember, you got a sister." The notion that there was a link between my behavior and how I could expect my sister to be treated has served as a painfully clear guide ever since. And, in the current romantic and sexual climate, I like to think it's saved me some trouble. "You can get by, but you can't get away."

Claude values experience. I remember going with him in search of a family attorney. He decided against several without saying why, before suddenly settling on a firm right there in the office. On the way home he explained: "I was looking for a 'Daddy' kind of man. Somebody who's been through some battles, who's raised children. He had those pictures up of his grandchildren. That tells me what he values. And I think he's already made most of his mistakes." When I asked him where he had acquired all this insight, he laughed. "I didn't get to be fifty and black by being stupid. You go around enough times, you begin to catch on."

Claude doesn't put a lot of stock in what he calls book learning. He says, "College never made anybody smart." But he has financed about $100,000 worth of book learning—and endured its being thrown in his face until the thrower had to return, hat in hand, for one kind of aid or another.

This leads to another basic law: "Be realistic." Claude sees the world very clearly, and what he sees is often not pretty. "It was like this when I got here, and it's going to be like this when I leave, so I'm not going to worry about it." I'm coming to see the wisdom in this. Young people often have to experience the world for many years before they have a hint of understanding human nature and, more important, history. For this reason, they often misread the world. They do not understand that poverty, war and racism have always been conditions of human life. Worse, when confronted by the unrelenting intractability of these problems, they often abandon smaller, but equally worthy, goals.

Claude likes to say, "If everybody would clean up his yard, the rest of the world would take care of itself." That statement verges on oversimplification, but as a way of recognizing one's true responsibilities in the world it makes irreproachable sense.

This is probably the key to the world according to Claude—the power of limited objectives. By being realistic about our goals, we increase our chances of success in the long run. "Anything we do is going to be hard, and if it isn't hard, it's going to be difficult. But that just means it's going to take us a little longer." To me, this acceptance of the world and life as they are, and not as we would have them be, is the key to becoming an adult.

And so I am forced to acknowledge that the world according to Claude is increasingly, in my experience, the world as it is. I realize you can't put a price on a clear conscience, as Claude loves to say; very often the ability to live with one's self is all one can hope for. I'm beginning to see the power in, to spin a metaphor, not needing to play every single golf course on the planet; Claude has built a putting green in his back yard and mastered that. He has made his peace with the world, and that is enough.

Most of all, I realize that every time Claude said, "Nobody can tell you nothing," he went ahead and told me something—and it was always the truth. Except maybe once. We were arguing, and I took exception to what I perceived as highhandedness. "You should respect me," I said. "We're supposed to be friends."

He looked at me gravely. "We are not friends. I am your father."

I haven't quite figured this out, because he is far from being my best friend. Sometimes I'm not sure we even know each other. But it seems he is the truest friend I have had and can expect to have. ∎

Walton, Anthony. "The World According to Claude." *Reader's Digest* Jan. 1990: 133–136. Reprinted with permission from the January 1990 *Reader's Digest*.

C: Post-Reading

Discussion Questions/Suggestions

Remembering

1. What was Claude's job? *steele factory worker*

2. How much money did Claude spend on his children's education? *$100,000.00*

3. How did Claude choose a lawyer? *Saw pictures of grandchildren; wanted a "daddy man."*

Analyzing

1. Share the aphorisms you underlined, highlighted, or wrote down while reading "The World According to Claude," and then discuss the value of these aphorisms with your peers.

2. What is the author's purpose? What does he want readers to do or think about after reading "The World According to Claude"?

Discovering

1. How are education and intelligence different? What do they have in common? Can a person be very smart in one way and not in another? Share examples of this with your peers.

2. Are there people you know who are very successful but who never went to college? What do these people do? How did they get started?

3. Often what the reader thinks of while reading is more important than what the author of the reading writes. There are ideas you had or aphorisms you remembered while reading this selection. Discuss these with your peers.

D: Vocabulary Building

1. Words related to *faith*

Fidelity: "His values—**fidelity**, simplicity and frugality—are spurned by younger people. . . ."

Walton: "The Word According to Claude"

What do the name of your dog, the heroine of Beethoven's only opera, and the motto of the U.S. Marine Corps all have in common?

The noun *fidelity* comes from the Latin word *fidelis*, "faithful," a form of the adjective *fides*, which comes into English as the noun **faith**. The English adjective **faithful** literally means "full of faith." The related abstract noun is **faithfulness**. The Latin phrase *semper fidelis* "always faithful" is used as the motto of the U.S. Marine Corps.

In the noun *fidelity*, and in most words related to it, "faith" is not used in a religious sense, but more in the sense of keeping one's promise or honoring obligations. *Fidelity* has also come to mean "faithful to an original," as in a **high-fidelity** recording, often abbreviated to **hi-fi**. Many characters in literature are named some variation of *fidelis* to indicate their faithfulness. For example, in Beethoven's opera *Fidelio*, the heroine (of the same name, naturally) is devoted to the rescue of her husband from unjust imprisonment. And let's not forget the name of man's most "faithful" friend, **Fido**.

could try it, and he asked me if I knew how to get into a canoe. I said I did because it seemed simple—just jump in and start paddling. I was eight years old.

Anyway, the canoe was tied to the dock, and I untied it and jumped in. I didn't know canoes were so tippy. I didn't know I needed to step into the middle of the boat, keep my weight low, and grab a hold of both sides of the boat. So when I got in, I did it wrong. It was like being on rollerskates for the first time. The canoe flipped completely over before I knew what was happening. I got pitched right into the lake. My sister, Judy, was standing on the dock laughing her head off.

I climbed onto the dock, soaking wet. Grandpa was there, and I said, "I guess I don't know how to get into a canoe." Grandpa said, "When in doubt, ask." Then he told me how to get into a canoe without tipping it over. Luckily it was eighty degrees out, and I was wearing a swimsuit. That day I learned how to get into a canoe.

> Your Chosen Aphorism: _Life's a journey, not a destination_
>
> Example Situation: _Selena always dreamed of becoming a lawyer. She believed that's what she was destined to do for a living. She was very materialistic, and so she liked the idea of making a lot of money, plus she worked very well with people. She went clear through school, and became a lawyer_

Pre-Writing Activity 2: Describing the People and Their Emotions

Once you have completed Pre-writing Activity 1, pick the people out of what you wrote. In the sample, the people are (1) the eight-year-old, (2) his or her grandfather, and (3) his or her sister. Then, for each person in your example situation, write two kinds of details. The first are descriptive details—tell what the person looked like. The second are emotion details—describe an emotion this person was feeling.

For example, look at the details below concerning the sister:

Descriptive details: Judy was ten years old and rather chubby. She wore a red swimsuit with shorts over it, and she was eating an ice cream sandwich.

Describing an emotion: When the canoe tipped over, Judy dropped her ice cream, put her head back, put both hands on her round tummy, and laughed so loud everybody on the lake heard her.

Person One: _Selena_

Descriptive Details: _Selena was 28 years old, and rather small. She wore a ~~cellule~~ grey business suit with a black blouse under it. She was sitting at her desk in her 21st floor office in Seattle, talking on the phone._

Describing an Emotion: _When she told her mom of the problems she was having with her job, she was sobbing ~~xxxxxxxxxx~~ endlessly, and reaching for the box of kleenex on the corner of her desk._

Person Two: _Selena's mother_

Descriptive Details _Selena's mother was 46 years old at the time, and she was a medium sized woman. She wore a green sweatsuit, and was smoking a cigarette on the back porch._

Describing an Emotion: When Selena began crying, she felt very bad for her, but tried to be strong for Selena's sake. The advice she gave her daughter, was the same advice she often heard from her own father when she was growing up.

Person Three:_____

Descriptive Details_____

_____

_____

_____

_____

Describing an Emotion:_____

_____

_____

_____

_____

_____

DRAFTING

B: Writing a First or Initial Draft

Once you have completed the pre-writing, write for thirty to forty minutes about your aphorism. Usually a saying's meaning becomes clearer when the reader can see a situation in which someone uses a particular aphorism to communicate an idea to someone else. What you write, therefore, might include descriptions of situations from your experience. For example, if an aphorism you choose is one your mother or your brother uses, write about a situation in which your mother or brother might say that aphorism. You do not have to write a story, but you may if you like. Please try to include at least some details that show emotions. Be sure to write your first draft all at once. Do not worry about spelling and grammar while you write; just write. You will probably work more on this piece of writing later to make it even better. You are the expert here; it's your paper. So concentrate on making what you are saying clear to a reader. At the same time, write quickly. Most people find that they get more and better ideas down on paper when they write quickly. While writing, if you want to look back at some of your pre-writing, please do.

SECTION

3

Revising for Details of Emotion

A: Details of Emotion

Communication involves much more than just words. When two people communicate by talking, they can see one another's facial expressions, hand gestures, and body language. They can also hear and understand more about what the other is saying by the tone of voice that person is using.

When we write, we tend to lose these other resources for communication. Aphorisms such as "It's not what you say but how you say it" and often-heard comments such as "You had to be there" point to this problem. We communicate our thoughts, but we also communicate our emotions. In fact, our thoughts and our emotions blend to form our ideas, attitudes, and opinions.

A part of this business of communicating fully in writing, then, is including some emotional content when we write. In English we have many words for emotions. "Love," "hate," "anger," "happiness," and "jealousy" are familiar examples. "Rude," "arrogant," "pleasant," "warm," and "cold" are also words we use to indicate emotions or emotional states.

These words, however, do not seem to communicate very much. "Anger," for instance, comes in many degrees and is expressed in many ways. Some people may express anger by clenching their teeth, wrinkling their brow, shaking their fist, or kicking a piece of furniture. Some people, when they get really angry, quit talking. Some stomp their feet while leaving. So just to write that a person was angry doesn't communicate very much. The good news is that emotional content need not be lost when we communicate in writing. We can describe emotions rather than only naming them. Look at the following pairs of examples.

Example One: Naming Versus Describing Emotions

Naming an emotion: When Carol saw her mother she was really <u>happy</u>.

Describing an emotion: When Carol saw her mother, she hurried toward her, her arms reaching out, and the corners of her mouth went up like rockets.

Example Two: Naming Versus Describing Emotions

Naming an emotion: When the boss asked him to work an extra hour, David replied <u>rudely</u>, "Yeah, sure."

Describing an emotion: When the boss asked him to work an extra hour, David rolled his eyes, snickered, and said, "Yeah, sure."

The difference is that naming emotions <u>tells</u> the reader what to think, while describing the emotion <u>allows the reader to figure out</u> the emotion from the details. Describing provides information; describing communicates more.

B: Revising Drafts of Student Essays

Presented here are three drafts of student essays written about aphorisms. The students were asked to pick an aphorism and tell why this particular aphorism was meaningful to them.

Read the following student draft, "Don't Judge a Book by Its Cover." While reading, look for places where the writer names rather than describes emotions.

Student Draft: "Don't Judge a Book by Its Cover"

DON'T JUDGE A BOOK BY ITS COVER

The aphorism "Don't judge a book by its cover" is a very common quotation. People judge a book by its cover in everyday stereotyping.

The meaning for "Don't judge a book by its cover" is basically saying don't just look at the outside of a particular thing in life but yet look at the inside also. Judging people for how they are rather than what they are is a very good example.

This quotation reminds me of a time in my life when I was very young and egocentric. I had a pompous attitude toward life and didn't respect too many people.

I was really hung up on first impressions when it came to meeting people I didn't know. Most new people that I met were classified the first time I looked into the whites of their eyes.

For example, one day I was meeting a complete stranger that I had never seen before. The first thing that came to mind was that he didn't have any money at all because of the way he dressed. This was very important to me during this time of my life. I usually treated people that dressed poorly in a very rude manner. Even before the innocent kid could utter a single word from his lips, I already had a stamp pegged on his head as if he were merchandise. I never ever really sat down and got to know a person until later in my life when I matured to an older age.

That's where the quote "Don't judge a book by its cover" comes in.

I usually judged people for what they looked like, how they talked, and how much money they had. I was ignoring the whole person. There are so many more qualities and values than that. I really didn't take the time to find out what people's attitudes and personalities were like. I usually just labeled a person, and I went on with my life. I didn't even give that person a chance to get to know me.

I learned a very valuable lesson by having this pompous attitude. I finally woke up and smelled the roses and took a good look at myself when a person asked me why I didn't have any friends. As I grew older I finally realized that I was the one that was being judged by other people. It taught me to look at people as real human beings and like them for who they were and not what I wanted them to be. It also taught me to have a more open mind toward new friends.

Judging a book by its cover is very common. I think everyone in this world overlooks things and doesn't care to recognize the obvious. Life is too short to not take a good look at the inner and outer surroundings of everyday life.

Andrew N.

Now look again at the following version of the same piece of writing. In this version, words that name emotions have been underlined; then language that describes the underlined emotion words has been added in *italics*.

Revised Student Draft: "Don't Judge a Book by Its Cover"

DON'T JUDGE A BOOK BY ITS COVER

The aphorism "Don't judge a book by its cover" is a very common quotation. People judge a book by its cover in everyday stereotyping.

The meaning for "Don't judge a book by its cover" is basically saying don't just look at the outside of a particular thing in life but yet look at the inside also. Judging people for how they are rather than what they are is a very good example.

This quotation reminds me of a time in my life when I was very young and egocentric. I had a pompous attitude toward life and didn't respect too many people. *For example when my high school history teacher asked me to do something, I'd look him right in the eye and say, "Why should I?" You see he was just a school teacher, and I knew teachers didn't make much money.*

I was really hung up on first impressions when it came to meeting people I didn't know. Most new people that I met were classified the first time I looked into the whites of their eyes.

For example, one day I was meeting a complete stranger that I had never seen before. The first thing that came to mind was that he didn't have any money at all because of the way he dressed. This was very important to me during this time of my life. I usually treated people that dressed poorly in a very rude manner. *When the person at the gas station wearing those greasy blue coveralls with the name embroidered in red over the pocket asked me a question like, "Can I check your oil?" I wouldn't even look at him, or, if I did, I'd read his name and then say something like, "What did you say, Dave?"* Even before the innocent kid could utter a single word from his lips, I already had a stamp pegged on his head as if he were merchandise. I never ever really sat down and got to know a person until later in my life when I matured to an older age.

That's where the quote "Don't judge a book by its cover" comes in.

I usually judged people for what they looked like, how they talked, and how much money they had. I was ignoring the whole person. There are so many more qualities and values than that. I really didn't take the time to find out what people's attitudes and personalities were like. I usually just labeled a person, and I went on with my life. I didn't even give that person a chance to get to know me.

I learned a very valuable lesson by having this pompous attitude. I finally woke up and smelled the roses and took a good look at myself when a person asked me why I didn't have any friends. As I grew older I finally realized that I was the one that was being judged by other people. It taught me to look at people as real human beings and like them for who they were and not what I wanted them to be. It also taught me to have a more open mind toward new friends. *I learned to really listen when someone spoke to me, and if I didn't understand somebody I would smile at the person and say, "Tell me what you think." When I'd say that, most people would smile back and start talking, like they're happy to have somebody listen to them.*

Judging a book by its cover is very common. I think everyone in this world overlooks things and doesn't care to recognize the obvious. Life is too short to not take a good look at the inner and outer surroundings of everyday life.

Andrew N.

Practicing Revising for Details of Emotion

Following are two more drafts of papers written by students on the topic of aphorisms.

Revising Activity 1: A Penny for Your Thoughts

Working with others or alone, revise in the spaces provided the student draft "A Penny for Your Thoughts" by adding language that describes the underlined emotion words. Use your imagination and remember to employ as many descriptive details as possible.

Student Draft: "A Penny for Your Thoughts"

A PENNY FOR YOUR THOUGHTS

"A penny for your thoughts" is a good aphorism. It means that when a person wants to know what you are thinking, it means he/she cares. It tells a lot about what could be said if people had enough courage to say what they think.

Right now there are a lot of people who don't say what they feel or think. They probably could be the only ones with a question on the subject matter. They could be having trouble with a problem, so they won't speak up. They probably think someone else is having the same problem and will say something for them. For example, in our English class I notice that people do not talk about the homework we were supposed to have done. Maybe they are <u>nervous</u> or <u>scared</u> to talk out loud.

nervous ~~and think the~~ because they think it is a stupid question, or scared to talk out loud, because they think people might look at them funny.

I know that if I had something to say about an issue, I wouldn't be too sure that I would say something, but I would at least talk around to see if everyone has got the same ideas or somewhat of the same ideas. For example, I used to work at a drug store, and every time the supervisor would tell me to fix an end of an aisle, I would always get a second opinion from another supervisor on how to do it. I was never quite sure on how to fix it if there wasn't a second opinion. It always had to be perfect, or we got pink slips which meant that we had messed up.

Another reason for "a penny for your thoughts" would be if you're married. You have got to let your spouse know that there is <u>a little conflict</u> starting to arise between the both of you or at work.

<u>at work, when you come home</u>
<u>and walk right past them</u>
<u>~~because you~~ as if you don't</u>
<u>even know them.</u>

✳

If one does not tell the other about the problem, either spouse might get the wrong idea and think that they don't care for each other anymore. For example, whenever I am home, my brothers and friends and I would go play basketball just to stay in shape. Now when I go home and we want to play basketball, my brother has got to ask his fiancé to see if it's ok. I know one of these days he is going to <u>blow up</u>,

... <u>in her face, with the look he</u>
<u>used to give me when I made</u>
<u>him really mad. His face gets</u>
<u>bright red, and his eyes get</u>
<u>all squinty.</u>

I mean, how does a relationship last if there is no communication?

REVISING

> The same idea would be true if you had a good friend who was of the opposite sex. She started to like you, but you didn't know that. You only considered her as a friend, and suddenly you find out that she has a crush. He/she better tell the one who is in love that all they can be is friends. You have got to tell that person what's on your mind.
>
> "A Penny For Your Thoughts" is a good aphorism to me because I heard it from a very special person. She asked me that because she cared, and that made me feel great inside.
>
> Wally R.

Revising Activity 2: If You Can't Say Anything Nice . . .

Working with others or alone, revise the student draft paper "If You Can't Say Anything Nice . . ." in the following way:

1.   Underline or highlight the emotion words in the draft.

2.   In a sentence or two, describe the emotions that the writer only names.

Student Draft: "If You Can't Say Anything Nice . . ."

> IF YOU CAN'T SAY ANYTHING NICE . . .
>
> Being the individual human beings that we are, each and every one of us lives our lives in different ways. Our lifestyles are greatly influenced by our physical environment as well as our mental environment. What I mean is that emotions play a great role in our daily lives, and they affect our actions and attitudes. That is why it is important that people think before they speak and don't say anything that will hurt another's feelings.
>
> Here's an example of what I mean. Picture a person who just got a new permanent, and it is quite curly. This person is not sure whether he or she likes it or not because it is a change to his or her appearance, and this person is still trying to get used to it. So, some jerk comes up and says, "What did you do, stick your finger in a light socket?" Even if the statement was made in jest,

it may bring tears to their eyes and leave them worried,

it still hurts the other person. You must realize that the person with the new permanent is now feeling self-conscious about his or her appearance, and his or her self-esteem probably just went down several notches. This person might feel worse, all because of somebody else's inconsiderate statements. *& holding their head down when in public.*

he or she will be constantly watching other people's faces as they walk down the street, making sure they aren't laughing

Thus, if you can't say anything nice, don't say anything at all. However, there is more to this aphorism than meets the eye. A person must also listen. Listening is not only a physical sound, but it is also a sight, as in body language. Let me make an example.

In the previous situation with the new permanent, physical listening was occurring. What if the situation had occurred differently; someone actually meant what his or her statements said, but what if the body language said differently? Maybe this person wasn't able to look the other person in the eyes and say, "Your hair looks good." Instead the speaker was looking everywhere but at the individual, and it was obvious that the words were only hot air. Well, in this situation, it would again have been better if nothing was said at all.

In conclusion, if you can't say anything nice, please don't say anything at all. Since, as humans, our life-styles and attitudes are greatly affected by our emotions, it is obvious that saying mean things or making statements that we don't truly mean will only cause harm to others. Consideration of others should be the utmost in everyone's mind, and it is sad to see the emotional turmoil that inconsiderate people place upon individuals.

Scott M.

C: Revising Your Draft

Working with others or alone, revise the draft you have just written in the following ways. These are revision strategies you have already used in this chapter.

1. Underline or highlight the emotion words in the draft you have written about "Aphorisms."

2. In a sentence or two for each, describe three or four of the emotions that you underlined or highlighted in your draft.

D: Helping Others to Revise Their Drafts

Exchange drafts of aphorism papers with another writer. Read the other person's draft. Then do activities C.1 and C.2 above on each other's papers. Here you will need to make up details about people and situations you do not know. Have fun doing this. Writing that is fun to do tends to be fun to read.

SECTION
◄►
4

Final Editing for Commas and Coordinating Conjunctions

When children first begin to write, each sentence is a single, self-contained thought. Adults, however, often want to emphasize the connection between related complete ideas by putting them inside the same sentence. An important way of doing this is by joining two (or more) smaller whole sentences with the coordinating conjunctions *and*, *but*, and *so* to form a single larger sentence.

Using coordinating conjunctions to join closely related sentences in our writing seems quite natural because we do the same thing in our spoken language all the time. However, there is a major problem in writing because of a special convention that we must follow: **when we use a coordinating conjunction to join whole sentences, we must use a comma in front of the coordinating conjunction.** Since this comma does not correspond to a pause in the spoken language, our ear does not guide us in using this comma. Nor do we use a comma in writing when we join words or phrases with coordinating conjunctions.

To use this comma correctly, we must develop a new final editing practice. We must consciously check each coordinating conjunction to see if it joins two smaller sentences inside the larger sentence. If it does, then we must put a comma in front of the coordinating conjunction. Many students find that it takes a surprising amount of self-discipline to carry out this check. Nevertheless, since leaving off this required comma is one of the most common punctuation errors for beginning college writers, checking for commas with coordinating conjunctions is a habit all writers must develop. The editing exercises in this chapter are designed to encourage this proofreading habit.

A: Omitting Commas with Coordinating Conjunctions

A helpful trick for identifying a complete sentence is to see if the words can be turned into a question that can be answered *yes* or *no*. (The opposite of a *yes/no* question is an information question—a question that begins with words such as *who, when, where, why*.) Only a complete sentence has a corresponding *yes/no* question. For example, we can show that the following words are a sentence:

1.   I think that this is a sentence.

We can turn this into a grammatical *yes/no* question:

1a.   Do I think that this is a sentence?

We can use the *yes/no* test to check whether or not a coordinating conjunction joins two complete sentences. If the coordinating conjunction joins two complete sentences, there will always be two *yes/no* questions—one for each of the smaller complete sentences within the larger sentence. If the coordinating conjunction is **not** joining two complete sentences, there will be only one complete sentence. Here are examples of the *yes/no* test applied to several sentences from Walton's article "The World According to Claude":

2.   I kept hearing my father's voice, **and** it was annoying.
      Yes/no test 1: Did I keep hearing my father's voice?
      Yes/no test 2: Was it annoying?

3.   He continued wrenching **and** whanging on a pipe.
      Yes/no test 1: Did he continue wrenching and whanging on a pipe?

As you can see, the coordinating conjunction *and* in sentence (2) joins two smaller sentences. When we apply the *yes/no* question test to sentence (2), we create two *yes/no* questions—one from each of the smaller sentences. However, when we apply the *yes/no* question test to sentence (3), we create only a single *yes/no* question because *and* is not joining two complete sentences. In this particular case, *and* joins the two verbs *wrenching* and *whanging*.

Editing Activity 1: Using the Yes/No Question Test to Identify Complete Sentences

The following sentences have been taken from Walton's "The World According to Claude." All commas have been removed from coordinating conjunctions that join complete sentences, and the coordinating conjunctions have been put in bold. Apply the *yes/no* test to each sentence. If the coordinating conjunction joins two complete sentences, put a comma in front of the coordinating conjunction, and draw a circle around

EDITING

both the comma and the coordinating conjunction. The first two questions are done as examples.

---

1. I often thought it sounded like a threat **but** now I see that he was challenging me to see the world as it is.
   Answer:
   1. I often thought it sounded like a threa(, **but**)now I see that he was challenging me to see the world as it is.
   Did I often think it sounded like a threat?
   Do I now see that he was challenging me to see the world as it is?

2. I wanted my father to call it a day **and** get on with the festivities.
   Answer:
   2. I wanted my father to call it a day **and** get on with the festivities.
   Did I want my father to call it a day and get on with the festivities?

3. One day I asked him why, **and** he looked at me as if I had rocks in my head.
   Did I one day ask him ~~call~~ why?
   Did he look at me as if I had rocks in my head?

4. Recently, searching for a new lawn tractor, he went to three different dealers **and** got three different prices for the same machine.
   _____
   _____

5. He then went to a fourth dealer **and** purchased a larger tractor for less money.
   _____
   _____

6. It was like this when I got here **and** it's going to be like this when I leave **so** I'm not going to worry about it.
   _____
   _____
   _____

7. I gain more respect for such an accomplishment **and** the unblinking steadiness it takes.
   _____
   _____

8. Anything we do is going to be hard **and** if it isn't hard, it's going to be difficult.
   _____
   _____

9. His values—fidelity, simplicity and frugality—are spurned by younger people **but** I am beginning to see that these are the very values that keep a society functioning.

   _____

   _____

10. The notion that there was a link between my behavior **and** how I could expect my sister to be treated has served as a painfully clear guide ever since.

    _____

    _____

11. Claude sees the world very clearly **and** what he sees is often not pretty.

    _____

    _____

12. I'm reminded of the television family "All in the Family" **and** how much of the humor was directed at the willfully uninformed, purposely contrary Archie Bunker.

    _____

    _____

Editing Activity 2: Adding Commas to Coordinating Conjunctions That Join Whole Sentences

In the following student essay, the coordinating conjunctions _and_, _but_, and _so_ are in bold type. Apply the _yes/no_ test to help you decide whether each coordinating conjunction joins a complete sentence. If the coordinating conjunction joins two complete sentences, put a comma in front of the coordinating conjunction, and draw a circle around both the comma and the coordinating conjunction.

EDITING

Kimberlee S.
English Writing, Sec 6
May 4, 1993

NO PAIN, NO GAIN

The aphorism "No pain, no gain" is a statement that everyone should live by. It helps those who aren't satisfied with just getting by **but** who don't seem to be getting anywhere. This phrase says that there is hope for anyone **but** it is true only if the individual makes it work for them.

Throughout my years playing softball, I have seen **and** experienced the proof of this statement. The softball team that I have played on for over ten years recently won a league championship **and** then went on to place fourth in the state championships. Most of us played together throughout little league **and** high school. When we started out in grade school, we definitely needed a lot of coaching **and** practice. Throughout the years players would come **and** go **but** the ones who kept practicing **and** didn't give up are the ones who were finally rewarded. My coach would often say "No pain, no gain" after telling us to run three miles around the track on a hot spring afternoon. We always moaned **and** groaned about it **but** in the long run the pain obviously paid off. We became stronger **and** more disciplined as a team. On long, tiring afternoons we were able to take an extra base **and** win a close game because we were stronger than the other team. We won a close game once because a tired outfielder was able to chase down a ball **and** hold the batter to a triple instead of a home run. It turned out that the runner never did score **so** we won the game by a run.

Another example of enduring pain while trying to succeed is going to high school **and** getting your diploma. Nowadays it is almost impossible to get a decent job that you like **and** that pays enough to live on without getting your high school diploma. Looking back, those four years seemed to last forever **but** now I know it was worth it. I was great at putting off studying for tests **and** I always procrastinated on my homework. I can remember the times when I had book reports due in my English class. We would have about a month to read the book **and** write the paper

> **but** I would always wait until the last minute **and** end up
> working on my paper until four or five o'clock in the
> morning. I always got the job done **but** the papers were
> never as good as they could have been. I still have a
> problem with putting things off **but** I have learned to get
> the important things done on time no matter how painful
> it is to do them because I know that I will be much better
> off in the long run.

Editing Activity 3: Editing a Student Paper for Commas Omitted from Coordinating Conjunctions That Join Complete Sentences

Find the coordinating conjunctions *and*, *but*, and *so* in this student essay. The total number of coordinating conjunctions in each paragraph is given in parentheses at the end of the paragraph. Check each coordinating conjunction to see if it joins complete sentences. If it does, add the necessary comma, and then (a) circle both the comma and the coordinating conjunction, and (b) underline the complete sentences that are joined by the coordinating conjunction you have circled.

Dave L.
English Writing, Sec 6
February 12, 1993

TREAT OTHERS AS YOU WOULD BE TREATED

Have you ever gone to a party where everyone is telling jokes? Then somebody decides to use you as the target of his jokes. Now you become the hit of the party. Everyone is using your name and your character in his or her jokes. This becomes very annoying as the party goes on and you can't even talk to people without their laughing in your face. You decide to leave the party and go home. Next Monday at school nearly everyone who attended the party tells you they didn't mean it and asks your pardon but the kid who started it won't let up and is still at it! You confront him in the hall and tell him to stop but all he does is pace back and forth and mumble some words. Finally he sticks his tongue out at you and runs away so you are left standing there like a total jerk. (12)

"Treat others as you would be treated" is an aphorism that is known and used throughout the world. When meeting or talking to foreign visitors, we would treat them the way that we would like to be treated if we were in their country. We would try to make them comfortable and feel at home. On the job good employers do their best to make all employees feel that they are respected and that their jobs are important. (3)

Back home, I had a friend who would clown around and do crazy things like make funny faces and voices and, in general, act like a total fool. He had a way of always making you laugh when you were in a bad mood and didn't feel like laughing. He would make fun of others and sometimes of his best friends. I didn't think this was so funny but he loved it. A few times I would get so angry that I would grit my teeth and just walk away in disgust. Maybe he didn't mean any harm but he couldn't let up. This kid had an attitude: he could not stand being made fun of himself and having jokes made at his expense. This made me really think about the aphorism "treat others as you would be treated." (9)

B: Incorrectly Adding Commas with Coordinating Conjunctions

The most common mistake beginning writers make with coordinating conjunctions is leaving off the comma when the coordinating conjunction joins two complete sentences. The second most common mistake is the reverse: adding a comma when the coordinating conjunction is followed by only a part of a complete sentence—usually a verb phrase (the verb and whatever follows the verb). To see what causes the second problem let's look at an example from the passage in the reading in which the author, Anthony Walton, describes Claude's shopping around for the best buy on a tractor. The simple sentences underlying the joined sentence the author used are these:

4.   He then went to a fourth dealer.

5.   He purchased a larger tractor for less money.

Walton could have joined the simple sentences with a comma and a coordinating conjunction like this (joined sentences underlined):

6.   <u>He then went to a fourth dealer</u>, **and** <u>he purchased a larger tractor for less money</u>.

Instead, Walton dropped the subject from the second simple sentence and joined the two verb phrases with <u>and</u> (verb phrases underlined):

7.   He then <u>went to a fourth dealer</u> **and** <u>purchased a larger tractor for less money</u>.

Do you see the difference between (6) and (7)? In sentence (6) what follows the coordinating conjunction *and* is the complete sentence *he purchased a larger tractor for less money*. Since *and* joins two complete sentences, a comma is required. However, in sentence (7) what follows the coordinating conjunction *and* is only a part of a sentence— the verb phrase *purchased a larger tractor for less money*. Since *and* is not joining two complete sentences, no comma can be used.

Now, the very fact that both sentences (6) and (7) meaning exactly the same thing makes it easy to get mixed up and incorrectly add a comma when the repeated subject is dropped from the second underlying sentence:

7a.   * He then went to a fourth dealer, and purchased a larger tractor for less money.

Sentence (7a) is incorrect because the *and* does not join two complete sentences: on the left of the comma is a complete sentence, but on the right there is only a piece of a sentence (the verb phrase). When you combine smaller sentences that have the same subject to make up a larger sentence, be sure to check the following: (1) if you keep the subject in the second smaller sentence, **add a comma**; (2) if you drop the subject from the second smaller sentence, **do not add a comma** because you are not joining two complete sentences.

Editing Activity 4: Combining Sentences With and Without the Repeated Subject

Combine the following pairs of sentence in two different ways. (a) Combine the sentences without dropping the subject from the second underlying sentence. (You may need to change the subject of the second sentence to a pronoun.) Be sure to add the comma before the coordinating conjunction. (b) Combine the sentences by deleting the subject from the second underlying sentence. Since the coordinating conjunction does not join two complete sentences, do not use a comma. The first sentence is done as an example.

1. Sam sat down with his cousin.
   Sam asked her what had really happened to the cat.

   a. *Sam sat down with his cousin,* **and** *he asked her what had really happened to the cat.*

   b. *Sam sat down with his cousin* **and** *asked her what had really happened to the cat.*

2. John gathered up all the canceled checks.
   John then balanced his checkbook.

   a. _____

   b. _____

3. Clark looked up and down the street.
   Clark ducked into a phone booth.

   a. _____

   b. _____

4. I had a bad attitude toward school.
   I didn't floss my teeth.

   a. _____

   b. _____

5. The lawyers approached the bench.
   The lawyers asked the judge for a postponement.

   a. _____

   b. _____

6. People should think before they speak.
   People should not say things they don't mean.

   a. *People should think before they speak, and ~~people~~ should not say things they don't mean.*

   b. *People should think before they speak and should not say things they don't mean.*

7. She had some computer training.
   She wanted to work in an academic environment.

   a. _____

   b. _____

8. I asked Scrooge for help.
   I got some good advice.

   a. _____

   b. _____

9. The salesclerk answered the phone.
   The salesclerk took out an order pad.

   a. _____

   b. _____

10. Claude built a cage in his back yard.
    Claude began importing parrots.

    a. _____

    b. _____

Editing Activity 5: Editing a Final Draft for Commas and Coordinating Conjunctions

Following is the final draft of a student essay on the topic of aphorisms. The essay is free from errors except for an appalling number of mistakes involving commas and coordinating conjunctions. Find all of the errors, and correct them in whatever way you think is best for the paper. The number of errors in each paragraph is given in parentheses at the end of the paragraph.

Marcy W.
English Writing, Sec 6
January 28, 1993

BE YOURSELF

I'm in the Student Union just about every day at eleven o'clock and I always see this one guy just standing around minding his own business but he continuously gets stared at by most everybody there. Well, people do watch each other while they spend time in the Student Union but this poor guy seriously gets stared at, and made a fool of. He's about 5'8" or so and I guess he would be about 150 pounds. His hair is dark brown, and appears to be naturally wavy. Basically, his hair is very short all over but I guess you could say that it is pretty much on the radical side, much like that of the Jonny Depp character portrayed on the hit show *21 Jumpstreet* because of the long bangs that cover his right eye completely, but expose his left eye just enough to make him look as if he were playing a game of peek-a-boo. (8)

Judging from the clothes he wears, you can certainly tell that he is a true individual. He seems to love wearing his one old, beat-up military jacket that looks as if it has been used to scrub the streets of Spokane. It has holes in both sleeves on the elbows, a big rip in the lower left pocket that looks as if a pit bull got hold of it and must have refused to let go and all the buttons appear to have been ripped completely off. It looks like he buttoned the jacket up, and then proceeded to rip it off, leaving behind little holes and threads where the buttons used to be. (2)

This guy has a gorgeous, sexy smile that he flashes at just about everybody who gives him a chance but there are only a few nerdy types that do. Most of the people give him the eye when they are far away from him but as soon as they get close to him, they tend to either look down at the floor or around at the building until they pass him by and then they resume looking straight ahead. It is obvious that he tries to interact with people but the reaction he gets is a measly smile, at best. (4)

The people who treat him the worst are the jocks and the preppies. The jocks are the type that like to show off how strong they are by doing some ridiculous stunt like squeezing oranges under their arms or taking turns punching each other in the arm to see which guy can take the most punches, and be known as the "real" man. The jocks like to watch him as he stands there and then they try to mess with him. They laugh and hit one another as they look over at the guy to see if they get a reaction from him. All this guy does is look down at the ground as if nothing was happening. (2)

The preppies are the type who have to wear the "in" clothes that everybody else in their crowd is wearing and they criticize individuals like this lonely guy who doesn't "dress to impress." The preppies call him petty names such as "the Goodwill guy," "homeboy," and "Mr. Nobody." (1)

When I see this kind of thing happening to this guy from day to day, I feel sorry for him but at the same time I feel a kind of admiration toward him because he continues to stand there, and take this abuse. If I were in his shoes, I probably would have given up long ago. I would have gone off to a dark corner someplace, and made my own little world where nobody could hurt me anymore but this guy just keeps on going and doesn't give up. (4)

I just don't understand why or how people can be so cruel and petty. It seems that if you are different, you are going to be the target for teasing. I always felt that being an individual, being yourself, was a good thing but I have witnessed that being different isn't very easy. (1)

EDITING

THE
SECOND
SHIFT

Problems and Solutions
in Two-Income Households

SECTION

1

Reading about Two-Income Families

A: Pre-Reading

In the last fifty years people in this country have witnessed and experienced one of the biggest changes in the whole history of Western culture. For thousands of years men's and women's roles, in the home and in society, were relatively stable. Men worked outside of the home—on the farm, in the factory, and in the office. Women worked in the home—cooking, cleaning, and caring for their husbands, their children, and the elderly.

There were always some exceptions to this pattern. Certain professions, health care and teaching to mention two, have long included both women and men in their workforces. In addition, there have always been some female scientists, artists, and political leaders, women whose power, influence, and talents have served to shape the world we know.

Many people believe that women have always been the most powerful shaping force in society. They have nurtured and trained each generation of children and taught the values and life skills necessary for success and even survival. This kind of thinking rings true. Still, until the second half of this century, in this country most women worked in the home, and most men worked outside the home.

Many books have been written on how and why this pattern has changed. Certainly World War Two (1939–1945) was a factor in this change. With most of the men in the armed forces, women were needed in the offices, on the farms, and in the factories, and many took jobs traditionally held only by men. More effective birth control methods, widely available starting in the early 1960s, were also factors. In addition the Civil Rights Movement, the Women's Liberation Movement, the Sexual Revolution of the 1960s and 1970s, and increased access to education also served to open the doors to previously male-dominated work places and careers.

This major movement of women into the out-of-the-home workforce continues, but the transition is not without problems. How we think of marriage, how we raise children, and how we care for the elderly are questions that arise from this transition. Smaller concerns, such as who will do the laundry, the cooking, and the cleaning in the home when both marriage partners work outside of the home, are also parts of this major social change. Basically, someone still needs to do all the work that used to be done only by women.

Pre-Reading Activities

Discussion

1. Working with others, brainstorm a list of benefits—for men, women, and children—that come when women work outside of the home. Then brainstorm a list of problems that arise or might arise when both marriage partners hold out-of-the-home jobs. Be sure to use plenty of details and examples in your discussion.

2. Some people enjoy doing some kinds of housework. Share with others a type of housework—such as cooking, cleaning, home repair, grocery shopping, or laundry—that you enjoy doing. Even if you are not enthusiastic about housework, there must be some type of housework that you find satisfying.

3. In an ideal marriage, how might the housework be divided equally between the marriage partners? Assuming that both partners work outside of the home, which partner might do which domestic tasks?

Reading Suggestions

(Keep these suggestions in mind while reading "The Second Shift: A Candid Look at the Revolution at Home" by Rebecca Allen.)

1.   Highlight or underline ideas or statements in the reading that you believe are true.

2.   Circle any ideas or statements in the reading with which you disagree.

3.   Assume that you will later write an essay about a problem connected to families in which both marriage partners work full-time jobs outside of the home. While you are reading, jot down some of your ideas about such a problem and how it might be solved.

4.   Rebecca Allen wrote the following book review. What is her purpose?

Vocabulary Preview

admonish: advise forcefully. (My mother always <u>admonished</u> me to do my best.)

enlightened: influenced by good judgment and experience. (He had an <u>enlightened</u> opinion about raising children.)

fragile: easily broken. (The crystal glasses were <u>fragile</u>.)

inflexible: fixed, difficult to bend. (Police officers tend to be <u>inflexible</u> about traffic violations.)

rationalize: make excuses. (He <u>rationalized</u> his anger by saying how tired he was.)

semblance: appearance. (They maintained the <u>semblance</u> of a happy family.)

stolid: quiet, uncomplaining. (She had a <u>stolid</u> attitude toward housework.)

trivial: unimportant, small. (My day was filled with <u>trivial</u> problems.)

B: Reading

"The Second Shift: A Candid Look at the Revolution at Home"

BY REBECCA ALLEN

Raising small children while working full time is very difficult. In many cases, it's too difficult, says sociologist Arlie Hochschild, who will be speaking in Seattle April 26 for the Seattle Kidsplace Forum Series.

Anyone with pre-schoolers knows just how hard it is to manage a job and then come home to the second shift of cooking meals, settling arguments, cleaning the house, reading stories, mowing the lawn, finding and keeping good day care. Oh, and still maintaining a good marriage and a semblance of family life, too.

Hochschild has taken a close look at 10 couples to see how they are coping with two full-time jobs and pre-school children in her new book *The Second Shift: Working Parents and the Revolution at Home*.

What she finds is a stalled revolution. Some men's and women's attitudes about housework and child care have changed, and a few have even managed to share. But society hasn't changed, corporations haven't changed and jobs haven't changed. If both parents work, they have to juggle the rest of their lives to do it, and something has to give. Very often it's the children, the marriage and the family that suffer, Hochschild finds.

Larger studies done in the 1960s and 70s showed that women who work outside the home did more housework and child care than their husbands. In fact, they worked an extra month of 24-hour days a year. This is what Hochschild calls the "second shift." And she saw many ways of coping with it.

Frank and Carmen Delacorte, a defiantly traditional couple, both believed that Carmen shouldn't have to work, but for financial reasons she did, and even though she thought she shouldn't, she enjoyed it. She didn't think Frank should work in the kitchen, but she needed him to, so she became "helpless" about some tasks. It became the family myth that Frank made better rice than Carmen, that he sewed because Carmen didn't know how. And even though she was running a day care business in her home, he could still tell his buddies that Carmen was really a stay-at-home mom. They had traditional ideas about their duties, but, in fact, Frank was doing almost half of the second shift.

On the other hand, Evan and Nancy Holt believed that they should share. But Nancy did almost all the second shift. Their family myth was that they had divided the work by dividing the house. Nancy took care of the upstairs, which included the house and most of the child care. Evan took care of the downstairs: the car, the garage and the dog.

They believed they were sharing equally. "I think they believed it because they needed to believe it, because it solved a terrible problem," Hochschild writes. "It allowed Nancy to continue thinking of herself as the sort of woman whose husband didn't abuse her—a self-conception that mattered a great deal to her. And it avoided the hard truth that, in his stolid, passive way, Evan had refused to share."

Hochschild also found couples who did share. The stories of Michael and Adrienne Sherman and of Art and Julia Winfield show men who are intimately involved with the day-to-day care of their children and their homes.

"The men who shared the load at home seemed just as pressed for time as their wives, and as torn between the demands of career and small children," she writes.

The book is an interesting, personal look at a problem faced by thousands of American families. The names and ages of the people are changed and their identities disguised. Even their children and jobs are changed, but what's true is the emotional flavor of their stories, Hochschild says.

"The point is to make the story clear," she says. "It's a shared story. And something we could do something about if we would."

She points out that the United States is the only developed country except South Africa with no national family policy. In Sweden, for example, every parent, male or female, is allowed 18 months' paid leave after a child is born. Part-time work is available to either parent when the child is small.

"They are light-years ahead of us," she says.

Studies show, however, that only 15% of Swedish parental leaves are taken by men. But the Swedish government is paying for a study to find out why and to encourage men to take them.

President George Bush has traditional ideas about the roles of men and women and is imposing them on a nation where three-quarters of mothers work outside the home, Hochschild says. "He is doing nothing to help the family."

The book has just the most general sort of solutions to the problem, but Hochschild is beginning a new study of companies that have enlightened policies.

"I would like to see parental leaves and jobs that are 60% to 80% time until the children are in school," she says. "It would require companies to be very creative about packaging work and still get the job done."

Her main concern is that families and children in particular are suffering under the current system.

"The family is already fragile," she says. "Sadly enough, a few working parents seem to be making cuts in the emotional care of their child. Trying to rationalize her child's long hours in day care, one working mother remarked about her 9-month-old daughter that she 'needed kids her age' and 'needs the independence.' It takes relatively little to cut back on house care, and the consequences are trivial. But reducing one's notions of what a baby needs—imposing the needs of a 14-year-old onto a 9-month-old baby—takes a great deal of denial and has drastic consequences."

And couples need time together. Families need relaxed time on their own turf, she says. "Sometimes we need to do productive labor together. Sometimes it can be nice to cook a meal together or paint a dog house together. It emotionally reinforces the idea of the family."

Hochschild studies families with pre-school children because "this is the most important phase in a family's life, and kids need their parents most in the tender years."

As a member of a two-job family, she was aware of the conflicts. An assistant professor at the University of California, Berkeley, she toted her first son along for office hours.

"I have been extraordinarily lucky, but, if with all my luck it is difficult, think how difficult it must be for people with inflexible jobs or with more than two children. People are trying so hard. It is a tough thing to do."

The book is sometimes a grim picture of what is happening in America today. But it is an accessible, interesting account of how real people live and how they cope with universal problems. Her conclusions may be ones that many people don't want to hear—that what we are doing may be too hard. That something has to give.

Hochschild writes that an honestly pro-family policy in the United States would give tax breaks to companies that encourage family leave for new fathers, job sharing, part-time work and flex time. Through comparable worth, it would pull up wages in "women's" jobs. It would institute lower-hour, flexible "family phases" for all regular jobs filled by parents of young children.

But in the meantime, she admonishes men to do their part. "In a time of stalled revolution—when women have gone to work, but the workplace, the culture and, most of all, the men, have not adjusted themselves to this new reality—children can be the victims. Most working mothers are already doing all they can, doing that extra month a year. It is the men who can do more."

Caring for children is the most important part of the second shift, and that's where men should concentrate their efforts, she says. "The effects of a man's care or his neglect will show up again and again through time—in the child as a child, in the child as an adult, and probably also in the child's own approach to fatherhood, and in generations of fathers to come." ∎

Allen, Rebecca. "*The Second Shift*: A Candid Look at the Revolution at Home." *Pierce County Parent* 3.4 (April 1990): 1–2.

Hochschild, Arlie, and Anne Machung. *The Second Shift*. New York: Viking Penguin, 1989.

C: Post-Reading

Discussion Suggestions/Questions

Remembering

1. What is the "second shift"?

2. According to Arlie Hochschild, at what age do children most need their parents?

3. What country is named as an example of one that has a national family policy?

Analyzing

1. Why would the authors of the book reviewed change the names and ages of the couples used as examples of different ways to split up the housework and child care duties in the households?

2. In this reading, most of the suggestions for change call for men to change. Why?

Discovering

1. Share with others the ideas or statements in the reading which you highlighted or underlined. Give reasons and examples why you believe these ideas and statements are true.

2. Share any ideas or statements you circled in the reading. Discuss with others why you disagree with these.

3. Rebecca Allen ends her essay—which is a review of a book by sociologists Arlie Hochschild and Anne Machung—by emphasizing three of the authors' recommendations. Review and discuss these three recommendations.

D: Vocabulary Building

1. Words related to *tri-*

2. Words using Latin numbers

Trivial: "The consequences are **trivial**."

Allen: "The Second Shift"

The adjective *trivial* means "of little importance." The word comes from a Latin word *trivium*, which originally meant "crossroads." The word *trivium* consists of *tri-*, "three," and *via*, "road"; literally, *trivium* meant a place where three roads met. Eventually, *trivium* was used to refer to commonplace and ordinary things that could be found at every crossroads. *Trivial* is related to the noun **trivia**, which originally meant unimportant things but which now means strange or insignificant factual information, as in a popular game called **Trivial Pursuit**. The related verb to **trivialize** means to treat something serious as through it were trivial. The noun **triviality** means the quality or state of being trivial. For example, a lawyer might dismiss a small, technical point of law as a "mere triviality."

The number *tri-* appears in a number of English words of Latin origin. Probably the oldest English word to use *tri-* is the noun **Trinity**, which refers to the Christian belief in the union of Father, Son, and Holy Spirit. A number of English words come from the adjective form *triplus*, such as **triple** and **triplet**. *Triple* means something that occurs three times. In baseball, for example, a *triple* is a three-base hit, and a *triple play* is when three outs are made in a single play. A *triplet* is a group of three things: for example, a group of three musical notes played as a unit or three children born together.

Vocabulary Building Activity 1: Different Uses of *Tri-*

In the left column are different words that use the prefix *tri-*. Match these words with their dictionary definitions in the column on the right. Some of the words you may not know, but you might guess what they mean by thinking about their parts.

Words	Dictionary Definitions
1. tripod	a. ____ A geometric figure with three sides
2. trident	b. ____ Something that is divided into three parts
3. triangle	c. ____ A three-pointed spear carried by a sea god
4. trey	d. ____ A playing card with three spots
5. tripartite	e. ____ A stand with three legs

Vocabulary Building Activity 2: Other Latin Numbers

The Latin words for the numbers up to eight appear in many English words. One area where you may know more about Latin numbers than you think you do is the names for groups of musicians. Fill in the blanks in the right column with the names of the groups of musicians on the left. The first question is done as an example. One name for a group of musicians does not fit the pattern of the others. What is it?

Number of musicians in a group	Name of group
2	*Duet*
3	_____
4	_____
5	_____
6	_____
7	_____
8	_____

Classification: "I belong to that **classification** of people known as wives."

Syfers: "I Want a Wife"

The noun *classification* consists of the noun **class** followed by two suffixes. The first suffix is *-ify*. This suffix changes nouns and adjectives into verbs. This suffix changes the noun **class** into the verb to **classify**, which means to put things into classes or groups. The second suffix is *-ication*. This suffix changes verbs into abstract nouns. Here *-ication* changes the verb *classify* into the abstract noun *classification*.

Now, why did the author go to all the trouble of changing the noun *class* into a verb and then changing that verb back into a noun? Couldn't she have used the noun *class* to begin with? Of course she could. She could have written "I belong to that *class* of people known as wives." *Classification* is not just a big word that means the same thing as the little word *class*. Each time a word is changed from one part of speech to another, a layer of meaning is added on. As a result, even though *class* and *classification* are both nouns, they don't mean exactly the same thing. To see why, let's look a little more closely at the process by which *class* evolves into *classification*.

Most prefixes and suffixes are pieces of words that can never stand alone as words. The suffix *-ify* is unusual in that it comes from a whole word—the Latin verb *ficare*, which meant to do or to make. The *-ify* ending means to make or do something connected to the meaning of the noun or the adjective that *-ify* is attached to. For example, to **beautify** means to make something more beautiful.

The second suffix, *-ication*, is a form of *-ation* and is used with many verbs formed by the suffix *-ify* (for example, **beautify/beautification**). When the suffix *-(ic)ation* changes verbs into abstract nouns, some of the meaning of the verb carries over into the meaning of that noun. For example, compare the nouns *beauty* and *beautification* in the following sentences: (a) We admired the *beauty* of the park; (b) We admired the *beautification* of the park. *Beauty* and *beautification* don't mean exactly the same thing. The park's *beauty* could be completely natural, but *beautification* implies that the park's beauty is the result of the effort that people put into making it beautiful.

The noun *classification* implies a class that people have created for their own reasons, as opposed to a permanent, natural *class* that cannot be changed. In other words, by using *classification* rather than *class*, Judy Syfers, the author of the article, is reminding us that although people have put her in the category of wives, it is a categorization she may or may not accept as permanent or valid. In fact, her article encourages us to think about what the classification of wife really means.

Vocabulary Building Activity 3: Using *-ify* and *-ication*

The words in the left column are adjectives and nouns that can be changed into verbs by adding the suffix *-ify*. In the second column, write the verb created by *-ify* suffix. After the verb, write what the verb means. Finally, in the third column, turn the verb into an abstract noun by using the *-ication* suffix. The first question is done as an example.

Adj or Noun	Verb	Abstract noun
1. glory	*glorify, "to make something glorious"*	*glorification*
2. false		
3. simple		
4. person		
5. clear		

Adj or Noun	Verb	Abstract noun
6. identity	_____	_____
7. diverse	_____	_____
8. electric	_____	_____
9. liquid	_____	_____
10. ample	_____	_____

E.1: Additional Reading

The following essay first appeared in the first issue of Ms. magazine in 1971. In the essay Judy Syfers lists the activities and attitudes of a traditional "ideal" wife. Millions of people have read, enjoyed, and discussed this essay. You are here invited to join in this reading, enjoyment, and discussion.

"I Want a Wife"

BY JUDY SYFERS

I belong to that classification of people known as wives. I am a Wife. And, not altogether incidentally, I am a mother.

Not too long ago a male friend of mine appeared on the scene fresh from a recent divorce. He had one child, who is, of course, with his ex-wife. He is looking for another wife. As I thought about him while I was ironing one evening, it suddenly occurred to me that I, too, would like to have a wife. Why do I want a wife?

I would like to go back to school so that I can become economically independent, support myself, and if need be, support those dependent upon me. I want a wife who will work and send me to school. And while I am going to school I want a wife to take care of my children. I want a wife to keep track of the children's doctor and dentist appointments. And to keep track of mine, too. I want a wife to make sure my children eat properly and are kept clean. I want a wife who will wash the children's clothes and keep them mended. I want a wife who is a good nurturant attendant to my children, who arranges for their schooling, makes sure that they have an adequate social life with their peers, takes them to the park, the zoo, etc. I want a wife who takes care of the children when they are sick, a wife who arranges to be around when the children need special care, because, of course, I cannot miss classes at school. My wife must arrange to lose time at work and not lose the job. It may mean a small cut in my wife's income from time to time, but I guess I can tolerate that. Needless to say, my wife will arrange and pay for the care of the children while my wife is working.

I want a wife who will take care of *my* physical needs. I want a wife who will keep my house clean. A wife who will pick up after my children, a wife who will pick up after me. I want a wife who will keep my clothes clean, ironed, mended, replaced when need be, and who will see to it that my personal things are kept in their proper place so that I can find what I need the minute I need it. I want a wife who cooks the meals, a wife who is a *good* cook. I want a wife who will plan the menus, do the necessary grocery shopping, prepare the meals, serve them pleasantly, and then do the cleaning up while I do my studying. I want a wife who will care for me when I am sick and sympathize with my pain and loss of time from school. I want a wife to go along when our family takes a vacation so that someone can continue to care for me and my children when I need a rest and change of scene.

I want a wife who will not bother me with rambling complaints about a wife's duties. But I want a wife who will listen to me when I feel the need to explain a rather difficult point I have come across in my course of studies. And I want a wife who will type my papers for me when I have written them.

I want a wife who will take care of the details of my social life. When my wife and I are invited out by my friends, I want a wife who will take care of the babysitting arrangements. When I meet people at school that I like and want to entertain, I want a wife who will have the house clean, will prepare a special meal, serve it to me and my friends, and not interrupt when I talk about things that interest me and my friends. I want a wife who will have arranged that the children are fed and ready for bed before my guests arrive so that the children do not bother us. I want a wife who takes care of the needs of my guests so that they feel comfortable, who makes sure that they have an ashtray, that they are passed the hors d'oeuvres, that they are offered a second helping of food, that their wine glasses are replenished when necessary, that their coffee is served to them as they like it. And I want a wife who knows that sometimes I need a night out by myself.

I want a wife who is sensitive to my sexual needs, a wife who makes love passionately and eagerly when I feel like it, a wife who makes sure that I am satisfied. And, of course, I want a wife who will not demand sexual attention when I am not in the mood for it. I want a wife who assumes the complete responsibility for birth control, because I do not want more children. I want a wife who will remain sexually faithful to me so that I do not have to clutter up my intellectual life with jealousies. And I want a wife who understands that *my* sexual needs may entail more than strict adherence to monogamy. I must, after all, be able to relate to people as fully as possible.

If, by chance, I find another person more suitable as a wife than the wife I already have, I want the liberty to replace my present wife with another one. Naturally, I will expect a fresh, new life; my wife will take the children and be solely responsible for them so that I am left free.

When I am through with school and have a job, I want my wife to quit working and remain at home so that my wife can more fully and completely take care of a wife's duties.

My God, who *wouldn't* want a wife? ■

Syfers (Brady), Judy. "I Want a Wife." *Ms.* 31 Dec. 1971: n. pag. Rpt. as "Why I (Still) Want a Wife." *Ms.* July-August 1990: 17.

E.2: Additional Reading

Sometimes when both parents work outside of the home, they simply do not have much time or energy to monitor their children's schoolwork. The following brief article contains suggestions for parents who want to help their children to do better in school. The article appeared in *The Washington Water Power Gazette* 266 (Jan. 1991). The *Gazette* is a consumer newsletter that is included in the monthly billing mailing from this power company. Read it for fun. Read it because it contains some pretty good advice.

"Invest in Your Children's Future"

Children need more than pencils, paper and books to learn at home. They need support and encouragement from their parents.

For parents, no investment is more rewarding than the time spent with your children. Every hour invested with your children can nurture the seeds of learning, responsibility, listening, self-esteem and confidence.

As a parent, you can plant these seeds early by encouraging sound homework habits. Here are some family suggestions to build a solid homework foundation:

WORK WITH YOUR CHILDREN

▲ Ask leading questions such as, "What three things did you learn in social studies today and how does that apply to your homework?"

▲ Don't do your children's work. Just help them find the answers.

▲ Everyone likes praise, but praise must be earned and honest. False praise leaves a hollow feeling.

SET TIME ASIDE

▲ Create a homework schedule.

▲ Discuss classwork.

▲ Check to see if homework is completed.

LIMIT DISTRACTIONS

▲ Create a quiet and comfortable place to work.

▲ Television is a powerful distraction. Keep it off.

▲ Many students study well with some background music. If the music is too loud or distracting, however, turn it off.

▲ Restrict student phone calls during the study period.

If homework assignments are unclear, contact your child's teacher. Teachers know the value of parent involvement with learning and would appreciate your call. ■

SECTION
◄►
2

Drafting to Identify a Problem and Suggest a Solution

A: Pre-Writing

You have already done several kinds of pre-writing for your essay about a problem connected to families in which both marriage partners work full-time jobs outside of the home. You have read, thought, and talked about some of the problems such families might face. Here you are asked to do one more kind of pre-writing. Remember that pre-writing helps writers to gather ideas, examples, and details that they might or might not include in the essays they write. Pre-writing also helps writers to organize their thoughts.

Pre-Writing Activity: Problems and Solutions

This pre-writing activity asks you to choose, from your reading, discussions, and thinking, three problems encountered in families in which both adults work outside of the home. List these problems on the left side of the following grid. Then, on the right, suggest three solutions to each problem. One of the three might be silly. "Silly" here means a solution that is not practical or reasonable, an option that might solve the problem but that might also either cause other problems or require that people do things they are unable or unwilling to do. Look for a moment at the following example.

Example Problem:	Example Solution 1:
After working all day then coming home and cooking dinner, neither Helen nor Jesse wants to wash the dirty dishes.	They could put a little money aside each month until they could buy and install an automatic dishwasher.
	Example Solution 2:
	They could teach their eight-year-old daughter and six-year-old son to wash dishes.
	Example Solution 3 (Silly):
	They could buy a new set of dishes every three or four days and simply throw dirtied dishes in the garbage after each meal.

Now complete your pre-writing grid, identifying three problems relevant to this chapter's theme and suggesting three solutions for each of the three problems.

DRAFTING

Problem 1_____   Solution 1:_____

_____   _____

_____   _____

_____   _____

_____   Solution 2:_____

_____

_____

_____

Solution (Silly) 3:_____

_____

_____

_____

_____

Problem 2_____   Solution 1:_____

_____   _____

_____   _____

_____   _____

_____   _____

Solution 2:_____

_____

_____

_____

_____

Solution (Silly) 3:_____

_____

_____

Problem 3_____

Solution 1:_____

_____

_____

_____

Solution 2:_____

_____

_____

_____

Solution (Silly) 3:_____

_____

_____

_____

DRAFTING

B: Writing a First or Initial Draft

Once you have completed the pre-writing grid, read the following essay prompt. This prompt specifies a topic and suggests a form that your essay <u>might</u> take. Following the prompt are two essays written by students who used the form suggested in the prompt. There are other ways you might organize your essay, but this suggested form fits the topic fairly well.

"Second Shift" Essay Prompt

I.   Topic:

Write an essay about a problem connected to families in which both of the marriage partners work full-time jobs outside of the home. The problem could concern child care responsibilities, money management, house cleaning, or cooking, for example. Other kinds of problems are okay, but the problem you choose to write about must concern difficulties in households in which both adults work outside of the home.

II.   Form:
Organize your essay in the following way:

Title_____

1. Describe a scene that shows the problem happening.

   _____

   _____

   _____

2. Specify the problem.

   _____

   _____

   _____

3. Suggest a solution.

_____

_____

_____

4. Name an objection—something someone else might say who disagrees with your solution—and then answer that objection.

_____

_____

_____

5. Repeat your solution in your conclusion.

_____

_____

_____

_____

_____

P.S. This is a topic that might lend itself to humor.

DRAFTING

Sample Student Essay: "Working for a Compromise"

DRAFTING

WORKING FOR A COMPROMISE

When I walked into my sister's house, I was shocked. The normally clean and tidy house my sister Peggy and her husband John have lived in for the last three years was in shambles. Their one son, John Jr., was screaming, yelling, and throwing toys everywhere. This had never happened before. I could just not understand why it was happening now. I would have asked both my sister and her husband, but they were still at work.

The problem with John Jr. was that he wanted more attention from his parents. The baby sitter that comes in every day while Peggy and John are at work is getting tired of the temper-tantrums by John Jr. Therefore, the baby sitter ignores John Jr. more than normal. Peggy and John are both gone by 6:30 a.m. and do not return until after 7:00 every night. It is difficult for the two of them to spend time with John Jr. except for the weekends. Since John Jr. is angry, he expresses his unhappiness through his actions.

It's obvious that John and Peggy have a problem in the household. The amount of time spent at home with John Jr. is not sufficient. Therefore, one or both of them need to make a sacrifice. John and Peggy both need to sit down with their work schedules and come to a compromise, a compromise that would be adequate for their jobs and income. John and Peggy agree that John Jr. is being neglected. Because of their tremendous spending habits, it is not possible for only one of them to work. Consequently, along with the cutting back in hours they need to cut back on the amount of spending they do.

Many of John and Peggy's friends tell them there is nothing wrong with leaving John Jr. home with a baby sitter every day. They say that John Jr. is going through the cranky stage. He is also experiencing new changes, such as new foods, walking, and teething. John and Peggy were asked if they thought John Jr.'s actions would stop if they spent more time at home with him.

John Jr.'s actions were obviously brought on by the feeling of neglect. It is very important that a child be with a parent during the critical growing years. No matter if you are a child or an adult, knowing that you have the feeling of love makes you feel more secure. John and Peggy's time is very valuable to John Jr. John Jr.'s time spent with his parents will make him able to deal with the new everyday changes that he experiences. Feeling secure allows one to feel comfortable in exploring all new paths of life.

Katey D.

DRAFTING

Sample Student Essay: "Getting More Help at Home"

GETTING MORE HELP AT HOME

You've had a rough day at work. You have a migraine that is pulsating painfully against every inch of your skull. As you pull in the driveway, you notice that the leaves need to be raked, the dogs and cats need to be fed, the garden looks like a huge pile of dead weeds, the dogs have once again scattered garbage across the yard, and all you ask for in life is to pop a few extra-strength Tylenol and crawl into bed. Your wife still isn't home from her job, the kids need to be fed and bathed, and the laundry is piled sky high. There are just not enough hours in the day to accomplish all the daily household tasks.

In American society today parents have no time to relax, and the term "vacation" is literally extinct. There is no way to escape the long hard struggle of raising a family; everyone fights for security, comfort and happiness. However, the good news is once you get through the headache of daycares and dirty diapers, things start to become easier. The trick is to teach your kids early on how to rake the leaves, cook for themselves and wash their dishes, and remember not to fall for "learned incapacity." It's instinct for all boys and girls to try and get out of their chores, but their efforts will subside if you reward them for doing their share. For example, my brother and I had a set plan of chores we had to complete every day for our daily allowance. My father would come home from work, and if we had our homework finished and all the chores done by the time he got home, he would put fifty cents apiece in two piggy banks. We never forgot or neglected our chores because we were always saving up for the next trip to Toys-R-Us.

Raising a family, having a nice yard, a clean home, and yearly vacations are virtually impossible, unless of course you have inherited millions or won the lottery and can afford live-in maids and nannies. The best advice I can offer is to wait before you jump into starting a family. Things will go a lot smoother if you have a stable career with an incoming paycheck large enough to support your family's needs. There is no such thing as the "Perfect Parent," but you can come closer after many years of practice; by then of course you'll probably be a grandparent.

Lisa W.

DRAFTING

After you have read the prompt and the sample student essays, review your pre-writing grid and choose <u>one</u> of your problems to write about. Then, following the form suggested (if you choose to follow the form), write a first or initial draft of your essay.

SECTION

3

Revising to Add Qualifiers

A: Categorical Statements and Qualifiers

Essays, by definition, discuss opinions. They almost always cover topics or issues about which people disagree. Two major purposes for essays are to inform and to persuade readers; the writer wants readers to read and consider the contents of his or her essay.

Because the writer wants to communicate, he or she should not accidentally offend the readers. One way to offend readers is to make what are called "categorical statements." A categorical statement presents an opinion as though it were a fact. For example, a categorical statement might be, "All men are spoiled by their mothers and think they don't have to do housework." The writer might believe this statement, but the reader might be or know a man who enjoys doing housework. This reader might, therefore, be offended by the writer's categorical statement.

Categorical statements can easily be revised to make them less offensive. One can simply add a qualifier. Qualifiers take many forms. Commonly used qualifiers are such words as "some," "perhaps," "often," "many," "usually," and "sometimes." Qualifiers can also take the form of phrases. For example, "I think," "I believe," or "I feel" before a categorical statement qualifies the statement. Starting a sentence with "Many people think," "People say that," or "Some people believe" also will qualify a statement.

Rather than saying "All men are spoiled by their mothers and think they don't have to do housework," the writer could write "<u>Some</u> men are spoiled by their mothers and think they don't have to do housework." Or a writer could write, "<u>Some people believe</u> that men are spoiled by their mothers and think they don't have to do housework." By using qualifiers, writers make themselves look more fair and reasonable. Verbs can also serve to qualify a statement. "Could be" and "might be" are examples of such verbs. For example, "All men <u>might</u> <u>be</u> spoiled by their mothers and think they don't have to do housework."

Look at the following examples. Notice how the meanings of the categorical statements are "softened" by the use of qualifiers.

Categorical statement: Men complain about dirty dishes but won't lift a finger to wash them.

Qualifier added: Men complain about dirty dishes but <u>frequently</u> won't lift a finger to wash them.

Qualifier added: <u>Some</u> men complain about dirty dishes but won't lift a finger to wash them.

Qualifier added: Men complain about dirty dishes, but <u>many</u> won't lift a finger to wash them.

Categorical statement: Women complain that they have to do all the housework.

Qualifier added: <u>Sometimes</u> women complain that they have to do all the housework.

Qualifier added: <u>Many</u> women complain that they have to do all the housework.

Qualifier added: Women complain that they have to do <u>most</u> of the housework.

The idea is sometimes to use qualifiers in your essays. Of course if every sentence you write contains a qualifier, your essay will be less effective. Statements of fact, for example, need not be qualified.

B: Revising Drafts of Student Essays

Presented here are drafts of three student essays written about a problem connected with families in which both of the marriage partners work full-time jobs. Read the first essay, "Just Say No," by Syrece S. While reading, underline or highlight two or three sentences to which qualifiers might be added to make the writer appear more reasonable or fair.

REVISING

Student Draft: "Just Say No"

JUST SAY NO

After today I was ready to quit. I am not just referring to my job, but everything. That includes being an employee, mother and wife. It all started this morning at five a.m. and proceeded to get worse. Little Kimmy and Bobby were determined not to get along at all. Trying to be the great arbitrator between the two caused me to get a late start for work. Its effect was I was rushed. As soon as I had walked in the door, Mr. Tabor handed me a thick file of notes. He said, "Hey babe, try to make sense out of it because I need this by the end of the day. Sorry to lay this on ya at such a short notice, but I know you're my best worker, and if anyone can do it, you can."

Needless to say, I was late getting off work, even though I skipped my lunch break. When I pulled into the school ground an hour later than usual, I saw little Kimberly in tears and Bobby patting her back trying to comfort her like a parent should. I felt terrible for being late. I apologized to these little naive eyes that didn't understand.

When our trio had walked in the door of the house, the answering machine revealed that Brad, my husband, would not be home until eight tonight, and Bobby was already whining about being hungry. I gave him a package of Twinkies to hold him and his sister until the Kraft macaroni and cheese was done. No sense to making a big meal if everyone wasn't going to be here. So I threw a load of laundry in the washer and started picking up the scattered toys in the house, making a mental note to ask Brad to do the dishes while the children bathed because I had a summary statement due first thing in the morning. Hopefully this weekend I can spend some quality time with Brad and the kids.

Is this what a family should be? If it is, I am afraid that you can count me out. There are enough problems today without trying to be the typical family. In today's world there is the stress of a job and also there is the problem of time with your spouse, let alone time for yourself when raising children. In today's rat race, children are from dysfunctional families because of the lack of time for families. There are always other people who are glad to populate the earth.

A normal family consists of husband, wife and children. That is the common way of thinking. The idea of having children is to carry on the family name and for them to love their parents unconditionally. Women say having children is a maternal instinct born in them. Another common reason for having kids is for a tighter bond in a family or a marriage.

I believe the only solution for this problem is not to have kids, even though some people disagree. Without kids people have time for themselves. They also can make time for a companion if they get lonely. This would also solve the world's overpopulation problem. I am not saying all people should not have children, but it isn't convenient anymore in today's society.

In society today children are more of a problem than they are worth. Children detract from a normal day with added stress.

Syrece S.

REVISING

Now, look back at the two or three sentences you underlined or highlighted. Then, in the spaces below, rewrite these sentences and add a qualifier to each.

1. _____

   _____

   _____

   _____

2. _____

   _____

   _____

   _____

3. _____

   _____

   _____

   _____

More Practice Adding Qualifiers

Two more student drafts of essays written in response to this chapter's prompt follow. While reading them, underline or highlight sentences to which you might add qualifiers. Also, look for places where the writer of each draft might add details or examples to make the essay better. Underline or highlight places where more details or examples are needed.

Student Draft: "The Second Shift Marriage"

THE SECOND SHIFT MARRIAGE

In recent years the concept of the "second shift" marriage is becoming more and more popular. This is a marriage where both the husband and wife have full-time jobs. Second shift marriages are becoming popular because of the high cost of living. Families can't afford to live off of one salary alone; therefore, the remaining husband or wife is forced to go to work also.

When both marriage partners are faced with full-time jobs, they find it hard to spend time together and with their children. When a person has just got off of a full day at work, that person is too tired or upset to spend quality time with the rest of the family. This lack of time and communication with one another leads to tension in their relationship.

I feel that in order to have a good relationship in a marriage you must spend a certain amount of time together every day. It is hard to spend this time together when both partners are working eight hours every day. A solution to this problem is setting out a certain time where a couple can be alone together every day without worrying about their jobs. For example, every day after work the two of them could sit down and have a meal together, go out to dinner, or even go to a movie. This short time together every day would mean a lot for their relationship.

Couples say that when they both have jobs and they don't get to see each other often, it keeps them from getting into arguments and fighting with each other. A marriage such as this already has problems, and these people need some extra time to work things out. If the couple still can't get along, they shouldn't be together in the first place.

Chan E.

REVISING

Student Draft: "The Long Walk"

THE LONG WALK

It is eight o'clock at night, and poor little Billy is waiting for his ride home from soccer practice. At Billy's house, five miles away, his mom is just getting home from picking up Billy's little sister. Ten minutes later Billy's dad gets home from a hard day at the office. Billy is still waiting for his dad at the school. Billy's dad goes through the ritual of hugs and kisses with his wife; meanwhile, Billy realizes it is going to be a long walk home.

The problem we have here is simple. The two parents did not discuss the transportation for their kids. This does not mean they don't love or care; it means that they are busy too. Both parents working full-time jobs have a lot to think about at work. This is all added to the dozen things they are thinking about when they get off work.

A solution for this may not be so easy. The parents can't stop thinking about their jobs. Sure, one could add that all they need to do is discuss it before they leave in the morning. This would be easy if the parents had nothing to think about all day, but parents who work are busy all day with their jobs. This is all to be added to what they must do after they punch out.

My solution to the problem is easy as cherry pie. The kids must do some of the thinking for their parents. All they must do is give their parents a call during the day to remind them that practice gets over at seven-thirty. This will save a lot of soles of shoes.

I can hear it now: "If parents can't remember their kids, they must not love them." This is definitely said by people who don't have kids and who do nothing more than change T.V. channels all day. I will totally disagree with those people who think that way. Think back to when you were at your girlfriend's house. You were having so much fun that you just forgot what time you were supposed to be home. This did not mean you didn't love your parents.

So to conclude my paper about being left at soccer practice, all one has to do is reach out and touch someone. Give them a call to let them know what time practice is over. If this doesn't do the trick, then you can always remind yourself, while walking the five miles home, that you are getting some good exercise.

Monte Z.

C: Revising Your Draft

Working alone or with others, revise the essay you wrote about a problem concerning families in which both marriage partners work full time outside of the home. Pay special attention to qualifiers in your revision, but also make any other kinds of revisions you think will make your essay better. Caution: It is possible to put too many qualifiers in an essay. Try to find a balance in your essay between qualified and unqualified statements. Adding two or three qualifiers will probably be enough.

D: Helping Others to Revise Their Drafts

Often it is easier to see places where revisions are needed in a paper you didn't write than in one you did. Exchange essay drafts with another writer, and offer each other suggestions for revisions.

E: Optional Revision

The "second shift" essay you have written may also benefit from your doing the revising strategy—Revising for Details of Emotion—found in Chapter 4.

REVISING

SECTION
◄►
4

Final Editing for Punctuating Subordinating Conjunctions and Conjunctive Adverbs

Subordinating conjunctions (such as *since*, *because*, *if*, and *although*) and **conjunctive adverbs** (for example, *however*, *nevertheless*, *moreover*, and *thus*) both show the relationship between clauses. However, they are very different in how they work and how they are punctuated. In addition, it is easy for writers to confuse subordinating conjunctions with conjunctive adverbs and use the punctuation appropriate for one kind of word with the other kind. In this section we will first look at subordinating conjunctions and how they are punctuated and then look at conjunctive adverbs and how they are punctuated. Finally, we will look at some simple tests that will keep you from confusing subordinating conjunctions with conjunctive adverbs.

A: Punctuating Subordinating Conjunctions

A subordinating conjunction begins a type of dependent clause called a **subordinate clause.** (You may recall that a **dependent clause** is a clause that can never stand alone—it must always be attached to an independent clause.) Subordinate clauses beginning with subordinating conjunctions are like big, overgrown adverbs that modify the verb in the independent clause that they follow. Look at the following sentence.

1. <u>I returned your call</u>   **as soon as** <u>I got your message.</u>
    Independent clause   **Subordinate clause**

The subordinate clause *as soon as I got your message* modifies the verb *returned* in the independent clause *I returned your call* and tells **when** the speaker returned the call.

We can divide subordinating conjunctions into four families according to meaning: **time, reason, condition,** and **contrast.** Here is a list of the more common subordinating conjunctions grouped by meaning with an example of each. In the examples, the subordinating conjunction is in bold, and the whole subordinate clause is underlined. Notice that the subordinating conjunction is always the first word in the subordinate clause.

EDITING

Time: after, as, as soon as, before, since (meaning "after" or "when"), until, when, whenever, while

Example: I need to use the car **before** I go to work.

Reason: as, because, since (meaning "because"), so that

Example: We stopped to get some gas **since** there are no stations in the mountains.

Condition: if, even if, unless

Example: I'll pull over and let you drive **if** you feel up to it.

Contrast: although, even though, though

Example: We decided to stop for the night, **even though** it was still early.

The normal position for a subordinate clause is after the independent clause it modifies. Generally, when a subordinate clause is in its normal position following the independent clause, we do not use a comma to separate the two clauses. There is, however, one exception to this rule: subordinate clauses that have the meaning of **contrast** (clauses that begin with the subordinating conjunctions *although*, *even though*, and *though*). We use commas with these subordinate conjunctions to signal the reader that the meaning of the subordinate clause is contrary to what the reader might expect. The use of a comma to signal a contrasting idea is quite common; for example, we normally use a comma for contrasting phrases beginning with *not*: *Some economists believe that the problem is unemployment*, **not** *inflation*.

Moving Subordinate Clauses in Front of the Independent Clause

One of the key features of subordinate clauses (like any kind of adverb that modifies the verb) is that they can be moved from their normal position following the independent clause to a position in front of the independent clause. For example, in the following set of sentences, the single-word adverb *frequently*, the adverb prepositional phrase *on Mondays*, and the subordinate clause **whenever** *I have to go shopping* all modify the verb *drive* in the independent clause.

2.   I drive to work frequently.
      I drive to work on Mondays.
      I drive to work **whenever** I have to go shopping.

All three adverb expressions can be moved from their normal place following the independent clause *I drive to work* to a position in front of the independent clause:

2a.   Frequently I drive to work.
       On Mondays I drive to work.
       Whenever I have to go shopping, I drive to work.

Notice that the adverb expressions are punctuated differently. Single-word adverbs (*frequently*) and short adverb prepositional phrases (*on Mondays*) are not usually set off from a following independent clause by a comma. However, when a subordinate clause (*whenever I have to go shopping*) is moved in front of an independent clause, it **must** be set off from the independent clause with a comma. One large research study found that failure to use a comma after subordinate clauses that have been moved in front of an independent clause was the single most common punctuation error in the writing of college students.

Editing Activity 1: Punctuating Adverb Subordinate Clauses at the End and at the Beginning of Independent Clauses

Combine the adverb subordinate clause on the second line with the independent clause on the first line in two ways:

1. Put the subordinate clause at the end of the independent clause, adding a comma only for contrastive subordinate clauses.

2. Move the subordinate clause in front of the independent clause, and add the required comma. The first question is done as an example.

---

1. The phone rang.
   As I was getting into the shower
   End: *The phone rang **as** I was getting into the shower.*
   Front: *__**As** I was getting into the shower, the phone rang.__*

2. I can't pay my tuition.
   Until I get my student loan
   End:_____
   Front:_____

3. We got dehydrated during the race.
   Because we didn't drink enough water
   End:_____
   Front:_____

4. I had to get home early.
   Since it was my turn to fix dinner
   End:_____
   Front:_____

5. He still couldn't finish his paper.
   Even though he had done all the research
   End:_____
   Front:_____

6. That lamb followed Mary.
   Wherever she went
   End:_____
   Front:_____

7. They decided to stay home.
   Since the roads were getting icy
   End:_____
   Front:_____

8. I am still gaining weight.
   Although I eat nothing but carrot sticks
   End:_____
   Front:_____

9. They will do the deck too.
   If there is enough paint left
   End:_____
   Front:_____

10. I will assume you are not coming.
    Unless I hear from you
    End:_____
    Front:_____

11. I think I should stay in school.
    Even if I could get a job now
    End:_____
    Front:_____

Now you are able to spot and correct the common error that occurs when we use subordinate clauses beginning with a subordinating conjunction: leaving off the comma that must be used when a subordinate clause has been moved in front of the independent clause.

Editing Activity 2: Identifying and Correcting Subordinate Clause Comma Errors in an Essay

The following student essay is ready for final editing. It is free of errors except for a number of comma errors with adverb subordinate clauses. The number of errors in each paragraph is given in parentheses at the end of the paragraph. Do the following:

1. Circle every subordinating conjunction.

2. Underline the entire clause that the subordinating conjunction begins.

3. Correct any comma errors that you find.

EDITING

Melinda H.
English Writing, Section 6
January 18, 1993

DAN AND JAN: THE WORKING COUPLE

Jan has many responsibilities as a working mother with three children. Since she works full time during the week she is exhausted by the weekend. Every weekday Jan gets up at seven, makes breakfast for the children, gets them up, helps the little ones get dressed, and gets them ready for school or the baby-sitter, before she has a chance to get herself ready for work. After her paying job is finished she comes home and starts her second shift. She cooks dinner for the family, does some house cleaning, and takes care of the children, until it is time for them to go to bed. (4)

Jan's husband Dan takes little part in taking care of the children or in doing household chores. Because he has an "old-fashioned" way of thinking he feels it is a wife's responsibility to take care of the children and the house. If he doesn't have anything else to do after work he will pick up the children from the baby-sitter's house, but that is the extent of his involvement. When Dan was growing up it seemed normal for his mother to do everything around the house. But times have changed; they couldn't keep their family farm without Jan's income. Although Dan must realize that Jan's job is absolutely necessary for both of them somehow Dan still thinks that her job doesn't count. He doesn't realize that all the jobs that his mother did during the day as her full-time job his wife now has to do after her full-time job is finished. (4)

Since Dan is an "old-fashioned" kind of man he may dislike the idea of his having to cook dinner and clean the house. He may feel that these jobs should be done by the woman of the house because it is the man's job to work outside the house. Although Dan may feel this way it doesn't change the fact that someone has to take care of the children and the house and that Jan isn't able to do it all alone. Since Jan's income is a necessity for their survival there are really only two alternatives: either Dan must do a lot more around the house or they must hire some part-time help. Even though they would have to give up some things they like to do or sacrifice some luxuries they really do have enough money to pay for a part-time housekeeper, because both of them are working full-time. (5)

If a housekeeper came to their home, say, every Tuesday and Thursday Jan would only have to worry about cooking dinner and cleaning the house three times during the week. While this won't solve all their problems it would mean that they would have more time to relax. Because they would have more free time they would be able to spend more time with their children and with each other. I believe that this kind of "quality time" is essential in every family. (3)

B: Punctuating Conjunctive Adverbs

Conjunctive adverbs act as "sign-posts" that show the reader how the ideas in the second of two independent clauses relate to the ideas already expressed in the first independent clause. There are three types of relationships signaled by conjunctive adverbs:

1. Some conjunctive adverbs signal that the ideas in the second independent clause are a continuation of the ideas in the first independent clause. We will call "sign-post" words of this type **"in addition"** conjunctive adverbs.

2. Some conjunctive adverbs signal that the ideas in the second independent clause are a result or consequence of the ideas expressed in the first independent clause. We will call "sign-post" words of this type **"as a result"** conjunctive adverbs.

EDITING

3. Some conjunctive adverbs signal that the ideas in the second independent clause contrast with or even contradict the ideas expressed in the first independent clause. We will call "sign-post" words of this type "**on the other hand**" conjunctive adverbs.

Here is a list of the more common conjunctive adverbs:

"in addition"	"as a result"	"on the other hand"
again	accordingly	however
also	consequently	nevertheless
besides	hence	nonetheless
further	then	otherwise
furthermore	therefore	still
likewise	thus	
moreover		
similarly		

Below are pairs of related independent clauses. Each of the second independent clauses contains a conjunctive adverb (in bold) that shows the relation of the ideas in the second clause to the ideas in the first clause. There are three important points to notice in these examples:

▲ The independent clauses are punctuated as separate sentences.

▲ Conjunctive adverbs can be used at the beginning of a sentence, in the middle of a sentence, or at the end of a sentence.

▲ Conjunctive adverbs are **always** set off from the rest of their clause by commas.

"In addition"

3. The experiment had failed. **Moreover,** it had damaged the equipment in the process.

4. The doctors diagnosed the problem. They were able, **furthermore,** to recommend a treatment.

5. Jones blocked a punt. He recovered a fumble, **besides.**

"As a result"

6. There has been a 20% increase in acreage under cultivation. **Hence,** food production has also increased in the region.

7. The legislature has set new limits on enrollment. Each school, **accordingly**, must review its admissions policies considering the new limitations.

8. Interest rates have fallen dramatically. Bond prices have increased, **therefore**.

"On the other hand"

9. Please pay your bill immediately. **Otherwise**, we will be forced to take court action.

10. Sam decided to take one last, desperate gamble. His luck, **however**, had run out.

11. Dark clouds were gathering ominously. We felt we must go on, **nevertheless**.

Editing Activity 3: Using Conjunctive Adverbs to Show the Relation of the Ideas in an Independent Clause to the Ideas in a Preceding Independent Clause

Pick a subordinating conjunction from the preceding list according to the type indicated in parentheses. Use the subordinating conjunction in all three positions in the second independent clause: (a) at the beginning, (b) in the middle, and (c) at the end. Be sure to separate the conjunctive adverb from the rest of its clause by commas. The first two questions are done as examples.

1. John's situation was hopeless.
   He didn't give up. ("on the other hand")

   a. *John's situation was hopeless.* **However**, *he didn't give up.*

   b. *He,* **however**, *didn't give up.*

   c. *He didn't give up,* **however**.

2. The discovery was a complete surprise.
   There was new interest in the topic. ("as a result")

   a. *The discovery was a complete surprise.* **Consequently**, *there was new interest in the topic.*

   b. *There was,* **consequently**, *new interest in the topic.*

   c. *There was new interest in the topic,* **consequently**.

3. The house was in good condition.
   The garage needed repainting. ("on the other hand")

   a. The house was in good condition. _____

   b. _____

   c. _____

4. The mine timbers were rotten.
   Some flooding was evident. ("in addition")

   a. The mine timbers were rotten. _____

   b. _____

   c. _____

5. The police wanted Sam.
   Sam decided to leave town. ("as a result")

   a. The police wanted Sam. _____

   b. _____

   c. _____

6. The problem was widespread.
   Nothing had ever been done about it. ("on the other hand")

   a. The problem was widespread. _____

   b. _____

   c. _____

7. The sample was too small.
   It was not even from the right population. ("in addition")

   a. The sample was too small. _____

   b. _____

   c. _____

8. The court was still wet.
   We played on it anyway. ("on the other hand")

   a. The court was still wet. _____

   b. _____

   c. _____

9. Tank led the league in home runs.
   He will renegotiate his contract. ("as a result")

   a. Tank led the league in home runs. _____

   b. _____

   c. _____

10. The driver was drunk.
    His license had already been suspended. ("in addition")

    a. The driver was drunk. _____

    b. _____

    c. _____

11. We ate out every night.
    I gained five pounds. ("as a result")

    a. We ate out every night. _____

    b. _____

    c. _____

In all of these examples, we used a conjunctive adverb to show how the ideas in the second independent clause related to the ideas in the first independent clause. Since the ideas in the two independent clauses are very closely related, a natural way to express this closeness would be to join the two independent clauses together within one sentence. When we put two independent clauses inside a single sentence without using a coordinating conjunction, **we must join the two independent clauses with a semicolon (;) to avoid creating a run-on sentence.** Here is where many less experienced writers make a mistake: they think that since they have used a conjunctive adverb in the second independent clause, they can just use a comma to join the two clauses. Wrong! Conjunctive adverbs relate ideas, but they have no grammatical power to join independent clauses. Conjunctive adverbs are only adverbs; they are not conjunctions. For example, the following sentence is still a run-on, even though the second independent clause begins with the conjunctive adverb *moreover*:

12.   * The experiment had failed, **moreover**, it had damaged the equipment in the process.

The correct way, of course, to join the two independent clauses in this sentence is with a semicolon:

12a. The experiment had failed; *moreover*, it had damaged the equipment in the process.

You are now ready to do the final editing of a paper containing conjunctive adverbs. Remember that the most common error is a run-on: using a comma instead of a semicolon to join the two independent clauses. Another common error is the failure to use a comma to set off the conjunctive adverb from the rest of its clause.

Editing Activity 4: Editing for Conjunctive Adverb Errors

The following student essay is ready for final editing. It is free of errors except for errors involving conjunctive adverbs. Underline the independent clauses containing conjunctive adverbs, and supply the correct punctuation. The number of conjunctive adverb errors in each paragraph is in parentheses at the end of the paragraph.

David D.
English Writing, Sec 6
February 13, 1993

PLANNING FOR TIME AND MONEY

The problem starts with two full-time working parents. Both parents have eight-hour jobs and long commutes, consequently there is not a lot of time for family bonding. The kids feel that they are being ignored, the fact is, however that both parents must work in order to support the family. Taxes, food, clothing, transportation, and housing cost more all the time, besides everyone in the family has their own personal needs and wants. The kids want the newest toys that their friends all have. The teenagers want clothing that is up to date, also they will just die if their athletic shoes are six months behind the current style. (4)

There really is no solution to the problem of the family spending so much time apart, nevertheless there are some things that could help the situation when they are together. One thing is to make the time they do have together count for more; for example, they could try to have dinner together once in a while and actually talk to each other for a change instead of each person grabbing a snack at whatever time that is most convenient for him or her. They could sit down and play a game like Monopoly, likewise, even watching television together is better than nothing. Another thing that would help the situation would be to get more realistic about expenses. Sure, the basic expenses of food and housing are unavoidable, however a lot of things really aren't that important. If the kids really want the latest clothing or shoes, let them earn the money to buy it with. The parents could give the children chores to do around the house and pay them for the work they do. The children learn self-reliance from having to earn their own money, moreover they learn responsibility from having to manage it. (4)

EDITING

> Some people say that since the parents work so hard to support their children, their children should not bother them when they come home from work exhausted, however this is not right. Children need to know that their parents care about them and about what they do, consequently both the parents and children have to work out ways that they can support each other. My conclusion is very simple. Families must keep in close contact, furthermore they must show that everybody in the family watches out and cares for each other. Both the parents and children must plan to spend time with each other. On the money side of things, if children want extras, they can do chores around the house to earn the money to pay for them. The family needs to set a realistic budget and stick to it, besides this way everyone benefits when Christmas and birthdays come around. (4)

C: Testing for Subordinating Conjunctions and Conjunctive Adverbs

Since both subordinating conjunctions and conjunctive adverbs are words that express relationships between ideas, it is easy to mix up subordinating conjunctions and conjunctive adverbs. Fortunately, the two types of words and the clauses they are part of have distinctly different movement characteristics that we can use to tell them apart.

Subordinating conjunctions are used to create subordinate clauses. We can easily move subordinate clauses from their normal position following the independent clause to a position in front of the independent clause. On the other hand, we can never move an independent clause containing a conjunctive adverb in front of the other independent clause. Compare the following examples of subordinating conjunctions and conjunctive adverbs.

Subordinating Conjunction

13.   John was in an accident **after** he has taken driver's education.

13a.   **After** he has taken driver's education, John was in an accident.

Conjunctive Adverb

14.   John was in an accident; **however**, he was not hurt.

14a.   * **However**, he was not hurt, John was in an accident.

The subordinate clause *after he has taken driver's education* in sentence (13) can be moved in front of the independent clause in sentence (13a). But the independent clause *however, he was not hurt* in sentence (14) cannot be moved in front of the first independent clause in sentence (14a). Thus, a simple and highly reliable test for identifying a subordinating conjunction is to see if you can move it (and its clause) in front of the independent clause. Conjunctive adverb clauses will always fail this test.

There is a second movement test that conjunctive adverbs pass, but subordinating conjunctions fail. Subordinating conjunctions are adverbs. Like many other adverbs, conjunctive adverbs can be moved around **inside** their clause. Compare the following sentences:

Conjunctive Adverb

15.   John was in an accident; **however,** he was not hurt.

15a. John was in an accident; he was, **however,** not hurt.

15b. John was in an accident; he was not hurt, **however.**

Subordinating Conjunction

16.   John was in an accident **after** he has taken driver's education.

16a. * John was in an accident he, **after,** has taken driver's education.

16b. * John was in an accident he has taken driver's education, **after.**

We can easily and routinely move the conjunctive adverb *however* in sentence (15) around inside its independent clause. But we cannot move the subordinating conjunction *after* in sentence (16) around inside its clause. A reliable test for conjunctive adverbs is, therefore, to move them to the middle or end of their clause. Subordinating conjunctions will always fail this movement test since they can be used only at the beginning of their clause.

Editing Activity 5: Distinguishing between Subordinating Conjunctions and Conjunctive Adverbs

The following sentences contain either a subordinating conjunction or a conjunctive adverb in bold.

1.   Write **Sub Conj** above subordinating conjunctions and **Conj Adv** above conjunctive adverbs.

2.   Supply any needed punctuation to the existing sentence.

EDITING

3. Show that your identification is correct by applying the appropriate test. For subordinating conjunctions, move the whole subordinate clause in front of the independent clause. For conjunctive adverbs, move the conjunctive adverb to a different place inside its clause. Be sure to punctuate the new sentence correctly. The first two questions are done as examples.

1. Sam had caught the killer **before** the police even knew there was a murder.
   Answer: **Sub Conj**
   *Sam had caught the killer **before** the police even knew there was a murder.*
   (No change in punctuation.)
   Test: ***Before** the police even knew there was a murder, Sam had caught the killer.*

2. Sam caught the killer **moreover** he collected a big reward.
   Answer: **Conj Adv**
   *Sam caught the killer; **moreover,** he collected a big reward.*
   Test: *Sam caught the killer; he collected a big reward, **moreover.***

3. The coach was really upset **because** we had played so poorly.
   Test:

   _____

   _____

4. I stopped off at the party, **even though** it was getting pretty late.
   Test:

   _____

   _____

5. Sam gets upset because he never wins **when** we play *Clue.*
   Test:

   _____

   _____

6. The judge was forced to postpone the trial **inasmuch as** the prosecution's key witness was sick.
   Test:

   _____

   _____

7. We are ready to leave **unless** there is something else you need to do.
   Test:

   _____

   _____

EDITING

8. The students couldn't identify conjunctive adverbs **thus** the professor was forced to flunk them all.
   Test:
   _____

   _____

9. We couldn't get to sleep at all **as** the mosquitoes were out in full force.
   Test:
   _____

   _____

10. The accident had taken place right in front of us **consequently** we were all interviewed by the police.
    Test:
    _____

    _____

11. The referee allowed the shot to count, **although** the buzzer had already sounded.
    Test:
    _____

    _____

12. You must get approval from the zoning board **otherwise** there is no deal.
    Test:
    _____

    _____

REVIEW: In this unit we have examined the punctuation of subordinating conjunctions and conjunctive adverbs. Subordinating conjunctions create subordinate clauses. When these subordinate clauses are used in their normal position following the independent clause, they are not set off from the independent clause by a comma—with one exception: subordinate clauses that begin with the contrastive subordinating conjunctions *although*, *even though*, and *though* are all set off with a comma.

We can easily move subordinate clauses in front of the independent clause. When we do this, we must set them off from the independent clause with commas. The failure to use a comma after a subordinate clause moved to the beginning of a sentence is the single most common punctuation error in the writing of college students.

Conjunctive adverbs are "sign-post" words that tell the reader how the meaning of that second independent clause is related to the meaning of the independent clause in front of it. Conjunctive adverbs must always be set off from the rest of their clause by commas. Quite commonly when we use conjunctive adverbs, we join the independent

EDITING

clause containing the conjunctive adverb together with the preceding independent clause to make a single sentence. When we do so, we must separate the two independent clauses with a semicolon. A common mistake is joining the two independent clauses with only a comma; doing this results in a run-on sentence. Conjunctive adverbs are not like coordinating conjunctions: conjunctive adverbs have no power to join clauses together.

Subordinating conjunctions and conjunctive adverbs have such similar meanings that they can be confused. A simple test for identifying a subordinate conjunction is to move it (along with the whole subordinate clause) in front of the independent clause. A simple test for identifying a conjunctive adverb is to move it around inside its clause.

Editing Activity 6: Final Editing for Punctuation of Subordinating Conjunctions and Conjunctive Adverbs

The following student essay is ready for final editing. It is free of errors except for punctuation errors of subordinating conjunctions and conjunctive adverbs. Find and correct the errors in the way that best fits the essay. The number of subordinating conjunction and conjunctive adverb errors in each paragraph is given in parentheses at the end of the paragraph.

Tracey L.
English Writing, Sec 6
March 2, 1993

MOTHER'S "JOB"

Finally, when a long week of work, athletic events, ballet lessons, and Boy Scouts has ended the family has some time to spend together. Then Mom, who has been working full time for only a few months, discovers that the house that she used to be able to keep clean during the week is a total disaster, moreover there is laundry and grocery shopping still to do. Saturday is the only time that the household chores and shopping can be done, however her husband, her teenage kids, and her two-year-old find better things to do. Dad is kicked back watching TV, although there is nothing on except re-runs. While the kids are out playing with their friends doing who-knows-what the two-year-old is in the bathroom playing in the toilet. With a heart filled with black thoughts, Mom proceeds to clean the house by herself while everyone else is enjoying their Saturday afternoon off. Somehow they seem to have forgotten that Mom has already put in 40 hours at work this week. (4)

In a busy home like this, the mother and father need to make up a list of chores and divide them among the family members, also they must set up a schedule for the jobs. Although different members of the family cannot do every job equally well all of them can contribute in their own way. For example, Mom is the cook in the family. Since she does the cooking every night it is only fair that she should not be expected to do all the cleaning up afterwards. This is a good job for the teenagers, besides this would be a chance for them to spend a little time around their mom. While Dad already spends some time taking care of the car and the lawn he could do his fair share by taking care of the grocery shopping on the weekends. If everybody does their fair share of the work Mom will have time to do some things that she would like to do, furthermore she will have the opportunity of spending a little quality time with the rest of the family. (7)

Another important thing is to involve even small children in family chores. I had a friend whose little sister loved to help her mom dust. To the little girl, of course, it was more a game than a chore, nevertheless the little girl was trying to make her contribution to the family. Although the child was probably more of a nuisance to her mother than she was a help it is important for the child to be involved in helping around the house, after all we can't expect older children to help around the house when they have never done it as young children. If we can teach our children, especially our sons, that they are capable of helping with household chores they will think it is normal to help around the house when they get older, moreover when they become adults, they will realize that they should help their wives around the house. (5)

CHAPTER 6

SERVICE INDUSTRY JOBS

SECTION

◄►

1

Reading for Examples That Support Generalizations

A: Pre-Reading

Most people in this society have jobs. A few people are independently wealthy, having money and property either inherited from a family member or won in a lottery, but most people need jobs to make a living. Most people go to work five or six days a week and work thirty-five to fifty hours each week.

These days, many students have jobs in addition to their schoolwork. They attend classes, study, read, and write papers; they also work ten to forty hours per week to earn money for food, rent, utilities, books, and tuition. Often the jobs students have in addition to their studies offer low wages and not much social status. For example, students often have jobs in convenience stores, restaurants, hotels and motels, and service stations. These kinds of jobs are called "service occupations" because the people who do these jobs work directly with the public.

Working with the public can be very stressful. Sometimes customers are impatient and even impolite. A particular customer, say in a restaurant, may have had a stressful day on his or her job, so this person doesn't treat the waiter or waitress very kindly. Some people think it is okay to be rude to people in service occupations; some people just ignore service occupation workers and act like these employees are not really people. This is wrong, but it happens. All human beings deserve to be treated with respect, no matter what jobs or how little money they have.

When you think about it, all sorts of jobs are service occupations and include working with the public. People who work in banks work with the public. People who work in schools—teachers, staff, and administrators—work with the public. In fact, most jobs include at least some regular interaction with the public. It is likely that most people will, at some time in their lives, do a service occupation job. In this chapter you will be asked to think, read, and write about jobs that require working with the public.

Pre-Reading Activities

Discussion

1. In small groups, talk about service occupation jobs you or people you know have had. Share details about these work experiences. For example, if you worked in a restaurant, what did you actually do?

2. Most people who have worked with the public have stories they tell about things that have happened on the job. Talking with others, share one story each about something good that happened at work and one story each about something that you learned about yourself or about others during this work experience.

Reading Suggestions

(Keep these suggestions in mind as you read "Inside the Golden Arches" by Marcus Mabry.)

1. Marcus Mabry writes about both good and not-so-good aspects of working in the fast-food industry. What are some of the good things about this kind of work?

2. Underline, highlight, or copy on a separate sheet of paper examples that the author includes in this essay that help the reader to remember that real people do these jobs.

3. What is the author's purpose? What does he want the reader to think, feel, or do as a result of reading this essay?

4. What kinds of pre-writing did Marcus Mabry do before writing this article?

Vocabulary Preview

absentee: never around, not in residence. (The building was owned by an <u>absentee</u> landlord.)

donning: putting on. (<u>Donning</u> her helmet, the cyclist prepared to start the race.)

novices: inexperienced people. (The <u>novices</u> had to attend three days' worth of training before working for the company.)

provocative: stimulating, causing further thought and discussion. (Many people disagreed with the speaker's <u>provocative</u> statements.)

B: Reading

"Inside the Golden Arches"

BY MARCUS MABRY*

Mariza Castro arrived in the United States from Honduras just three months ago—and she already has a job. She works behind the counter at McDonald's. Greeting a customer, she takes the order and punches it into a computer. She speeds to the shake machine—weaving through four co-workers headed in different directions—moves to the burger bin and sprints to a machine where she grabs a bag of fries. Then she brings it all back to the customer—with a smile. Mariza performs these tasks hundreds of times a day. Is she getting a golden opportunity to learn valuable skills? Or is she being exploited under the Golden Arches?

McDonald's is not only the biggest and best-known fast-food chain in America; it's also the nation's largest corporate employer of youth. About half of the more than 400,000 workers in McDonald's restaurants are under 20—and more than 60,000, or 13 percent of the total, are black. That's more minority and other kids than any other U.S. company—and many a government job program—employs. But how good a job is it? Critics have long held up McDonald's as a symbol of low-wage, dead-end work. The writers of "The 100 Best Companies to Work for in America" sum up this view: "The profit squeezed out of the business depends crucially on low wages (as low as possible) and an assembly-line operation that leaves the employee with little or no free time to think. McDonald's seemed to embrace a system geared to exploiting people in the lower ranks."

Yet in a provocative recent article, an editor for a prominent conservative journal comes to the defense of McJobs. Writing in *Policy Review*, a publication of the Heritage Foundation, Ben Wildasky says working at McDonald's can teach kids the discipline and skills they need for a productive future—particularly minorities and low-income employees who may lack a structured home life. "Far from sticking its employees into an inescapable rut," Wildasky writes, "McDonald's functions as a de facto job-training program by teaching the basics of *how* to work."

Which of these descriptions captures the reality behind the counter? A day spent working at a McDonald's on the Upper West Side of Manhattan—and weeks of interviews with McDonald's employees—suggested that the truth is somewhere between the two. There's little doubt that working at McDonald's gives employees a sense of pride. Just donning the uniform makes you feel important, part of a great American institution. Workers all like to talk about how important their jobs are— and how well they do them. Johnny DeJesus works the grill at the Upper West Side outlet, the dirtiest job in the store. But he trains novices with visible relish: how to run a complicated contraption that makes Egg McMuffins, how to put together a Big Mac quickly but neatly.

It's also wrong to assume that McDonald's jobs are menial. Some are quite demanding. The "bin man" is a kind of fast-food economist, balancing supply and demand. As customers come into the store, he estimates how many sandwiches will be needed in the next few minutes and calls orders to the grill. A miscalculation can result in angry customers, or wasted food and lost profits. Even jobs that don't carry that much responsibility are more complicated than you might expect. Working the frying machine, the apple-pie machine, even cleaning the bathroom, all involve mastering precise steps that have been laid out in company manuals.

Getting Respect.   For workers who show initiative, McDonald's offers opportunities for quick advancement. In just a few months, 17-year-old Ameer Abdur-Razzaaq worked his way up to crew chief, managing a good part of the kitchen operation. "Where else can I go at my age and be over this many people?" he asks. Ameer says the job has earned him respect at home in Harlem: "They call me 'Young Crew Chief' around my block." Ameer still isn't sure that he wants to stay on after he graduates from high school, but he's thinking about it. McDonald's has a long tradition of promoting on the basis of skill and hustle, not academic credentials. More than half of its corporate executives never graduated from college.

Yet for all the success stories, statistics suggest most McDonald's workers will never get promoted to manager. They'll continue to work the crew, or more likely— given the annual turnover rate of more than 70 percent—go on to other jobs. And many of those who stick it out will find the pressure hard to take. Employees who work the counter are expected to serve customers in under one minute. They're timed, and the results are stored in a database kept by the store manager. During a busy lunch hour, a counter worker can feel like a mouse on a treadmill.

It's also clear that McDonald's hires so many young people—and an increasing number of senior citizens—precisely so that it can pay them low wages. Until recently, most stores started crew members at the old minimum wage of $3.35 an hour. (Most now offer about 90 cents more than the newly legislated minimum of $3.80 because of growing labor shortages.) Former employee Edward Rodriguez worked for almost a year at a Los Angeles McDonald's, starting at the minimum wage and getting only a 10-cent raise. "I used to joke that it's the closest thing to slave labor," he says. "They expect a lot and pay very little." He went on to the University of California, Berkeley—then went back for a four-month stint when he was strapped for cash—but says the job did nothing to prepare him for college. "You couldn't look forward to that job," he says.

The quality of the McDonald's experience can depend heavily on whom you work for. McDonald's Corp., headquartered in Oak Brook, Ill., runs only 25 percent of the restaurants. The other 75 percent are owned by independent franchisees. Some owners—like Art and Anita Polner, who run the Upper West Side store—get high marks for bringing along young workers. But others are criticized for taking advantage of kids' inexperience and lack of other job options. Joseph Kim, a former employee from Redlands, Calif., says, "A friend of mine worked the 60 hours he had been assigned by the manager. He was then told that he wouldn't be paid for more than 40 hours, the legal limit." Company spokesman Stephanie Skurdy says that all of the franchisees are hands-on, rather than absentee, and that regional offices regularly monitor all of the operations.

Working at "McD's" is also a very different thing for suburban kids, who are mostly white and middle class, and inner-city kids, who are usually poorer and black or Hispanic. For the suburbanites, it's usually a way station on the road to college, a ticket to more clothes or maybe a car. Whether they learn discipline may not matter; they'll go on to better things anyway. For unskilled city kids, it may be one of the only games in town. If they don't work out, they'll be on the street. And if they do, the easy paycheck may keep them from taking risks to get more advanced skills. Carmen Cruz, an order taker at McDonald's, used to attend a community college. But she found it impossible to work, study and raise her two young kids at the same time. So she dropped out and has no immediate plans to go back.

Important Lesson. Of course, McDonald's can't be held responsible for Carmen's choice: it only offered her a job. In fact, given the shortage of opportunities for unskilled young people, McDonald's can only be credited for hiring so many of them. But in the end it's a business, not a training program. The lesson it teaches kids—particularly minorities—is that no one is going to help them get ahead; they have to make it happen for themselves. In today's job market, that's an important lesson to learn. ∎

Mabry, Marcus. "Inside the Golden Arches." *Newsweek* 18 Dec. 1989: 46–47.

C: Post-Reading

Discussion Suggestions/Questions

Remembering

1. What portion of McDonald's corporate executives never graduated from college?

2. According to Marcus Mabry, what are some of the kinds of people who work for McDonald's?

Analyzing

1. List the kinds of pre-writing the author did or might have done before writing "Inside the Golden Arches."

2. Share the examples you underlined, highlighted, or wrote on a separate sheet of paper while reading this article. What point does the author make with each example?

3. What is the author's purpose? What does he want the reader to do, think, or feel as a result of reading this essay?

Discovering

1. Talk about some of the good aspects of service industry jobs. In addition to those mentioned by Marcus Mabry, are there others you can think of?

2. Often what the reader thinks of while reading is more important than what the author of the reading writes. There are ideas you had while reading this selection. Discuss these with your peers.

D: Vocabulary Building

1. Latin phrases used in writing

De facto: "McDonald's functions as a **de facto** job-training program."

Mabry: "Inside the Golden Arches"

De facto is a Latin phrase that means "in fact" or "in reality." It consists of the preposition *de*, "from," and the noun *facto*, "fact." We use **de facto** when we want to emphasize the difference between the actual reality of something and the way it is supposed to be in theory. For example, in the following sentence, "Even though all facilities were legally open to the public, the schools still practiced de facto segregation," the use of *de facto* points out the difference between legal rights and actual practices. Often *de facto* is contrasted with **de jure**, a Latin phrase which means "by law." For example, we might write the following, "Equal access to public facilities was required **de jure**, but **de facto** there was segregation everywhere."

Despite the fact that Latin has been a dead language for well over a thousand years, we still use an amazing number of Latin words and phrases. For example, Latin is used for the technical names of most of the parts of the body, and all newly discovered plants, insects, fish, and animals are given a formal scientific name in Latin. A number of Latin phrases are used in law. For example, the Latin phrase **habeas corpus** (part of a longer phrase which means "you are ordered to produce this person") is a term for the right of any arrested person to appear before a judge. A number of Latin phrases occur in the writing and speech of educated people, such as **sine qua non** "without which not," which means an absolutely indispensable thing, as in "The **sine qua non** of being a media personality is appearing on a major talk show." Another example is **persona non grata** "not acceptable person," a term often used by governments to ban unwelcome foreigners from entering their countries.

Vocabulary Building Activity 1: Latin Phrases Used in Writing

In the left column are Latin phrases commonly used in English. Match these phrases with their literal translations and dictionary definitions in the column on the right.

Words	Literal Translations and Dictionary Definitions
1. status quo	a. _7_ "by the day," service paid for on a daily basis
2. per capita	b. _1_ "state of something," the existing state of affairs
3. et cetera	c. _5_ "for form," something done or carried out as an empty formality
4. quid pro quo	d. _3_ "and others," and more of the same
5. pro forma	e. _4_ "something for something," something done or given in order to get something else back
6. non sequitur	f. _6_ "it does not follow," a statement that does not logically follow from what has been said before
7. per diem	g. _2_ "by head," for each unit of a population

2. *-ee* and *-or* pairs

Franchisee: "The other 75 percent [of McDonald's restaurants] are owned by independent **franchisees**."

Mabry: "Inside the Golden Arches"

In the sense that it is used in the article, a **franchise** is a right or a license granted to a person to market a company's services. In this case, of course, it is the right to operate a McDonald's restaurant. The person who receives a franchise is called a **franchisee**. The company that grants a franchise is a **franchisor** (also spelled **franchiser**). The *-ee* ending often means a person who receives some benefit or obligation. The *-or* ending is just the opposite. It means the person giving the benefit or imposing the obligation. Often the two endings go together: where there is an *-ee*, there is an *-or* (*-er*). For example, a **grantee** is a person who receives a grant; a **grantor** is the person (or agency) giving the grant.

Sometimes only one-half of the pair exists as a recognized word. Nevertheless, our sense of the *-ee* (receiver)/ *-or* (giver) relationship is so strong that we can make up an understandable word to supply the missing half of the pair. For example, a person who gives a contribution is a **contributor**, but there is no existing word that means a person who receives a contribution. No problem; we can make up a new word, **contributee**, for just this meaning. A word of warning, however: made-up words, even words that follow this clear-cut pattern, are nonstandard. They may be acceptable as part of the technical jargon of some specialized trade or field, but they will usually be out of place in formal writing. At the very least, they run the risk of striking the reader as comical.

Vocabulary Building Activity 2: *-ee* (Receiver) and *-or* (Giver) Pairs

The words in the left column are verbs. In the spaces provided, see if you can turn these verbs into their corresponding *-ee* (receiver) and *-or* (giver) noun forms. Not all verbs have both *-ee* and *-or* forms, and some of the words have spelling changes. The first question is done as an example.

Verb	-ee (receiver)	-or (giver)
1. advise	advisee	advisor
2. appoint	*appointee,*	*appointor ?*
3. assign	*assignee*	*assignor (er)*
4. deposit	*depository*	*depositor*
5. designate	*designation*	*designator*
6. distribute	*distribution*	*distributor*
7. donate	*donation*	*donator*
8. employ	*employee*	*employor*
9. inherit	*inheritance,*	*benefactor*
10. lease	*leaser?*	*leaser*

DRAFTING

Verb	-ee (receiver)	-or (giver)
11. license	*licensee*	*licensor*
12. nominate	*nominee*	*nominator*
13. supervise	*supervision ?*	*supervisor*

Drafting with Supporting Examples

A: Pre-Writing

There are many ways people prepare themselves to write. Marcus Mabry, author of the article "Inside the Golden Arches," mentions in the article that he worked one day at a McDonald's in Manhattan. He also mentions "weeks of interviews with McDonald's employees," so he did the job and talked to others who had done or were doing the job to gather more information. Also, as pre-writing, he read articles other people had written about McDonald's. Doing, talking, and reading are excellent ways to pre-write an essay.

You will soon be writing an essay about working. Since everybody knows about the not-so-good features of working—not enough pay, getting up in the morning without wanting to, angry bosses, unhappy customers, and having to do things that aren't very interesting—here you will be asked to write about the good parts. Think about jobs you have had. Then think about parts of one of those jobs that were fun or that taught you something.

Essays are the kind of writing students are most often asked to do. Basically, an essay is made up of the writer's ideas and opinions about a subject or topic (the subject here, for example, is "the fun or learning aspects of working") and facts, descriptive details, examples, and logic that "support" or "back up" the writer's ideas and opinions.

Normally, essays are about subjects on which people have different opinions. You wouldn't, for example, write an essay arguing that trees are good for the environment or that automobiles pollute the air. Everyone agrees on these things. <u>Essays are usually about things that are in doubt</u>. The essay writer's job is to share his or her ideas and opinions on a subject or topic and include enough facts, details, and examples in the essay for the reader to understand the writer's ideas and opinions and see the writer's perspective.

Pre-Writing Activity 1: Describing the Aspects of Working

The first kind of pre-writing here is to decide which working experience from your life you will write about. Then think a little about that experience, asking yourself what was good about it. After some thought, fill out the following grid. On the left side list the fun or learning aspects of your working experience. Then, on the right side, write out an example that supports or illustrates each aspect you have listed on the right. Try to write two fun aspects of the job and examples of them and two learning aspects of the job and examples that let the reader see what actually happened.

Aspects of the Working or Learning Experience

Sample aspect: *A fun part of working at the car wash was playing with the water.*

Examples That Support or Illustrate This Aspect

Sample example: *After the automatic wash cycle, two employees worked together, one with a pressure hose and one with a soapy washrag, to get the dirt that was left over. The person with the pressure hose would try to soak the other person. The other person tried to dodge the water, so you had to get the water to ricochet off the car just to get a hit.*

Aspect 1 (fun) _A fun part of working at the frog was the occasional food fights._

Example 1 _every once in awhile, when it was really dead, someone would throw tomatoes or something as juicy at someone else & start a food fight._

Aspect 2 (fun) _another fun part of working at the frog was coming together w/ so many different kinds of people._

Example 2 _our staff was made up of football players, wallflowers, stoners, prepies, etc. & we all learned to respect eachother & like eachother for who & what we were._

both!

Aspect 3 (learning) _____

Example 3 _____

Aspect 4 (learning) *I learned many good social skills. ✓ ✓ (& once I was in charge - priority)*

Example 4 *I learned how to interact w/ all different kinds of customers. Learned how to be very friendly & even the strangest people I've ever seen.*

Pre-Writing Activity 2: Discovering New Ideas

Next, think about what fun or learning aspect of your working experience was really different or unexpected. Most people think meeting new people and receiving paychecks are fun aspects of working. What other fun aspects of your experience can you think of? In small groups, share these different or unexpected features of your experience.

Notes on Essay Form

Many things can be said about essay form, but two things really stand out:

1. **An essay has a point.**
   Some people call the "point" of an essay the "focus." An essay's focus normally has three interconnected parts—an issue, the writer's opinion, and an intended audience.

   a. An "issue" is what the essay is about.

   b. The writer of an essay has to take a stand on the issue. This normally takes the form of an opinion.

   c. Essays are written with specific audiences in mind.

The following examples and figure serve to illustrate the concept of focus:

Essay Subject:
Some problem or annoyance connected to the campus on which you are studying

Possible Issue	Writer's Opinion	Intended Audience
The bookstore is not open in the evening.	It should be open.	The manager of the bookstore.
The copy machines at the library don't work.	They should.	The Head Librarian.
The dormitory rooms are too cold in the winter.	Students shouldn't have to freeze.	The Director of Student Services.

From Elder, Dana C. *Writing to Write: Process, Collaboration, Communication*. New York: Macmillan, 1990: 37.

2. **An essay has a beginning, a middle, and an end.**

   a. The beginning is called the "introduction." It lets the reader know what you will write about and what point you will make. The introduction is normally one paragraph long.

   b. The middle part of an essay is called the "body" of the essay. The body of an essay can be as few as two or three or as many as twenty paragraphs long. It is the biggest part of the essay. It is where the writers put details, examples, facts, and reasons that make their points sound good to their readers.

c. The end of an essay is called the "conclusion." Many things can be said about essay conclusions, but at the end of an essay a reader should know what the writer's point is.

B: Writing a First or Initial Draft

1. After you have completed the pre-writing for your essay, look back over this work. With all of these ideas and examples in mind, write a first draft of your essay. Don't worry about spelling, punctuation, or grammar—just write. Try to include examples that support or illustrate the ideas and opinions you write about. If you get stuck, look back at what you did on the grid in pre-writing activity 1. Maybe you can put some of that work into your essay. Remember that an essay contains <u>your</u> ideas and opinions and your details and examples. <u>You</u> are the expert on this experience.

2. Sometimes it is easier to write an essay assignment when you have an outline, when you can see a way to organize your essay. In addition, it sometimes helps if you can see an essay someone else wrote for the same assignment. You do not have to follow the outline, but you may if you like. It represents one way to organize your essay. Following the outline is an essay written by a student who used the outline. Following the student essay is another essay form outline. You may choose to use the second essay form.

Service Industry Job Prompt

I.   Topic:
Write an essay about the fun and/or learning aspects of a service industry job.

II.   Form Option 1:
You <u>may</u> choose to organize your essay in the following way:

DRAFTING

Title

1. (Introduction)
People talk about the negative aspects of work at _Señor Froggy_
They say. . . . .

    a. negative aspect _if you work around fast food all the time, you'll gain weight._

    b. negative aspect _you only get paid minimum wage._

    c. negative aspect _you have to work some weekend nights till late._

    d. negative aspect _you have to dress in uniform_

2. (Body)
But there are fun and/or learning aspects of this job, and the one I think is most important is _working with a variety of people._

    a. example plus explanation _learning responsibility; (being on time; in charge etc.)_

    b. example plus explanation _I had a super boss who related to his employees_

    c. example plus explanation _if you do your job right, & stick w/ it long enough, they may offer you a raise._

3. (Body)
Other good features of this job could be highlighted.

    a. good feature _you learn to associate politely w/ even the strangest customers._

    b. good feature _you learn a lot about priority. (especially once in charge)_

    c. good feature _you become fast & more consistant at work._

4. (Conclusion)
For me, however, the most important is _the people I work with_ because _all of us respect eachother for the way we are, even though we are all very different._

Student Essay: "Make My Day"

MAKE MY DAY

Certified nurses' aides or CNAs tend to concern themselves with all of the negative aspects at the Davenport
hospital. All the employees complain about the poor wages
for the amount of work; we only get five-fifty an hour
starting wage, and that is only after paying three hundred
sixty dollars for the college class required for the
certification for the job. Another common complaint is the
administration. Sue, the administrator, is a registered
nurse and hasn't any ideas of how to run the hospital. Her
lack of education causes very inappropriate scheduling.
For example, I worked two double shifts in a row, sev-
enteen hours per day, and then she switched me to nights.
That caused me to work twenty-four hours straight without
any sleep, and then I worked a double shift at night. That
was fifty-eight hours in three days. Another common complaint for all hospitals and nursing homes is a CNA
doesn't have time for the little things for people like
putting makeup on the elderly ladies, reading letters to
them, and putting lotion on them. This impersonality
causes a worker to be a machine and not a person who has
time to treat the elderly as people, but regardless of
these problems I still love the job.

   I love being a CNA mostly because I can make an elderly
person's day. If I work extremely hard and skip my given
breaks, I can do the little things that make a person
smile. If I have time, I will put makeup on the elderly
ladies. Most of these ladies haven't had makeup on in
years, although when they were able to, before coming to
the nursing home, they wore it often. To them putting
makeup on is like taking a stroll down memory lane. Some
of the residents aren't able to see as well as they used
to, so time for letter reading is needed. Nothing excites
residents more than getting mail from loved ones that they
aren't able to be around anymore. To put lotion on their
bodies is a comfort. They get lotion once a week, but the
old dry out so easily that they could use the lotion more
often. My reward is to hear them say it feels good, a
smile, a glitter in their eye, or a thank you. The
gratitude is the most rewarding, although there is more.

Other benefits are also received in the nursing home or hospital. The work is so physically demanding that a CNA receives adequate exercise. I also cherish my health more fully. The job made me extremely considerate to the handicapped and grateful I haven't any handicaps. Teamwork is a necessity in a hospital. It is a great skill to learn. It is learned by the two-man transfer which requires two people, and during feeding time all of us CNAs make an assembly line for a quick, efficient way to pass out trays. For me, though, the most rewarding is being able to do the little things.

To me being able to do the little things has made me a better person. Now I try to obtain my goal to help people as a way of life. To me every day is a day to make a person smile, giggle, or laugh.

Syrece S.

III.   Form Option 2

Another way to organize an essay is the standard five-paragraph form. This form is easy to use, and it can be very handy when a person has only a short time to complete an essay. For example, in an essay exam situation the five-paragraph form helps a writer to organize his or her answer quickly. You may use this form while writing your essay on "the fun and/or learning aspects of a service industry job."

Title

First paragraph: (Introduction)

There are three fun and/or learning aspects of working at_____.
They are _____
_____
_____ .

Second paragraph: (Body)

The first is _____ .
(add example plus explanation)_____
_____
_____

Third paragraph: (Body)

The second is _____ .
(add example plus explanation)_____
_____
_____

Fourth paragraph: (Body)

The third fun and/or learning aspect of working at _____
is _____ .
(add example plus explanation)_____
_____
_____

Fifth paragraph: (Conclusion)

These three aspects of working at_____
made the job better for me because_____
_____
_____ .

Because this five-paragraph essay form is taught in grade schools, junior highs, high schools, community colleges, and universities, most people know it. Some think that because it is a "fixed" form, this form limits what a writer can write, or they think that because they have seen it so often, it is boring. Five-paragraph essays can be dull. Many are.

On the other hand, many fine five-paragraph essays have been written. Many really good five-paragraph essays are written every day, and not just in schools. Making a point, giving three reasons, and repeating your point is a good strategy for writing or for speaking.

You may choose to use the first or the second essay form. You may also choose to write using a completely different form—one you provide. In any case, write an essay that is about two full, typed, double-spaced pages long.

SECTION

3

Revising for Supporting Examples

A: Adding Examples

Examples are a writer's best resource. They are excellent resources for communication, whether spoken or written. For example, many students ask other students about courses and instructors when they are trying to decide which courses to take. One student might say, "I took Economics 101, and it was really great." If the person that student is talking to asks, "What was great about it?" that person is asking for examples, for more specific information. Words like "great" and "fun" and "wonderful" and "interesting" mean different things to different people. Examples offer more information.

Marcus Mabry, in the article "Inside the Golden Arches," writes about particular people. Mariza Castro, Ameer Abdur-Razzaaq, Edward Rodriguez, Joseph Kim, and Carmen Cruz are all included in the article as examples of young people who work or have worked at McDonald's. Rereading that article, you will note that every opinion or idea in it is supported or illustrated by an example. This is a good strategy. Good essays are rich in examples.

B: Revising Drafts of Student Essays

The following are three drafts of three different student essays about the fun or learning aspects of working. Read the first one. While reading, look at the examples Cynthia T. includes, and look for places where other examples might be added.

Student Draft: "Why Working Is Fun to Me"

WHY WORKING IS FUN TO ME

Working is a part of everyone's life. Working is something one has to do everyday throughout his or her lifetime. I feel that people should have to make work fun for themselves since they will work for most of their lifetimes. However, there are those who do not like to work or do not like their careers and just make life miserable for themselves because of this. From my experience with working I feel that people have to find some kind of work that they like to do because if a person doesn't do that, life can be really hectic. Working is fun to me because it keeps me from being bored, it gives me the opportunity to meet interesting and important people, and I get to learn many new things when working different jobs.

A prime example to show how work kept me from being bored is to think about my early teenage years. Life then was beginning to become very boring. I was at the early teen stage in which playing outside and playing games were over with, and I was simply ready to be a young adult. My grandmother would always tell me she was tired of looking at me watching television and talking on the phone most of the day, which are favorite pastimes of teenagers, but to me that's all there was to do besides playing sports and doing homework. When the time came and I was old enough to work, I went out and found myself a job at Wendy's Hamburgers. When I got this job I said to myself, "Hey, now I won't be bored, and now I can make money too." Working and going to school kept me really busy and kept me from being bored.

Another reason why working is fun to me is because it gives me the opportunity to meet interesting and important people. Depending on what kind of job you have, you can meet all kinds of important people. Take for instance my job last summer. I was a technical clerk for Westinghouse Hanford Company at FFTF. I worked in a department called "quality assurance," which consisted of the top engineers of the company who made sure everything was being done right. At first I was nervous working with these people, but throughout the summer I got to know them better, and they taught me a lot. I was constantly going to meetings with my boss, Jim, and on one occasion I got to meet the president of the company, John Noland, and talk with him about the summer program I was in. I was thrilled to meet this man. This example clearly shows that you can meet very interesting and important people if you take time to find the right kind of job.

Last but not least, working is fun to me because I can learn many new things with every job I get. Take for instance my job last summer again. The program that I was in required that one have certain skills such as typing, being able to use a word processor, and so on. When I started working in quality assurance, I was taught many new skills also. I was taught how to use different programs on a computer, such as Data Base III. I learned how to use a dictaphone and how to write in shorthand. These and various other skills have helped me in college.

Cynthia T.

Now look again at the same piece of writing. In this version, ideas and opinions not already supported or illustrated by examples have been underlined. Then examples that support these ideas or opinions have been added in italics. Cynthia T. has already included several good examples, but a few more make her essay even better.

Student Draft: "Why Working Is Fun to Me" (Revised)

WHY WORKING IS FUN TO ME (REVISED)

Working is a part of everyone's life. Working is something one has to do everyday throughout his or her lifetime. I feel that people should have to make work fun for themselves since they will work for most of their lifetimes. However, there are those who do not like to work or do not like their careers and just make life miserable for themselves because of this. From my experience with working I feel that people have to find some kind of work that they like to do because if a person doesn't do that, life can be really hectic. Working is fun to me because it keeps me from being bored, it gives me the opportunity to meet interesting and important people, and I get to learn many new things when working different jobs.

A prime example to show how work kept me from being bored is to think about my early teenage years. Life then was beginning to become very boring. I was at the early teen stage in which playing outside and playing games were over with, and I was simply ready to be a young adult. My grandmother would always tell me she was tired of looking at me watching television and talking on the phone most of the day, which are favorite pastimes of teenagers, but to me that's all there was to do besides playing sports and doing homework. When the time came and I was old enough to work, I went out and found myself a job at Wendy's Hamburgers. When I got this job I said to myself, "Hey, now I won't be bored and now I can make money too." <u>Working and going to school kept me really busy and kept me from being bored</u>. *At Wendy's I was in charge of the salad bar. I had to fill the bowls with lettuce or potato salad or bacon bits, and I had to clean up all the spills people made. I'd just get all the bowls filled and start to clean when some of the bowls were empty again. Wendy's kept me running for four hours a night, and then I still had to go home and do my homework.*

Another reason why working is fun to me is because it gives me the opportunity to meet interesting and important people. Depending on what kind of job you have, one can meet all kinds of important people. Take for instance my job last summer. I was a technical clerk for Westinghouse Hanford Company at FFTF. I worked in a department called "quality assurance," which consisted of the top engineers of the company who made sure everything was being done right. At first I was nervous working with these people, but throughout the summer I got to know them better, and they taught me a lot. I was constantly going to meetings with my boss, Jim, and on one occasion I got to meet the president of the company, John Noland, and talk with him about the summer program I was in. I was thrilled to meet this man. This example clearly shows that you can meet very interesting and important people if you take time to find the right kind of job.

Last but not least, working is fun to me because I can learn many new things with every job I get. Take for instance my job last summer again. The program that I was in required that one have certain skills such as typing, being able to use a word processor, and so on. When I started working in quality assurance, I was taught many new skills also. I was taught how to use different programs on a computer, such as Data Base III. I learned how to use a dictaphone and how to write in shorthand. <u>These and various other skills have helped me in college</u>. *I write my papers on a computer, I take lecture notes in shorthand, and I'm not so nervous around the teachers. I knew that school prepared people for work; now I know work prepares people for school.*

Cynthia T.

Practicing Revising by Adding Examples

Following are two more drafts of essays written by students about the fun or learning aspects of working.

Revising Activity 1: "Work as Fun"

Working with others or alone, revise the student draft "Work as Fun" by adding examples in the spaces provided. You will need to make up these examples, so use your imagination.

Student Draft: "Work as Fun"

WORK AS FUN

Although it is hard to believe, in some ways working can be fun. The first highlight that most people think of when the word "work" is mentioned is money._____

_____

_____

Although making money is a nice part that comes with working, in my opinion the most practical and fun parts of holding down a job are coffee breaks and vacation time.

You may be asking yourself how can a coffee break keep you from falling asleep at your desk? But for many people a fifteen-minute coffee break is the only breather in a long, eight-hour day. How many times do you get to sit around and B.S. with your friends while drinking an A&W and get paid for it? What a great idea. Whoever came up with the idea of a coffee break in my opinion should win the Nobel Peace Prize. What would the average working man or woman do without these fifteen minutes of freedom away from the boss? If it were not for coffee breaks, the average number of employers killed by their employees would go up drastically. In my opinion the best part about a coffee break is not the maple bar or the opportunity to talk with your fellow coworkers, but the fact that your employer has to pay you for spending fifteen minutes doing absolutely nothing constructive. I only wish that the entire workday could be one long coffee break.

Another fine luxury in the job force is the almighty vacation time. A person earns vacation time by working a certain number of hours per month, and if you work for the right company, you may even get paid for spending a few days in the sun. So when you're working your tail off, all that you have to do is think of all the vacation time you are earning, and it is guaranteed to put you in a better mood. You might get in trouble for daydreaming at the office, but it would be worth it to be able to have some way of retaining your sanity. Wouldn't it be great if for every eight hours you put in at work you earned eight hours of paid vacation? Heck, I would settle for four hours of paid vacation. While you and your family are on your two-week fun-in-the-sun vacation, compliments of the boss, it is not only a great time to relax or get the perfect tan, but can you think of a better time or place to complain about your boss and fellow coworkers? I mean it is not like any of them will ever hear you._____

_____

_____

_____

   If it were not for an occasional two weeks of complete relaxation and corndogs, surfboards, and beachballs, many people would be pale-faced, keyed-up, time bombs just ready to explode._____

_____

_____

_____

They would never get the opportunity to wear stupid hats, smack their children in the back of the head for body surfing during high tide, or say unkind things to people they love. Could you imagine never having had the opportunity to meet MICKEY MOUSE in person?
   If it were not for the always wonderful coffee break and the vacation with the family once a year, your average nine-to-five worker would probably kill his or her boss, or go from town to town and from job to job looking for a break in the hectic schedule. I only wish that there were more coffee breaks in the day and longer vacations. Who knows, maybe someday the employers of this country will get a heart and learn to appreciate all of us hard-working employees. They might even let us have as many paid breaks as they have.

                                        Erin M.

REVISING

Revising Activity 2: "Work's a Beach"

Working alone or with others, revise the student draft "Work's a Beach" in the following way:

1. Underline or highlight three places where the writer states an idea or opinion and doesn't include an example.

2. Then, in two or three sentences, add an example for each idea or opinion you highlighted or underlined. You will need to make up these examples, so be creative. Try to make examples that you think this writer might use.

Student Draft: "Work's a Beach"

> WORK'S A BEACH
>
> Working in this day and age is pretty tough on your average person. I bet the majority of the people that I have known and know now don't find much pleasure in it. With both learning and working there is a lot of time that you must use to do assignments or assigned paper work. This seems to make people irritable and like their jobs less and less. I, being the more leisure type of person, prefer sleeping or lying on the beach instead of work. But yet I have to work to keep going in this modern world with all these expensive little toys that I would like to have. So I work on. Right now I don't have a job, and I wish I had one because right now I am a poor college student who would basically do anything for a buck—well, almost anything. Thinking about my situation I seem to find that work could be fun to people. If you work hard enough, you can get all those things that you want—a nice place to live, a nice car, nice furniture, and a big screen television. Jet skis would be nice for the summer. I think a boat would be very interesting also.
>
> I guess that when it comes down to pleasure in the work place, I think that there is some fun in it. In my past experiences I have had some interesting jobs. I used to work at a swim and tennis club in Wenatchee, Wa. I found this job especially interesting because it was something I liked to do. Of course you know what they do at places of this sort; you basically play racquetball and tennis and play around. It wasn't all fun and games, but it wasn't working in the apple orchards.

I have found that you meet a lot of people at the work place that you would have never met otherwise. I have met many girls at work. I have been a lifeguard for the past three years, so I am at the beaches of Lake Chelan all the time. I enjoy being on the beach and suntanning. Teaching little kids how to swim really makes me happy. When I can teach a person how to swim well, it makes me look good. It also makes me confident that I am doing my job well. Plus little kids are a ball to work with because they enjoy being in the water and are fun to kid around with.

All in all, I personally think work is a social evil, and it's too bad that we can't just eat and sleep. But we live in a high-strung society that is a capitalistic money machine. If you don't keep up with the pack, you'll get left with the rotten meat. But you can't say that all the work that you have done in the past is all bad. I think it's just how you look at it. If you want to go into it negatively, you will work in a negative fashion. But if you look to the brighter side of things, you will see the impact that you yourself have on the job or work you do, and then you will be able to work for the benefit of others and not just for materialistic things. Still, I'd rather be sitting at home in front of the television instead of working.

Jamie D.

C: Revising Your Draft

Working alone or with others, revise the draft of your essay about fun or learning aspects of working by adding three examples. Use the revision strategies you have already practiced in this chapter:

1. Underline or highlight places in your essay where you have written an idea or opinion but not included an example.

2. Then write examples that support or illustrate those ideas or opinions.

D: Helping Others to Revise Their Drafts

Exchange drafts of essays on the subject "The Fun or Learning Aspects of Working." Then complete activities C.1 and C.2 above on each other's drafts. Try to make the examples you add sound like the other writer wrote them.

E: Optional Revision

The essay you have written on the fun or learning aspects of working may also benefit from your using the revision strategy—Revising for Details of Place—presented in Chapter 2.

SECTION 4

Final Editing for Wrong Choice of Verb Tense

Wrong choice of verb tense means choosing the wrong verb tense to convey the meaning you want.[1] Three sets of tense choices often cause writers problems: (1) past and present tense shifting errors, (2) failure to use the perfect tenses when called for, and (3) failure to shift tense in indirect quotation. We will deal with each of these problems in turn.

[1] See pages 264–265 for list of verbs with irregular past or past participle forms.

A: Past and Present Tense Shifting Errors

There are two mistakes writers make with the present and past tense: shifting from one tense to the other when they shouldn't and, conversely, not shifting from one tense to the other when they should. Here is an example in which the writer incorrectly shifted from the past tense to the present tense:

1.   * I **grabbed** my coat and **go** out for a sandwich.
         Past   **Present**

Here is an example of the reverse situation in which the sentence is ungrammatical because the writer didn't shift from past tense to the present tense.

2.   * Last year we **visited** Disneyland, which **was** near Los Angeles.
              Past   **Past**

In order to see why these sentences are wrong and to know when to shift between the past and present tenses in your own writing, you need to know a little about the meaning of the past and present tenses. The basic difference between the past tense and present tense is not just a difference between past time and present time: the two tenses are really in two different dimensions altogether. Let's begin with a brief discussion of the meanings of these two tenses so that you can see what is involved in tense shifting.

Past Tense

The most common use of the past tense is for narration—telling a story or relating an incident. Narration describes an event or a series of events that were completed at some specific time or during some period of time in the past. Here are some examples from Mabry's article "Under the Golden Arches" that illustrate these two uses of the past tense.

Event That Happened at a Point of Time in the Past

3.   Mariza Castro **arrived** in the United States from Honduras just three months ago.

Event That Happened over a Period of Time in the Past

4.   In just a few months, 17-year-old Ameer Abdur-Razzaaq **worked** his way up to crew chief, managing a good part of the kitchen operation.

EDITING

Present Tense

Despite its name, we rarely use the present tense to refer to the actions taking place at the present moment of time. Instead, we usually talk about what is happening at the present moment by using the **present progressive** tense—a compound tense with *be* as a helping verb together with a main verb ending in *-ing*:

5. Just a minute, I'm **talking** on the phone.

6. The children **are playing** in the back yard now.

7. Close the windows; it's **raining**.

We use the present tense in three different ways, for (a) statements of fact; (b) generalizations; and (c) habitual or customary actions.

Statements of Fact

The trick about this use of the present tense is that "present" doesn't mean just at this moment; it means a span of time ranging from a single moment to all eternity, depending on what is relevant to the topic. For example, compare the relevant spans of time in the following sentences:

8. It **is** 11:45.

9. Today **is** Tuesday.

10. In the Chinese calendar, this **is** the year of the monkey.

In sentence (8) the span of time for which this statement is true is only one minute—in another minute it will be 11:46. In sentence (9) the span of time is a day, and in sentence (10) it is a year.

This use of the present tense often implies that the "present" time will stretch into the indefinite future until something comes along to change the existing situation, as in this example:

11. Sacramento **is** the capital of California.

This sentence implies that we expect Sacramento to continue to be the capital of California for the foreseeable future.

The "present" can even stretch to include forever when we describe things that are true by definition. Examples follow.

12. Two plus two **is** four.

13. Hawks **are** members of the class of raptors.

Often we use this type of present tense to describe an ongoing state—whether temporary or permanent, as in the following examples:

14.   Billy **has** a headache.

15.   Sam **hates** his job.

16.   Sally **loves** peach ice cream.

Note that the implied span of time for these three ongoing events is quite different. Billy in sentence (14) will probably be over his headache in a matter of hours. Sam in sentence (15) hates the way his job is now, but that might change if his job were to get better. However, Sally in sentence (16) will probably continue to love peach ice cream all of her life.

Generalizations

A second important use of the present tense is for making generalizations (as, for example, in this sentence, and the following examples):

17.   Life **is** unfair.

18.   The main cause of unemployment **is** our inefficient tax system.

19.   Good study habits **are** the most important skills a student can have.

Generalizations are different from statements of fact. Generalizations are statements of opinion that must be supported. For example, in the following quotation from "Inside the Golden Arches," Mabry makes a generalization:

> Working at "McD's" **is** also a very different thing for suburban kids, who **are** mostly white and middle class, and inner-city kids, who **are** usually poorer and black or Hispanic.

In the remainder of the paragraph in which this quotation appears, Mabry gives various facts and arguments to support this generalization. The important point here is that this sentence is not a statement of fact; it is a statement of opinion that must be supported by further argument and evidence. Since both statements of fact and generalizations use the present tense, you need to be clear in your own mind whether you are stating facts that can stand by themselves without further support or you are giving generalizations that require evidence and support for the reader to accept.

Habitual or Customary Actions

The third common use for the present tense is to describe actions that are habitual or customary (as opposed to single, specific events that we would use the past tense to describe). For example, in the sentence

EDITING

20.   I **shop** at Safeway.

the use of the present tense *shop* means that it is the speaker's regular habit to go shopping at Safeway. It has nothing to do with the present moment of time. The speaker could say sentence (20) even if he or she were at home, sick in bed, and hadn't been out of the house in a week. Here are good examples of the use of the "habitual" or "customary" present tense from Mabry's article:

> She **works** behind the counter at McDonald's. Greeting a customer, she **takes** the order and **punches** it into a computer. She **speeds** to the shake machine—weaving through four co-workers headed in different directions— **moves** to the burger bin and **sprints** to a machine where she **grabs** a bag of fries. Then she **brings** it all back to the customer—with a smile. Mariza **performs** these tasks hundreds of times a day.

The present tense in this paragraph is not describing what Mariza is doing now, at this present moment of time, nor is it a generalization about Mariza's job. The present tense is used to describe what she normally does every day in her job routine.

In this section on the present tense we have seen three important ways in which the present tense is used: (1) to make statements of fact; (2) to make generalizations that must be supported by argument and evidence; and (3) to describe habitual, customary actions. Notice that none of these uses of the present tense means "now, at this moment of time."

Editing Activity 1: Identifying Uses of the Present Tense

The following paragraph is from Mabry's article "Inside the Golden Arches." Each use of the present tense appears in bold. In the space provided following the paragraph, tell which of these three meanings best describes each use of the present tense: **statement of fact, generalization**, or **habitual/customary action**. The first question is done as an example.

It's also wrong to (a) **assume** that McDonald's jobs (b) **are** menial. Some (c) **are** quite demanding. The "bin man" (d) **is** a kind of fast-food economist, balancing supply and demand. As customers (e) **come** into the store, he (f) **estimates** how many sandwiches will be needed in the next few minutes and (g) **calls** orders to the grill. A miscalculation can result in angry customers, or wasted food and lost profits. Even jobs that (h) **don't** carry that much responsibility (i) **are** more complicated than you might expect. Working the frying machine, the apple-pie machine, even cleaning the bathroom, all (j) **involve** mastering precise steps that have been laid out in company manuals.

EDITING

1. (a)   assume
   Generalization _____

   (b)   are

   _____

   (c)   are

   _____

   (d)   is

   _____

   (e)   come

   _____

   (f)   estimates

   _____

   (g)   calls

   _____

   (h)   do

   _____

   (i)   are

   _____

   (j)   involve

   _____

To Shift or Not to Shift

The present and past tenses have fundamentally different meanings. The main use of the past tense is for narration—telling about an actual event that took place at some specific time or over some period of time. The present tense is essentially "timeless." We use the present tense (1) to make statements of fact; (2) to make generalizations; and (3) to describe habitual or customary actions, none of which are tied to any specific moment in time. Since the past and present tenses have totally different functions, it is not at all surprising that we shift back and forth between the present and past tense depending on what we are saying. Here is an example of this kind of tense shifting from Mabry's article:

> For workers who **show** initiative, McDonald's **offers** opportunities for quick advancement. In just a few months, 17-year-old Ameer Abdur-Razzaaq **worked** his way up to crew chief.

In the first sentence the author uses the present tense (*show* and *offers*) to make a generalization. In the second sentence the author supports this generalization by a specific example in the past tense (*worked*). This particular combination of tenses—the present tense for a generalization, followed by a shift to the past tense for an example that illustrates or supports the generalization—is very common in academic writing.

Editing Activity 2: Selecting Past or Present Tense

The following paragraph is taken from Mabry's article "Inside the Golden Arches." However, each of the present or past tense verb forms has been replaced by the dictionary form in parentheses. In the space provided, pick either the present or the past tense form of the verb in parentheses; then compare your answers with the original. The first verb has been done as an example.

It (be) *is* also clear that McDonald's (hire) _____ so many young people—and an increasing number of senior citizens—precisely so that it can pay them low wages. Until recently, most stores (start) _____ crew members at the old minimum wage of $3.35 an hour. (Most now [offer] _____ about 90 cents more than the newly legislated minimum of $3.80 because of growing labor shortages.) Former employee Edward Rodriguez (work) _____ for almost a year at a Los Angeles McDonald's, starting at the minimum wage and getting only a 10-cent raise. "I (use) _____ to joke that it (be) _____ the closest thing to slave labor," he (say) _____. "They (expect) _____ a lot and (pay) _____ very little." He (go) _____ on to the University of California, Berkeley—then (go) _____ back for a four-month stint when he (be) _____ strapped for cash—but (say) _____ the job did nothing to prepare him for college. "You couldn't look forward to that job," he (say) _____.

Let's now look again at the two sentences at the beginning of this section with tense shifting errors and see what the problem is.

1.   [*] I **grabbed** my coat and **go** out for a sandwich.

Sentence (1) is part of a narration; the writer is relating a series of actions. Even though the two events are not simultaneous (first the speaker grabbed his coat and then he went out for a sandwich), both actions are part of a single event completed in the past. Since these actions are specific, time-bounded events, we must use the past tense for both of them. Consequently, the shift of tense of the second verb (*go*) from past to present is incorrect. The proper form of the sentence is the following:

1a.   I **grabbed** my coat and **went** out for a sandwich.

Here is the second example of a tense shifting error:

2.   [*] Last year we **visited** Disneyland, which **was** near Los Angeles.

Sentence (2) requires a shift in tense. The first verb (*visited*) is in the past tense because it is part of a narration that describes specific events that took place at a specific time in the past (*last year*). The second verb (*was*) is an incorrect use of the past tense because it implies that Disneyland's location is also an event that took place last year. In other words, the past tense *was* ties Disneyland's location near Los Angeles to a specific time period in the past with the implication that it may not be near Los Angeles today. The use of the past tense incorrectly restricts the statement of fact about Disneyland's location to the past. We need to express statements of fact in the "timeless" present tense. Here is the corrected form of this sentence:

2a.   Last year we **visited** Disneyland, which **is** near Los Angeles.

An extreme example that demonstrates that we cannot use the past tense for statements of fact is the following:

21.   [*] Two plus two **was** four.

Using the past tense in sentence (21) ties the statement of fact to the past and implies that two plus two may not be four at the present time or at some time in the future.

Likewise, stating a generalization in the past tense implies that the generalization was true only at that time in the past—that it is not necessarily true at the present time. For example, the following past tense sentence is grammatical:

22.   The main cause of poverty **was** a weak educational system.

However, the use of the past tense restricts the generalization to the past. If the writer meant to make a generalization that also included the present (and the foreseeable future), then he or she should have used the present tense for a "timeless" generalization:

EDITING

22a. The main cause of poverty **is** a weak educational system.

Editing Activity 3: Correcting Tense Shifting Errors

The following sentences contain errors in tense: the sentences either shift tense when they shouldn't or don't shift when they should. In the space provided, rewrite the corrected form of the sentence. The first question is done as an example.

1. Einstein **showed** us that time **was** relative.
   Corrected: *Einstein **showed** us that time **is** relative.*

2. The main thing we **remember** today about Herbert Hoover **is** that he **is** president during the beginning of the great depression.
   Corrected: _____

3. I **stepped** into the street and a kid on a bicycle nearly **runs** me over.
   Corrected: _____
   _____

4. We **hiked** along the river that **flowed** into Lake Coeur d'Alene.
   Corrected: _____
   _____

5. My job **was** to write down all the information whenever somebody **calls** with a complaint.
   Corrected: _____
   _____

6. In Washington, we **visited** the National Gallery, where there **were** many famous paintings.
   Corrected: _____
   _____

When you are writing, you sometimes have a choice between narrating an event in the past tense or making a "timeless" present tense generalization about the event. Either choice is acceptable, but once you have decided which way to do it, you must be consistent. For example, either of the following is grammatical:

23. Past: Whenever my brother **made** a fuss about something, he always **got** his own way.

24. Present: Whenever my brother **makes** a fuss about something, he always **gets** his own way.

Sentence (23) is a narration—the telling of an event or an episode that took place in the past. There is no necessary implication that the writer's brother still gets his way now. Sentence (24) is a "timeless" generalization about the writer's brother. What you cannot do, however, is shift from one tense to another without a reason for doing so:

25.   * Whenever my brother **made** a fuss about something, he always **gets** his own way.

25a.   * Whenever my brother **makes** a fuss about something, he always **got** his own way.

Now you are ready to identify and correct tense shift errors on your own. The key point to remember about shifting present and past tense is the following: don't shift unless there is a reason to, but if there is a reason, then you must shift. If you are writing about a specific event or series of events that has a beginning and an end, almost certainly you should use the past tense. If you are making a statement of fact or a generalization or are describing something that is habitual or customary, almost certainly you should use the present tense.

Editing Activity 4: Identifying and Correcting Tense Shifting Errors

The following is a student paper that contains many tense shifting errors. Underline the incorrect tenses, and then correct them in the way that you think works best for this essay. The number of tense shifting errors in each paragraph is given in parentheses at the end of the paragraph.

Renee S.
English Writing, Sec 6
April 19, 1993

WORKING AS A RED CROSS VOLUNTEER

In the summer of 1991, I volunteered for the Red Cross at Madigan Hospital on Fort Lewis Army Base. I work in the Chemistry Lab doing many different jobs such as filing lab reports, typing lab samples into the computer, and handling lab samples. The samples we dealt with are people's urine and blood. (2)

On the computer I had to learn the abbreviations of the tests they ran, and then I have to figure out the results. Learning the abbreviations was easy except when the letters are combined together. Most of them were based on the periodic table, and since I had had chemistry in high school, I already know most of the symbols. (3)

At first, working in the lab gives me a sense of insecurity because I am the youngest one in there at that time. I guess that you could say that I am the new kid on the block for a couple of weeks. I was very intimidated by the knowledge the technicians possessed because I could tell by their actions that they know what they are doing. While watching them, I notice the intense expressions on their faces. That showed me how serious the job was and how much responsibility is demanded of me then. (7)

Becoming a member of their team was challenging but worthwhile. After a while I feel like a puzzle piece that fit right into the picture. I could honestly say then that I like working with that team instead of working individually because they needed each other to carry out the job so that the final outcome would be correct. Unity and dedication on everyone's part are how to make a team. If someone is not doing his or her job (and it only takes one person), the team broke apart. I liked working in that fast-paced atmosphere with all the excitement surrounding me, knowing that I am important because they needed me. (5)

> Working in the chemistry lab that summer is quite
> enjoyable. The techniques, skills, and information gained
> through observing others and learning to do it myself
> teaches me a lot about communicating with people and about
> depending on people to fulfill their duties. Now I felt
> that the experience will be rewarding in the future. (3)

B: Failure to Use the Perfect Tenses

The second tense problem we will examine is the failure to use the perfect tense when it is called for. The perfect tense form always consists of two verbs: the helping verb *have* in some form (past, present, or future) followed by a second verb in the past participle form. For regular verbs, the past participle form ends in *-ed*, such as *talked*, *worked*, and *smiled*. Don't be confused by the fact that the *-ed* past participle form of regular verbs looks just like the past tense *-ed*. When a verb follows the helping verb *have*, that verb is always a past participle, not a past tense. See the Appendix for a list of verbs that have irregular past participle forms.

The helping verb *have* can be used in any one of the three tense forms: present, past, or future:

26.   Fred **has** <u>finished</u> his homework.
      present perfect

27.   Fred **had** <u>finished</u> his homework before he went out.
      past perfect

28.   Fred **will have** <u>finished</u> his homework before class.
      future perfect

What's so "perfect" about the perfect? Nothing. The term *perfect* in its grammatical sense means "completed, finished"; it does not mean "terrific." The key to understanding the perfect is to remember that in a perfect tense, one action or event is completed or finished before a second action or event begins. In other words, the perfect is used to show the time relation between two different events or actions.

In the rapid give and take of the spoken language, we sometimes fail to use the perfect tenses correctly because we do not have sentences completely worked out in our heads before we start talking. One of the big differences, of course, between writing and speaking is the fact that when we write, we have time to plan our sentences and to go back over what we have written and correct errors. Here are some examples of the failure

EDITING

to use the perfect tenses that we might not even notice in speaking but that we must correct in writing.

29.   *Holmes quickly **searched** the victim's pockets because he **noticed** something odd about his appearance.

30.   *We **will cover** the entire book by the end of the term.

To see what is wrong with the above sentences and to ensure that you will be able to use the perfect tenses correctly in your own writing, we need to look separately at each of the three different tense forms of the perfect (past, present, and future) and see how they work.

Present Perfect

The basic use of the present perfect tense is to describe an action that began at some point in the past and which continues in an unbroken way up to the present. This meaning will be clearer if we compare it with the past tense. The past tense describes an event or action that began in the past and ended in the past. The past tense is for past events or actions that are finished and done with in the past. The present perfect, however, emphasizes an action that began in the past and that continues right up to the present time (and may even continue into the future). Here are two examples of past and present perfect sentences that illustrate this difference:

31.   I **lived** in that house for five years. (past)

31a.   I **have lived** in that house for five years. (present perfect)

The past tense in sentence (31) implies that the speaker does not live in that house any more. The present perfect in sentence (31a) implies just the opposite: that the speaker has lived in the house continuously over the past five years and still lives there now. In addition to **continuous past action**, there are two other, slightly different uses of the present perfect: **repeated actions** and a **recent event that affects the present**.

Repeated Actions

A closely related use of the present perfect is for specific events that have occurred repeatedly over a span of time right up to the present, as shown in the following sentences.

32.   It **rained** earlier this week. (past)

32a.   It **has rained** nearly every day this week. (present perfect)

The past tense in sentence (32) is for a specific event (*raining*) that occurred at a particular time in the past—a one-time-only event that is now finished. The present perfect in sentence (32a) is for a series of repeated events occurring over the past week right up to the present (with an implication that it may continue into the future).

Recent Event that Affects the Present

Even a single event can be described in the present perfect, but only with the implication that the event happened very recently and that the consequences of the event directly affect the present. Compare the following sentences:

33.   I **lost** my car keys yesterday. (past)

33a. I **have lost** my car keys. (present perfect)

33b.* I **have lost** my car keys yesterday. (present perfect)

The past tense in sentence (33) describes a single past event that is now over. The present perfect in sentence (33a) also describes a single past event, but it is both a recent event and an event that immediately affects the present. The use of the present perfect is ungrammatical in sentence (33b) because the adverb *yesterday* means that the event is not recent—one of the conditions for this use of the present perfect.

Editing Activity 5: Identifying the Uses of the Present Perfect

Each of the following sentences contains a present perfect verb in bold. Identify which of the three uses of the present perfect best describes the use of the present perfect in each of these sentences. In the space provided, label each sentence as *continuous action*; *repeated events*; or *single recent event*. The first question is done as an example.

1. Susan **has delegated** the project to Matthew.
   single recent event
   _____

2. The court **has issued** five separate injunctions in this case.
   _____

3. The Senator **has campaigned** in every district in the state this year.
   _____

4. The company **has** just **shut** down its plant in Chicago.
   _____

5. I **have worked** for them all summer.
   _____

6. Maintenance **has adjusted** the thermostat a dozen times, and it still isn't working.
   _____

EDITING

Past Perfect

The past perfect is used in situations in which one past action or event was completed before a second past event took place, as shown here:

34.   The South **had lost** the war long before Lee **surrendered**.
       Past perfect   **Past**

Often with the past perfect, there is an implication that the first event caused or directly affected the second event, as in this example:

35.   They **had had** a big fight about money before they **broke** up.
       Past perfect   **Past**

The past perfect can also be used to describe an action that continued for some span of time in the past before it was interrupted or stopped by some other event, as shown in the following example:

36.   The house **had been** empty for years when we **bought** it.
       Past perfect   **Past**

Often we put the part of the sentence containing the past tense (usually a subordinate clause) in front of the part containing the past perfect (the independent clause). When you do this, remember to be sure to use a comma after the subordinate clause that has been moved in front of the independent clause. Here are the three preceding example sentences in reversed order:

34a.   Long before Lee **surrendered**, the South **had lost** the war.
                      Past   **Past perfect**

35a.   Before they **broke** up, they **had had** a big fight about money.
                    Past   **Past perfect**

36a.   When we **bought** the house, it **had been** empty for years.
               Past   **Past perfect**

Editing Activity 6: Using the Past Perfect

Below are pairs of simple sentences written in the past tense. Combine the two sentences, and change one of the past tenses to a past perfect to show the time relation of the two events. There is more than one way to combine the sentences, so explore the alternatives to find the one that you think works the best. The first question is done as an example.

1. The owner **fired** the coach.
   The team **lost** every game last season.
   Answer:
   *After the team **had lost** every game last season, the owner **fired** the coach.*

2. The official **stopped** the race.
   Several runners **jumped** the gun.

   _____

   _____

3. The governor **called** out the national guard.
   The river **broke** through the sand banks.

   _____

   _____

4. The lawyer **requested** a new trial.
   The lawyer's client **was** convicted.

   _____

   _____

5. We **finished** dinner.
   We **asked** the waiter for the check.

   _____

   _____

6. Watson **wrote** up the case in his memoirs.
   Holmes **solved** the crime.

   _____

   _____

Future Perfect

The future perfect is a way of talking about the time by which some future action will be completed. The future tense, by way of comparison, merely indicates that an action will take place in the future. For example, compare the following sentences:

37.   Next Tuesday the contractor **will finish** the kitchen. (Future)

37a.   By next Tuesday, the contractor **will have finished** the kitchen. (Future perfect)

In sentence (37) the future tense (together with the adverb of time *next Tuesday*) tells us that a future action (*finishing the kitchen*) will take place at a specific time in the future (*next Tuesday*). In sentence (37a) the future perfect tense and adverb of time *by next*

Tuesday tell us that a future action (*finishing the kitchen*) will be completed no later than a specific time (*by next Tuesday*). The future perfect must always be used with some expression of time that functions as a cut-off point by which time the action will be completed.

Editing Activity 7: Using the Future Perfect

Each of the following sentences contains a future tense verb in bold. Below each sentence is an expression of time in parenthesis. In the space provided, combine the sentence and the time expression to form a new sentence with a future perfect tense, using the time expression as a cut-off point. The first question is done as an example.

1. The computer **will start** the new procedure.
   (by noon)
   Answer: *The computer **will have started** the new procedure by noon.*

2. I hope that the roofers **will fix** the leak.
   (before the next storm)

   _____

3. I **will get** you a permit.
   (by the time you park)

   _____

4. They **will complete** the project.
   (before you finish the paperwork)

   _____

5. They **will install** the new lock.
   (before closing time)

   _____

6. The students **will turn** in their papers.
   (by no later than noon)

   _____

Using the Perfect Tenses Correctly

Now we can see what the problems were with the two sentences at the beginning of this section. Here is the first sentence:

29.   * Holmes quickly **searched** the victim's pockets because he **noticed** something odd about his appearance.

In sentence (29) the writer has used the past tense for both verbs as though both actions took place at the same time. This is incorrect because first Holmes noticed something odd about the victim's appearance, and then, as a result, he searched the victim's pockets. Here are some ways the writer could have used the past perfect to show the correct relationship between the two events:

29a.   Holmes quickly searched the victim's pockets because he **had noticed** something odd about his appearance.

29b.   Because Holmes **had noticed** something odd about the victim's appearance, he quickly searched his pockets.

Here is the second sentence that fails to use a perfect tense:

30.   * We **will cover** the entire book by the end of the term.

In sentence (30) the writer probably had not planned the whole sentence when he or she used the future tense *will cover*. The future tense would have been correct if the sentence ended with a different kind of time expression, for example:

30a.   We **will cover** the entire book **this term**.

However, if the writer wants to use the time expression *by the end of the term*, then the writer must change the verb to the future perfect because this particular time expression serves as a cut-off point, and when we use a cut-off point referring to the future, then we must use the future perfect tense:

30b.   We **will have covered** the entire book **by the end of this term**.

Now you are ready to use the perfect tenses correctly on your own. Here is a student essay for you to edit.

Editing Activity 8: Supplying Necessary Perfect Tenses

In the following student paper, the writer has failed to use the perfect tense when it was needed. Underline the incorrect tenses, and then supply the correct form of the perfect tense. The number of errors in each paragraph is given in parentheses at the end of the paragraph. In a few cases, other interpretations of the sentence would not require a shift to the perfect tense.

Toshihito Y.
English Writing, Sec 6
May 5, 1993

WORKING AS A SITE SUPERVISOR

Before I came to the United States last year, I worked for the previous six months for my father in his architecture company. At first my father was opposed to my going to school abroad, but eventually he agreed on the condition that I earn three thousand dollars, enough to pay for an airplane ticket and the first quarter's tuition. At that time I never had a part time job, so I didn't know what to do. My father offered to let me work for him at the rate of four dollars an hour. Before I started, I only knew that my father drew building plans. However, after I worked for him for six months, I knew a lot more about what he did. (4)

One day my father told me to start working as a field supervisor. Next morning I went to a building site where I had to wait for the subcontractors--electricians, carpenter, and painters. My father told me to begin cleaning up the site. After I worked about an hour, five carpenters showed up. They told me to help them bring in new material. After I finished helping them carry in the stuff, I had to start cleaning the site all over again because of the mess that we made bringing the stuff in. I felt like a slave, not a field supervisor. Then the painters told me how important cleaning up was. If nobody cleaned up the site, then the next group of workers couldn't do their job. Then I understood why my father asked me to help clean up the site. (5)

That afternoon while I was working, three electricians came. They asked where the power source was and where they should put the lights. I told them to call my father, but they couldn't reach him. After they called, they began complaining about the wiring plans. Just because they didn't know enough to understand the plans, they began complaining about how the plan was drawn. I became very angry with them because my father drew that plan. We got into a big argument, and I told them to leave if they didn't know what they were doing. After they left, I felt that I did a terrible thing because I sent them away without any real authority from my father. (4)

> When I got back home that night, I told my father what
> happened at the site that day. He told me not to feel bad
> about what I did because I was just a young man. He said
> that when I became an adult, I should be careful not to
> show my anger in front of people because when adults get
> angry, they look stupid and immature. I realize now that
> my father taught me many things when he sent me to the
> building site by myself. (2)

C: Failure to Shift Tense in Indirect Quotation

Indirect quotation is when we tell somebody what another person said. Indirect quotation is not the same as direct quotation. Compare the following examples:

Direct Quotation

31. Sam said, "Miles Archer **is** my partner."

Indirect Quotation

31a. Sam said that Miles Archer **was** his partner.

Notice these important differences between direct and indirect quotation:

Direct Quotation

▲ uses a comma after the verb of reporting (*said*, in this case)

▲ uses quotation marks around the reported speech

▲ uses reported speech that is word-for-word exactly what the person said

Indirect Quotation

▲ does *not* use a comma after the verb of reporting

▲ does *not* use quotation marks around the reported speech

▲ introduces the reported speech with *that*

▲ **back-shifts the tense of the reported speech if the verb of reporting is in the past tense.** Present tense back-shifts to the past tense, and past tense back-shifts to the past perfect.

Here are some more examples of back-shifting in indirect quotation:

Present Back-Shifted to Past

Direct quotation: He said, "I always **watch** daytime soaps."

Indirect quotation: He said that he always **watched** daytime soaps.

Direct quotation: He said, "I **will** watch the game tonight."

Indirect quotation: He said that he **would** watch the game that night.

Direct quotation: He said, "I **am** watching TV now."

Indirect quotation: He said that he **was** watching TV then.

Past Back-Shifted to Past Perfect

Direct quotation: He said, "I **watched** TV last night."

Indirect quotation: He said that he **had watched** TV that night.

Direct quotation: He said, "I **was** watching TV last night."

Indirect quotation: He said that he **had been** watching TV that night.

Beginning writers often get direct and indirect quotation mixed up. Here is a very reliable test to tell them apart: see if you can put *that* between the verb of reporting and the reported speech.

If you **can** insert *that*, then the reported speech is an indirect quotation: don't use a comma; don't use quotation marks, and do use back-shifting if the verb of reporting is in the past tense (as it usually is).

If you **cannot** insert *that* between the verb of reporting and the reported speech, then the reported speech is a direct quotation: use a comma; use quotation marks; and don't back-shift the tenses in the reported speech.

Editing Activity 9: Direct and Indirect Quotations

Convert the following utterances to (a) their direct quotation form and (b) their indirect quotation form. Use a past tense form of the verb of reporting for both forms of quotation. Assume that Sam is the speaker in all sentences. The first question is done as an example.

1. Utterance: *I **know** where it **was** hidden.*
   (a) Direct quotation: Sam said, "I **know** where it **was** hidden."
   (b) Indirect quotation: Sam said that he **knew** where it **had been** hidden.

2. Utterance: *Effie is my secretary.*
   (a) Direct quotation:

   _____

   (b) Indirect quotation:

   _____

3. Utterance: *She is taking the day off.*
   (a) Direct quotation:

   _____

   (b) Indirect quotation:

   _____

4. Utterance: *She will be back tomorrow.*
   (a) Direct quotation:

   _____

   (b) Indirect quotation:

   _____

5. Utterance: *The captain brought me a package.*
   (a) Direct quotation:

   _____

   (b) Indirect quotation:

   _____

6. Utterance: *I may have to call the police.*
   (a) Direct quotation:

   _____

   (b) Indirect quotation:

   _____

7. Utterance: *Joel Cairo searched my office.*
   (a) Direct quotation:

   _____

   (b) Indirect quotation:

   _____

8. Utterance: *The Fat Man was looking for the Maltese Falcon.*
   (a) Direct quotation:

   _____

   (b) Indirect quotation:

   _____

9. Utterance: *Miles always was a sucker for a pretty face.*
   (a) Direct quotation:

   _____

   (b) Indirect quotation:

   _____

10. Utterance: *A man has to stick up for his partner.*
    (a) Direct quotation:

    _____

    (b) Indirect quotation:

    _____

Verbs with Irregular Past or Past Participle Forms

Simple Form	Simple Past	Past Participle	Simple Form	Simple Past	Past Participle
arise	arose	arisen	fling	flung	flung
be	was/were	been	fly	flew	flown
bear	bore	borne/born	forbid	forbade	forbidden
beat	beat	beaten/beat	forecast	forecast	forecast
become	became	become	forget	forgot	forgotten
begin	began	begun	forgive	forgave	forgiven
bend	bent	bent	forsake	forsook	forsaken
bet	bet	bet	freeze	froze	frozen
bid	bid	bid	get	got	gotten
bind	bound	bound	give	gave	given
bite	bit	bitten	go	went	gone
bleed	bled	bled	grind	ground	ground
blow	blew	blown	grow	grew	grown
break	broke	broken	hang	hung	hung
breed	bred	bred	have	had	had
bring	brought	brought	hear	heard	heard
broadcast	broadcast	broadcast	hide	hid	hidden
build	built	built	hit	hit	hit
burst	burst	burst	hold	held	held
buy	bought	bought	hurt	hurt	hurt
cast	cast	cast	keep	kept	kept
catch	caught	caught	know	knew	known
choose	chose	chosen	lay	laid	laid
cling	clung	clung	lead	led	led
come	came	come	leave	left	left
cost	cost	cost	lend	lent	lent
creep	crept	crept	let	let	let
cut	cut	cut	lie	lay	lain
deal	dealt	dealt	light	lit/lighted	lit/lighted
dig	dug	dug	lose	lost	lost
do	did	done	make	made	made
draw	drew	drawn	mean	meant	meant
eat	ate	eaten	meet	met	met
fall	fell	fallen	mislay	mislaid	mislaid
feed	fed	fed	mistake	mistook	mistaken
feel	felt	felt	pay	paid	paid
fight	fought	fought	put	put	put
find	found	found	quit	quit	quit
fit	fit	fit	read	read	read
flee	fled	fled	rid	rid	rid

Simple Form	Simple Past	Past Participle	Simple Form	Simple Past	Past Participle
ride	rode	ridden	steal	stole	stolen
ring	rang	rung	stick	stuck	stuck
rise	rose	risen	sting	stung	stung
run	ran	run	stink	stank/stunk	stunk
say	said	said	strive	strove	striven
see	saw	seen	strike	struck	struck/stricken
seek	sought	sought	string	strung	strung
sell	sold	sold	swear	swore	sworn
send	sent	sent	sweep	swept	swept
set	set	set	swim	swam	swum
shake	shook	shaken	swing	swung	swung
shed	shed	shed	take	took	taken
shine	shone/shined	shone/shined	teach	taught	taught
shoot	shot	shot	tear	tore	torn
show	showed	shown/showed	tell	told	told
shrink	shrank/shrunk	shrunk	think	thought	thought
shut	shut	shut	throw	threw	thrown
sing	sang	sung	thrust	thrust	thrust
sit	sat	sat	understand	understood	understood
sleep	slept	slept	undertake	undertook	undertaken
slide	slid	slid	upset	upset	upset
slit	slit	slit	wake	woke/waked	woken/waked
speak	spoke	spoken	wear	wore	worn
speed	sped/speeded	sped/speeded	weave	wove	woven
spend	spent	spent	weep	wept	wept
spin	spun	spun	win	won	won
spit	spit/spat	spit/spat	wind	wound	wound
split	split	split	withdraw	withdrew	withdrawn
spread	spread	spread	wring	wrung	wrung
spring	sprang/sprung	sprung	write	wrote	written
stand	stood	stood			

EDITING

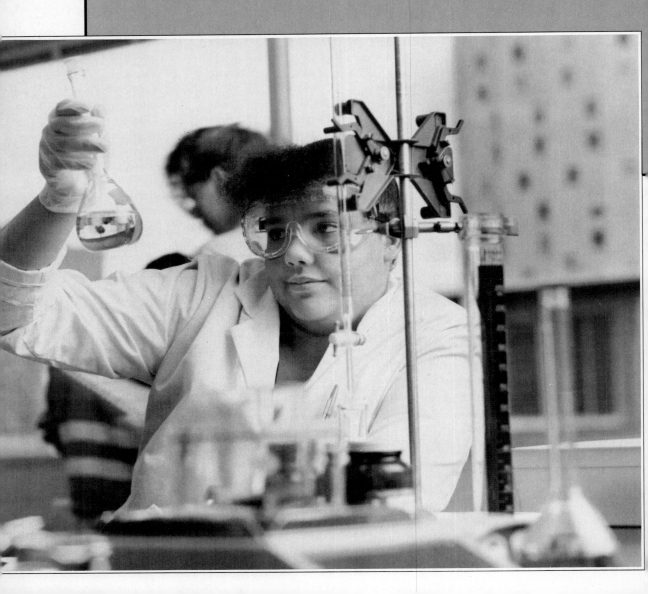

CAREER TRAINING OPTIONS

SECTION ◄► 1 Reading About Career Training Options

A: Pre-Reading

Continuing education is the time-honored solution for people who want more employment challenges and opportunities and more income—for those who want more promising careers. That much is simple, but that is where the simplicity ends and the complex decision making and hard work start. Many types of training are available in technical schools, community colleges, universities, and professional schools. This training can be completed in anywhere from one year to fifteen, and there is no guarantee that once the training is completed the person who has invested time, energy, and money in that training will get the job he or she has prepared for. Nor is there any guarantee that, once on the job, the individual will enjoy the career he or she has chosen.

Still, a person's chances for success can be dramatically increased by careful research and planning. Knowing the training options and understanding the work different kinds of training may lead to are the keys to making an informed decision.

In this chapter you will be asked to become a researcher, asked to investigate a career training option. Then you will be asked to write about the results of your research.

Pre-Reading Activities

Discussion

1. One possible measure of success in a career is how much a person enjoys the work. Some people believe that a truly successful individual wakes up in the morning and wants to go to work, actually looks forward to starting the day's tasks and to interacting with coworkers. Such people are fortunate. Whether by chance or by design, they have found careers that fit their talents and their personalities. Take a few minutes and brainstorm a list of activities you really enjoy. Then think about why you find these activities enjoyable. Do you prefer to work alone, or do you normally share tasks with others? Given the choice, would you spend time in a city, a small town, or a national forest? With others, share some of your ideas.

2. Think for a minute about all the people you know. Then ask yourself which of them seems to enjoy his or her job, which of these people you consider "successful." Choose one of these people, and then write a few notes about what this person does, what this person likes about his or her work, and what kinds of training this person completed to qualify for this kind of work. Share your ideas with others.

Reading Suggestions

(Keep these suggestions in mind as you read "Careers 101" by Neale Baxter.)

1. "Careers 101: Occupational Education in Community Colleges" appeared in the *Occupational Outlook Quarterly*, a publication of the U.S. Department of Labor, Bureau of Labor Statistics (BLS). The BLS gathers and disseminates information about trends in employment and opportunities for career training. Who is the intended audience for "Careers 101"?

2. While reading "Careers 101," please underline or highlight the following:

   a. facts that you find interesting or surprising

   b. any statements that look like advice to individuals considering career training options—especially those regarding sources of information

   c. specific types of careers that might be of interest to you or to someone you know

3. Often what a reader thinks about while reading is more important than the information and ideas that person reads. Note down some of your ideas while reading the essay in this chapter.

Vocabulary Preview

decade: ten years. (After a decade of high unemployment, the economy began to grow.)

diverge: become separate, different. (Most people complete high school, but then their educational and career paths diverge.)

initiated: a. started. (The company initiated an on-the-job training program.)
b. made a member. (The club initiated new members at a formal ceremony.)

internship: on-the-job training. (Many career training paths include internships.)

post secondary: after high school. (There are many post secondary educational opportunities available.)

B: Reading

"Careers 101: Occupational Education In Community Colleges"

BY NEALE BAXTER

One day, a high school sophomore was walking down the street and came to a signpost. One sign said, "Short Road." Tacked to it was a notice warning of delays and detours ahead. Another sign said, "Interstate 4." The Interstate led to some interesting places, people said, but you had to drive pretty far before you got to them. The third sign said, "Community Highway." It also went to some interesting places and had connections with the Interstate further down the road, according to a map in a nearby gas station. The student thought things over for a long time and then said, "That first road doesn't look like it will get me anywhere. And that second one is kind of long. But the third one is just right."

In some ways, today's educational programs to prepare people for employment are similar to the three roads in the fable above. The actual situation is more complicated, of course, with back roads, detours, short cuts (that turn out to take longer), and many other paths leading to almost any career. But still, the occupations open to people often depend on the education they have received.

JOBS THAT REQUIRE EDUCATION AFTER HIGH SCHOOL

Millions of jobs can be entered by high school graduates who have no additional training. Many of these jobs, however, hold out very little opportunity for advancement. Other jobs require at least 4 years of education after high school. Only about 25 percent of all high school graduates, however, complete college within 5 years after receiving their diploma. But a third kind of occupation offering many jobs—challenging jobs, jobs with a future—also exists. These are occupations that require 1 or 2 years of additional education after high school, the type of education provided by the nation's 1,400 community colleges and other 2-year institutions.

As long ago as 1964, the National Advisory Committee on the Junior College noted that "the two-year college offers unparalleled promise for expanding educational opportunity through the provision of comprehensive programs embracing job training. . . ." Such a promise may never be completely fulfilled, but the expansion of occupational programs in community colleges shows that they continue to make job training an important part of their mission.

The need for the kind of training provided in community colleges has been growing recently. During the past couple of decades, this country has produced more than enough college graduates for the jobs available. It is likely to continue to do so, according to projections of the Bureau of Labor Statistics. The situation for jobs that require education and training in a community college is less clear. These occupations have been growing rapidly and several are expected to be among the fastest growing between now and 2000. The schools are ready to provide the training, but will they have the students? "The important shortfall that may materialize is the lack of individuals with the education needed to qualify for the necessary post secondary education or training," according to Ronald Kutscher, the head of the BLS Office of Employment Projections.

These occupations include nursing and other health disciplines, technical specialties such as electronics technician, and administrative fields such as bookkeeping. Additional occupations are listed in Tables 1 [on pages 273–274] and 2 [on page 275]. Many other smaller fields can be learned about by contacting community colleges in your area.

In occupations such as these, pay is often closer to that of jobs requiring a degree from a 4-year college than to jobs that require no training. For example, inhalation therapists and radiologic technicians—who usually enter these occupations with an associate's degree—and the average college graduate have similar starting salaries. Frequently, these occupations also offer better prospects for advancement than do occupations that require no training. The major attraction of these jobs, however, is the nature of the work. They combine the need to keep abreast of a complex body of information and solve difficult problems with hands-on tasks that provide the satisfaction of seeing the results of one's work. This is a combination especially appealing to young people who enjoy a mental challenge but like to see the immediate relevance of what they learn.

The diversity of occupations that can be entered by people who have education after high school other than a college degree is reflected in the diversity of programs offered by community colleges. The accompanying chart, "At Least 4,000 Associate Degrees Were Awarded in These Fields in 1987" [on page 272], shows some of the more common fields. The chart does not reveal the great variety of programs available, however.

COLLEGES AS DIVERSE AS THEIR COMMUNITIES

High school students who explore community colleges will quickly learn that no two schools are alike. With so many community colleges, each trying to tailor its programs to the needs of the local area, the only standard is variety. For example, Santa Fe Community College in Florida has a program in zoo animal technology. Maryland's community colleges offer dental assisting, early childhood development, human services assistant, chemical technology, construction inspection, aviation

READING

At Least 4000 Associate Degrees Were Awarded in These Fields in 1987–1988 (disciplines in which fewer than 4000 such degrees were awarded are not listed)

Field	Degrees awarded
Engineering technologies other than construction	==================================
Nursing, general	===========================
Business administration and management	==================
Secretarial and related programs	=============
Miscellaneous business and office	==========
Marketing and distribution	==========
General business and management	=========
Miscellaneous business and management	=======
Mechanics and repairs	======
Business data processing	======
Home economics	=====
Precision production	=====
Computer and information sciences	====
Education	===
Criminal justice administration and studies	==
Agriculture and natural resources	==
Accounting	==
Law enforcement and security services	==

```
0      10,000  20,000  30,000  40,000  50,000
     (number of degrees awarded in this time period)
```

maintenance, electrodiagnostic technology, and medical laboratory technology. Michigan students can choose from a wide variety of programs related to manufacturing technology. One indication of the diversity of these schools is the accompanying description of programs that won the Secretary of Education's Award for Outstanding Vocational-Technical Education Programs in 1990.

You might think of a community college as a transportation hub. People from all

Table 1   Occupations in Which at Least 10 Percent of the Workers Needed Junior College or Technical Institute Training to Qualify for Their Current Job, 1983

Occupation	Percent Who Needed Community College or Technical Institute Training
Inhalation therapists	46
Radiologic technicians	39
Dental hygienists	38
Licensed practical nurses	34
Registered nurses	29
Electrical and electronics technicians	25
Data processing equipment repairers	25
Clinical laboratory technologists and technicians	24
Real estate sales occupations	23
Drafting occupations	22
Sales engineers	20
Office machine repairers	20
Barbers	20
Dental assistants	19
Computer programmers	19
Aircraft engine mechanics	17
Eligibility clerks, social welfare	16
Stenographers	15
Sheriffs, bailiffs, and other law enforcement officers	15
Heating, air-conditioning, and refrigeration mechanics	15
Computer operators	15
Secretaries	14
Management-related occupations not elsewhere classified	14
Optical goods workers	13
Engineering technicians not elsewhere classified	13
Stationary engineers	12
Purchasing agents and buyers	12
Physical therapists	12
Hairdressers and cosmetologists	12
Actors and directors	12

Table 1 (Continued)

Occupation	Percent Who Needed Community College or Technical Institute Training
Teachers, prekindergarten and kindergarten	11
Teachers' aides	11
Payroll and timekeeping clerks	11
Nursing aides, orderlies, and attendants	11
Designers	11
Police and detectives	10
Mechanical engineers	10
Interviewers	10
Electronic repairers, commercial and industrial equipment	10

Source: Carey, Max, and Alan Eck. "How Workers Get Their Training." *Occupational Outlook Quarterly,* Winter 1984. New data were collected in January 1991; the date and form of their publication have not been determined.

sorts of backgrounds enter the hub, make various connections, and then move on.

Many students use the college to connect them with a 4-year college. Most community colleges have agreements with at least a few 4-year schools in their state or region. These agreements detail the courses that a student should take in order to be accepted as a transfer student in a particular major. A student who successfully completes the course of study in the 2-year school is guaranteed admission into the 4-year school. Following such a course of action is much more likely to lead to success than would taking a bunch of courses and then applying to a four-year school. Local community colleges can give you pamphlets or booklets that detail exactly what you will need to do to qualify as a transfer student.

But community colleges are far more than way stations on the road to a 4-year degree. They also offer a wide choice to a student who wishes to pursue occupational education. A student could simply take some adult education courses. More wisely, a person could earn a certificate or an associate's degree in an occupation-related subject. (Certificates can be earned in 1 year or less, while associate's degrees usually require 2 years of full-time study.)

Even for a single occupation, more than one choice may be available. For example, one school offers both a diploma and a certificate program in air-conditioning and refrigeration, and the certificate program can be pursued either full time in 3 semesters or in the evenings for 6 semesters. Similarly the school offers both a certificate

Table 2 Fifteen Occupations with the Largest Number of Workers Who Need Junior College or Technical Institute Training to Qualify for Their Current Job, 1983

Occupation	Number with Junior College or Technical Institute Training (thousands)	Percent of Employment in Occupation
Secretaries	530	14
Registered nurses	372	29
Managers and administrators not elsewhere classified	242	5
Bookkeepers, accounting and auditing clerks	172	9
Licensed practical nurses	148	34
Nursing aides, orderlies, and attendants	136	11
Real estate sales occupations	113	23
Accountants and auditors	91	8
Supervisors and proprietors, sales occupations	89	3
Computer operators	80	15
Computer programmers	75	19
Electrical and electronics technicians	75	25
Hairdressers and cosmetologists	73	12
Clinical laboratory technologists and technicians	65	24
Typists	63	7
Drafting occupations	57	22
Automobile mechanics	55	7
Supervisors, production occupations	49	4
Receptionists	48	8
Electricians	45	8
Administrative support occupations not elsewhere classified	42	8
Radiologic technicians	42	39
Teachers, elementary school	42	3
Teachers' aides	40	11
Dental hygienists	39	38

Source: Carey, Max, and Alan Eck. "How Workers Get Their Training." *Occupational Outlook Quarterly*, Winter 1984. New data were collected in January 1991; the date and form of their publication have not been determined.

program for medical laboratory assistants and a longer program leading to an Associate in Applied Science Degree for medical laboratory technicians. Programs like these may be the same for the first year but then diverge, with the degree program requiring more specialized courses.

Yet another option available in some fields at some schools is cooperative education. Students in these programs alternate time in the classroom with time in the workplace. See "Cooperative Education: Working Towards Your Future," in the fall 1988 issue of the *OOQ* for more information about co-oping.

These 10 programs received the Secretary of Education's Award for Outstanding Vocational-Technical Education Programs from the U.S. Department of Education in 1990. The programs were judged on factors such as the following:

▲ The integration of the vocational curriculum with a quality academic program.

▲ The use of objective standards to measure students' competency and evaluate progress in attaining basic skills and training.

▲ Cooperation with secondary and post secondary schools.

▲ Placement of graduates in jobs.

▲ Replicability.

They show the great variety of programs available in the nation's community colleges.

Region 1
Greater Lowell Regional Vocational Technical School
Tyngsboro, Mass.
Contact: F. Nelson Burns (508)454-5411

The program offers intensive occupation-specific retraining and placement services in computer, business, drafting, and electronics technologies. More than 90 percent of graduates have been placed in jobs with employers such as Wang and Honeywell.

Region 2
Bergen County Technical Schools District
Hackensack, N.J.
Contact: Leonard Margolis (201)343-6000

The program is a cooperative effort among the school district, the Wakenfern Food and Shop-Rite Supermarkets, and Cornell University's Food Industry Training Program. Currently, 51 educationally disadvantaged students receive in-store and classroom training in five basic supermarket employment areas.

Region 3
Prince Georges Community College
Largo, Md.
Contact: Rosemary Swartwood (301)322-0699

Entry-Level Police Officer Training Program initiated to meet the region's need for trained law enforcement officers. Graduates of the 17-week program master 336 skills in areas such as criminal investigation and emergency care. The program is run in cooperation with the Maryland Police and Correctional Training Commission.

Region 4
Valencia Community College
Orlando, Fla.
Contact: Hugh Rogers (407)299-5000

The college offers on-site computer technology training and places specialists in jobs requiring less than a bachelor's degree. Begun in 1987, the program will train more than 1,000 students in the 1990-91 school year. Martin-Marietta Corp. and Stromberg-Carlson are major partners in the program.

Region 5
Thief River Falls Technical College
Thief River Falls, Minn.
Contact: Orley Gunderson (218)681-5424

The college's Aviation Maintenance Technology Program offers basic skills and training for new students as well as upgraded training for certified technicians. Internships are offered with Northwest Airlines.

Region 6
Kiamichi Area Vocational-Technical School
McAlester, Okla.
Contact: Rebecca Nichols (918)426-0940

The school's child care program integrates basic skills training in reading, math, and science with child care skills. Private sector involvement was spurred by the need for child care providers. More than 65 percent of graduates are placed in the field, while 10 percent continue their education.

Region 7
Longview Community College
Lee's Summit, Mo.
Contact: Karen Kistner (815)763-7777

The college's Automotive Technology program has cooperative partnerships with Ford, General Motors, and Toyota. Curriculum is updated regularly to keep pace with industry advances. The program boasts a 95-percent placement rate.

Region 8
Weber State College
Ogden, Utah
Contact: Jane Van Valkenburg (801)626-6120

The college's Radiological Science Cluster Program focuses on four areas: radiography, nuclear medicine, ultrasound, and radiation therapy. Fully accredited by the American Medical Association, the program serves 24 hospitals in Utah and surrounding areas.

Region 9
East San Gabriel Valley Regional Occupational Program
West Covina, Calif.
Contact: Myrna Craig-Evans (818)960-1424

The Apparel and Accessories Program reinforces basic academic skills through hands-on-learning experiences in store layout, merchandising, and marketing. Although the region has a 40-percent high school dropout rate, every student completing the 2-year program in 1988-89 was employed or continued in school.

Region 10
Spokane Community College
Spokane, Wash.
Contact: Wayne Elinger (509)536-7148

One of only 15 fluid power technology programs in the country, it prepares students for work in four major areas: machine maintenance, fabrication and installation, sales, and system design. Fluid power is the combined use of hydraulics, pneumatics, and electronics in machinery and equipment. Job placement is nearly 100 percent. ■

Baxter, Neale. "Careers 101: Occupational Education in Community Colleges." *Occupational Outlook Quarterly* Spring 1991: 13–15, 19–21.

C: Post-Reading

Discussion Suggestions/Questions

Remembering

1. What percentage of all high school graduates complete four-year college degree programs within five years of graduating from high school?

2.   Of the ten programs that received the Secretary of Education's Award in 1990, which has the highest percentage of post-training job placement?

Analyzing

1.   Why is this article entitled "Careers 101"?

2.   Share with others (a) the interesting or surprising facts, (b) advice to individuals considering career training options, and (c) specific types of careers that might be of interest to you or to someone you know that you underlined or highlighted while reading "Careers 101."

3.   Consider the communication situation of the article. Who is the intended audience for "Careers 101" by Neale Baxter? In twenty words or fewer, what is the "point," or message, of the article? What kind of a person does the author, Neale Baxter, who is the managing editor of the *OOQ*, seem to be?

Discovering

1.   Share and discuss with others ideas you had while reading this article.

2.   People choosing careers think about wages, working conditions, job security, benefits, location, and opportunities for advancement. Which of these is the most important to you and why? Share your thoughts with others.

3.   Some people who have very little post secondary education have very successful careers. How do these people get to be so successful?

D: Vocabulary Building

1. Occupational terms ending in *-er, -ist,* and *-ian*

The reading for this chapter includes many names for trades and occupations. These names are created in three main ways. The oldest way of creating a trade or occupational name was to add **-er** (also spelled **-or**) onto the verb that describes the professional activity. For example, a **baker** is someone who bakes; a **sailor** is someone who sails; a **weaver** is someone who weaves; a **painter** is someone who paints. Most of these *-er* occupational names are so old that they pre-date family names. In the Middle Ages in England, many people took the name of their trade as their family or last name, so that Rolf the weaver became Rolf Weaver; William the baker became William Baker, and so on. In fact, the most common family name in English is an occupation name—Smith (as in blacksmith, goldsmith, and silversmith.)

Although we continue to use the old ending *-er* (sometimes spelled *-or*) to describe modern occupations (**buyer, repairer, operator**), we often use two more recent endings for occupational titles: **-ist** and **-ian**. Here are some examples of the *-ist* ending: someone who types is a **typist**; someone who lobbies is a **lobbyist**; someone who provides physical therapy is a **physical therapist**. Here are some examples of the *-ian* ending: someone who works in a clinic is a **clinician**; someone who works with electricity is an **electrician**; someone who works in the field of beauty is a **beautician**.

A disadvantage of having three common ways of making up words for occupations (*-er*, *-ist*, and *-ian*) is the difficulty of predicting which of the three forms will be used. About the only guideline is that older trades or occupations are more likely to use the *-er* ending.

Vocabulary Building Activity 1: Occupational Terms ending in *-er*, *-ist*, and *-ian*

In the left column is a list of activities. For each activity, write in the occupational name of a person who does that activity in the appropriate column. The first question is done as an example.

Activity	-er	-ist	-ian
1. draws cartoons		*cartoonist*	
2. farms			
3. fits pipes			
4. fixes roofs			
5. plays music			
6. provides a technology			
7. provides hygiene			
8. sells flowers			
9. styles hair			
10. provides diets			

2. Noun/verb stress shifts

Produce: "This country has **produced** more than enough college graduates for the jobs available."

Baxter: "Careers 101"

The verb *produce* comes from the Latin verb *producere*, which meant "to produce." The word *producere* has two parts, a prefix *pro-*, which meant "forward," and the verb stem *ducere*, which meant "to lead." This verb stem appears in a number of English words; for example, it is in any word using **duct**, as in **conduct**, **deduct**, and even the word *duct* by itself in the sense of the **duct work** in a building (because ducts "lead" air or water through the building). It also appears in the word **duke** ("leader") and in the term **Il Duce**, the term the Italian Fascist leader Mussolini adopted for himself.

The verb *produce* has two slightly different meanings. The older meaning is to put something in front of the public—to exhibit something. We still keep this meaning when we talk about how someone will produce a play or movie. The person who produces a play or movie is a **producer**. The result—the play or the movie—is a **production**.

The second meaning of the verb *produce* is to manufacture something, as in the sentence "The manufacturer produces 100,000 widgets a day." Related to this meaning of the verb *produce* are the nouns **product** and **produce** (what we buy in the fruit and vegetable section of the grocery store as opposed to the verb to *produce*.) Notice that the noun "the produce" is pronounced differently than the verb "to produce."

Vocabulary Building Activity 2: Noun/Verb Stress Shifts

Often the same word can be used as either a noun or a verb. A number of two syllable words (such as *produce*) have a special feature: although the verb and the noun forms are spelled the same way, they are not pronounced the same way—they have different stress. The verbs are stressed on one syllable; the nouns on the other syllable. The words listed below have different stress. Say each pair of words aloud, and mark which syllable is stressed. (Be sure also to say *to* and *the*, or else you may get confused about whether you are saying a verb or a noun.) When you are finished, state the stress rule. The first question is done as an example.

Verb	Noun
1. to *record*	the *record*
2. to suspect	the suspect
3. to subject	the subject
4. to object	the object
5. to relay	the relay
6. to export	the export
7. to permit	the permit
8. to survey	the survey
9. to protest	the protest
10. to contract	the contract

3. Changing *d* in verbs to *s* in nouns

<u>Provision:</u> "The 2-year college offers unparalleled promise for expanding educational opportunity through the **provision** of comprehensive programs."

Baxter: "Careers 101"

The word *provision* in the quoted sentence means "something that has been given or **provided**." The noun *provision* comes from a Latin word, *provisus*. *Provisus* is actually a form of the verb *providere*, "to *provide*," used as a noun. Certain forms of Latin verbs could be used as nouns in much the same way that the *-ing* forms of English verbs can be used as nouns. For example, from the verb **sing** we can create the noun **singing**, as in the sentence "The *singing* of the choir is an important part of the service." The verb system of Latin was quite complicated. It had many classes of irregular verbs, each of which followed its own pattern. One pattern affected certain verbs that had a *d* sound. When these verbs changed into their noun forms, the *d* sound changed into an *s* sound. Several of the verbs that followed this pattern were quite common, and, consequently, the change of a *d* in verbs to an *s* in nouns is also quite common. Many English words derived from Latin show the same change; for example, compare the *d* in the verb to **provide** with the *s* in the related noun **provision**.

Vocabulary Building Activity 3: Changing *d* in Verbs to *s* in Nouns

The verbs in the left column all contain a *d*. They have noun forms in which the *d* changes to an *s*. In the space provided, write in the noun form for each of the verbs. The first question is done as an example.

Verb	Noun
1. collide	*collision*
2. concede	
3. conclude	
4. decide	
5. divide	
6. evade	
7. include	
8. intercede	
9. invade	
10. recede	

SECTION

2

Drafting for Clarity and Completeness of Information

A: Pre-Writing

Imagine that you have received a letter from a friend or relative. This person is living in a place where there are no telephones, no libraries, no schools, few newspapers, and no televisions. This person has been in this place—Alaskan fishing trawler, South American jungle village, Australian "outback"—for over a year.

In the letter, this person has asked you to research a kind of career training offered by a community college, technical school, or university. You get to choose which kind of career training. It may be something in which you are especially interested, or it may be a career option someone you know is considering. Either way, you need to become a "career detective." You need to track down as much information about this career as possible. You will then write a letter in which you share this information. You will need to include several pieces of information in your letter:

1. School information—the name of the school that offers the program, its address, and the name and title of the person in charge of the program.

2. The requirements of the training program—admissions policies, courses, internships, examinations, and so on.

3. The costs of the program—tuition, books, and fees.

4. The availability of courses in the program—are they offered during the day or during the evening hours? Are they offered year around or only at certain times? Are they offered in sequence—does one have to start in the fall, for example, and then complete the courses in a certain order? How long does it normally take a person to complete the training?

5. Employment opportunities once the training is completed—does the school or program offer a career placement service? Do graduates of the program actually get the jobs they have been trained to do?

You may have other questions about the program you select. See if you can find answers to these questions also.

Resources

The pre-writing for this project will depend on the career option you choose. There are, however, several kinds of resources that will offer valuable information:

1. Libraries are excellent resources. Most have collections of catalogues for both community colleges and four-year schools. Most libraries also subscribe to the *Occupational Outlook Quarterly* and other useful publications.

2. The schools themselves are perhaps your best resource. Campuses have offices of admissions, general advising, career counseling, and cooperative education. All schools have catalogues that describe their programs and courses. These catalogues are free or available for a small fee.

3. There may be people you can contact who work in the career you are researching. Employers could tell you what kinds of training they are looking for in the people they hire. A person who has completed training and is working in the career you are investigating might have all sorts of useful information.

4. You may have other ideas on how to obtain information you need. Try them out.

Pre-Writing Activities

1. Decide which career training option you will investigate.

2. Discuss with others your choice and what you might do to find the information you need.

3. Begin your information search. Remember to take notes on your research activities. It is important to know where each piece of information comes from, so note down the source of each. Notes on information from a person should include the person's name, title, place of employment, and address. Notes from published sources—catalogues, magazines, newspapers, and so on—should include the name of the author (if known), the title of the article, the title of the publication (magazine or newspaper, for example), and the date of publication. You would be wise to photocopy larger clusters of information such as degree requirements. Note on the photocopies where you got this information. Careful note taking will save you time in the long run.

4. Once you have gathered the information, put it in order using the following outline:

a.   Program identification: _____

1. Name and address of school _____

2. Name of program and name, address, and phone number of contact person (program director or supervisor) _____

_____

_____

_____

_____

_____

b.   Program requirements _____

_____

_____

_____

_____

_____

_____

1. Admissions requirements _____

_____

_____

_____

_____

_____

DRAFTING

DRAFTING

2. Required courses and internships _____

_____

_____

_____

_____

_____

_____

_____

3. Program costs—tuition, books, and fees _____

_____

_____

_____

_____

_____

c.   Schedule information—when the courses are offered and in what order

_____

_____

_____

_____

_____

_____

_____

d.   Employment opportunities for people who have completed the training

_____

_____

_____

_____

_____

_____

e.   Other information and ideas you have gathered _____

_____

_____

_____

_____

_____

_____

_____

_____

_____

DRAFTING

B: Writing a First or Initial Draft

Using the information you have located and the preceding outline, write a letter to someone you know, to someone you made up, or to yourself in which you share the results of your research.

SECTION

◄►

3

Revising for Clarity and Completeness of Information

A: Clarity and Completeness of Information in Career Option Letters

The writing assignment in this chapter is both informative and informal. "Informative" means that its primary purpose is to inform, to provide information. "Informal" here means "casual" or "relaxed." You have written a personal letter to a friend or acquaintance, and personal letters are informal. Including personal comments like "Hope to see you soon," and questions like "How's that old cat of yours doing?" is appropriate in a personal letter. In more formal writing, like essays for instance, such personal comments or questions are not normally included.

Since this piece of writing—the letter you have written—is mostly informative, the clarity and completeness of the information you provide are very important. You need to answer all the questions your reader might have.

REVISING

B: Revising Drafts of Student Career Option Letters

One way to check for completeness and clarity of information is to ask someone else to read your letter and do the following two things.

1. Mark places in the letter where he or she doesn't understand the information offered by writing **Clear?** next to them.

2. Mark places where he or she would like more information by writing **More?** next to them.

Following is a student draft a reader has marked in these two ways.

Student Draft: Film Producer

May 26, 1993

Dear Sally,

   To be a film producer, you had better go to the university and have a degree. I think it is the best way to know the process of film making. In my opinion, California State is a good place to study film making because Hollywood is in California, so you can feel the sense of how to make movies there. Here is a great university I would recommend for you: University of Southern California, which is located five miles from downtown Los Angeles and was founded in 1880. This university has good majors which you might take--Motion Picture Technology, Radio and Television, Radio and Television Technology. These are kind of similar, but I would suggest you take Motion Picture Technology as your major because you should know everything about film making. You will learn how to use the camera, how to write the script, how to direct, and lighting techniques. It is necessary for you to know these kinds of things if you want to be a film producer.

   The University of Southern California is well-known as having a good Motion Picture Technology degree because George Lucas graduated from there. He gave money to the school to help to teach directors who will be like him. Actually, there are a lot of wonderful students who might be following George. Therefore, you would be very smart to involve yourself in this program. There is great teamwork needed to make a film, so you must not be shy, you have to have strong opinions, and you must keep good relationships with the people you are working with.   ***Clear?***

   The tuition at the University of Southern California is about $13,446 per year. Room and board are $5282. Books and supplies are $532, and other costs will be about $1314. Therefore, the total will be about $20,574 each year. I know it costs a lot, but 80% of undergraduate students have scholarships from the school. In   ***More?*** addition, this school is located near a large city, so it will cost you more than if you go to a school which is in a small town.

> I do not know how much money you will make since we do
> not know how many people will watch your movies or if you
> will have a good sponsor or not. However, you   ***More?***
> will make tons of money if you succeed.
>
> The University of Southern California has some dorms
> --men's, women's, and coed--so you can make a lot of
> friends there. This university has many activities that
> you can participate in--film, magazine, radio, drama,
> musical theater, and opera. I think you should get in-
> volved in one of these because you might find someone who
> has the same goal as you. In addition, your English skills
> will be going up.
>
> The admissions closing date is May 1, so do not be late
> to apply. The address is Dr. Robert Biller, Dean of
> Administration and Financial Aid, University of Southern
> California, 666 Childs Way, Los Angeles, CA 90089-0911.
>
> Study hard and good luck. I hope your movies will be
> shown everywhere and people will like them. My favorite
> movies are love stories, like Pretty Woman. I know that
> a movie is never true and will not happen to us, but the
> movies give us dreams. In addition, my favorite actor is
> Arnold Schwartzenegger, so I hope you are going to work
> with him. I think it is very funny to see him in a love
> story movie.
>
> Sincerely,
>
>   Ayako S.

Practice Marking a Letter for Clarity and Completeness of Information

Below is another student draft. Read this draft, alone or with others, and practice writing ***Clear?*** in places that are confusing and ***More?*** in places where you would like to see more information.

Student Draft: Translators and Interpreters

November 12, 1993

Dear Shoko,

   Being a translator is a very exciting job for a person who can speak many languages. I am also interested in it and thinking about what I am going to be in the future. My interest too is in being a translator, so I was very glad to receive your letter. I want to help you as much as I can, so I wrote all the information I could get. I hope that it helps you.

   There are two kinds of translators. These are called "interpreter" and "translator." An interpreter orally translates what has been said into another language while people are talking. The interpreter translates orally either while a speaker is talking or after a speaker has finished. Interpreters may do escort work, conference work or court interpreting. On the other hand, a translator transfers meaning in written form from one language to another. The translator becomes familiar with subject matter and produces written translations of literary or technical materials by capturing their style and sense. A translator also provides written summaries of meetings, books, articles, etc. Translators scan materials for future translation.

   Usually a bachelor's degree is required. Training on the graduate level is becoming more common for interpreters and translators. A good background in foreign languages and cultures or relevant experience may be substituted for formal training. I am going to give you some examples of types of college courses:

   Foreign-language Translators and Interpreters: two or three common languages or one rare language; current use rather than literature, linguistics.

   Interpreters: history, English, philosophy, economics, political science, public speaking.

   Translators: English composition, math and sciences, business administration, literature.

No formal occupational training is required in most cases. The UN trains BA's for three to nine months before they take the qualifying exam for being an interpreter. Time spent abroad and jobs in business and government are good occupational training.

Linguistic ability and good memory are needed. Interpreters need the ability to work under pressure and deal with a variety of people, quick reflexes and good voice and hearing. Translators need self-discipline, general and technical knowledge, good writing style, and accuracy. These are personal qualifications.

The following skills are required: public speaking, writing, gathering information, conducting research, analyzing, interpreting, evaluating, quick thinking, memorizing, and the command of two or more languages. Foreign travel and broad cultural background are helpful. For UN work, you should know three of the five UN languages (French required).

A beginning language specialist in the federal government earns less than $26,000 a year. Staff jobs are not usually open to beginners, who can develop experience as freelancers. Outside government, less experienced interpreters earn $100 a day or more. The average government pay for a language specialist is $34,000 a year. At the United Nations, experienced interpreters/translators start at about $31,000–$35,000 a year. Average earnings at the State Department are $42,000 a year. Freelance escort interpreters earn $100 to $135 a day. Freelance translators earn $80 to $92 per 1,000 words. Top earnings in the federal government and the UN are usually about $45,000 a year. A few earn considerably more. In-house translators and interpreters working for large corporations can earn $50,000 to $65,000 a year. Interpreters working with difficult/exotic languages, perhaps with technical terminology, can earn up to $600 a day. Similarly, translators can earn up to $160 per 1,000 words. However, earnings depend on difficulty of language(s) learned, type of material (general, specialized, highly technical), skill, and amount of time worked.

REVISING

Employment outlook is poor because there are more applicants than jobs open; very few full-time positions are available. The UN employs about 100 interpreters and 250-300 translators; the State Department has a staff of twenty interpreters and uses a roster of about 1,900 freelance escorts for short-term assignments. Prospects for French and Spanish jobs are especially limited. Nevertheless, as business becomes increasingly international in orientation, the demand for linguists should grow; there is already strong demand for those with good Japanese and Russian skills (about 3,900 employed).

You will be employed at these places: UN and other world organizations, U.S. Government and Courts, publishers, private business and large cities. Interpreters may advance from escort to conference work. Translators may become proficient in a specialized area or may supervise others. In general, advancement is very limited.

If you want to find out more information, you can write a letter or visit the following places:

▲ American Translators' Association
109 Croton Ave.
Ossining, NY 10562

▲ The American Society of Interpreters
P.O. Box 9603
Washington, D.C. 20016

▲ The American Society of Language Specialists
Suite 9, 1000 Connecticut Avenue, N.W.
Washington, D. C. 20036

I hope this information helps you, and good luck!

Sincerely,

Kazuyo K.

C: Revising Your Letter About a Career Training Option

Working with others or alone, read or have someone else read your letter and mark unclear places with the word "Clear?" and places where more information might be added with the word "More?". If possible, have two people other than yourself read and mark your draft.

Now look at the marked places, and clarify or add information where you think you should. You may need to do more research—find more information—at this point. You want the information you provide to be as clear and complete as possible.

D: Optional Revision

The letter you have written might be made even better by your also using the revision strategy—Revising for Details of Place—presented in Chapter 2.

SECTION

4

Final Editing for Subject-Verb Agreement

When the subject of a sentence is a **third person singular pronoun** (*he*, *she*, or *it*) or a singular noun (which amounts to the same thing as a third person singular pronoun because a third person singular pronoun can always replace a singular noun), a special form of the verb called the **third person singular form** is required to agree with the third person singular subject.

In the present tense, the third person singular form of the verb is spelled with an -*s* (or -*es* if the verb ends in an *s* or *s*-like sound, as in *rush/rushes*, *kiss/kisses*, *buzz/buzzes*, and the like). The helping verbs *can*, *may*, *must*, *shall*, and *will* are the only exceptions. These five verbs do not change form to agree with third person singular subjects; that is, for historical reasons there is no distinctive third person singular -*s* form of these verbs:

EDITING

*cans, *mays, *musts, *shalls, and *wills. Here is an example of a sentence with the verb *love* in its third person singular present tense form:

1.   He/she/it/Sam **loves** corn-dogs and sauerkraut.

In the past tense, only the irregular verb *be* has a special form that agrees with a third person singular subject: *was* (rather than the form *were*, which is used with all other subjects except "I"). Here is an example of a sentence with the verb *be* in its third person singular past tense form:

2.   He/she/it/Sam **was** eating corn-dogs and sauerkraut.

A **subject-verb agreement error** is a mismatch between the subject noun (or pronoun) and the verb. The third person singular form of the verb is incorrectly used with a plural subject, as in the following example:

3.   * The <u>children</u> <u>loves</u> corn-dogs and sauerkraut.
          Plural   3rd
                    person
                    singular

A non-third person singular form of the verb (a form without the *-s*) is also incorrectly used with a third person singular subject, as shown here:

4.   * The   <u>girl</u>   <u>love</u>   corn-dogs and sauerkraut.
          Singular   Non-3rd
                      person
                      singular

Since subject-verb agreement errors can happen only with present tense verbs (with the exception of the five helping verbs previously discussed) and the past tense forms of the verb *be* (*was* and *were*), these verb forms are the only forms that you need to check for subject-verb agreement. Let's call these verb forms that have the potential for subject-verb agreement error **high-risk** verb forms.

One of the most striking features of subject-verb agreement errors is the fact that most of the errors in high-risk verb forms occur in only three situations. Your ability to do final editing for subject-verb agreement errors will be greatly improved if you are aware of the following situations and take special care to check high-risk verbs in these situations:

▲ "Lost subject" error: sentences in which the writer either loses track of what the subject actually is or forgets whether the subject is singular or plural

▲ "All of the above" error: sentences in which a singular verb refers to a plural subject as an "all of the above" collective singular

▲ *There is/there was* error: sentences in which the verb *is* or *was* incorrectly follows *there*, meaning "there exists"

We will deal with each of these types of error in turn.

A: "Lost Subject" Error

Research has shown that "lost subject" type agreement errors are most likely to occur when long and/or complicated phrases separate the subject and verb. In these cases the writer can lose track of the subject and make one of two different kinds of subject-verb agreement errors.

One kind of error results when the writer mistakenly makes the verb agree with a nearby noun rather than with the more distant actual subject. This kind of error is most likely to occur where the **subject noun phrase** (the subject noun together with all of its modifiers) is lengthy, forcing the writer to hold many words in mind before he or she comes to the verb. In this situation there is a strong tendency to remember the most vivid or specific noun as being what the sentence is about rather than the word that is the actual grammatical subject. Here is an example of such an error from a student essay:

5.   *A well-rounded education with different **classes** in everything from art to zoology **help** the student decide what major field he or she would like to enroll in.

Although it is impossible to tell for sure what is going on in someone else's mind, the odds are pretty good that by the time the writer of sentence (5) got to the verb *help*, the writer was thinking about the more specific noun *classes* rather than the vague noun *education*. The writer then made the verb *give* agree with the nearer and stronger noun *classes* rather than the actual subject *education*.

A second kind of error results when the writer correctly remembers which noun the subject is but forgets whether the number of the subject noun is singular or plural. This type of "lost subject" error occurs in sentences with long subject noun phrases and with subject nouns that the writer can make either singular or plural without affecting the meaning of the sentence. By the time the writer reaches the verb, he or she has forgotten which form of the noun he or she actually picked, and then the writer inadvertently makes the verb agree with the unpicked alternative. Here is an example of this kind of error from a student essay:

6.   *My **chances** of getting a job over somebody who does not have a college education **is** better.

In sentence (6), the writer had a choice of writing either *my chances* or *my chance*. There is really no difference in meaning between the two alternatives. By the time the writer reached the verb, however, the writer had forgotten that he or she had actually written the plural form *chances* rather than the singular form *chance*. The writer of sentence (6) probably thought that he or she had written this grammatically correct sentence:

6a.   My **chance** of getting a job over somebody who does not have a college education **is** better.

The best way to check your writing for both types of "lost subject" subject-verb agreement errors is to strip away all of the words that come between the subject noun and the high-risk verb. When you put the subject noun and the verb side by side, you can easily detect any subject-verb agreement errors. Finding the actual subject is surprisingly simple: **the subject is always the first noun (or pronoun) in the subject noun phrase— the noun in the subject noun phrase that is furthest away from the verb**. To check for "lost subject" error, always follow this procedure:

a. Identify every high-risk verb form.

b. For each high-risk verb form, find the first noun (or pronoun) in the subject noun phrase. Underline (with a pencil or just in your mind) every word between the high-risk verb and the first noun.

c. Delete (with a pencil or in your mind) all of the words you have underlined.

d. The subject is now side by side with the high-risk verb, ready for you to check for subject-verb agreement.

Just to give this procedure a name that is easy to remember, we will call it the **strip search test** for "lost subject" agreement error. Here is the strip search test applied to sentences (5) and (6). In both sentences, steps (a) and (b) have already been carried out: the high-risk verb and the first noun in the subject noun phrase are identified in bold, and the words between them have been underlined.

5.   * A well-rounded **education** with different classes in everything from art to zoology **help** the student decide what major field he or she would like to enroll in.

We are now ready to carry out step (c) in the strip search test—deleting the underlined words:

5a.   * A well-rounded **education help** the student decide what major field he or she would like to enroll in.

When *education* and *help* are side by side, we can easily see that there is a subject-verb agreement error. In sentence (5), as in most cases, we would correct the error by changing the verb to agree with the subject:

5b.   A well-rounded **education helps** the student decide what major field he or she would like to enroll in.

Here is the second example of a "lost subject" error:

6.   * My **chances** of getting a job over somebody who does not have the college education **is** better.

Step (c)—delete the underlined words:

6b.   * My **chances is** better.

We can now easily correct the error by making *is* agree with *chances*:

6c.   My **chances are** better.

Editing Activity 1: Using the Strip Search Test to Identify "Lost Subject" Error

Use the following procedure to identify and then correct the subject-verb agreement error in the following sentences:

▲ Circle the high-risk verb and the subject noun or pronoun.

▲ On line (a) copy the sentence, deleting all the words between the subject word and the high-risk verb.

▲ On line (b) correct any subject-verb error.

The first question is done as an example.

1. The **number** of accidents caused by drunk drivers **increase** at night.

   (a) *The **number increase** at night.*

   (b) *The number **increases** at night.*

2. Another reason to justify this work are the opportunities to meet others.

   (a) _____

   (b) _____

3. The best way to check for errors are to hope and pray.

   (a) _____

   (b) _____

4. These types of error in subject-verb agreement is common in writing.

   (a) _____

   (b) _____

5. The opportunities that will mean the most often comes unannounced.

   (a) _____

   (b) _____

6. The plans on file in the clerk's office is the only record.

   (a) _____

   (b) _____

7. The drive to achieve your goals in life are critical to success.

   (a) _____

   (b) _____

8. The life experience learned in college justify any expense.

   (a) _____

   (b) _____

9. The advantage of a college education are obvious.

   (a) _____

   (b) _____

10. The needs within myself has led me to pursue a higher education.

    (a) _____

    (b) _____

Editing Activity 2: Using the Strip Search Test to Check High-Risk Verbs for "Lost Subject" Agreement Errors

The following is part of a personal letter describing a training program at a local community college. All high-risk verbs are shown in bold. For each high-risk verb, go through all the steps of the strip search test for "lost subject" agreement errors. Circle the subject, and lightly cross out all of the words between the subject word and the high-risk verb. When you find a subject-verb agreement error, correct the error in the way that you think fits this letter best.

Dear Jay,

How**'s** it going? The heavy diesel equipment courses that you asked me about **is** offered at Spokane Community College. Six quarters of work at SCC **is** the equivalent to two years of college. The credits that you **receive** at SCC for equipment repair **transfers** to Oregon Institute of Technology, where you can finish your BA in diesel equipment repair. Students who **go** through the SCC program **has** a good chance at a job if that **is** what they want. Most of the students coming out of this program **was** successful in finding the job they wanted.

Before I **get** into the classes, I should mention all the electives in this program that **is** required: first aid, technical writing, mathematics, leadership development, effective listening. I won't talk about these elective courses because they **do**n't make any difference for the program that you **are** interested in. I will go through each class and explain what the course requirements **are** and give you a perspective of the course through the instructor's eyes.

<u>Basic Electrical Theory</u> This class **deals** with the basic theory of low voltage DC electricity and its application to electrical equipment and air conditioning. The main topics that we **cover** in this class **is** the following: ignition systems, vehicle wiring, starting systems, charging systems, and auxiliary electrical/electronics components. This course, like most of the classes, **consist** of two parts--a lecture part and a hands-on lab part.

<u>Basic Principles of Engine Theory</u> This class **is** an introduction to the repair of heavy equipment. Students who **take** this class **is** expected to become familiar with engine systems and their component parts. The study of gasoline engines and two- and four-stroke diesel engines **are** the main focus of the course. One of the most important features in the class **are** diagnostic systems for carburetors, fuel injectors, and diesel fuel systems.

Ron W.

B: "All of the Above" Error

A surprisingly large percentage of subject-verb agreement errors occurs when a writer uses a third person singular verb to refer to a plural subject as though the plural subject were a collective singular unit. This kind of error is unlike a "lost subject" error. In a "lost subject" error, the writer uses the wrong verb form because the writer has mistakenly made the verb agree with a noun that is not actually the subject or the writer has forgotten whether the subject is singular or plural. In an "all of the above" type error, the writer knows exactly what the subject is. The problem is that the writer has chosen to treat what is technically a plural subject as though it were a singular subject and uses a singular form of the verb to refer to "all of the above" as the collective subject. The most common type of "all of the above" error occurs when there is a **compound subject.** (A compound subject is a subject noun phrase with two subject nouns (or pronouns) joined by *and*.) Let's begin with two examples of sentences in which it is marginally acceptable to treat a compound subject as a collective "all of the above" singular subject:

8.   **Ham and eggs is** my favorite breakfast.

9.   **The salt and pepper is** already on the table.

In these two sentences, the singular verb *is* is acceptable only because we could think of *ham and eggs* and *salt and pepper* as things that go together to make single, collective units. However, the singular verbs in sentences (8) and (9) are quite exceptional. The normal rule is that **compound subjects require a plural verb**, as shown here:

10.   My **mother** and **father have** been married 30 years.

The verb *have* is plural in agreement with the compound subject *mother* and *father*. Even though *mother* and *father* make up a single unit, a married couple, they are treated as two different grammatical entities. They are two separate subjects that require a plural verb. The use of a singular verb with them would be ungrammatical:

10a.   * My mother and father **has** been married 30 years.

Here is an example from a student essay that illustrates the problem of "all of the above" verb agreement:

11.   * **Intelligence** and **knowledge is** a very worthwhile tool that can be used on every occasion.

In sentence (11), the writer uses the singular verb *is* to bundle together the compound subject *intelligence and knowledge* as an "all of the above" singular unit. While we can debate whether *intelligence* and *knowledge* make up a single logical unit, we cannot debate the grammatical correctness of the use of the singular verb *is*: it is unacceptable. The sentence must be corrected by making the verb agree with the compound (plural) subject:

11a.   **Intelligence** and **knowledge are** a very worthwhile tool that can be used on every occasion.

We might also consider changing the singular noun *tool* to be consistent with the plural subject:

11b.   **Intelligence** and **knowledge are** very worthwhile **tools** that can be used on every occasion.

Here are some more examples of "all of the above" subject-verb agreement errors taken from student essays:

12.   * All the hard **work, pain**, and **suffering is** evidence enough that the student has learned valuable skills.

13.   * **Breaking the bonds with parents** and **controlling one's own life makes** one realize what being out on one's own really means.

14.   * **Being able to have a slight edge in the work force, having the security of a possible career,** and **just being knowledgeable in many areas is** worth all the time, expense, and investment of energy.

As part of your regular procedure of final editing, you need to check every high-risk verb for both "lost subject" and "all of the above" errors. Fortunately, "all of the above" subject-verb agreement errors are relatively easy to spot: you need to be on the lookout for the coordinating conjunction *and* in the subject noun phrase. When you find an *and*, check to see if it is joining two or more nouns (or pronouns) together to form a compound subject. If there is a compound subject, then you must use a plural verb.

Here is good way to simplify a sentence with a compound subject to see what the high-risk verb should be: replace the entire compound subject noun phrase with the plural pronoun *they*. Any subject-verb error will then be easy to see and correct. Here are the three example "all of the above" sentences. Underneath each example is a version of the same sentence in which the pronoun *they* has replaced the entire subject noun phrase. The "all of the above" error is corrected in the third sentence of each set:

12.   * All the hard **work, pain**, and **suffering is** evidence enough that the student has learned valuable skills.

12a.   * _____ **They** _____ is evidence enough that the student has learned valuable skills.

12b.   **They are** evidence enough that the student has learned valuable skills.

13.   * **Breaking the bonds with parents** and **controlling one's own life makes** one realize what being out on one's own really means.

13a. *   <u>They</u>   **makes** one realize what being out on one's own really means.

13b. **They make** one realize what being out on one's own really means.

14. *<u>Being able to have a slight edge in the work force, having the security of a possible career,</u> and <u>just being knowledgeable in many areas</u> is worth all the time, expense, and investment of energy.

14a. *   <u>They</u>   is worth all the time, expense, and investment of energy.

14b. **They are** worth all the time, expense, and investment of energy.

Editing Activity 3: Checking High-Risk Verbs for "All of the Above" Subject-Verb Agreement Errors

Underline the entire subject noun phrase, and circle the high-risk verb. On line (a) rewrite the sentence, replacing the underlined subject noun phrase with the plural pronoun *they*. On line (b) correct the "all of the above" subject-verb agreement errors. The first question is done as an example.

1. The expense and time commitment required by college **is** worthwhile.

   (a) *They is worthwhile.*

   (b) *They are worthwhile.*

2. Your time and money is at stake.

   (a) _____

   (b) _____

3. A comma error and a run-on is too many mistakes in one sentence.

   (a) _____

   (b) _____

4. A hamburger and a soft drink costs about $3.00.

   (a) _____

   (b) _____

5. A layer of cotton and a layer of wool keeps you warm.

   (a) _____

   (b) _____

6. A good defense and an aggressive offense makes you nearly unbeatable.

   (a) _____

   (b) _____

7. Increasing tuition fees and higher housing costs makes college expensive.

   (a) _____

   (b) _____

8. Living on campus and making new friends is an important part of college.

   (a) _____

   (b) _____

9. Finding a place to live and getting moved in was my highest priority.

   (a) _____

   (b) _____

10. Two and two is four.

   (a) _____

   (b) _____

When there are two or more subject words (nouns or pronouns) in the subject noun phrase joined by *or*, the rules for subject-verb agreement are completely different. **The verb agrees only with the nearest subject word**. Compare the following sentences:

15.   Mary or her **sisters are** returning the car.

16.   Mary's sisters or **Mary is** returning the car.

In sentence (15), the verb is plural because it agrees with the nearest noun *sisters*, while in sentence (16) the verb is singular because it agrees with the nearest noun *Mary*.

Editing Activity 4: Editing for "All of the Above" Errors and Correct Agreement with Or

The following is part of a letter describing a training program at a local community college. All high-risk verbs have been set in bold. Check for "all of the above" errors by seeing if the subject noun phrase contains compound subject words. If there is a compound subject, use the *they* paraphrase to help find the right form of the verb. If two or more subject words are joined by *or*, remember that the verb agrees only with the nearest subject word. Correct subject-verb agreement errors in the way that you think fits this letter best. There are also a few "lost subject" errors in the letter.

Dear Ron,

   Spokane Community College and the Diesel/Heavy Equipment Maintenance Program **offers** a two year AA degree. The tuition and lab fees for this program **totals** $325 per term for in-state residents. In order to be admitted to the program, applicants must be high school graduates or have GEDs. The applicants' high school record and performance on an assessment test **allows** the school to place applicants in the right academic program. Math classes or an English lab **are** required if an applicant's test scores or record in high school **are** not high enough. In addition to the technical courses in equipment maintenance, the requirements for an AA degree at SCC **includes** a sequence of courses in humanities. Communication skills in written and spoken English **is** especially important for technical communication.

   The classes in the Diesel/Heavy Equipment Maintenance Program at SCC **has** both a lecture component and a lab component. The lecture component and the lab component of a course **fits** together so that students **get** both the theory and the practice. In the theory portion of classes, students **acquire** the basic knowledge that the labs then **build** on. Diesel/heavy equipment mechanics **are** no longer men or the occasional woman who just **follow** the same maintenance check list day after day. More high-tech mechanical equipment and more complicated electronic gear **means** that mechanics **have** to become technicians. Reading technical drawings and getting information from technical manuals **is** something that every technician must be able to do in the future. A good foundation in electrical/mechanical systems and the ability to learn **is** what will get us jobs in the future.

                                                        Mark L.

C. *There Is/There Was* Error

Notice the special use of "there" in the following sentences:

17. Waiter, **there is** a fly in my soup.

18. **There are** some presents under the tree.

19. **There was** a knock at the door.

20. **There were** ninety-nine bottles of beer on the wall.

The basic meaning of *there* in these sentences is "existence." That is, all of these sentences point out the existence of the noun following the verb. For example, in sentence (17) the speaker is pointing out to the waiter the existence of a fly in the speaker's soup. In sentence (18) the speaker is pointing out the existence of the presents under the tree, and so on. An important point about these **"there exists"** sentences (as we will call them) is the fact that the subject **follows** right after the verb and that the verb must agree with this following subject.

The problem for writers is that in informal speech, we often treat the *there* in "there exists" sentences as though *there* were a singular pronoun like the pronoun *it* in sentences beginning with "*it is* . . ." or "*it was* . . ." In other words, in informal speech we tend to use only a third person singular verb in "there exists" sentences no matter what the grammatical subject actually is. For example, notice how normal the following sentence sounds when we read it aloud:

21.   * There **is** some soft drinks on the table.

The grammatical subject of verb in sentence (21) is the plural noun *some soft drinks*. The grammatically correct form of this sentence requires a plural verb to agree with the actual plural subject:

21a. There **are** some **soft drinks** on the table.

Not surprisingly, beginning writers carry over into their writing the habits they have developed in their informal speech: they tend to use *there is* and *there was* as fixed phrases no matter what the actual subjects of their sentences really are. Note that this error goes only one direction: we tend to substitute the singular forms *is* and *was* for the plural forms *are* and *were*, but rarely do we commit the reverse error of using plural forms for singular ones. Therefore, we do not need to worry much about checking to see if our use of *there are* or *there were* is correct, but we do need to check very carefully for subject-verb agreement every time we use *there is* or *there was*.

EDITING

Editing Activity 5: Checking *There Is* and *There Was* "There Exists" Sentences for Subject-Verb Agreement

All of the following are "there exists" sentences. Circle the actual grammatical subject in each "there exists" sentence. If the subject in the "there exists" sentence is plural, change the verb to make it agree with the subject. If the sentence is already correct, write *okay*. The first question is done as an example.

1. There is some special tools needed for working on this equipment.
   *There **are** some special **tools** needed for working on this equipment.*

2. There was a million things for us to learn.

3. There was a few problems with the initial design of the building.

4. There is things to do beyond college.

5. Even if the job market for graduates is poor, there is many good reasons for going to college.

6. There is a good reason for being concerned about getting a job.

7. There is things that make the expense and trouble of college worthwhile.

8. There is many ways of stretching tuna fish.

9. There is always the advantage of lower tuition fees and fewer expenses.

10. It's always possible that there is some jobs out there waiting just for you.

11. I feel that even if I don't receive a job when I leave, there was lots of things that were worth coming here for.

Review

In this unit the verb forms that have a distinctive third person singular form are called **high-risk** forms. High-risk forms are all the present tense verb forms (except for five helping verbs that have no third person singular -s form) and the past tense of *be* (*was* and *were*). In this unit we have examined three situations in which subject-verb agreement errors are most likely to occur.

1. **"Lost subject" errors**. When the subject noun phrase is long or complicated, the verb may agree with the nearest noun rather than with the more distant grammatical subject. The only way to check for this "lost subject" error is to simplify the subject noun phrase so that the subject noun is side by side with the verb. A good technique for doing this is to use the **strip search test**:

    a. Identify every high-risk verb form.

    b. For each high-risk verb form, find the first noun (or pronoun) in the subject noun phrase. Underline every word between the high-risk verb and the first noun.

    c. Delete all of the underlined words.

    d. The subject is now side by side with the high-risk verb, ready for you to check for subject-verb agreement.

2. **"All of the above" errors**. An "all of the above" agreement error occurs when a writer has used a third person singular verb form to agree with a plural compound subject in order to treat the compound subject as though it were a single, collective unit. "All of the above" errors are different from "lost subject" errors in that the writer knows exactly what the correct grammatical subject is. The problem is that the writer is using a nonstandard technique (a third person singular verb with a plural subject) to get across the idea that a plural subject is a single entity. A good way to figure out the correct form of the verb when the subject noun phrase contains a compound subject is to substitute the plural pronoun *they* for the compound subject.

    When the subject noun phrase joins two or more nouns with *or*, the verb agrees only with the nearest subject word.

3. ***There is/there was* errors**. In informal speech, we have a tendency to use only the singular forms *is* and *was* in sentences beginning with *there*, meaning "there exists," no matter what the grammatical subject actually is. The subject in a "there exists" sentence follows the *is* or *was*. Accordingly, we need to check the noun following each use of *there is/there was* to see whether the subject is singular or plural. If the following subject is plural, then we need to change the verb to *are* or *were* to make it agree with the actual subject.

Editing Activity 6: Final Editing for Subject-Verb Agreement Errors

The following essay contains a number of subject-verb agreement errors of the types discussed in this unit: "lost subject" errors, "all of the above" errors, and *there is/there was* errors. Circle the high-risk verbs in the following essay, and then circle the subjects of the high-risk verbs. Wherever there is a subject-verb agreement error, correct the error in the way that you think works best for this essay. The number of subject-verb errors in each paragraph is given in parentheses at the end of the paragraph.

Clara B.
English Writing, Sec 6
March 27, 1993

NURSING AS A CAREER

Nursing is one of the most demanding, yet rewarding fields that one can pick. There is many fields and specialty areas to choose from. For example, surgical nurses work in operating rooms. All the specialized instruments and equipment for operating on and caring for patients is their responsibility. Nurses working in a pediatric ward helps with the delivery of babies and cares for the newborn children. Most nurses, however, are general duty nurses who take routine care of sick and injured patients. Giving shots, supervising medication, making sure that patients are getting proper nourishment, and keeping a general eye on patient progress is their main responsibility. More and more, the duties of a nurse in a modern hospital supplements what a doctor alone used to do just a few years ago. All this additional work and responsibility means that there is both more pressure on and more reward for nurses today. (8)

There is three main types of programs for training nurses: associate degree programs, diploma programs, and baccalaureate programs. The time needed for students to complete their programs vary from two to five years depending on the type of program. Associate degree programs in a community college typically takes two years. Diploma programs is usually offered by a school or other education institution that are part of a hospital. These programs usually requires two or three years of study. A baccalaureate program, offered by four year colleges and universities, lead to a college degree and usually take four or five years to complete. These kinds of programs requires general university courses in sciences and humanities as well as specialized courses in nursing. While there is many nurse training programs with lots of differences in the amount of academic work required, every one of these programs have a strong component of hands-on practical training at hospitals, clinics, or health agencies that is associated with the academic program. (12)

EDITING

CULTURAL DIFFERENCES

SECTION

◄►

1

Reading About Cultural Differences

A: Pre-Reading

A special feature of our culture is the generally held belief that people have the right to have and share their own opinions. This is called "freedom of speech." We believe that each person has the right to think and that each person has the right to say or write what he or she thinks. Of course, as with any right, this one also implies some responsibilities. Our right to our own opinions and to expressing them is limited. One cannot, for example, tell or write lies about someone else. Telling lies about someone else is called *slander*. Writing lies about someone is called *libel*. Slander and libel are crimes. It is also illegal to advocate the violent overthrow of the government or to tell people to go home, get their shotguns, and shoot any law enforcement officer or politician they see. Freedom of speech ends where criminal acts begin.

A third limitation on our freedom involves discrimination. It is illegal to judge people as members of a group. For example, one should not say that all members of a racial, religious, gender, or age group are lazy or stupid. The best reason not to make such judgments is the fact that they are not true. Every person is different. Every person is valuable. Every person has strengths and weaknesses.

Discrimination is also illegal because it creates or reinforces prejudice. *Prejudice* means to "judge beforehand," to pre-judge. Prejudice is a kind of nonthinking. Prejudices keep people from seeing other people as valuable, keep them from seeing each person as a separate, unique, and important member of the human race.

Prejudice is looking at the differences among people and thinking those differences are bad. Usually differences are just differences. Quite often, different ways of thinking or living can become resources for better thinking and living.

The best antidote or cure for prejudice is understanding. Each person needs to understand and accept people who are different. The theme of this chapter is understanding and accepting differences. Two readings are presented. One is a speech by a Native American, Four Guns, which he gave in 1891. The second is an essay written by a Native American student, Debbie Louie, in 1991.

Too often when people think of differences, they think of discrimination and prejudice; they think of differences as negative. The truth is that many differences are positive.

Our country is great because we have been willing to accept differences. All kinds of people have contributed to our greatness. Young and old have contributed. Men, women, and children have contributed. People from every race and from all other cultures have added good ideas and attitudes to our culture.

Pre-Reading Activities

Discussion

1. Too often when we talk or write or read about cultural differences, we think about problems associated with these differences. Working with others or alone, brainstorm some cultural differences that are positive. For example, some Latin American peoples take a nap, a "siesta," at about two o'clock every afternoon. Some non–Latin Americans think this is a great idea. Other cultures have different ideas about older people and children. Each culture has its own ideas about what "good food" is. While brainstorming, try to think of customs we don't have that would be good to have.

2. Just as cultures have differences, so do families. Think about customs or rituals your family or families you knew practiced when you were growing up. For example, some families have rituals concerning dinner. In some families, family members have had to be seated at the dinner table, with clean hands and faces, at six o'clock every evening. This custom of sitting, eating, and talking every evening helps them to feel like a family, helps them to communicate. Every family is different. Share some good differences with one another.

Reading Suggestions

(Keep these suggestions in mind as you read Four Guns' speech and Debbie Louie's essay, "Time Peace.")

1. The term *dominant culture* is sometimes used to refer to people in our country who have money, education, and good jobs. The dominant culture is the group of people who seem to make the rules and the important decisions. What attitudes do Four Guns and Debbie Louie express toward the dominant culture? Underline or highlight some of these attitudes.

2. Four Guns gave his speech in 1891. Debbie Louie wrote her essay in 1991. Four Guns was a member of the Oglala Sioux tribe. Debbie Louie is a member of the Colville tribe. Do these two Native Americans share any attitudes or ideas? How do their ideas differ?

3. What are some differences between adaptation and assimilation?

4. Often what a reader thinks about while reading is more important than the ideas that person reads. Note some of <u>your</u> ideas while reading the speech and the essay in this chapter.

Vocabulary Preview

adaptation: change made in response to a different situation. (I made many <u>adaptations</u> in my lifestyle when I moved from Arizona to Miami, Florida.)

analogy: a comparison that stresses similarities. (Life is like football—every time you are knocked down you have to get up and keep playing.)

assimilation: the process of becoming the same as something else. (Parents who migrate to the United States sometimes fear that their children will lose the old customs and values through <u>assimilation</u>.)

concurrently: at the same time as something else. (The two weddings were scheduled <u>concurrently</u>, so I had to choose which one to attend.)

disrupt: confuse, interfere with. (The accident <u>disrupted</u> the flow of traffic on the interstate.)

equilibrium: balance. (The medication affected my <u>equilibrium</u>.)

B.1: Reading

Four Guns' Speech *

FOUR GUNS

I have visited the Great Father in Washington. I have attended dinners among white people. Their ways are not our ways. We eat in silence, quietly smoke a pipe and depart. Thus is our host honored. This is not the way of the white man. After his food has been eaten, one is expected to say foolish things. Then the host feels honored. Many of the white man's ways are past our understanding, but now that we have eaten at the white man's table, it is fitting that we honor our host according to the ways of his people.

Our host has filled many notebooks with the sayings of our fathers as they came down to us. This is the way of his people; they put great store upon writing; always there is a paper. But we have learned that though there are many papers in Washington upon which are written promises to pay us for our lands, no white man seems to remember them. However, we know our host will not forget what he has written down, and we hope that the white people will read it.

But we are puzzled as to what useful service all this writing serves. Whenever white people come together there is writing. When we go to buy some sugar or tea, we see the white trader busy writing in a book; even the white doctor as he sits beside his patient writes on a piece of paper. The white people must think paper has some mysterious power to help them on in the world. The Indian needs no writings; words that are true sink deep into his heart where they remain; he never forgets them. On the other hand, if the white man loses his papers, he is helpless. I once heard one of their preachers say that no white man was admitted to heaven unless there were writing about him in a great book. ■

*Four Guns, Oglala Sioux Indian judge, with two other judges, Pine Tree and Running Wolf, were guests in 1891 at a dinner given by anthropologist Clark Wissler.

(Four Guns. "Four Guns' Speech." *Indian Cavalcade*, ed. Clark Wissler (New York: Sheridan House, 1938). Reprinted in *I Have Spoken: American History through the Voices of the Indians* 217, ed. Virginia Irving. (Chicago: Swallow Press, 1971): 130.

B.2: Reading

"Time Peace"

BY DEBBIE LOUIE
WINTER 1991

What is life? It is the flash of a firefly in the night. It is the breath of a buffalo in the winter time. It is the little shadow which runs across the grass and loses itself in the Sunset.*

Crowfoot, 1877

I knew I was raised in a manner much different than main-stream America. I expected the society I was walking into would have alternative views on even the simple aspects of life. <u>Expecting</u> a difference, I believe, keeps the mind open. Expecting a difference makes it easier for one to learn and understand another's ways. I believe that when a difference is overlooked, a myth is created in that place. I am here to destroy a long-held myth about "Indian Time." The myth, surprisingly, is one which is held by many of us Native Americans, and not by the dominant society. It is the notion that American Indians are unreliable concerning appointments and deadlines, that they do not understand time. This is not true. Native Americans understand time, but they understand it differently.

Indian Time is not a standard of measurement per se, but more a manner by which one lives. Instead of the person being manipulated by when a project is to be <u>completed</u>, one manipulates <u>how</u>, <u>why</u>, and <u>when</u> a project is undertaken. For example, in lieu of worrying about when a hand-made shirt for someone else is to be <u>completed</u>, one contemplates: <u>How</u> it is to be done—which material? which pattern? what color is favored? etc. <u>Why</u> is it to be done—simply because you like the person? because you are the best at shirt making? because you owe the person a favor? etc. <u>When</u> is it to be worked on—when you are happy? quiet? reflective? feeling strong-willed? (These things are taken into consideration because many believe hand-made items absorb the energies and emotions emitted by the craftsperson as the item is being created.) For me, making the transition from being the manipulator to being manipulated by an intangible, external, human-created "force" called "time" was difficult but necessary.

*Quotation from *Touch the Earth. A Self-Portrait of Indian Existence*. Comp. by T. C. McLuhan. (New York: Outerbridge & Dienstfrey, 1971), p. 12. (Dist. by E. P. Dutton & Co.)

I have been a college student for several years now, and quite a successful one too I might add (having made the Dean's List twice). I came straight from the back woods of the Colville Reservation to the college scene. Along the way I met many of my own people who proclaimed that Indian Time does not function in unity with the concept of Time that is held by main-stream America. I disagree. Indian Time can, and does, work well "out here."

I think the easiest way for me to describe Indian Time is to compare it to how main-stream America views and uses time.

First we will examine three basic assumptions concerning time (the basic units of time, the smallest units of time, and one's focus along the line of time) and how the cultural differences cause discomfort for many Native Americans. After these are discussed, we will look at (1) how one's focus on the time line relates to the completion of a task, (2) working in a human-manipulated environment in contrast to working with Nature, and (3) the desire and need to adapt versus the fear of assimilation.

The basic unit of time for main-stream society is the hour. Compare that to the month which is the basic unit of time for most Native Americans. There is more than length that is different. The length one chooses to function under creates a mind frame. When one must think in terms of hours instead of months, one gets a sense of urgency and/or impatience when thinking about things that need to be done. Many Native Americans find this constant sense of urgency hard to deal with. I think it is this constant pressure of the new shortness of time that initially disrupts a Native American's ability to function at a comfortable level.

When I had a month to complete a writing project, I was at ease in considering the whole project and its components. I had lots of room (time) for brainstorming and exploring ideas on the relevant material. This allowed me to develop several ideas concurrently. Now, in college and hard driven to complete an in-class essay final in one hour, I am forced to focus on only one concept, and I am not allowed to "play" with it and explore how really relevant it is to my life.

The smallest practical unit of time for main-stream society is the minute. For the Native American it is the day. This, for the Native American, causes even more pressure. And it does another thing: The demand to focus on such a small detail of time forces one to concentrate more on <u>time itself</u> rather than on the project at hand. Some members of the dominant culture can tell where they will be and what they will be doing every minute of the day. They make schedules for their days and even their work weeks. Some make schedules that tell them how to spend their weekend time also—up at seven A.M., one hour to shower and dress, eat breakfast at eight A.M., etc. These people may even leave a task unfinished because it is time for the next one on the list. The point seems to be getting many things "done," rather than doing a few things well.

I think that for many Native Americans it is unnatural to have to be aware of time in such small portions. Having to focus so frontwardly on time itself distracts one's attention from the project. And, as I have been taught, a proper job is one which, in the making, has no distractions. When one's attention is distracted, so too is one's heart. If one's heart is not in the project, it is a project that should not be done.

The third assumption is the difference in the focus one keeps concerning the time line itself. For main-stream society, the focus is on the deadline—when a project is to be <u>completed</u>. For the Native American, the focus is on when a project is to be <u>started</u>— the completion of a project takes care of itself. The best analogy I can think of is relating focus to eyesight.

To focus on a starting time can be related to being near-sighted (not to be confused with being short-sighted!). Attention is focused on the nearest part of the time line— when a project is to be begun. This may sound natural to Native Americans. However, the new society which he or she is walking into is, by and large, far-sighted. In this place one pays attention to the part of the time line which is furthest—when a project is to be completed. The required change in focus is the second disorienting and discomforting issue for many Native Americans. Not simply because the focus must change, but also because one's view of the project is changed.

When one is allowed to concentrate on starting a project, one tends to view it as a <u>whole</u> because one is watching for when all circumstances are just right to <u>do</u> the project. Yet in main-stream America one must think about a project in terms of when it must <u>end</u>. I feel that with this kind of view one tends to trip and stumble over the beginning or front-end of projects. If one were to stand on railroad tracks and hear a train coming, one would take note of the <u>front</u> of the on-coming train. What would it matter how far away the last car was? It is the front end that must be dealt with. Yet I often feel I am working in a society which is concerned with getting off the track only when the last car passes.

Because the dominant society has the tendency to break the day down into hours, minutes and seconds, people of that society also have the tendency to break down a project into parts. This, I feel, is also contrary to the Native Americans' tradition of viewing projects as a whole—not parts. This is the third issue which disrupts a Native American's ability to function at a comfortable level.

I don't think Native Americans are too comfortable with doing one part of a job at a time because, for one thing, we come from an environment which allows us to complete a whole project all at once. For example, when one goes fishing one either fishes until he or she has enough fish or until the prime time for fishing is over—either way, that is the <u>whole</u> of it. Another example would be that one weeds the garden until all the weeds are taken care of or until one reaches the part of the day when conditions no longer allow any further activity in the garden.

Here is where a big distinction must be made between these two cultures/environments. Main-stream American society is largely a human-manipulated environment. By this I mean that within the businesses and institutions it is <u>humans</u> who set the pace at which they function—not nature. In Nature you cannot hurry the roots nor berries to grow. One needs only to be prepared to dig and pick. But in main-stream society, the individual <u>can</u> hurry him or herself to do an appointed task. Many of the things people in main-stream society do are not even remotely connected to nature. Even day and night are not considered because homes and businesses have electric lights. Most people do not farm, hunt, or fish. Most jobs remain about the same summer, fall, winter, and spring. Natural time is hardly even considered. Deadlines take control. Even members of the dominant culture who are their own bosses face deadlines—they simply create their own.

Native Americans have struggled for years to adjust to this other form of time. Because our grandparents and parents were struggling for survival within a "new" world, and were dealing with the highly emotional issues of being the fragmented remains of a destroyed way of living, understanding the newer concept of time was of little concern. Now that we, the new generation of Native Nations, have gained some semblance of equilibrium, we can look to understanding and adapting to the new requirements for functioning competently within this developing society.

It is this issue of adapting that brings us back to business. Adapting should not be confused with assimilation. I remember working myself through this confusion. For many, though not all, Native Americans, assimilation into the Non-Native way of doing and thinking is undesirable. Yet I have learned that simply because I can DO things in a Non-Native way does not mean I am no longer Native American. It just means that I can be competent in <u>two</u> realms. Being competent in both realms, the Native American and the dominant culture, has been my number one priority.

In closing I just want to say to the Native American readers, "Don't panic and become discouraged when learning to function within this new time orientation." "They" have had century upon century to develop and live within this orientation. We have had only a few generations. If you feel your pride in yourself or your culture slipping, take heart. We have survived worse. And to <u>all</u> readers I want to say, "When one can come to <u>appreciate</u> a different culture, one can then become a communications link between the two cultures. One can foster understanding between the two cultures and the growth of both, as well as grow and better understand one's self." ■

C: Post-Reading

Discussion Suggestions/Questions

Remembering

1. Why does Four Guns say Native Americans don't need writing?

2. What does Debbie Louie mean when she writes that the dominant culture is "far-sighted?"

Analyzing

1.   Debbie Louie gave the date of her essay as "Winter 1991." Why might she have done that instead of giving the day and the month?

2.   Debbie Louie writes about two kinds of time. Does she think one kind is better than the other? Use quotations from her essay to support your opinion.

Discovering

1.   Is there really a "dominant culture" in the United States? Do most people in this country have the same customs and attitudes? Discuss some attitudes and customs that most people in this country share.

2.   Discuss with others some of the attitudes expressed by Four Guns and Debbie Louie. In what ways are these attitudes attractive, healthy, or positive?

3.   Often what a reader thinks about while reading is more important than the ideas that person reads. There are ideas you had while reading these selections. Share some of these with your peers.

D: Vocabulary Building

1. Words relating to *domus,* "house"

> **Dominant:** "The myth, surprisingly, is one held by many of us Native Americans, and not by the **dominant** society."
>
> *Louie: "Time Peace"*

Dominant is an adjective that means governing or controlling. *Dominant* is a form of the Latin verb *dominari,* which means "to control." The Latin verb, in turn, is related to the noun *domus,* the word for house. The connection between *domus,* the noun for house, and *dominari,* a verb meaning to control, is the noun *dominus,* which means "the master of the house." In Roman culture, the head of the house had absolute authority over the household, and everyone and everything in it was his personal property. For example, if he wished to, he could even sell his adult children into slavery.

English has a few words related to *domus,* house. For example, the legal term in English for a person's residence is **domicile,** and you may live in a **dormitory.** The adjective **domestic** means "things relating to a house or family." For example, an animal that lives with humans (as opposed to an animal that lives in the wild) is a **domestic animal.** A

domestic wine is a wine that is produced in the home country as opposed to a wine that is imported from a foreign country.

English has many words related to *dominus*, master of the house. The verb **dominate** means "to control or rule over." The abstract noun form of *dominate* is **domination**, which means "to have control of something or someone," as in the sentence "England's *domination* of shipping was one of the causes of the American Revolution."

Vocabulary Building Activity 1: Words Related to *Domus*, "House"

Write in the word from the left column that best fits in each blank space in the sentences in the column on the right.

---

1. dormitory   a. Usually _____ cheese is cheaper than imported cheese.

2. domination   b. In Napoleon's time, France _____ all of Europe.

3. dominated   c. Students are required to stay in a _____ on campus during their freshman year.

4. dominant

5. domestic   d. There are two kinds of inherited genes: _____ and recessive.

           e. A monopoly is the complete _____ of an industry by one company.

---

2. Different meanings of the prefix *dis-*

Disorienting: "The required change in focus is the second **disorienting** and discomforting issue for many Native Americans."

     Louie: "Time Peace"

Disorienting is an adjective form of the verb **disorient**, which means to cause someone to lose his or her sense of direction. *Disorient* is the negative form of the verb to **orient**, which means to get your bearings or locate yourself in relation to a landmark, the points of the compass, or a frame of reference. The verb *orient* comes from a form of a Latin word that referred to the direction of the rising sun—in other words, the east.

The prefix **dis-** is a Latin prefix with two historically related but basically different meanings: (1) "not," and (2) "to reverse" or "to do the opposite of." A clear example of the first meaning is the adjective **disloyal**, which means "not loyal." An example of the second meaning is the verb **disinfect**, which means "remove the infection" or "do the opposite of infecting." The verb to **disinfect** does not mean "not infect."

"not"	**"to reverse" or "do the opposite of"**
disbelieve	disconnect
dishonest	disenchant
disobey	dismount
disorder	disown
disuse	disqualify

Note that the words in the column in which **dis-** means "not" are a mixture of nouns, verbs, and adjectives but that all the words in the column in which **dis-** means "to reverse" or "do the opposite of" are verbs.

Vocabulary Building Activity 2: Different Meanings of the Prefix *Dis-*

The prefix *dis-* has two basic meanings: (1) "not" and (2) "to reverse" or "do the opposite of." Below are words formed by adding the prefix *dis-* to an existing word. In the columns provided, put an X to indicate whether the prefix dis- has the meaning "not" or whether it has the meaning "to reverse" or "do the opposite of." The first two questions are done as examples.

Word	"not"	"to reverse/to do the opposite of"
1. disable		X
2. disagree	X	
3. disapprove		
4. disarm		
5. discontinued		
6. disassemble		
7. disinherit		
8. dislocate		
9. disorderly		
10. disrobe		

3. Words derived from *prior/primus,* "first"

Priority: "Being competent in both realms, the Native American and the dominant culture, has been my number one **priority**."

Louie: "Time Peace"

Priority comes from the Latin word *prioritas,* a form of the word *prior,* an adjective that meant going first—either in time or in order of rank. We often use *prior* in reference to time—for example, a prior event is an event that takes place before something else—but there are many related words that refer to the order of rank. The noun *priority* itself means the rating or rank that something has. The verb to **prioritize** means to put things in order of rank.

The Latin *prior* is the root of dozens of English words, not through the basic form of the adjective, but through its superlative form *primus*, which means "first of all." Like words derived from *prior*, words derived from *primus* can refer either to first in time or to first in order of rank. For example, a **prime coat** of paint is the first layer of paint put on a wall before the color coat is applied, but a **prime minister** is the most important official in a government. *Prime* can also mean "basic" or "fundamental," as in a **prime number**—a number than cannot be derived from another number. *Prime* can also be "first" in the sense of "best." For example, in the jargon of television, **prime time** means the most important or popular viewing hours. The related word **primary** has both meanings. For example, the word *primary* means first in time in such phrases as **primary election** or **primary grades**. But in the phrase the **primary reason**, *primary* means first in importance.

In a few words derived from *primus*, the meaning of first in time can have negative twists. For example, the word **primitive** implies "crude" or "unsophisticated," as in the phrase **primitive life form**.

Vocabulary Building Activity 3: Words Derived from *prior/primus*

The four different meanings of words derived from *prior/primus* are given in the left column. In the right column are sentences that use words (in bold) derived from *prior/primus*. In the space provided after each sentence, indicate which of the meanings of *prior/primus* is being used in that sentence. The first sentence is done as an example.

Meaning	Example of Meaning
a. "First in time"	1. He is the **prime** suspect in the crime. <u>b</u>
b. "First in rank or importance"	2. Our cabin is pretty **primitive**. ____
	3. The Italian phrase "**prima** donna" literally means "leading lady." ____
c. "Crude"	
d. "Fundamental" or "basic"	4. He is in the **preliminary** event. ____
	5. The fruit is of **prime** quality. ____
	6. There are three **primary** colors. ____
	7. A **primer** is a small book used for teaching children to read. ____
	8. In many religions, the head bishop or leader is called the **primate**. ____

SECTION 2

Drafting with Details and Examples of Positive Cultural or Familial Differences

A: Pre-Writing: Comparing and Contrasting

There are many ways people prepare themselves to write. Reading, thinking, and talking to others are all good ways to prepare to write. Using the materials in this chapter, your own ideas, and ideas shared by your peers, you have been preparing to write about positive differences among people or families. You will soon be asked to write an essay. Essays include facts, examples, ideas, and opinions. Normally in an essay, facts and examples are used to support the writer's ideas and opinions. In thinking, facts and examples often come before ideas and opinions. In writing, the writer needs to include all four. Doing so helps the reader to understand the writer's message.

Another way to prepare to write your essay is to do the pre-writing activities here. Basically, you are asked to describe a different custom. This can be a custom that is different because your family practices it and other families do not, it can be different because it used to be practiced and now is not, or it can be different because it comes from a culture unlike the dominant culture. Keep in mind that you are looking for a custom that is both different and positive.

Pre-Writing Activity 1: Analyzing Student Essays

Because this kind of essay often uses comparing and contrasting—old custom versus new custom, one family's tradition versus other families' traditions, one culture's custom versus another culture's custom—it might be useful to list the similarities and differences between two customs or traditions.

Before making this list, look at the two essays written by students about the topic "positive cultural or family differences." While reading, think about what makes these essays good.

Student Essay: "Sunday Dinners"

DRAFTING

SUNDAY DINNERS

In today's world both parents have to work to keep up with the high costs of living or raising a family. In our household times were rough when our mom and dad both worked forty to fifty hours a week and raised five children who all had busy schedules. The boys had football practice, one daughter had volleyball practice, another had work, and no one was around to watch our little sister. Finally dinner hour came. If our mom wasn't going to be home, she would prepare something ahead of time that was microwavable. On those nights we never attempted to sit down as a family. On the nights our mom was home she prepared dinner for seven people, and as we all sat around the table, the noise level was high. Most of the time there was a lot of arguing going on. It was beginning to feel like we never had any quality family time.

My grandmother caught on to this. She understood that not only were my parents busy, but my aunts' and uncles' families were busy also. She knew our parents worked hard, long hours to give us a roof over our heads and food on our table. In my parents' case, they worked so much to put their kids through school and college. My grandmother wanted to come up with a way for our entire family to spend some quality time together. She came up with Sunday being family dinner night.

Now we have family dinner night established. My grandmother usually takes care of the main dish and one of the side dishes, like ham and baked beans, pot roast and potatoes, spaghetti and meatballs, chicken and dumplings, or, sometimes, usually in the summer, we barbecue. Everyone else is responsible for bringing desserts, salads, and dinner rolls and for doing the clean-up duties.

Having thirty people for dinner is a lot of work and a lot of clean up. The clean-up duties are clearing the table of all the dirty dishes and condiments, washing all pots and pans, putting all the dirty dishes in the dishwasher, and wiping off all counters and the table.

We have a system of who brings what and who has clean-up duties, so it changes every week.

My grandmother thinks her plan for quality time is the best thing next to sliced bread. She enjoys having us all around to visit with.

Sunday family dinner night has become a pretty big tradition in our family. It's brought a lot of unity and closeness to our family. Whenever there is a tragedy, we come together and give support to each other, like when my grandfather died. We all wanted to be by our grandmother's side and give her the love and support that she needed.

As I look back on coming from a large family that had a get-together once a week, I guess I'm thankful. If I didn't have my aunts, uncles, parents, brothers, sisters, and cousins, I don't know what I would do if I were ever in trouble. I know if I ever needed anything, I could turn to any of them. I have a lot of trust in all of my relatives and, most of all, my parents.

This help doesn't happen by accident; the time to prepare a family for open communication comes before a crisis, not during it. Experience suggests several guidelines for doing this preparation.

A family tradition should be regular, not whenever you feel like having a get-together. You should have a set time and day of the week when you have your get-together. It shouldn't be canceled if Billy has a football game. He simply will be late, or he won't make it. If two people are having inter-personal conflicts, they either work out their problems, or they don't go. One of the most important things is to make sure the work is divided up equally, that it is not put on only one person's shoulders. Everyone should be involved. By the way, isn't that the way family unity is created?

Laurie W.

Discussion Suggestions for "Sunday Dinners"

1. Laurie W. writes about a problem and a solution. What is the problem? What do you think of her family's solution?

2. "Sunday Dinners" is a pretty good essay. What is it that makes it good?

Student Essay: "Simplify America"

SIMPLIFY AMERICA

A loud blare of noise rushes out, devouring my dreams: "It is six-o-eight in the morning on your favorite hits station, B98." I tumble out of bed to meet the monotonous routine of a school day. I crawl up the stairs to feed my stomach, otherwise known as the bottomless pit. I swing open the cupboard door. I am quite intent on my survey of food. A foreign exchange student from Denmark who is residing with my family, Anne, comes up behind me and nudges me hard enough to make me fall. This is her affectionate way to say hello in the morning. Anne is an odd but special girl in my heart. She dresses in a simple, sophisticated way. She is a short, plump girl who is as cute as a button with her blond hair and blue eyes. Her attitude, like the Hobbit depicted by J. R. R. Tolkien, is meek, level-headed, and proud. I must admit I respect her greatly for her ways, which Americans should consider adopting.

Anne said it best in explaining the difference in our lives: "There is a difference between me and most Americans. My ways are so much more simple, and America is so flashy. Why is it?" I have pondered that question since she asked it, and I still don't have an answer. Anne also asked another question that I had never fathomed: "Why do Americans buy so many gadgets that they seldom use?" Again I didn't have an answer while various gadgets flew through my head like the pasta maker and the food dryer on the bottom shelf of the pantry covered with dust. Anne caused me to question what I have. See, like most Americans, I have never questioned the illogical areas of American culture--like our being the largest consumers of products in the world.

Being the largest consumers in the world may explain why Americans buy practically useless objects, like wonton wrapping machines, radish-rose cutters and mellon ball makers. How often does an American use a wonton wrapper or any of these devices? Or how about that pink fluorescent jacket that was purchased and was one of those things a person had to have but was worn for three months before going out of style? And don't forget the hair crimper your

DRAFTING

little sister now uses on her Barbie Dolls. These are only a few examples of wasteful consuming or a typical American way of life.

Americans are even wasteful and illogical in the way they eat compared to the Danes. Anne always ate raw oatmeal and milk for breakfast while I always ate my microwavable Jimmy Dean's breakfast biscuit. For lunch Anne always wanted a roll and a salad; I would eat my hamburger that dripped grease, salty french fries, and a delicious chocolate milkshake. Anne couldn't even think of eating that because of the salt, grease, and sugar. Anne got to the point that she would beg me to fix something lighter to eat, and she brainwashed me that grease is ugly.

Her Danish wardrobe was also practical like her Danish food preference. She had a leather jacket that she had worn for years and still would wear for at least three more years, and here I was pouting because I had to wait a month before I got my annual winter coat. I never saw the obvious until Anne came to live with me. We Americans are wasteful. Here every year I go out and spend about fifty dollars on a new jacket, even though at the end of the year it is stained and well used. What I did not think of was getting a darker color so the stains would not show and getting a higher quality coat for one hundred fifty dollars that would last me about five years. Running shoes are the same way; like greedy ogres, Americans feel they must purchase new ones every spring.

I know it isn't just me being greedy. It is the society because when I confronted my parents with the idea of spending more now to get a better coat that would last me longer, they declined on the grounds that they did not have enough money to purchase it. My parents were figuring that they would have to buy that expensive of a coat every year, even though I explained it. Some of the solutions are so logical, and still when the stupidity of our ways is confronted, we accept them as the way we were brought up.

Their comfort and style are also more logical. Danes wear baggier clothes, which allow unrestricted movement, while the tight jeans that Americans wear look spray-painted on. Americans still wear these jeans, even though they cause poor circulation and are close to impossible to move around in. The versatility of Danish clothing is limitless. Americans must have dress clothes, running outfits, business clothes and casual outfits. What is wrong with a blazer, plain cotton top and baggy blue jeans? This typical Danish outfit is practical for almost every occasion. The clothes being so versatile would solve many girls' dilemmas of being appropriately dressed.

The Danes eat and even dress more practically. Wake up, America! Smell the coffee, and get in gear. As I have pointed out, the Danish culture is more logical than our own. We could be more money-wise and practical by simply changing a little of our wonderful American culture. I have tried to adapt to some of the Danish culture, and I confess it is difficult not to think "Go buy it," but overall it has helped me with my life. I am proud to say the changes I have made please myself and definitely help me save money.

Syrece S.

Discussion Suggestions for "Simplify America"

1. Syrece S. thinks that people in America could learn some lessons from people in Denmark. What are these lessons? Are they good ones?

2. "Simplify America" is a good essay. What makes it good?

Pre-Writing Activity 2: Compare and Contrast Lists

By now you should have a few ideas to write about. Choose one of them. Since you will write about cultural or family differences that are positive, you will need to think about both how things are and what can be changed. Write at the top of the following grid the idea or topic you have chosen to write about. Then list details and examples about how things related to your different custom are now or have been. Also list details and examples about the difference you think is positive.

DRAFTING

Positive Difference Compare and Contrast Grid

I. The idea or topic I will write about is _____

_____

_____ .

II. On the left, list details and examples concerning the way things are. Then, on the right, list positive details about and examples of the different custom.

Details and examples of the way things are now

Positive details and examples of the different custom

A. _____   A. _____

_____   _____

_____   _____

_____   _____

_____   _____

_____   _____

_____   _____

B. _____   B. _____

_____   _____

_____   _____

_____   _____

_____   _____

_____   _____

_____   _____

DRAFTING

C. _____

_____

_____

_____

_____

_____

_____

_____

_____

D. _____

_____

_____

_____

_____

_____

_____

_____

_____

C. _____

_____

_____

_____

_____

_____

_____

_____

_____

D. _____

_____

_____

_____

_____

_____

_____

_____

_____

DRAFTING

B: Writing a First or Initial Draft

Once you have completed the pre-writing, look over all you have done. Then write a first or initial draft of your essay about cultural or family differences that are positive.

SECTION
◄►
3

Revising by Adding Transitions

A: Adding Transitions

While talking, we all tend to jump from one idea to another or from one topic to another. When the person we are talking to loses track of what we are saying, that person asks us to explain or repeat what we are saying. This is normal. While writing, however, we need to signal readers to changes in direction or "jumps" in ideas or topics. These signals are called *transitions*. Transitions are bridges between ideas. Usually a reader and the writer whose work that reader reads are not sitting together; they are separated by both time and space. To help the reader follow what you write, you need to have transitions.

It is the long-standing custom for each paragraph to focus on a new idea or supporting point in an essay. Transitions serve to connect paragraphs, so transitions are normally found at the beginnings of some but not all paragraphs. Not every paragraph needs to begin with a transition, and many times good transitions are already in a first or initial draft of an essay.

B: Revising Drafts of Student Essays

Presented here are drafts of three student essays on the topic of cultural or family differences that are positive. Read the first student draft, "Traditions." While reading, look carefully at the beginning of each paragraph and ask yourself, "Does the writer use a transition to connect this paragraph to the one just before it?" If not, ask yourself if a transition is needed. Then mark with square brackets—[ ]—those places you think could use a transition.

In addition, since some paragraphs in a first or initial draft already include good transitions, underline or highlight the good transitions you see in the student essay "Traditions."

Student Draft: "Traditions"

REVISING

TRADITIONS

How many of the people whom I pass each day on this campus have no fond memories of the family's getting together on a regular basis? Maybe there just isn't enough time in our busy day. It could be related to the fact that families are smaller now.

We no longer see the "Ma and Pa Kettle" type of family--a large truck coming into town for the monthly supplies and twelve kids piling out the back of the truck in various types of hand-me-down clothing. With a large family such as this, you would need some regimentation in order to operate. There would be no such thing as "coming and going" at mealtimes, something that would drive the cook crazy trying to "short order" for so many people. Everyone would have an assigned seat at the table, and certain individuals might even be given tasks that were theirs alone to carry out. The oldest child might be responsible for making sure everyone was at the table on time while the next oldest might be responsible for making sure that the table was set correctly as well as that hands had been properly cleaned. It all sounds so uniform for today's "scattered schedules," and maybe we could use more of it in our society.

It might have something to do with what Americans believe in. When racing through a typical day, do we have time to actually stand for something? It would appear that this could be hard to do for several reasons. When pressured hourly to meet deadlines, we have no time to reflect on what our decisions are based on. Don't you need a little time to make sure that, whatever you do, your action is based on some principle? If I had been responsible for making sure my brothers and sisters were at the table on time, I would have learned leadership skills and gained a sense of accountability to my parents. If I'm running past the kitchen and Mom passes me a "nuked" sandwich, what kind of traditions are forming? None, if done on a regular basis. With no time to share with my mom, what does she become to me? A part of the microwave, I suspect.

It is fashionable to have an old-fashioned Christmas now among the wealthy few--a chance to bring back old memories, eat quality food, and just smell the aromas of Christmas. It fits into the lifestyle of these people because you can order one up just like fast food. Hey, FAX me an old-fashioned Christmas. You don't have to do it until the evening of the 24th. Do people actually go out into the forest to cut down a tree? Does anyone bake until all hours of the day and produce mass quantities of cookies, breads, and sweet treats? Only a few people today are familiar with sending a Yule log wrapped in red ribbon to special friends with candy canes tied to the log in order to be picked off before the log is ceremoniously tossed on the fire to warm grateful hearts. It's a traditional gift of warmth from one friend to another, and it does not cost much!

I will create traditions in my family in the years to come. I might even modify a few old ones to slow our lifestyle down. How about actually sitting at the table together for an hour for meals? We could be gaining some relaxation time on this one! Maybe if we observe traditions in the family, our children will do the same. They will have a few traditions to stand on when it comes time to make a decision. It might be easier when they have to ask that all important question, "Who am I?"

Joe T.

One good way to build a transition is to read the last sentence of the preceding paragraph, then take a word or idea from that sentence and include it in the first sentence of the next paragraph. That sentence _is_ the transition; it helps the reader to see a connection or bridge between the two paragraphs.

Now look again at the following revision of "Traditions." In this version, connecting words, or transitions, that are already in the essay have been underlined. Places where transitions are needed have been marked with square brackets—[ ]. After the square brackets, the writer has added transitions in italics.

Revisions for "Traditions"

TRADITIONS

How many of the people whom I pass each day on this campus have no fond memories of the family's getting together on a regular basis? Maybe there just isn't enough time in our busy day. It could be related to the fact that <u>families</u> are smaller now.

We no longer see the "Ma and Pa Kettle" type of <u>family</u>--a large truck coming into town for the monthly supplies and twelve kids piling out the back of the truck in various types of hand-me-down clothing. With a large family such as this, you would need some regimentation in order to operate. There would be no such thing as "coming and going" at mealtimes, something that would drive the cook crazy trying to "short order" for so many people. Everyone would have an assigned seat at the table, and certain individuals might even be given tasks that were theirs alone to carry out. The oldest child might be responsible for making sure everyone was at the table on time while the next oldest might be responsible for making sure the table was set correctly as well as that hands had been properly cleaned. It all sounds so uniform for today's "scattered schedules," and maybe we could use more of it in our society. [ ]

Why do we have these scattered schedules? It might have something to do with what Americans believe in. When racing through a typical day, do we have time to actually stand for something? It would appear that this could be hard to do for several reasons. When pressured hourly to meet deadlines, we have no time to reflect on what our decisions are based on. Don't you need a little time to make sure that, whatever you do, your action is based on some principle? If I had been responsible for making sure my brothers and sisters were at the table on time, I would have learned leadership skills and gained a sense of accountability to my parents. If I'm running past the kitchen and Mom passes me a "nuked" sandwich, what kind of traditions are forming? None, if done on a regular basis. With no time to share with my mom, what does she become to me? A part of the microwave, I suspect. [ ]

Modern conveniences like the microwave are probably part of the problem. It is fashionable to have an old-fashioned Christmas now among the wealthy few--a chance to bring back old memories, eat quality food, and just smell the aromas of Christmas. It fits into the lifestyle of these people because you can order one up just like fast food. Hey, FAX me an old-fashioned Christmas. You don't have to do it until the evening of the 24th. Do people actually go out into the forest to cut down a tree? Does anyone bake until all hours of the day and produce mass quantities of cookies, breads, and sweet treats? Only a few people today are familiar with sending a Yule log wrapped in red ribbon to special friends with candy canes tied to the log in order to be picked off before the log is ceremoniously tossed on the fire to warm grateful hearts. It's a <u>traditional</u> gift of warmth from one friend to another, and it does not cost much!

I will create <u>traditions</u> in my family in the years to come. I might even modify a few old ones to slow our lifestyle down. How about actually sitting at the table together for an hour for meals? We could be gaining some relaxation time on this one! Maybe if we observe traditions in the family, our children will do the same. They will have a few traditions to stand on when it comes time to make a decision. It might be easier when they have to ask that all important question, "Who am I?"

Joe T.

REVISING

Practicing Revising for Transitions

Following are two more student drafts on the topic of positive cultural or family differences.

Revising Activity 1: Grandpa's Tradition

Working alone or with others, revise the student draft "Grandpa's Tradition" by adding transitions in the spaces provided. If you like, make other changes in the draft to make it even better.

Student Draft: "Grandpa's Tradition"

REVISING

GRANDPA'S TRADITION

Music creates an atmosphere of its own; the atmosphere it creates is an escape from our surroundings. This is especially true in a car. I'm sure that all of us have seen idiots driving down the road more aware of their music than of the traffic around them. You know the idiots I'm talking about--the ones playing the drums on the steering wheel, the ones pretending to be the lead singer exciting a crowd at a concert, the ones you can hear before you see. These idiots are not uncommon.

The sad part is that I am one of these idiots, but only under special circumstances. These special circumstances consist of when I am so tired that I have the tape player all the way up just to stay awake. The thing that is wrong with this is that I begin to wake up in another world, and this world is going as fast as my speedometer. This happens to be too fast for my insurance rates. I have always thought that the Surgeon General should put a warning on the cover of tapes. It should read like this: "Surgeon General's Warning: Listening to Music by People in Automobiles has been Proven to Increase Risks of Speeding Tickets and Accidents."

_____

_____

_____

_____

Music can be so self-indulging that it completely takes over your concentration. All your thoughts start to focus on the music and the feelings, memories, and reflections it can dredge up in your mind. This is more obvious when there is someone in the car with you. When music is playing in a car with more than one person in it, it can be a distraction from "the fine art of conversation." It is easy to ignore people when you have your music to listen to. And if it's your parents, or anyone else whose music taste varies greatly from yours, then it can become a wall between you and them.

This wall is even worse when there's a person in the back seat. Here's the situation: there are two people in the front seat, one person in the back seat, the radio is louder in the back than in the front, and the person in back is attempting to talk with the people in the front. Does this situation sound typical? Well, Joe in the back has finally gotten tired of sitting in the middle of the seat, leaning forward trying to listen and stay in the conversation. He sits back and starts staring out the window, and then Brad in the front yells, "Isn't that right, Joe?" And Joe replies, "What?" Then Brad and Phil have to explain the situation to Joe, and the conversation seems to go around in this cycle, ending where it started, with Joe again getting tired of sitting in the middle and leaning forward.

_____

_____

_____

My Grandpa doesn't like radios in cars, and he never has. He always thought that a radio turned on meant that you weren't concentrating on what you were doing. He also thought that radios were rude. My Grandpa removed all the radios from the vehicles on the farm. His idea was if you were by yourself, then you could use the silence, and if you were with someone else, then you could talk to that person without any distractions. This is not that bad of an idea. It seems that our society focuses so much on being entertained by radios, tape players, and T.V.'s, that we need to learn how to accept silence and how to talk with others. Besides, driving with the music on is dangerous; just ride to school some morning with me.

John L.

REVISING

Revising Activity 2: "The Good New Days"

Working alone or with others, read the following student draft, "The Good New Days." Then read it again, the second time doing two things:

1.   Mark places where transitions are needed with square brackets—[ ].

2.   Write transition sentences, and add them to beginnings of paragraphs where you think they are needed.

Student Draft: "The Good New Days"

THE GOOD NEW DAYS

As we discussed in class the positive differences between family "cultures," I noticed that the majority of the conversation led back to "the good old days." I enjoyed hearing about the many family traditions that have survived. However, there are new traditions being forged by today's single-parent homes. These traditions may have been developed out of necessity, but they do have a positive side. There is a tradition being forged of both girls and boys learning car maintenance and yard upkeep. There is a "team spirit" being forged, which is replacing the old "team spirit." Traditional meals have changed, too; no more days are spent in the kitchen preparing a meal that will take twenty minutes at the most to consume.

Because many youngsters come home to an empty house, they are learning at an early age how to care for themselves, including the preparation of meals. Both boys and girls are learning at an early age how to cook simple meals. My brothers have been cooking macaroni and cheese since they were old enough to operate the stove safely. My eleven-year-old brother has developed an incredible recipe for omelettes in the microwave. My seventeen-year-old brother can make a mean plate of spaghetti!

Because my father didn't live with us, he taught me to do maintenance and repair on my own car, repair horse corrals, and many other "handy-PERSON" tasks so that I could take care of myself and teach my mother to do the same. One winter, my mother and I had to repair a section of corral fence almost daily. We kept doing it the way Dad had showed me, but the horses, or maybe the wind, kept knocking it down. Finally we did it Mom's way, which is "more is better." We took a bucket full of nails and two hammers and we put so many nails in that section of fence that I swear it changed the earth's magnetic field. It still stands.

The old family spirit of "All for one and one for all
. . . but, Dear, you stay in the kitchen, and I'll work
on the car" is gone. In my family, as well as many other
single-parent homes, there are many things to get done and
only half of the adult power to do them. My mom organizes
parties that all of her children are expected to attend.
We have a couple of "Leaf Raking Parties" per year and
a couple of "Barn/Corral Cleaning Parties" per year.
Last summer, we had a "House Painting Party." My mom, she
really knows how to have a good time! This fall, I
extended invitations to family members to my "Apartment
Painting Party," and everyone showed up, even two friends
of my brother!

Last but not least the microwave, prepackaged meals and
fast food places are rapidly replacing home-cooked, sit-
down meals. I have often heard this lamented. However,
such meals are convenient, allowing us more time to be
involved in other activities. Our family does make it a
point to attend most Little League games, ballet recitals, Jazz Band concerts, etc. These quick meals enable us
to have our own activities as well as supporting the
activities of each other.

All in all, these new "traditions in the making" may
be different, but some of them are good. Time marches on,
and often times our way of life changes. In order to be
happy, one must adapt and develop the good in the changes.

Veronica P.

C: Revising Your Draft

Working alone or with others, find places in <u>your</u> draft where transitions are needed, and then add those transitions. Feel free to make other changes in your draft that make it even better.

D: Helping Others to Revise Their Drafts

It is often easier to see places in someone else's draft where transitions are needed. Using the skills practiced in this chapter, suggest places where another writer might add transitions to his or her draft. You may even suggest transition sentences to this other writer.

E: Optional Revision

The essay you have written might benefit from your also using the revision strategy—Revising by Adding Qualifiers—presented in Chapter 5.

SECTION

◀▶

4

Final Editing for Pronoun Problems

In this unit we will deal with four different types of pronoun problems: **wrong pronoun form in noun compounds, unclear pronoun reference, using indefinite *you***, and **using *they* to refer to a singular antecedent**. We will deal with each type in turn.

A: Wrong Pronoun Form in Noun Compounds

One of the most common pronoun mistakes is using the wrong form of the pronoun in a **noun compound**. (A noun compound consists of two nouns or pronouns joined together by *and*.) An example of this kind of error is using the object form *me* instead of the subject form *I* in the noun compound that serves as the subject of the following sentence:

1. * <u>John and **me**</u> fixed the flat tire.
    Noun compound

The following personal pronouns have different forms when they are used as a subject and when they are used as an object of a verb or preposition. Compare the following forms:

Subject	Object of verb or preposition
I	me
he	him
she	her
we	us
they	them

Here is an example of subject and object forms using the pronouns *I* and *me*:

2.   Subject: **I** saw Jane.

2a. Object of verb: Jane saw **me**.

2b. Object of preposition: Jane gave a party for **me**.

Nobody (except possibly Tarzan) would mix up the subject and object forms in these sentences:

3.   Wrong subject: * **Me** saw Jane.

3a. Wrong object of verb: * Jane saw **I**.

3b. Wrong object of preposition: * Jane gave a party for **I**.

However, in the case of pronouns in noun compounds, we seem to lose our effortless ability to pick the correct subject or object form of pronouns. In noun compounds we tend to use a subject pronoun form where we should use an object form and to use an object form where we should use a subject form. Here are examples of this kind of error:

Subject Pronoun Incorrectly Used As an Object of a Verb

4.   * Jane saw <u>Tarzan and **I**</u>.

Subject Pronoun Incorrectly Used As an Object of a Preposition

5. * Just between <u>you and **I**</u>, Tarzan's grammar is terrible.

Object Pronoun Incorrectly Used As a Subject

6. * <u>Tarzan and **me**</u> are going to check out the jungle.

All of these pronoun errors have two important features in common:

a. The incorrect pronoun is always the second element in a noun compound, and

b. the first element in the compound is a word that never changes form. It is either a noun or a pronoun like *you* that doesn't have different subject and object forms.

For whatever reason, we seem to have great difficulty in picking the proper personal pronoun in noun compounds. It is as though the unchanging form of the first element in the compound blocks us from naturally and effortlessly selecting the correct form of the second pronoun that does change form.

Fortunately, there is a simple substitution test that will instantly show if the pronoun in a compound is correct: substitute the correct plural pronoun (*we/us* or *they/them*) for the entire noun compound. Our sense of which plural pronoun is correct is very strong. If the correct plural pronoun substitute for the noun compound is the subject form *we* or *they*, then the correct singular pronouns within the noun compound is the subject form *I*, *he*, or *she*. Conversely, if the correct plural pronoun substitute for the noun compound is the object form *us* or *them*, then the correct singular pronoun within the noun compound is the object form *me*, *him*, or *her*.

Here is how we would use this **plural pronoun substitution test** on the example sentences above—first to discover the error of the incorrect pronoun form and then to help us pick the correct pronoun form:

4. * Jane saw <u>Tarzan and I</u>.
   them

Since *them* in sentence (4) is an object pronoun, the corresponding correct singular pronoun must be the object form *me* rather than the subject form *I*:

4a. Jane saw <u>Tarzan and **me**</u>.
   them

Here is the second example sentence:

5. * Just between <u>you and **I**</u>, Tarzan's grammar is terrible.
   us

Since *us* in sentence (5) is an object pronoun, the corresponding correct singular pronoun must be the object form *me* rather than the subject form *I*:

5a.   Just between <u>you and **me**</u>, Tarzan's grammar is terrible.
                       us

Here is the third example:

6.   * <u>Tarzan and **me**</u> are going to check out the jungle.
          We

Since *we* in sentence (6) is a subject pronoun, the corresponding correct singular pronoun must be the subject form *I* rather than the object form *me*:

6a.   <u>Tarzan and **I**</u> are going to check out the jungle.
         We

Editing Activity 1: Using the Plural Pronoun Substitution Test to Check for Wrong Pronoun Form in Noun Compounds

All of the following sentences contain compounds in which a pronoun is the second element. Underline the compound, and then put the correct form of the plural pronoun under the compound. If the plural pronoun substitution test shows that the pronoun in the compound is wrong, write out a correct form of the sentence on the line below. If the plural pronoun substitution test shows that the pronoun in the noun compound is correct, write "okay." The first two questions are done as examples.

1. My sister and me used to be very close.
   Answer:

   1.   <u>My sister and me</u> used to be very close.
        We
        My sister and I used to be very close.

2. They gave it to you and me.
   Answer:

   2.   They gave it to <u>you and me</u>.
                         us
   okay _____

3. Tarzan and she want to be partners.

   _____

4. I hope that Jane and him can learn to like bananas.

   _____

5. After Cheetah and me came, we had to add an extra room to the hut.

   _____

6. Above Cheetah and me, there was a huge bunch of bananas.

   _____

7. We are late because Tarzan and me got lost.

   _____

8. Our visitors went with Jane and me to the river.

   _____

9. Only you and me would have been there at that time.

   _____

10. The elephant came toward Tarzan and they.

    _____

11. Why did Jane ask you and I to sit outside?

    _____

B: Unclear Pronoun Reference

The term **pronoun reference** means the noun that a particular pronoun refers to. In the following example, the pronoun *he* in the second sentence refers to the noun *clerk* in the first sentence:

7.   I talked to the **clerk** at the post office. **He** gave me a change of address form.

The noun that a pronoun refers to is called the **antecedent** of that pronoun. [The term *antecedent* literally means "one that goes before."] In sentence (7), the noun *clerk* is the antecedent of the pronoun *he*. When the reader cannot tell which of several possible nouns is a pronoun's antecedent or when there is literally no noun that could serve as a pronoun's antecedent, then that pronoun has **unclear pronoun reference**.

When we are talking to someone we know, we can afford to be a little careless about pronoun antecedents because the listener knows us and knows enough about the situation we are describing to make a pretty good guess about what a pronoun's antecedent must be. However, when we write, we write to strangers who know nothing about us or the situation we are describing. Consequently, in writing we need to be much more careful about clearly spelling out every pronoun's antecedent.

One of the main functions of final editing is to see our papers with the eyes of a reader instead of with the eyes of an author. As authors, we tend to see what we mean to say and not see what we actually wrote. For example, we know exactly what we mean when we use a pronoun. The problem is that the reader might not have any idea of what that pronoun refers to. Once we, as authors, have recognized that a pronoun has unclear pronoun reference, clarifying the pronoun's antecedent is easy; the problem is recognizing that a pronoun has unclear reference in the first place.

In this section we will examine two kinds of unclear pronoun reference: **ambiguous pronoun reference** and **vague pronoun reference**.

Ambiguous Pronoun Reference

Ambiguous reference is when a pronoun could equally well refer to more than one noun as its antecedent, such as in the following example:

8.   * John called the office and talked to his boss. **He** wanted to know when they should be at the airport.

Does *he* refer to *John* or to *his boss*? The problem here is that the writer has a scene in his or her mind in which one person is talking to another. This scene is so vivid in the writer's mind that the writer forgets that the scene is not clear in the reader's mind. The only thing the reader knows is the words that the author has put on the paper. The reader creates from these words a scene that may or may not be the same scene in the writer's mind. It is the writer's responsibility to make sure that the words on the paper provide all of the information necessary for the reader to create the scene that the writer wants to communicate to the reader.

Once the writer has recognized a case of ambiguous pronoun reference, the problem is easily solved by replacing the ambiguous pronoun with the appropriate noun or with a pronoun whose antecedent is unambiguous. For example, in sentence (8a) below, it is unambiguous that John was the one who wanted to know when they should be at the airport, and in sentences (8b) and (8c) it is equally clear that it was his boss:

8a.   John called the office and talked to his boss. **John** wanted to know when they should be at the airport.

8b.   John called the office and talked to his boss. **His boss** wanted to know when they should be at the airport.

8c.   John called the office and talked to his boss, **who** wanted to know when they should be at the airport.

Notice that in sentence (8c) the use of the relative pronoun *who* to show that it was the boss (not John) who wanted to know when they should be at the airport.

Every time a writer uses a pronoun, the writer runs the risk of distracting the reader from what the writer is saying by forcing the reader to puzzle out the pronoun's antecedent. Careless pronoun use, even if it turns out that there is no ambiguity, causes the reader to lose track of what the writer is trying to communicate. One cause of reader uncertainty about pronoun reference is using the same pronoun to refer to two different antecedents in the same sentence, as in this example:

9.   * My relatives prepared elaborate holiday meals. **They** believed that **they** were something that helped keep the family together.

Here, the word *they* is used twice. After a little detective work, the reader will eventually realize that the first *they* must refer to *my relatives* and that the second *they* must refer to *elaborate holiday meals*. A much less confusing alternative would have been to use a noun to avoid the second use of *they*, for example:

9a.   My relatives prepared elaborate holiday meals. **They** believed that **these occasions** helped keep the family together.

Editing Activity 2: Correcting Ambiguous Pronoun Reference

In the following student essay, all non-possessive pronouns are in bold. Check each pronoun to see if the pronoun clearly and unambiguously refers to an appropriate noun. If the pronoun has more than one possible antecedent or if the same pronoun has several different antecedents in the same sentence, correct the error in the way that you think fits the essay best.

EDITING

```
                                        Jeff M.
                        English Writing, Sec 6
                           February 12, 1993

        FAMILY BONDING CAMPING TRIPS
```

   Every year my parents get the whole family together--my father Tom, my mother Linda, my brother Nick, my sister Tami, and **me**. **They** called these annual gatherings "family bonding" because **they** gave the family a chance to get together away from friends and relatives. The final days before **we** were to leave were always very hectic for **us**. **We** had to get everything together that **we** would need for the trip--tents, lanterns, stoves, sleeping bags, clothes, and all the food--and then pack **it** in the van. **It** always had a fresh tune-up before **we** began a trip.

   We never went to the same place twice. **We** went to places like Idaho, Montana, Utah and eastern Washington. **They** were always quite a long distance away from Vashon Island, the place **we** lived at the time. **It** is located between Seattle and Tacoma. **They** were all places that were different from the small, wet island where **we** lived.

   No matter where **we** went, **we** picked a camp site near a river, so **we** could play in **it** and fish. **Those** were the only things we did when **we** went camping. The worst part of being out in the boonies is camping in the rain. **I** always hated **it**. The other thing I hated about pitching a tent was that there was always a big rock in the middle of my back no matter where I put **it**.

   When **I** turned sixteen, I began to have many new interests. **They** didn't seem nearly so much fun anymore. My brother and sister felt the same way, so **we** finally put an end to **them**. However, when I look back on **it** now, I am glad that my parents made **us** go camping. **They** really did bring **us** together.

Vague Pronoun Reference

When a pronoun has no specific noun that serves as its antecedent, the pronoun exhibits **vague pronoun reference**. An example of a vague pronoun reference is the *they* we hear so much about in political discussions, for example:

10.   * **They** really ought to do something about health care.

Who is the antecedent of *they*? Congress? The President? The health care industry? Society in general? Since there is no expressed antecedent, the reader is forced to guess what is in the writer's mind (if anything).

The relative pronoun *which* must also have a specific noun as its antecedent. Sometimes, however, *which* is carelessly used to mean "all the above." Here are examples of the two different uses of *which* that illustrate the difference between *which* with a valid antecedent and a "vague" *which* that does not have any specific antecedent:

11.   The council rejected the motion, **which** the chair herself had introduced.

12.   *The council rejected the motion, **which** really upset the chair.

In sentence (11) *which* refers to its antecedent *motion*. In sentence (12), however, *which* has no antecedent. *Which* does not refer to the nearest appropriate noun, *motion*. The motion didn't upset the chair; what upset the chair was the fact that the council rejected the motion. Consequently, the use of *which* in sentence (12) is vague. We can correct sentence (12) by rewriting the sentence to make the first part of the sentence the subject in place of the "vague" *which*:

12a.   **The council's rejection of the motion** really upset the chair.

Under certain circumstances we can use the pronouns *it* and *they* and the demonstrative pronouns *this*, *that*, *these*, and *those* without a specific noun as their antecedent to mean "all of the above." For example, see the following sentence:

13.   When the President vetoed the bill, **it** didn't come as a shock to anyone.

Here the pronoun *it* is antecedent-less; *it* does not refer to either *President* or *bill*, the two nouns in the sentence that could serve as grammatical antecedents. Instead, *it* refers to all of the preceding part of the sentence taken together: *the fact that the President vetoed the bill*.

The antecedent-less pronoun *it* in sentence (13) is marginally acceptable because the reader can easily tell that the pronoun *it* means "all of the above." However, in most cases of antecedent-less pronouns, we can write much better sentences by making the "all of the above" part of the sentence the actual subject in place of the empty antecedent-less pronoun, as shown in this example:

13a.   **The President's veto of the bill** didn't come as a shock to anyone.

A basic problem of antecedent-less pronouns is that they force the reader to puzzle out what the writer is saying because the reader does not know if a pronoun is antecedent-less without first exhausting all possible antecedents. In other words, the reader has to check back to the first part of the sentence or read through the entire preceding sentence to see if the pronoun has an antecedent. Only after discarding all possible antecedents can the reader tell that the pronoun is antecedent-less. In longer and more complex sentences, this search becomes quite distracting—even annoying—as in this example:

14.   * Bosnian nationalists assassinated Archduke Ferdinand of Austria and Hungary in Sarajevo in June of 1914. **This** was one of the causes of World War I.

What does the pronoun *this* refer to? The reader is forced to work back through all of the first sentence looking for an antecedent for the pronoun *this*. Eventually the reader concludes that there is no specific noun that can serve as the literal antecedent of *this*. Then the reader knows that the writer really means *this* as an antecedent-less pronoun that refers to all of the first sentence taken together—the "all the above" meaning.

A better alternative would be to put a noun after the pronoun *this* so that the reader would not have to play a guessing game:

14a.   Bosnian nationalists assassinated Archduke Ferdinand of Austria and Hungary in Sarajevo in June of 1914. **This event** was one of the causes of World War I.

An even better alternative would be to eliminate the empty antecedent-less pronoun *this* altogether and turn the whole first sentence into the subject of the verb in the second sentence:

14b.   **The assassination of Archduke Ferdinand of Austria and Hungary by Bosnian nationalists in Sarajevo in June of 1914** was one of the causes of World War I.

An inherent danger of all antecedent-less pronouns is that they can be ambiguous—the reader can't tell if the pronoun has specific antecedent or is antecedent-less and refers to "all the above." Following is an example.

15.   * Last summer John worked at a summer camp. To his surprise, he discovered that he liked **it** a lot.

What is the antecedent of *it*? One possibility is that *it* refers to *summer camp*. Another possibility is that *it* is antecedent-less and refers to "all of the above." That is, the pronoun *it* refers to John's working at a summer camp. Here are some better alternatives that make the writer's intended meaning clearer:

15a.   Last summer John worked at a summer camp. To his surprise, he discovered that he liked **the camp** a lot.

15b.   Last summer John worked at a summer camp. To his surprise, he discovered that he liked **working at the camp** a lot.

The pronoun *it* has some special uses. Certain sentences require the use of an antecedent-less use of *it*, as in **It's raining** and **Let's call it** a day. Since an antecedent-less *it* is obviously correct (even required) in these and similar expressions, this kind of antecedent-less *it* cannot be replaced by a noun.

Editing Activity 3: Correcting Vague Pronoun References and Eliminating Antecedent-less Pronouns

In the following student essay, all non-possessive pronouns are in bold. The essay is free of errors except for a number of vague pronoun references and several unnecessary antecedent-less pronouns. Correct the vague pronoun references and unnecessary antecedent-less pronouns in the way that you think fits this essay best.

Jennifer F.
English Writing, Sec 6
February 22, 1993

FAMILY VACATIONS

In our family **it** is almost impossible to get everyone together. **This** is because our busy schedules keep **us** apart. Even when **I** was a child, my father was busy building his business into a big success. Dad always spent time with **us** individually, but **we** never got together and did anything, **which** meant that there was never any "quality time" for the whole family as a unit.

Now my parents are divorced. **This** is not unusual by today's standards: almost 60 percent of all marriages end in a divorce. **This** is so unfortunate for the many young children **who** miss the opportunity to have a full family life. In today's society **they** have to grow up choosing between their parents. **This** is an intense emotional strain that can leave marks on **them** for life. How **they** react to the divorce and the extent that **they** take the children into consideration make a big difference to the children's life. When **they** continually degrade their former spouses, children become very confused. **They** do not know what to think. Morality does not often take a major part in a custody battle--the more one parent can say to degrade the other, the better chance **he** or **she** has of keeping the children. In my case, **I** chose to live with my father, **which** is unusual for most eleven-year-old daughters.

> My family now consists of my dad, stepmother, my fourteen-year-old sister, and **me**. With all of **us** going different ways the chances of having all of **us** together for the "family dinner" are slim, though **we** would all like to do **it**. However, there is one special thing our family does to keep close--our family vacation. Every summer **we** rotate **who** chooses where **we** will go on vacation. For example, last summer **it** was my turn to choose, and **it** was Hawaii. **It** is a chance for our family to unite as one. With no telephones interrupting, my dad can relax and have time to talk to all of **us**. **It** is surprising how a week or two can bring a family together. **It** is a wonderful feeling. Between shopping and boating **we** had plenty of time to sort out our feelings. Talking with my sister about some problems and with my dad about others often took up a large portion of the day. After a long day together, **we** talked about how **we** were all going to make **it** rich and live in Hawaii, **which** will always be a dream of mine.

C: Using Indefinite *You*

Most languages have an indefinite "generic" pronoun that means something like "somebody/anybody/everybody/people in general." In British English the pronoun *one* plays this role as in the following sentence:

16.   Jane and Sue went to a cafe where **one** can get espresso.

Most Americans find this use of *one* slightly foreign. In informal conversations many Americans use the pronoun *you* as their indefinite pronoun of choice, as in this example:

17.   * Jane and Sue went to a cafe where **you** can get espresso.

Unfortunately, however, in formal writing this indefinite use of *you* is not acceptable. The only formally correct use of *you* is as a pronoun that actually refers to the hearer or reader, for example:

18.   Jane and Sue bought **you** [the reader] a present.

Accordingly, the pronoun *you* in sentence (17) is an incorrect pronoun reference because the second person pronoun *you* doesn't refer to anybody. It doesn't mean *you* the reader, and, of course, *you* can't refer to the subjects Jane and Sue.

We could use *they* in place of *you* to refer to Jane and Sue:

19.   **Jane and Sue** went to a cafe where **they** could get espresso.

Although sentence (19) is perfectly grammatical, it doesn't mean quite the same thing as the indefinite pronoun *one* in sentence (16). Since the pronoun *they* refers exclusively to Jane and Sue, sentence (19) has the unwanted implication that only Jane and Sue (but nobody else) can get espresso at the cafe, a meaning that the indefinite generic pronoun *one* in sentence (16) avoids.

A better alternative might be to use a general purpose noun like *people* to avoid using any pronoun:

20.   Jane and Sue went to a cafe where **people** can get espresso.

Still another alternative would be to duck the issue by rewriting the sentence entirely:

21.   Jane and Sue went to a cafe that serves espresso.

We are left with two alternatives, neither of them very satisfactory:

▲ learn to live with *one* as an indefinite pronoun, as in sentence (16), or

▲ abandon any attempt to use "generic" pronouns altogether in formal writing, and either substitute in their place "generic" nouns, as in sentence (20), or rewrite the sentence entirely, as in sentence (21).

You pay your money and take your choice. Unfortunately, the informal spoken language alternative of using *you* as an indefinite pronoun, as in sentence (17), is simply not acceptable in formal writing.

Editing Activity 4: Revising Sentences to Eliminate Indefinite *You*

All of the following sentences contain the indefinite *you* in bold. Replace *you* with *one* or a generic noun, or rewrite the sentence entirely to eliminate the need for a "generic" pronoun. Try to explore several alternative solutions. The first question is done as an example.

---

1. The amount of time **you** put into college is amazing.
   *The amount of time **people** put into college is amazing.*

2. How **you** get along with other people is very important.

   _____

3. All the time and effort **you** put into college should bring some reward.

   _____

4. Getting a college education does not guarantee **you** a job.

---

5. That kind of future can't help but excite **you**.

6. Everybody knows that **you** will get a ticket parking on Main Street.

7. A high school education may be the only option that **you** have.

8. With a good degree, **you** can always find some kind of a job.

9. We wanted a place where **you** could get some rest.

10. After college, **you** must develop a whole new set of skills.

11. The directions didn't make it clear what **you** should do.

D: Using *They* to Refer to a Singular Antecedent

One of the most common errors of pronoun reference in college writing is the use of the plural pronoun *they* (*they, them, their, themselves*) to refer to a singular noun or indefinite pronoun. Here are some examples of this error from student essays. Both *they* (in its various forms) and its antecedent singular noun or pronoun appear in bold.

22. * If a **person** sticks with it for a while, I think **they** will eventually find a job.

23. * If **anyone** attends college, graduates, and does not acquire a good job, **they** have wasted much time and effort.

24. * It is virtually impossible for **somebody** living on **their** own to put **themselves** through school.

25. * This is so the **child** can taste everything and see if **they** like it.

The key to understanding this kind of pronoun agreement error is to notice the kinds of nouns and pronouns that *they* refers to.

The nouns are all generic; that is, they refer to people in general, not to specific actual persons. For example, *person* in sentence (22) does not refer to any actual specific person; *person* really means "anybody." Likewise, *child* in sentence (25) refers to children in general, not to a particular child.

The pronouns are all generic indefinite pronouns such as *anybody*, *everybody*, or *somebody*.

In the past it was customary to refer to singular generic nouns with the masculine pronoun *he*. We can make the preceding sentences technically correct by replacing all the plural pronouns with the corresponding forms of the masculine pronoun:

22a.   If a **person** sticks with it for a while, I think **he** will eventually find a job.

23a.   If **anyone** attends college, graduates, and does not acquire a good job, **he** has wasted much time and effort.

24a.   It is virtually impossible for **somebody** living on **his** own to put **himself** through school.

25a.   This is so the **child** can taste everything and see if **he** likes it.

Most of us would feel uncomfortable with the masculine pronouns in sentences (22a) through (25a) because of the sexist implication that only men count in this world. A grammatically valid alternative is to use both masculine and feminine pronouns:

22b.   If a **person** sticks with it for a while, I think **he or she** will eventually find a job.

23b.   If **anyone** attends college, graduates, and does not acquire a good job, **he or she** has wasted much time and effort.

24b.   It is virtually impossible for **somebody** living on **his or her** own to put **him or herself** through school.

25b.   This is so the **child** can taste everything and see if **he or she** likes it.

The obvious disadvantage of using both masculine and feminine pronouns is the fact that it makes the sentences seem clumsy—the double possessive and reflexive pronouns in sentence (24b) are especially awkward.

In informal speech we have solved the problem of the inappropriate gender marking of the third person pronouns *he* and *she* when referring to generic nouns and indefinite pronouns by substituting the third person plural pronoun *they* (in all of its various forms) for the grammatically required third person singular pronoun because *they* (unlike *he* and *she*) refers equally well to males and females. If we look back to the original four sentences, (22) through (25), we can see that the writers of these sentences have used this strategy; these writers have substituted a form of the plural pronoun *they* to avoid using the third person singular forms *he/she* with their inappropriate gender markings to refer to singular generic nouns and indefinite pronouns.

The simplest and most satisfactory way to solve the problem of the inappropriate gender marking of *he* and *she* is to make the generic nouns plural to begin with; by doing this, the plural pronoun *they* will then be grammatically correct, and we have avoided the problem of inappropriate gender marking. Here is how the two example sentences with singular generic nouns could be rewritten with corresponding plural generic nouns:

22c. If **people** stick with it for a while, I think **they** will eventually find a job.

25c. This is so that **children** can taste everything and see if **they** like it.

The indefinite pronouns in the other two example sentences cannot be changed from singular to plural because indefinite pronouns are always singular—there is no such thing as a plural indefinite pronoun of this type. The only solution for these two sentences is to change the indefinite pronouns to a plural generic noun with a comparable meaning, as in these examples:

23c. If **people** attend college, graduate, and do not acquire a good job, **they** have wasted much time and effort.

24c. It is virtually impossible for **students** living on **their** own to put **themselves** through school.

Editing Activity 5: Correcting Agreement Error When *They* Refers to a Singular Antecedent

The following sentences were taken from student essays. All of the sentences contain some form of the third person plural pronoun *they* in bold. The third person pronoun refers to a singular antecedent. Correct this agreement error in the way you think works best for each sentence. The first question is done as an example.

1. While a person is furthering **their** own education, **they** also begin to pick up a large vocabulary.
   *While **students** are furthering their own education, they also begin to pick up a large vocabulary.*

2. Although a student might understand a problem, **they** might not be able to complete it on time.
   _____
   _____

3. Everyone should go to college at one point in **their** life.
   _____
   _____

4. If a student is going to invest in a college education, **they** should get **their** money's worth.
   _____
   _____

5. Each one will have **their** own opinion.
   _____
   _____

6. If a student sets **their** mind on becoming something special, **they** can take classes in that area.
   _____
   _____

7. If anybody sticks with it, I think **they** will eventually find a job.
   _____
   _____

8. Social science courses are offered to the student to help **them** realize that **they** are an important part of society.
   _____
   _____

9. The reason that everybody goes to a college is to help **themselves** get a good job.
   _____
   _____

10. The college student may find the working world quite different from **their** expectations.
    _____
    _____

Editing Activity 6: Correcting Indefinite *You* and *They* with a Singular Antecedent

The following student essay is ready for final editing. It is free of errors except for a number of incorrect pronoun references involving indefinite *you* and *they* used with a singular antecedent. Every *you* and *they* appears in bold. Check each one, and decide if it has an incorrect pronoun reference. If it does, correct it in the way that you think fits this essay best.

Chris G.
English Writing, Sec 6
May 27, 1993

THE ADVANTAGES OF A SMALL TOWN

I have lived just about all my life in the small town of Grand Coulee, Washington, population 4,500. I really love living there because everybody is friendly and will go out of **their** way to help **you**. For example, if **you** go into a store looking for something special and the owner doesn't have it in stock, **they** will order it special for **you**. An owner of a business in a small town has to struggle a lot because **they** have to pay higher prices for shipping. Also **they** have fewer customers because everybody goes into larger towns where **they** can get a wider variety of goods and cheaper prices. Nevertheless, I still like shopping in Grand Coulee because **you** will never get ripped off there the way **you** will in larger towns. Besides, the money that **you** spend in a little town stays there and helps everyone else in town--**they** have to make a living too.

I went to school at Lake Roosevelt High School. There were about ninety people in my graduating class. I knew who everybody in my class was and what **they** were like. In fact, I think I knew the name of every student in the school. In a small school like Lake Roosevelt **you** feel like **you** are part of a family; no student felt like **they** were an outsider the way **they** would feel at a larger school. A large school has cliques or groups that make **you** feel **you** have to be a part of in order to be anybody. **You** end up trying to show off an image rather than worrying about **your** schoolwork. A student at a small school doesn't have to worry about being in a special clique; **they** are accepted for who **they** are by the whole school.

In Grand Coulee there are no traffic lights. About the only thing **you** have to worry about driving in Grand Coulee is making sure that **you** stay on **your** own side of the road and watch out for an occasional elderly driver who never bothers to use **their** turn indicator when turning left in front of **you**. When I first came to Spokane I had to learn to deal with stop lights, weird traffic signs, and worst of all, the big city driver who seemed ready to run **you** over if **you** got in **their** way.

I really like living in a small town. It is the perfect place for **you** to raise **your** family. A kid growing up in a small town can always find plenty of things to do; **they** can fish, hunt, get involved in community sports, and go around town on **their** bikes with **their** friends. When I am done with college, I hope that I will be able to live in a small town again.

ESSAY EXAMS

READING

Reading About Essay Exams

A: Pre-Reading

Essay exams are a frequent feature of the college experience. Students are asked to write such exams in many of their courses. Chemistry, biology, history, sociology, physical education, political science, and literature professors all might require essay exams in the courses they teach. Students who think only English professors will ask them to write are mistaken. More and more professors, in all disciplines, have found that writing helps students to discover, organize, and remember course content; writing helps people to learn.

In this chapter you will learn about and practice skills you need to write even better essay exams.

Pre-Reading Activities

Discussion

1. Not everyone, but most people, have had frightening essay exam experiences. If you are comfortable talking about these living nightmares, share an experience that you or someone you know has had. For example, did you ever sit in a classroom and stare at an essay exam question that made no sense at all to you? Did you ever, when asked to answer three essay questions, hear the instructor ask for completed exams when you were still writing on the first question? Did you ever study chapters three and four of a textbook and then discover, when you read the essay exam questions, that the exam was over material presented in chapters five and six?

Such experiences can be positive if we learn from them. After sharing your experience, share what you learned from that experience.

2. Working with others, make a list of what you know about what it takes to write good essay exams. What tricks do you know or study strategies do you use to succeed on these exams? Discuss these ideas with others, using examples to illustrate them.

Reading Suggestions

(Keep these suggestions in mind while reading "Learning to Succeed Under Pressure: Essay Exam Strategies" by Christy Friend.)

1. Highlight or underline any advice included in the reading that addresses a problem you have had while preparing for or writing essay exams.

2. Circle any words or advice included in the reading that you find confusing.

Vocabulary Preview

coherent: logical, organized. (Instructors expect <u>coherent</u> written responses to essay exam questions.)

constraints: limits, boundaries. (My husband and I did not buy a new car because of financial <u>constraints</u>.)

irrelevant: not to the point, not important in this context or situation. (The traffic officer thought that the fact that I was late for class was <u>irrelevant</u>, and she wrote me a speeding ticket.)

B: Reading

"Learning to Succeed Under Pressure: Essay Exam Strategies"

CHRISTY FRIEND[*]

"I spent hours getting ready for my history midterm, but the professor didn't ask about any of the information I had studied. Most of the questions didn't look familiar, and I didn't know how to even begin an answer. What a nightmare!"

"My first essay on the philosophy final was great, and I was sure I'd get an 'A'." Then the instructor said, 'Fifteen more minutes,' and I realized that I had two more essays left to write. I ran out of time before I even got to the last question."

"I'm pretty good at doing term papers, but when I have to write under time pressure, I freeze. Last time I took an essay test, I wrote two pages before I realized that I'd left out something important. By the time I had scratched out and made changes, my paper was such a mess that even I couldn't decipher it."

Most of the material you've read so far in this book focuses on writing done outside of class over a period of days or weeks. Such assignments allow you time for brainstorming, planning, writing, and rewriting several drafts. The quotations above focus on a different kind of writing situation: the essay exam. Essay exams are in-class, timed tests in which you deal with information you have covered in a history, literature, biology, political science, or other class. When instructors give essay exams, they want to see how well you can relate and apply course material. They want to see if you can sort out important concepts from class lectures or readings and reconstruct these concepts in your own words. For these reasons, writing essay responses is a doubly challenging task. It requires not only that you know course information thoroughly, but also that you be able to put it into writing

---

[*] Christy Friend teaches writing at Southwestern University in Georgetown, Texas. She previously taught at the University of Oklahoma, where she was also Assistant to the Director of Instructional Development. Her area of interest is composition studies, and she has published essays on writing education, rhetorical theory, and essay-exam writing.

quickly and effectively. This is why many students, like the ones in the quotations, have difficulty mastering the essay-exam writing process. Some, like the student in the first scenario, have problems organizing and recalling appropriate information to include in their essay responses. Others, like the students in the second and third scenarios, find it stressful to work under time pressure. Still others encounter problems in studying, analyzing exam questions, budgeting time, or organizing their essay responses.

A COLLEGE SURVIVAL SKILL

Although essay exams are challenging, learning to succeed on them is essential. Consider essay-exam writing as a college "survival skill." In fact, researchers estimate that over 50% of the writing you do throughout school will take place on exams (Applebee 1984; Meiser 1982). More and more colleges across the country have begun to include substantial writing requirements not just in English but in many kinds of courses. The instructors of these courses often believe that an exam that requires you to write is the best way to assess what you have learned. Learning to write well in a time-pressured environment enhances your writing ability in general by helping you become comfortable with a wider variety of writing tasks.

HOW ESSAY EXAMS ARE DIFFERENT

Recognizing that writing essay exams is important, you may be wondering how to develop your skills in this area. You may ask, "How is it possible to write a polished essay in less than an hour?" or, "I always study hard for exams, but what if I'm just not good at taking tests?" An encouraging thing to remember is that you already know a lot about how to write well on an exam. Most of the writing assignments you've done in this book require you to write to a particular audience, in an organized way, using facts and examples to support your focus. A successful exam essay has these same qualities, so many of the skills you have in these areas are likely to be helpful on a test. For instance, you already know how to consider the characteristics and needs of your audience before you begin writing a paper. You can transfer this same knowledge successfully in a test situation by thinking about your instructor: What kinds of information is this instructor likely to be looking for? What topics in the course has the instructor stressed the most? Is this person likely to be more concerned with what is in the textbook or with your own interpretations and opinions? These kinds of questions can help you focus your exam responses in much the same way as thinking about the intended audience helps you focus an out-of-class paper.

However, essay exams differ from other types of writing in some fundamental ways, so not all the processes you use in writing out-of-class papers will be successful in a test situation. Three of these different skills are particularly important:

1.   learning to memorize and recall appropriate content material for the essay;

2.   learning to analyze the exam questions and tailor your essay to fit the question's requirements; and

3.   dealing with time pressure, anxiety and other restraints that are part of the test setting.

Being aware of these skills and using the following suggestions to practice them will help you refine your writing process to fit the essay exam situation.

THE ESSAY-EXAM WRITING PROCESS

Preparing for an Exam: Learning and Recalling Course Information

One unique aspect of essay-exam writing is that you have to rely solely on your memory for material to include in the essay. Think about the last time you wrote a paper outside of class. You may have used your memory to search for ideas or to explore your knowledge about the topic, but you also had access to other sources—the library, your textbook, or your classmates' input. In an exam, however, you are "on your own." This can be difficult, since most exams cover many pages of readings and lecture notes, and because you do not know beforehand exactly what the instructor will ask you to write about. Preparing for an exam, then, involves finding efficient ways to organize, memorize, and recall what you know.

Of course, no instructor expects you to remember every single fact covered in class. Instead, most educational research suggests that teachers want students to remember main ideas, key concepts, and a few supporting examples (Popken 1989; Breland 1983). These should be your focus as you prepare for an essay exam—figure out what these are and learn them first, saving less important information for later. How do you determine what the main points and key ideas in a course are? Sometimes these are obvious. Some instructors outline their lectures on the board or provide "study outlines" before a test, making it easy to know what material is essential. Even without such guides, though, most instructors provide clues about what they believe is central. Listen to the organization of course lectures to determine key concepts and the relationships between them, for instance:

> "the three stages of photosynthesis are . . . ; "there is a major educational debate between the proponents of evolution and those of creationism . . . ;" "four developments contributed to the re-emergence of English after the Norman invasion . . . ;" "the most important studies of gender-role development are . . ."

Look for similar divisions in your textbook and course readings, paying special attention to chapter summaries, subheadings, and highlighted terms. These clues not only help you choose what material to study, but also give you a framework for remembering the information, making the studying process more manageable.

Once you have an idea of the concepts and facts you will need to memorize, develop a study plan. If you are unsure about how to organize your study time, consider one or more of these suggestions.

1. Write down a few questions you think are likely to appear on the exam, then write practice responses. Show your practice responses to a classmate or to your instructor well in advance of the exam, and ask for feedback.

2. Review previous exams given by an instructor. Many schools maintain "test libraries" that can provide these.

3. If you cannot obtain a previous exam, most instructors are willing to answer general questions about the type, length, and number of questions they normally include on tests.

4. Many students benefit from studying with classmates in pairs or groups. Group studying provides practice in talking about course material to others; also, feedback from group members may give you new ideas or help fill gaps in your understanding.

Of course, there are study techniques that are likely to be ineffective for most students. Don't waste time trying to reread all the material several times; instead, focus on grasping main ideas and a few supporting details. Similarly, avoid unfocused studying. Go through your notes and decide which information you want to concentrate on learning before you try to memorize anything. Without a plan, you may not cover the material thoroughly or evenly. Also, avoid unreasonable studying schedules. Don't procrastinate until one or two nights before the exam. This rarely allows enough time to learn the material adequately, and the accompanying anxiety caused by having to "cram" can hurt your performance even more. Another common mistake is to stay up all night studying—experts warn that this can be worse than not studying at all since sleep deprivation hinders your ability to recall and process information. Perhaps the most serious mistake, however, is to neglect daily coursework.

These suggestions should give you a general idea of how to develop a successful study plan. Remember, however, that you should tailor your studying process to suit your strengths and weaknesses as a student. For instance, if sitting in one place for several hours makes you restless, study for short periods each day for a week rather than studying the entire day before the exam. If you tend to procrastinate, schedule a group study session well in advance of the exam. If you have trouble remembering specific names and dates, make index cards and spend extra time reviewing these during each study session.

Before You Write: Analyzing the Exam Question

Another important difference between an out-of-class paper assignment and an essay exam is that exams usually require much more narrowly focused responses. Recall some of the papers you have written this quarter or semester. In most cases, your instructor probably assigned a broad subject, such as "Write a research paper on a current political controversy," or "Describe a person who strongly affected your life." When writing papers like these, you are free to choose several possible topics and numerous possible approaches. In an essay exam, however, questions are designed to elicit much more specific responses. The instructor will ask you to recall a particular body of information and present it in a particular way. A typical question might look like this: "Trace the development of the Civil Rights movement from 1950–1965, identifying its major leaders, strategies, and opponents." Here the instructor has singled out a particular body of information (leaders, strategies, and opponents of the Civil Rights movement from 1950–1965) and expects you to write about it in a narrowly defined way (trace the historical development). A response that failed to do all these things—for example, an essay which did not include information about strategies, or which did not cover the entire time frame—would be less successful. Instructors also do not usually give credit for information outside the scope of the question—for instance, an essay that discussed developments after 1965 or people who were not leaders or opponents. Obviously, learning to analyze exam questions to determine what the instructor is asking you to do and tailoring your essay to fit those requirements are vital parts of the exam writing process.

Exam questions can be intimidating because of their length and complexity. Consider the following example:

> Write an essay identifying four cultures that influenced the English language before 1476. Discuss the historical events and important people that led to each influence, then summarize and illustrate the specific linguistic effects each culture had on English.

This question contains an overwhelming number of instructions, but it becomes more manageable if you examine it in terms of the purposes defined in the previous paragraph: its purpose is to get students to write about specific <u>bodies of information</u> in specific <u>ways</u>. Imagine that you have encountered this question on a test. How should you go about analyzing it?

First, to determine which bodies of information to include in the essay, pick out the <u>noun phrases</u> in the question—"four cultures which influenced English," "historical events," "important people," "linguistic effects."

Second, to know what to do with that information, underline the verbs in the question—"identify," "discuss," "summarize," "illustrate." Once you have identified these elements, you know what you need to include in your answer—you need to choose four influencing cultures, along with some supporting details about events, people and linguistic effects. The underlined words may even give you an outline for organizing your essay; you should probably divide the essay into four parts, one about each culture.

The other words in the question may help you focus your response further but are not essential—you can probably safely ignore them if you find them confusing. You can analyze any exam question by extracting the relevant noun phrases and verbs. This strategy will help you focus on what the instructor is asking you to do and will make complicated questions seem less complex.

Once you know how to analyze an exam question, you may experience another problem: you may become flustered by unfamiliar vocabulary used in exam questions. Instructors use very specific words in essay exams—if they ask you to "compare," they want you to talk about the similarities between two things or ideas. They don't want you to "discuss" or "evaluate." If they ask you to "illustrate," they want you to give concrete examples, not generalizations. And they are unlikely to reward a student who writes a lengthy discussion when asked to give a "list" or "outline." Students unsure about the meanings of words used on exams may include irrelevant information or use inappropriate organization simply because they do not understand what the instructor is asking. You can avoid this problem by familiarizing yourself with common exam vocabulary like the following: apply, argue, cite, compare, contrast, criticize, define, demonstrate, discuss, enumerate, evaluate, explain, identify, illustrate, interpret, list, outline, prove, review, and summarize.

If any or all of these words seem confusing, start by looking them up in a dictionary. Then consult old exams, classmates, or your instructor to find out exactly what is expected when a particular term appears on an exam. Think about how the terms are different from each other. For instance, "discuss" probably indicates a more extensive response than does "summarize." Having good working definitions of these terms will both improve your analysis of exam questions and help you approach the test day with confidence.

Writing Exam Responses: Dealing with Constraints

Let's suppose that you have organized the course material, studied it thoroughly, analyzed the exam questions, and know what information to include in your response. These preparations play a large role, but one more skill is necessary to guarantee success on an essay exam: You must be able to work within the confines of a test situation. Think about how you write papers outside of class. Although you have the pressure of a deadline, you can do the actual writing wherever and however you wish. In an exam, you have to write well in a classroom, in an extremely short time, with no time for breaks or major revisions.

Two kinds of constraints affect students in an exam situation: test anxiety and time constraints. Text anxiety often arises because the exam situation is unfamiliar. For instance, many students become anxious when the test questions do not look familiar at first glance. Others lose their train of thought in the midst of writing and panic because they can't remember what to write next. Many such problems can be avoided simply by being aware beforehand of the kinds of disasters that can happen in a test situation and anticipating ways to handle them. Try to recall any recurring difficulties you have experienced in taking tests; then brainstorm ways to prevent them. If you panic when test questions look unfamiliar, make a deal with yourself to close your eyes and count to ten after reading through the exam for the first time. Then read the questions a second time, and start writing on the one that looks easiest. If the mere idea of an exam makes you nervous, try timing yourself on a couple of practice exams to accustom yourself to performing under pressure, or consider arriving at the test early to allow yourself time to become calm. What is important is that you become aware of your own potential problems and anticipate solutions. This process will increase your confidence and decrease the likelihood that you will experience too much test anxiety.

Perhaps the hardest constraint to deal with in an exam is the lack of time. Most writers produce their best work only after several drafts. However, there is no time for major revision on most exams. Instead, you must focus on streamlining your writing process. Careful planning will help you do this. After you have analyzed the exam question carefully, take a minute or two to jot down a quick outline or a few organizational notes. This will help you as you write the essay by giving you a sense of direction and making sure you remember what points to cover. It will also speed the drafting process as you will not have to pause after each paragraph and decide what to include next.

Once you have a plan, decide how much time you have to complete the essay. Always budget your time wisely. Many students' grades have suffered because they slighted several questions in order to spend extra time on one. Divide the number of minutes you have to complete the exam by the number of points the question is worth to give you a time guideline (for example, on a question worth 40 of 100 points on a 60-minute exam you should spend around 24 minutes). Monitor the clock as you write, and skip minor points and details if you begin to run behind. If you cannot finish a response in the allotted time, stop. You may have time to return to it later. If not, write a brief note directing your instructor to your original notes or outline; let him or her know that you stopped writing because of time, not because you lacked knowledge of the topic.

You can also save time by eliminating writing features that are unlikely to enhance your grade. Don't bother to copy each exam question onto your paper; instead, write the number or a few key words that can serve as a cue to your instructor. Also, most instructors will not expect dramatic, polished opening and closing paragraphs or artistically constructed sentences. They would rather you concentrate on providing a clear thesis statement, then explain and illustrate your main points fully and coherently. Another effective technique is to double-space your essay. This leaves room to insert information or correct minor errors without having to tear out and recopy an entire page. Finally, even if you know a lot about a question, avoid writing more than is needed. Keep your response within the confines of the question. These techniques will help you concentrate on drafting the clearest, most purposeful response possible in the time allowed.

Facing Future Exams

Even if you follow all the suggestions offered in this chapter, you may still find essay-exam writing unfamiliar and uncomfortable for a while. Essay exams are a unique writing situation, and it takes experience and practice to develop a successful approach. It is worth the effort, though. You already know that well written essay exams can improve your grades in college courses. More importantly, however, essay exam skills give you new ways of learning, internalizing, and talking about the issues and ideas covered in your courses—thereby increasing what you get out of your education.

The exercises in the remainder of this chapter will give you additional opportunities to work on your essay exam skills. ■

WORKS CITED AND CONSULTED

Anderson, T. H. and B. B. Armbruster. "Studying." *Handbook of Reading Research*. Ed. P. David Pearson. New York: Longman Press, 1984.

Applebee, A. N. *Contexts for Learning to Write: Studies of Secondary School Instruction*. Norwood, New Jersey: ABLEX, 1984.

Breland, H. M. and R. J. Jones. "Perceptions of Writing Skills." *Written Composition* 1 (1983): 101–119.

Meiser, M. "Survival Skills: Learning to Write the Essay Exam." *Wisconsin English Journal* 21 (1982): 20–23.

Popken, R. "Essay Exams and Papers: A Contextual Comparison." *Journal of Teaching Writing* 8 (1989): 51–65.

Simon, H. A., and J. R. Hayes. "Understanding Complex Task Instructions." *Cognition and Instruction*. Ed. David Klahr. Hillsdale, NJ: Erlbaum, 1976.

C: Post-Reading

Discussion Suggestions/Questions

Remembering

1. What percentage of the writing that students do in school takes place in exam situations?

2. What two kinds of constraints affect well-prepared students in essay exam situations?

Analyzing

1. Christy Friend's essay is long and complex. Working alone or with others, make an outline of the essay that includes major concerns and subpoints she makes under each concern.

2. In small groups discuss any words or advice in the reading that you found useful or confusing. Use your outlines of the essay to guide your discussion.

Discovering

1. Christy Friend, the author of the reading, writes that one key to success on essay exams is good study skills. Working with others, make a list of strategies people use while studying for essay exams. Feel free to include strategies from the reading and from your own experience. To make your efforts more coherent, you might use the list below of resources for students. The question is how <u>you</u> make good use of each of these resources.

1. textbooks_____
   _____
   _____
   _____

2. lecture notes_____
   _____
   _____
   _____

3. study groups_____
   _____
   _____
   _____

4. the instructor_____
   _____
   _____
   _____

2.   Christy Friend mentions many ways students can waste time while studying for or writing essay exams. With others, talk about some of these "time wasters" and how you can avoid them.

D: Vocabulary Building

1. Two different meanings of *re-*

Reconstruct: "They want to see if you can sort out important concepts from class lectures or readings and **reconstruct** these concepts in your own words."

Friend: "Learning to Succeed Under Pressure"

The verb *reconstruct* consists of the prefix *re-*, "again," plus the verb to **construct**. The verb to *construct* comes from the Latin verb *construere*, which meant "to put together." This verb is also the source of the noun **structure**. The noun form of to *construct* is **construction**, and the adjective form is **constructive**, which means "positive" or "helpful," as in "We appreciated their constructive criticism."

The prefix **re-** is added to verbs. It has two different meanings. With some verbs, **re-** means to "do again" or to "start over again," as, for example, in the sentences "We **restarted** the engine," and "The officials **recounted** the ballots." *Restarted* means to start over again, and *recounted* means to count over again.

With other verbs, *re-* has a different meaning. With these verbs, *re-* means to "go back" or to "restore something back to its original condition." Here are some examples of these meanings. To **return** means to "go back," as in the sentence "I returned home." To **replace** means "to put something back in its original position," as in "Alice replaced the box on the shelf." Likewise, to **repossess** means to get back, as in "The loan company repossessed the car after I had missed some payments."

Sometimes the same verb can be used with either meaning of *re-*. For example, compare the two meanings of **recover** in the following sentences: (a) "We recovered the couch with new material," and (b) "The police recovered our couch from the burglars who had taken it." In sentence (a), *recover* means to "cover again." In sentence (b), *recover* means "to get back."

Vocabulary Building Activity 1: The Two Different Meanings of *Re-*

In the left column are sentences containing a verb beginning with the prefix *re-*. In the space provided, write "*Again*" if the basic meaning of *re-* is to do again or repeat; write "**Back**" if the basic meaning of *re-* is to restore or get back or go back. The first two questions are done as examples.

	Again/Back
1. We had to **recalk** the seams.	*Again*
2. We **reclaimed** our luggage.	*Back*
3. We **reconfirmed** our reservation.	_____
4. We **retraced** our footsteps.	_____
5. The officials had to **restart** the race.	_____
6. The tide was **receding**.	_____
7. The soldiers **reloaded** their rifles.	_____
8. We **repaid** the loan in full.	_____
9. I **reinjured** my ankle.	_____
10. I **regained** full motion in my ankle.	_____

2. Changing nouns to adjectives by adding *-ic*

> <u>Strategies</u>: ". . . identifying its major leaders, **strategies**, and opponents."
> *Friend: "Learning to Succeed Under Pressure"*

The noun *strategy* comes from a Greek word that meant "generalship" in the broadest sense of applying economic, social, and political forces to support a military policy or goal. We often use *strategy* to mean a carefully prepared overall plan for obtaining some goal, as in the sentence "The company developed a marketing strategy for its new product line." The adjective form of *strategy* is **strategic**. *Strategic* means something that is important in terms of the overall picture. For example, an army that engages in a strategic retreat is retreating, not because it was defeated by an enemy, but because some overall plan requires it to do so.

The **-ic** ending that changes the noun *strategy* to the adjective *strategic* comes from the Latin suffix *-icus*, which was one of the main ways of changing nouns to adjectives in Latin. Unfortunately for us, however, the process of changing nouns to adjectives with *-icus* was quite complicated, so that the resulting adjective forms come out in unexpected ways. Using *-ic* to change nouns into adjectives has some surprising results.

One kind of surprising result is in the different ways that the noun and the corresponding *-ic* adjective are pronounced. For example, compare the pronunciation of the nouns **mel**ody and **an**gel with their *-ic* adjective forms **mel**od**ic** and **an**gel**ic**. Most of the differences in pronunciation between nouns and *-ic* adjectives are due to a strange shift in the placement of stress with *-ic* adjectives. You can figure out the rule for placing stress with *-ic* adjectives from the following exercise.

Vocabulary Building Activity 2: Stress Rule for *-ic* Adjectives

The following are pairs of related words. Nouns are in the left column, and related *-ic* adjectives are in the right column. The stress is marked for all the nouns. Say the adjectives aloud, and underline the part of the adjective that is stressed. After you have worked through all the adjectives, see if you can state the rule that determines where the stress goes in *-ic* adjectives. The first two questions are done as examples.

Noun	Adjective
1. <u>I</u>taly	it<u>a</u>lic
2. <u>id</u>iom	idio<u>ma</u>tic
3. dip<u>lo</u>macy	diplomatic
4. <u>a</u>pathy	apathetic
5. <u>te</u>lephone	telephonic
6. ro<u>man</u>ce	romantic
7. <u>sa</u>tire	satiric
8. <u>al</u>cohol	alcoholic
9. <u>sy</u>mbol	symbolic
10. de<u>mo</u>cracy	democratic

A second way in which the *-ic* suffix is odd is that it may affect the spelling of the word it attaches to in unusual ways. For example, some adjectives insert the letter **t** between the noun and the *-ic* ending, as in **gene/genetic**. Other adjectives insert a vowel between the noun and the *-ic* ending, as in **idiom/idiomatic**. Probably the strangest is the change of the noun **giant** to the adjective **gigantic**.

Vocabulary Building Activity 3: Changing Nouns to Adjectives by Adding *-ic*

In the left column is a list of nouns. Change these nouns to adjectives by adding *-ic*. Write the *-ic* adjective form in the space provided in the right column. The first two questions have been done as examples.

Noun	Adjective
1. prose	*prosaic*
2. error	*erratic*
3. energy	
4. metal	
5. magnet	
6. system	
7. science	
8. number	
9. Asia	
10. theme	

SECTION 2

Understanding Essay Exam Prompts and Organizing Your Response

Another term for an essay exam question is a "prompt." Prompts take many forms, but prompts for essay exams always include key words that tell the student what is expected in his or her response. Since failing to understand the prompt is a major pitfall for students, the first goal here is to review some of the key words that appear in prompts for essay exams.

Of course, essay exam prompts can take many forms. Whole books have been written to help students practice responding to essay exam prompts. Here, however, the lessons will focus on the most common type of essay exam prompt, the type of prompt you will probably see the most often. Fortunately, many different key words in essay exam prompts ask for the same kind of response; they ask students to recall and illustrate concepts they have found in the material they studied.

For example, a teacher might ask students "to identify the three main ideas in Chapter 4 of the textbook and to illustrate each idea with an example." This prompt asks for an essay that takes the following form:

Paragraph 1 (introduction)
There are three main ideas in chapter four. They are
(1)_____   (2)_____   (3)_____
Paragraph 2
The first main idea is _____.
Define the main idea.
Give an example that illustrates or supports the idea.
Paragraph 3
The second main idea is _____.
Define the main idea.
Give an example that illustrates or supports the idea.
Paragraph 4
The third main idea is _____.
Define the main idea.
Give an example that illustrates or supports the idea.
Paragraph 5 (conclusion)
These three ideas are important (or useful) because _____.

Yes, this is the old five-paragraph essay form taught in schools for over one hundred years. It is simple. It is popular. It works. Even when the prompt asks for four, five, six, or eight "main ideas," "key concepts," or "important terms," this kind of response in this kind of form is appropriate. You simply have more paragraphs between your introduction and your conclusion.

Not surprisingly, most teachers give essay exams to find out if students have memorized and understood the contents of the material those students have studied. Therefore, while the words included in the prompts may vary, many prompts ask for the same kind of response.

Look now at the following prompts:

1. "List the key terms in Chapter 4 of your textbook, and apply each to a particular situation."

2. "Enumerate the main ideas in Chapter 4 of the text, and demonstrate each with an example from your own experience."

3. "Recall and discuss the main concepts presented in Chapter 4 of your textbook."

4. "Define and develop the important ideas included in Chapter 4 of your text-book."

Although the wording varies among these four prompts, all four ask for the same thing—for the student to define key ideas and give a supporting example for each that shows the teacher that the student understands the ideas.

Even when the prompt does not ask for examples, illustrations, applications, or discussion, teachers expect to see them.

Look at the following possible prompts:

1. "Enumerate the key concepts in Chapter 4."

2. "Outline the main ideas in Chapter 4 of your textbook."

3. "Discuss the important points presented in Chapter 4."

4. "Review the key terms presented in Chapter 4."

5. "Summarize the contents of Chapter 4."

6. "Explain the main ideas presented in Chapter 4."

All six of these prompts ask for the kind of essay form that names, defines, and then illustrates each term, idea, or concept with a supporting example.

SECTION

3

Studying for and Writing an Essay Exam

Pre-Writing Activity 1: Reading for Understanding

The following reading, "Packages," is a chapter from a college textbook entitled *Age of Propaganda: The Everyday Use and Abuse of Persuasion* by Anthony Prakanis and Elliot Aronson. This textbook is used in first year community college and university communications courses.

Please read "Packages." Since understanding a reading is the first step in studying it, have a notepad, pen or pencil, and dictionary handy while reading. Then, when you run across a word you do not know, write it down, look it up in your dictionary, and then copy down the dictionary definition. This takes time, but it is an excellent study strategy. Keep this list of words and definitions. You will use it soon.

*"Packages"** *

BY ANTHONY PRAKANIS AND
ELLIOT ARONSON

The cereal aisle at the local supermarket is the battleground for many a weekly war of words. The battle usually goes something like this: Seven year-old Rachel spots her favorite cereal, Lucky Charms, picks up a box from the shelf and quietly delivers it to the shopping cart. Her mom looks at the box in disgust. It is bright red. A leprechaun is sprinkling shining stars (must be sugar) over pink and purple marshmallow bits. On the back of the box she reads that a special pair of glasses is enclosed to be used in spotting hidden leprechauns.

Mom sternly announces, "Rachel, put that junk back on the shelf. It's loaded with sugar and nothing but empty calories."

Rachel replies, "But Mom, it tastes good. The other stuff tastes yukky."

Being a smart mom, she offers Rachel another choice and a little inducement, "Why not this one? It's 100% Natural. It's good for you. You'll be a big girl."

Rachel looks at the box. It is small, but heavy. The front features a bowl of light brown cereal set against a wood-grain background and a couple of stalks of unprocessed grains. On the back of the box is a lot of small print.

Rachel exclaims, "Yukko! I don't want to be a big girl."

How would you resolve the great breakfast cereal standoff? Would you side with the mother and opt for nutrition even though Rachel may not eat it? Or would you feel that Rachel, even at this young age, should be making her own decisions regardless of the consequences? Our recommendation may surprise you. The fight is for naught. Tell Rachel and her mom to buy the Lucky Charms because, quite truthfully, it is more nutritional than the "natural" cereal.

Every year Americans spend roughly $6.9 billion on breakfast cereals. In 1981, *Consumer Reports*, a highly respected source of consumer information, conducted a test of some of these breakfast cereals.[1] Their researchers fed young rats, which have nutritional requirements remarkably similar to humans, an exclusive diet of water and one of thirty-two brands of breakfast cereals for a period of fourteen to eighteen weeks. They found that the rats grew and remained quite healthy on a diet of such cereals as Cheerios, Grapenuts, Life, Shredded Wheat, and Lucky Charms. On the other hand, fifteen ready-to-eat cereals such as Captain Crunch, Corn Flakes, Product

DRAFTING

19, and Quaker's 100% Natural either prevented the rats from growing or were judged to be not sufficiently nourishing to support life.

A comparison between Lucky Charms and 100% Natural shows that Lucky Charms is lower in calories but slightly higher in sodium and sugar than 100% Natural, although the differences probably do not matter very much. 100% Natural, like many granola-style cereals, is higher in saturated fats, which raise blood cholesterol levels. Whereas Lucky Charms contains no saturated fat, a cup of 100% Natural is equivalent in fat content to about a half a rack of greasy spare ribs.[2]

What caused the disagreement between Rachel and her mom? It is clear that they used the cereal package (not the cereal) as what is technically called a *heuristic*—a simple cue or rule for solving a problem. In this case, the problem for Mom was to select a nutritious cereal; for Rachel the problem was to get a cereal that is fun and tasty. The bright colors, the cartoon character, and the kids' game on the box of Lucky Charms suggest that this cereal is for kids—and we all know that kids' food is junk food. On the other hand, the earth tones and pictures of unprocessed grains on the 100% Natural box indicate that this cereal is "all-natural" (even the brand name agrees). Nature is good and wholesome; this cereal must be nutritious. In both cases, the cereal packages were designed so that Rachel and her mom would infer certain attributes about the products—qualities that may or may not be present. Armed with these conclusions, the choice of which cereal to purchase can proceed without much additional thought; persuasion occurs in the peripheral route.

Marketers have been using packages to guide consumer decision making for nearly a century. Since the 1890s, Quaker Oats has been boxing rolled oats in a container with a picture of a religious Quaker to suggest the purity and consistency of their breakfast cereal. In 1898 a man named C. W. Post reinforced the image of a healthy breakfast food by enclosing a copy of the pamphlet "The Road to Wellville" in each box of Grape-Nuts cereal. Sales took off. Packaging is such a successful heuristic device that generic and store brands often try to take advantage of it by making their packages—the color of their labels, the shape of the container, and so on—resemble the bestselling national brands.

Other heuristics are also used to encourage consumers to infer product quality and thus buy a particular brand. Three of the most important are price, store image, and brand name. Each heuristic comes with its own rules for inferring product quality. For example, the higher the price, the better the quality—which is probably true when it comes to such products as Yugos and Rolls Royces, but not necessarily the case for wines, medicines, sport sneakers, prepackaged foods, and a host of other products. The same pair of jeans looks better in a high-class department store than in the local discount mart. Nationally recognized brand names are deemed superior to store brands and generics. In addition, advertisers spend vast sums of money to link their brand name to a brand-specific proposition, such as "Michelob is classy" or "Bud is for the everyday working Joe" to guide our supermarket visit.

DRAFTING

Persons can be packaged too. The first information that we typically pick up about a person—gender, age, race, physical attractiveness, and social status—is usually associated with simple rules and stereotypes that guide thought and behavior. Gender and racial stereotypes tell us "just how men and women differ" and "what a particular member of an ethnic group is like." Much research has demonstrated that beautiful people are assumed to be more successful, more sensitive, warmer, and of better character than less physically appealing persons and that we often act in accord with those assumptions. Persons of high social stature, often inferred by dress and mannerisms, are respected and held in high esteem. Is it any wonder that "get-ahead" self-help books often describe how to take advantage of these heuristics by urging their readers to "dress for success"—that is to wear the *right* clothes to create the *right* image or to use the *right* cosmetics to enhance their attractiveness?

Heuristics can also be used to judge whether a persuasive communication is worthy of acceptance and belief. In [a] prior section . . . we looked in detail at one such heuristic—the source of the message. We saw that, in general, the more credible, attractive, or expert the source, the more effective is the communication; we also saw that we are more likely to use the source to guide our opinions if we are operating in the peripheral, as opposed to central, route of persuasion.

There are other persuasion heuristics. For example, the advertisers John Caples and David Ogilvy argue that advertisements are most effective when they contain long compelling copy—in other words a long message with many arguments. Obviously, such a message would be more effective than a short message containing weak arguments—*if the message is read*. But what about cases where the message is only skimmed or not read at all? According to research in social psychology, when people are not thinking very carefully about an issue, long messages, regardless of whether they contain weak or strong arguments, are most persuasive.[3] It appears that we operate on the principle that "message length *equals* message strength." If the message is long, it must be important.

If you have watched commercial programming, those half-hour "shows" that feature knives, blenders, cleansers, and sandwich makers for sale, you have seen another persuasion cue in action. These shows inevitably feature a "daring" demonstration of the product—a knife cutting up an old tennis shoe and then slicing a tomato perfectly, a blender making mayonnaise from scratch, or a magic powder removing a difficult stain. What is the audience's reaction? At first there is murmuring, as disbelief fills the air with tension. And then the audience, acting as one, bursts into loud, thunderous applause.

The thunderous clapping and cheering serve as a *social consensus* heuristic—a cue that says "everyone accepts the conclusion of this message, so you should too!" Recognition of the power of the applause-makes-right heuristic leads politicians to schedule major talks in favorable settings, television producers to insert canned laughter and applause, advertisers to use testimonials and portray their products as being in great demand. Once again, the evidence shows, social consensus heuristics are most likely to have an impact when people are unmotivated to think about a message's meaning.[4]

Another common persuasion heuristic is based on the confidence of the speaker—the more self-assured and confident a communicator appears, the more likely that we will accept what is said. Research on trial testimony in courts of law, for example, has found that juries are more likely to believe testimony when it is given by an eyewitness or expert who exudes confidence. Similarly, nonverbal behavior that suggests confidence in the message, such as a low rate of speech errors, an authoritative tone of voice, and a steady body posture, are positively related to persuasion.

Another frequently used persuasion tactic is to load a speech with the "correct" symbols and buzzwords as a means of informing the recipient that the message is acceptable and worthwhile. For example, car dealers and politicians often appear with the flag or invoke God, as if to say, "My position is patriotic and religious, so it is worthy of acceptance." Of course, history reveals that just about any scoundrel can wrap him- or herself in the flag—usually for personal profit, not for the nation's best interest.

Often the symbols and buzzwords are tailored to a specific audience. One craze that is currently sweeping some regions of the country is "PC"—political correctness. PC is a fast-changing set of symbols, phrases, and actions that, when properly used, lets everyone know that the message is right and the communicator is doing the right thing. To gain acceptance, one should not wear fur in public; one should always say "he or she"—never the generic "he"; one should eat free-range chicken, not formula-fed, assembly-line chicken; one should never eat veal; one should use cloth, not disposable, diapers; one should demand paper bags at the grocery store—never plastic; above all, one should not provide a critique intolerant of PC.

Never mind that some of the rules are contradictory and ineffective. For example, if fur is unacceptable, why not forgo leather? It has been argued that paper bags, unless they are recycled, produce more environmental waste than plastic and that cloth diapers result in more pollution in their manufacturing and cleaning than do disposables and greatly disadvantage working and single parents. But that is the nature of heuristics—they aren't meant to be thought about, lest they appear as silly as applauding a sliced tomato.

Consider the case of McDonald's.[5] In the early 1970s, environmentalists launched a campaign criticizing McDonald's for its use of paperboard packaging. Ray Kroc, McDonald's founder, commissioned the Stanford Research Institute to conduct a study comparing the environmental impact of different forms of packaging. The study concluded that when all aspects of the issue were considered—from manufacturing to disposal—polystyrene is better for the environment than paper. When paper and cardboard are used for food, they must be coated with a plastic film, making them nearly unrecyclable. The manufacture of polystyrene uses less energy and conserves more natural resources than does the production of paper, and polystyrene takes up less room in landfills and is recyclable. The infamous McDonald's clamshell was born.

In the 1980s, environmentalists raised another, quite legitimate, concern: the manufacturing of polystyrene releases chlorofluorocarbons, which contribute to the destruction of the earth's ozone layer. In 1987, McDonald's directed its polystyrene suppliers to eliminate chlorofluorocarbons from their manufacturing process. However, the clamshell had become a symbol of environmental irresponsibility and McDonald's, in response to pressure groups, ceased using it in the early 1990s, returning to unrecyclable, plastic-coated paper wrappers. Ironically, McDonald's image of being "concerned about the environment" has suffered because it was responsive to environmental concerns. One of McDonald's competitors, which did not respond to earlier pressures to adopt the clamshell, actually ran ads claiming that they had always used cardboard out of concern for the environment. In truth, many American households and businesses would find it difficult to compete with McDonald's record on the environment. McDonald's earmarks 25% of its capital budget ($100 million) for purchasing recycled building materials (thus helping to create this industry), allocates $60 million to purchase recycled paper products, and recently announced forty-two initiatives aimed at holding down the volume of garbage at its restaurants by more than 80%. The destruction of the environment is a complex problem, requiring more than just symbolic finger-pointing and heuristic thinking to resolve.

Of course, as we have stressed earlier, persuasion does not have to be peripheral and decisions do not have to be based on heuristics. Rachel's parents could carefully read the ingredients on the cereal box, subscribe to a consumer magazine, or consult nutrition textbooks. Similarly, we could base our judgment of what a politician is saying not on buzzwords, audience reactions, and source demeanor, but on the actual content and implications of the message itself.

This raises an important question: What conditions are most likely to lead to heuristic rather than rational decision making? Research has identified at least five such conditions.[6] Heuristics are most likely to be used when we do not have *time to* think carefully about an issue, when we are *so overloaded with information* that it becomes impossible to process it fully, or when we believe that the issues at stake are *not very important*. Heuristics are also used when we have *little other knowledge or information* on which to base a decision and when a given heuristic *comes quickly to mind* as we are confronted with a problem.

A moment's thought will reveal that the persuasion landscape faced by Rachel and her parents contains many of the features that lead to heuristic decision making. If they are like most Americans, Rachel and her family are feeling increasingly pressed for time, since their leisure time has eroded considerably in the last ten years. As consumers, they face a message-dense environment complete with a choice of, for example, more than 300 different brands of cereal currently on the market. They probably have had little consumer education or training. They have been, however, the recipients of millions of advertisements each repeating and repeating a brand image so that this image will quickly come to mind in the aisles of the local supermarket. Given this state of affairs, it is a wonder that *all* decisions are not made heuristically.

One of the dilemmas of modern life is that with decreasing leisure time, increasing information, and increasing choices, we must rely more and more on heuristic decision making. Although relying on heuristics is sometimes a useful way of dealing with the onslaught of the message-dense, decision-rich environment, basing our decisions primarily on heuristics can present some problems.

First, the heuristic cues that we possess may be false. There is little reason to assume that brand images and ethnic stereotypes have a reliable basis in fact. Relying on such heuristics may result in the purchase of an unwanted product and the missed opportunity to hire a qualified employee or fall in love with that special person. Furthermore, a rule may be appropriate in certain situations, but be misapplied in others. For example, spontaneous, legitimate audience applause can signal that this is an entertaining show worthy of our attention. Canned laughter does not.

Another serious problem is that heuristics can be easily faked and manipulated. Cereal boxes can be redesigned to look increasingly wholesome. Laughter and applause can be dubbed into a broadcast. Politicians can be coached to exude winning mannerisms. Physical attractiveness can be improved with makeup and surgery. Speeches and advertisements can be peppered with buzzwords and symbols. Anyone with a little cash can buy a new blazer and a sincere tie. The essence of propaganda is a well-designed package.

What can be done to lessen our dependence on faulty heuristics? One attempt to forestall these concerns is to enact legislation to insure that the cues that we do use—for example, phrases on product labels such as "low calorie," "low sodium," or "100% nutritious"—are accurate and are applied correctly. In recent days, the Federal Trade Commission has attempted to establish guidelines for the use of such labels as "low fat" and "environmentally safe." (Currently they can mean just about anything.) This, along with other efforts to improve the quality of product information, is a step in the right direction. However, such efforts are unlikely to succeed in stamping out heuristic thinking. After all, no government, no matter how vigilant, can protect us from our own prejudices. In the long run, we must depend on our own knowledge of propaganda tactics and our own efforts to treat important issues as if they were truly important. ■

Prakanis, Anthony R., and Elliot Aronson. *Age of Propaganda: The Everyday Use and Abuse of Persuasion*. New York: W. H. Freeman and Company, 1991: 115–123.

WORKS CITED

1. "Which cereal for breakfast?" *Consumer Reports*, February 1981. 68–75.

2. Comparison based on "Eating to Lower Your High Blood Cholesterol," U.S. Department of Health and Human Services, NIH Publication No. 87-2920, September 1987. Saturated fats, such as animal fat, and some vegetable fats, such as coconut oil, cocoa butter, palm oil, and hydrogenated oil, have been shown to raise cholesterol levels. Cereal manufacturers sometimes use such fats, especially coconut, palm, and hydrogenated oil in their products. Many manufacturers are in the process of reformulating their cereals to remove such oils, so check the label before making a final decision.

3. Petty, R. E., and J. T. Cacioppo. "The Effects of Involvement on Responses to Argument Quantity and Quality: Central and Peripheral Routes to Persuasion." *Journal of Personality and Social Psychology* 46 (1984): 69–81.

4. Axsom, D., S. Yates, and S. Chaiken. "Audience Response As a Heuristic Cue in Persuasion." *Journal of Personality and Social Psychology* 53 (1987): 30–40.

5. Fierman, J. "The Big Muddle in Green Marketing." *Fortune* 3 June 1991: 91–101; Hume, S. "McDonald's." *Advertising Age* 29 Jan. 1991: 32.

6. Pratkanis, A. R. "The Cognitive Representation of Attitudes." *Attitude Structure and Function*. Ed. A. R. Pratkanis, S. J. Breckler, and A. G. Greenwald. Hillsdale, NJ: Erlbaum, 1989. 71–98.

Pre-Writing Activity 2: Studying Effectively

Writing good essay exams requires, first and foremost, good study skills. Understanding the information, identifying key concepts, and memorizing those key concepts are all very good study skills. A person learns these skills by practicing them, and that is what you are asked to do next.

Since organized information is easier to study and remember, make an outline of the textbook chapter, "Packages." Since this is a long and complex chapter, it might help you to know a few things about the chapter before you outline it:

1. The chapter is about "heuristics." The first step in making your outline, therefore, is to define the word "heuristics."

2. The authors present ten types of heuristics. You need to list and define each one. Including an example, either from the reading or from your own experience, with each heuristic on your outline will make each easier to remember.

3.   Late in the chapter, the authors discuss conditions in which heuristics work. List these in your outline.

4.   Finally, the authors suggest ways people can guard against heuristics. List these.

Pre-Writing Activity 3: Studying with Peers

In her essay, "Learning to Succeed Under Pressure: Essay Exam Strategies," Christy Friend suggests studying with your peers in small groups. Doing just that is the next pre-writing activity.

1.   In small groups of four to six people, share and discuss your outlines of "Packages." Include as many examples of each heuristic in your discussion as possible. These examples may come from the chapter studied, but examples from your own experience tend to be more interesting and more easily remembered.

2.   Next, still using your outlines, discuss where and why these heuristics work.

3.   Finally, share ideas about how people can guard against being misled by heuristics.

You don't need to be a weatherperson to see which way the wind blows. You have already figured out that your instructor will ask you to write an essay exam covering the ideas presented in the textbook chapter "Packages." Use the pre-writing strategies you have practiced here and any other study strategies you find helpful to prepare yourself for this exam. Review the essay exam form presented in the introduction to **Section 2** in this chapter.

You might also try to imagine what kinds of essay prompts you might be given for this exam and then make an outline of your responses to one or two of these prompts.

Your instructor will write the essay exam prompt and set the time for this exam. Remember to budget your study time well.

Final Editing for Relative Clauses

Relative clauses (also known as **adjective clauses**) modify nouns. Relative clauses begin with **relative pronouns** (*who/whom/whose*, *that*, and *which*). Here are some examples of sentences containing relative clauses. The relative clauses are underlined, and the relative pronouns are in bold:

1. They identified the person **who** who won the lottery.

2. She married a man **whom** she met at college.

3. They called the person **whose** turn was next.

4. The office **that** is on the fourth floor has a nice view of the lake.

5. Susan's office, **which** is on the fourth floor, has a nice view of the lake.

A: Punctuating Restrictive and Nonrestrictive Clauses

Notice that the relative clause in sentence (5) is punctuated differently from the relative clauses in the other four sentences. The relative clause in sentence (5) is separated from the noun it modifies by commas. There are two different ways of punctuating relative clauses because relative clauses have two completely different kinds of relationships to the nouns that they modify.

One type of relative clause actually **defines** the noun that it modifies. For example, let's compare sentence (4) with what the author might have written, sentence (4a):

4. The office **that** is on the fourth floor has a nice view of the lake.

4a. The office has a nice view of the lake.

The reason the author chose to write sentence (4) rather than sentence (4a) is that the writer would be afraid that the reader would not know **which** office the author was talking about. Therefore, the author **defined** which office he or she was writing about by adding the relative clause *that is on the fourth floor*. This type of relative clause is called a

EDITING

restrictive **relative clause** because it "restricts" or defines the meaning of the noun it modifies. **Restrictive clauses are never separated from the nouns they define by commas.**

The other type of relative clause does not define. This type of modifier provides supplementary information about a noun that has already been defined. Let's look again at sentence (5):

5.　Susan's office, <u>**which** is on the fourth floor</u>, has a nice view of the lake.

The reader of sentence (5) knows which office the author is writing about—it is **Susan's** office. Telling the reader that Susan's office is on the fourth floor doesn't further define which office the author is writing about (since we assume that Susan has only one office). Thus the relative clause *which is on the fourth floor* is supplementary, non-defining information about Susan's office. This type of relative clause is called a **nonrestrictive relative clause** because it does not restrict or define the noun it modifies. **Nonrestrictive clauses are always separated from the nouns they modify by commas.**

The punctuation of relative clauses makes it easy for the reader to tell whether a relative clause is restrictive or nonrestrictive. However, it is not so easy for an author to tell when a relative clause the author is writing is restrictive or nonrestrictive. The following scenario may help you make the correct choice in your own writing.

Imagine that you are writing a story in which you are describing a castle courtyard as it might appear by moonlight. The clause underlying the relative clause is in parentheses because you haven't yet decided whether it is restrictive or nonrestrictive.

6.　The moon **(the moon was just rising above the towers)** brightly lit the far wall of the castle courtyard.

In sentence (6) the underlying clause *the moon was just rising above the towers* modifies the noun *moon*. Since there is only one moon, the fact that the moon was just rising above the towers does not serve to further identify *which* moon we are talking about. Therefore, this relative clause is nonrestrictive and must be punctuated with commas:

6a.　The moon, **which was just rising above the towers,** brightly lit the far wall of the castle courtyard.

Now imagine that you are writing a science fiction story set on a planet that has three moons. Since there is more than one moon on this planet, the relative clause in sentence (6) takes on a completely different meaning. The relative clause tells us **which one** of the three moons lit the courtyard—it was the moon that was just rising above the towers (as opposed to the other two moons that were not rising above the towers at the moment). The clause is restrictive because it "restricts" or "narrows" the class of moons down to a single specific moon—the one that was just rising above the towers at this particular moment. Since the relative clause is restrictive, it cannot be separated from the noun it modifies by commas:

6b.   The moon **that was just rising above the towers** brightly lit the far wall of the castle courtyard.

The basic difference between a restrictive and a nonrestrictive modifier is this:

▲ A **restrictive** relative clause fundamentally changes the meaning of the noun it modifies by "restricting" the noun's meaning from a whole class to a specific, individual member of that class. Because it changes the meaning of the noun it modifies, a restrictive clause is permanently attached to the noun it modifies and can never be separated from it by commas.

▲ A **nonrestrictive** relative clause does not restrict the meaning of the noun it modifies because that noun already has a specific meaning independent of the relative clause. Therefore, the nonrestrictive relative clause is not permanently attached to the noun it modifies. The optional nature of the nonrestrictive clause is signaled by separating it by commas from the noun it modifies.

A helpful test for distinguishing between restrictive and nonrestrictive clauses in your own writing is the **who/what question test**. This test asks a *who* or *what* question about the noun being modified by the relative clause.

If the answer to the *who/what* question comes back **with the relative clause attached to the noun**, then the relative clause is a necessary part of the meaning of that noun. Therefore, this relative clause is restrictive and cannot be separated from the noun it modifies by commas.

If the answer to the *who/what* question comes back **without the relative clause**, then the relative clause is not a necessary part of the meaning of the noun. Therefore, this relative clause is nonrestrictive, and its optional nature must be indicated by separating it from the noun it modifies with commas.

Let's apply the *who/what* question test to two new sentences.

7.   Students **who didn't take the test** will get an incomplete.
      Who will get an incomplete?
      Answer: **Students who didn't take the test**.

8.   * My cousin Vinnie **who missed the test** got an incomplete.
      Who got an incomplete?
      Answer: **My cousin Vinnie**.

In sentence (7), the answer to the question *who will get an incomplete* is not just *students*, but *students who didn't take the test*. The relative clause *who didn't take the test* restricts the meaning of "students" to a small subclass of students—just those who didn't take the test. Therefore, *who didn't take the test* is a restrictive clause that cannot be cut off from the noun it modifies by commas. Sentence (7) is correctly punctuated as it is.

In sentence (8), the answer to the question *who got an incomplete* is just *my cousin Vinnie*. The relative clause *who missed the test* does not serve to restrict the meaning of the noun the clause modifies because that noun is already restricted to a single person—my

EDITING

cousin Vinnie. Therefore, the relative clause *who missed the test* is a nonrestrictive clause that must be set off with commas to show that it does not change the meaning of the noun it modifies. The correct punctuation for sentence (8) is the following:

8a.   My cousin Vinnie, **who missed the test,** got an incomplete.

Editing Activity 1: Using the *Who/What* Question Test to Identify Restrictive and Nonrestrictive Relative Clauses

Each of the following sentences contains a relative clause in bold. Write *restrictive* or *nonrestrictive* above each relative clause as appropriate, and add the necessary commas for nonrestrictive clauses. Apply the *who/what* question test to prove that your answer is correct. The first question is done as an example. In the first five questions, the *who/what* question is supplied. In the second five questions, you must write in the *who/what* test.

nonrestrictive
1. The result of the election **which came as no surprise** was a landslide.
   Answer: *The result of the election,* **which came as no surprise***, was a landslide.*
   who/what test: **What** was a landslide?
   Answer: *The result of the election.*

2. Somebody **who knows what he or she is doing** will have to fix this.
   who/what test: **Who** will have to fix this?
   Answer: _____

3. This church **which was built in 1220** is an excellent example of Norman architecture.
   who/what test: **What** is an excellent example of Norman architecture?
   Answer: _____

4. All students **who failed to turn in their papers** will receive an incomplete.
   who/what test: **Who** will receive an incomplete?
   Answer: _____

5. Aunt Sally **who does crossword puzzles** is a demon at Scrabble.
   who/what test: **Who** is a demon at Scrabble?
   Answer: _____

6. Senator Blather will never forget the first election **that he won**.
   who/what test: **What** will Senator Blather never forget?
   Answer: _____

7. The novel **which was also made into a movie** was very popular in the 1930s.
   who/what test: _____
   Answer: _____

8. Holmes was only attracted to crimes **that were out of the ordinary.**
   who/what test: _____
   Answer: _____

9. The pattern **that we picked** is an unusual one.
   who/what test: _____
   Answer: _____

10. Doyle **who grew very tired of writing about Holmes** tried to kill off his famous hero.
    who/what test: _____
    Answer: _____

11. The voters wanted a candidate **whom they could trust.**
    who/what test: _____
    Answer: _____

Editing Activity 2: Punctuating Restrictive and Nonrestrictive Relative Clauses

Each of the following sentences contains a relative clause. Write *restrictive* or *nonrestrictive* above each relative clause as appropriate, and add the necessary commas for the nonrestrictive clauses. The first question is done as an example:

nonrestrictive

1. Senator Blather **who is up for re-election next year** has been busy raising campaign funds.

   Answer: *Senator Blather, who is up for re-election next year, has been busy raising campaign funds.*

2. One of the books that I am reading for my literature class was written by a faculty member here.

3. My husband who is violently allergic to shellfish must be very careful when he eats seafood at restaurants.

4. The school board sent a flyer home with each student who attends elementary school.

5. Vincent Van Gogh who was a financial failure in his lifetime has become the most famous of the impressionist painters.

6. The people whom you don't know are friends of my roommate.

7. A quarterback who is confused by the defensive formation should always call time-out.

8. The quarterback who was confused by the defensive formation called time-out.

9. Painters who are just beginning their careers have a hard time getting exhibited.

10. Watson who is Holmes' slow-witted assistant narrates all the great detective's adventures.

11. The paper gave the names of all the people who are running for the school board.

B: Choosing Between *That* and *Which*

Many writers distinguish between the relative pronouns *that* and *which* as a way of telling the reader which relative clauses are restrictive and which are nonrestrictive. These writers always use *that* with restrictive clauses and *which* with nonrestrictive clauses. For example, compare the following sentences:

9.   I called a company **that is based in Chicago**.

10.   I called their head office, **which is in Chicago**.

The writer of these sentences has signaled that the relative clause in sentence (9) is restrictive in two ways: (1) by the fact the relative clause is not separated from the noun it modifies by commas and (2) by the use of the relative pronoun *that*. Likewise, the writer has signaled that the relative clause in sentence (10) is nonrestrictive in two ways: (1) by the fact that the relative clause is separated from the noun it modifies by commas and (2) by the use of the relative pronoun *which*.

It probably would be a good idea to recall here another use of *which*—the "vague" *which* discussed in the final editing section of Chapter 8. As you may recall, a vague *which* looks like the relative pronoun *which*. However, a vague *which* is not really a relative pronoun at all because *which* does not have any noun that it modifies. A vague *which* refers to everything that has gone before in an "all of the above" manner, as in this example:

11.   * The council rejected the motion, **which** really upset the chair.

In this case, *which* does not really modify the noun *motion*. *Which* refers to the whole preceding clause—it wasn't the motion itself that upset the chair but the fact that the council rejected the motion—an "all of the above" meaning. Although the vague *which* is common in informal conversation, it is unacceptable in formal writing. The entire sentence should be rewritten to eliminate the vague *which*:

11a. The fact that the council rejected the motion really upset the chair.

Editing Activity 3: Editing *Which* Clauses

All of the following sentences contain a clause beginning with *which*. If the clause beginning with *which* is nonrestrictive, write "okay." If the clause is restrictive, rewrite the sentence, replacing *which* with *that* and removing the commas. If the which is a "vague" *which*, rewrite the sentence to eliminate the *which* clause. The first question is done as an example.

1. I remembered some nails, **which** I had in the garage.
   *I remembered some nails **that** I had in the garage*

2. My car, **which** had been badly damaged in the wreck, was not worth fixing.
   _____

3. The storm finally broke the drought, **which** really made the farmers happy.
   _____

4. We agreed on the wording of the parts, **which** had been in dispute.
   _____

5. The few newspapers, **which** carried the story, supported the Mayor's decision.
   _____

6. Any game, **which** was played at home, would draw a big crowd.
   _____

7. We lost our last six games, **which** came as no surprise.
   _____

8. The Great Depression, **which** began with the crash of the stock market in 1929, was one of the watershed events of American history.
   _____

9. The neighborhood had really gone downhill, **which** didn't exactly improve the building's resale value.
   _____

10. Holmes found the weapon, **which** the murderer had used.
    _____

11. I bought a CB radio, **which** was a silly thing to have done.
    _____

C: Choosing Between *who* and *whom*

In formal writing, the most common error when the antecedent is a person is not the incorrect choice of *who* or *whom*, but the use of *that* to refer to people. Here are two examples in which *that* is used in place of *who* (sentence [12]) and *whom* (sentence [13]):

12.   *I met the children **that** live next door.

13.   *I met some children **that** you know.

Probably the main reason why we use *that* to refer to people in informal speech is to avoid choosing between *who* and *whom*.

The distinction between *who* and *whom* has nothing to do with whether the relative clause is restrictive or nonrestrictive. The choice between the relative pronouns *who* or *whom* is made solely on the basis of the role that the relative pronoun plays **inside** the relative clause:

▲ We use *who* when the relative pronoun is the subject of the relative clause.

▲ We use *whom* when the relative pronoun is not the subject of the relative clause.

Here are the correct forms of example sentences (12) and (13):

12a. I met the children **<u>who</u> live next door**.

13a. I met some children **<u>whom</u> you know**.

In sentence (12a), *who* is the subject of the clause **who** *live next door*. In sentence (13a) the subject of the relative clause is *you*—*whom* is the object of the verb *know*.

Here is a trick that you might find helpful in choosing between *who* and *whom* in relative clauses: **the personal pronoun test.** Turn the relative clause into a complete, free-standing sentence (an independent clause), and see what form of personal pronoun replaces the relative pronoun.

▲ If the relative pronoun changes into a subject personal pronoun (*he, she, we,* or *they*), then the correct form of the relative pronoun is the subject form *who.*

▲ If the relative pronoun changes into an object personal pronoun (*him, her, us,* or *them*), then the correct form of the relative pronoun is the object form *whom.* It may be helpful to know that the *-m* object marker in the personal pronouns *him* and *them* is the same *-m* object marker that appears in the object relative pronoun *whom.*

Here is the way we would use the personal pronoun test on the two preceding example sentences:

12b. I met the children. **<u>They</u> live next door**. (*they* = *who*)

13b. I met some children. **You know <u>them</u>**. (*them* = *whom*)

The personal pronoun test tells us that the relative pronoun in sentence (12a) plays the role of subject and that the relative pronoun in sentence (13a) plays the role of the object. Accordingly, *who* is the correct form of the relative pronoun in sentence (12a), and *whom* is the correct form in sentence (13a).

EDITING

Editing Activity 4: Using the Personal Pronoun Test for *Who* and *Whom*

Each of the following sentences contains a relative clause beginning with *who* (in bold). Decide if the relative clause should begin with *who* or *whom*, and make the necessary correction (if any). Show that your answer is correct by using the personal pronoun test (PPT). The first two questions are done as examples.

1. He is a teacher **who** everybody respects.
   Answer: *He is a teacher **whom** everybody respects.*
   PPT: *He is a teacher. Everybody respects **him**.*

2. There are teachers **who** love to diagram sentences.
   Answer: *There are teachers **who** love to diagram sentences.*
   PPT: *There are teachers. **They** love to diagram sentences.*

3. I have a baseball coach **who** my father had when he was in college.
   PPT:_____

4. The study monitored children **who** had a high level of exposure to lead.
   PPT:_____

5. The study monitored children **who** schools had identified.
   PPT:_____

6. The coach always looked for players **who** were natural athletes.
   PPT:_____

7. Reporters were highly critical of the candidates **who** the party officials had nominated.
   PPT:_____

8. A teacher **who** I had back in the ninth grade is my TA in English now.
   PPT:_____

9. The team's owner fired the coach **who** he had hired just the week before.
   PPT:_____

10. The stock was strongly recommended by a person **who** my cousin once knew.
    PPT:_____

11. The teacher **who** you know always seems nicer.
    PPT:_____

Editing Activity 5: Editing for Relative Clauses

In the following student essay on heuristics, all of the relative clauses are in bold. Identify which modifiers are restrictive and which are nonrestrictive, and punctuate accordingly. Be sure to use the correct relative pronoun.

Danny K.
English Writing, Sec 6
April 22, 1993

HEURISTICS

A heuristic **which is a simple rule for problem solving** is what we use for making small everyday decisions. We can't spend hours of our time thinking about the pros and cons of every small decision **that we have to make.** When we go grocery shopping, we see fifty different kinds of cereal filling up a whole aisle in the supermarket. If we weighed the advantages and disadvantages of each different box of cereal **which we saw on the shelves**, we would spend our entire day just getting something for breakfast. Instead, we sort through all the alternatives by turning to some heuristics: price, brand name, nutritional value, attractiveness of the package, etc. When we see a child **who is shopping with his or her mother**, the child wants the cereal **which is advertised on television.** The child's heuristics are simple; the child picks cereal based on the cartoon characters **who the child sees every morning on television.** The children **who are depicted on the TV program** have all that terrific fun and excitement eating Crunch Loops, so that child thinks that if his or her mom buys Crunch Loops, he or she will have fun and excitement too. This is not much of a heuristic, but is one **which makes General Mills rich.** Against her wishes Mom may be forced to buy Crunch Loops--a cereal **which has the nutritive value of sawdust.**

The mom's heuristics **that are drawn from an adult's experience** are more sophisticated than her child's, but they may not be any more accurate. Let's say that Mom has two main heuristics--cost and nutrition. A box of cereal **which has the words "giant economy size" on it** may or may not be cheaper than the same cereal in a smaller box. Even if two different brands of cereal are the same size, the box of cereal **which has the cheaper price** may have half the weight of the more expensive box because the cheaper box is filled with cereal **which has been fluffed up** so that the main ingredient in that cereal is air. As the article pointed out, the heuristics **which Mom relies on for evaluating nutrition** may not be more accurate than her child's. A cereal **which is low in sodium and high in fiber** is not necessarily a good thing. Tree bark is low in sodium and high in fiber, but that doesn't mean that it is nutritious.

Editing Activity 6: More Editing for Relative Clauses

The following student essay is free from mistakes except for a number of errors involving relative clauses. Make the corrections that you think fit this essay best.

Melissa M.
English Writing, Sec 6
March 12, 1993

HEURISTICS AS SELF-DEFENSE

The authors of the reading passage which was taken from the college textbook *Age of Propaganda: the Everyday Use and Abuse of Persuasion* by Anthony Prakanis and Elliot Aronson defined a "heuristic" as a simple cue or rule which one can use for solving a problem. They stated in the essay that many heuristics can be manipulated by people that want to take advantage of less sophisticated consumers. Advertisers that have a knowledge of consumers' heuristics can persuade people to buy things which they don't really want or need. For example, the case which is described in the reading dealt with the heuristics which Rachel and her mother used in buying a box of cereal. Rachel who was shopping with her mother was attracted to a box of cereal because of the visual qualities which it had. The box which showed a rainbow with stars, squares, moons and triangles prominently featured a green leprechaun. Her mother, on the other hand, wanted what she thought was a more nutritious cereal. This cereal was in a dull box which had 100% grain written on the front. Of course Rachel didn't want the cereal which was contained in the dull box because that box made the cereal look boring. The heuristic which the advertisers used here was visual persuasion. Children who the advertisers have targeted for this particular heuristic will be influenced by brightly colored packaging. Advertisers also know that mothers who are shopping with children would rather give in to their children than get into a fight about it.

Another heuristic which was in the essay was the half-hour TV show on knives. These knives are the sharpest thing which you have ever seen. The announcer who alternated between confidence in his product and astonishment at its performance cut through everything from tennis balls to metal rods. These are "daring" demonstrations which attract the viewer's attention by the risk of the product's failure. The advertiser that is hoping that the viewer will become hooked on the risky demonstration gets the viewer to sit still for a half-hour commercial as though it were an actual TV show. The idea is that the viewer who the advertiser knows is naturally suspicious of ads will identify with an audience that is just overwhelmed with amazement at the wonder of the demonstration. I know that when I watched one of these shows which promoted the sharpest knife in the world, I was nearly conned into purchasing one. I really had to force myself to think about the program which I was watching. What I was watching wasn't a docu-drama. It was nothing more than a sales pitch which was trying to get me to buy one more product which I didn't really need.

CHAPTER 10

STRESS
MANAGEMENT

| SECTION ◄► 1 | **Reading for Stress Management Strategies** |

A: Pre-Reading

Nearly everyone experiences stress. In small amounts, stress is actually beneficial. It's that nagging voice that keeps a person on task when the hour is late and energy levels are low. It's that touch of anxiety that tells a person to work harder, faster, and more efficiently. Stress is the normal companion of ambition. It is, for most individuals, present when a person does something he or she has not done before, does something he or she is not sure how to do.

Normally, people experience times of high stress followed by periods of low or no stress. Stress, basically, comes and goes. Sustained periods of high stress, however, do cause problems. Too much stress can keep people from doing their best and, in some cases, keep people from doing anything at all. Long-term unrelieved stress can negatively affect one's work performance, one's relationships with others, and one's health.

Like time and money, stress is one of those things most people need to learn to manage. In this chapter you will write about managing stress. Because there are so many types and sources of stress, and because so much thinking, research, and writing have been done about stress, you will be asked to find and read several articles about stress and stress management. You will then be asked to use quotations from these articles in your own essay about stress.

Pre-Reading Activities

Discussion

1. In small groups, talk about when and where you or people you know experience stress. Try to be specific rather than general. For example, if your present job is stressful, think about which parts of it are most stressful and why.

2. How can you tell when you are experiencing stress? Does it sneak up on you, or does it hit you all at once? Does stress change your behavior toward other people? Does

stress cause you to experience physical symptoms (e.g., a sore neck, tooth pain, headaches)? Using specific details, share your ideas with others.

3. Share with others activities you use to relieve stress. For example, some people build model airplanes, bake cookies, or paddle a canoe to help them relax. Also share what it is about these activities that makes them relaxing and restful.

4. Each occupation seems to have its own special kinds of stress. Students, for instance, face certain kinds of stressful situations. Law enforcement officers, healthcare workers, and people who work in the home or elsewhere with small children all experience their own brands of stress. With others, discuss some occupation-specific kinds of stress.

5. Someone said that money can both cause and relieve stress. Is this true? Are there other things that both cause and help to reduce stress? Discuss some of these with others.

6. Some people say that the older one gets, the more stress one experiences. Is this true? Discuss with others reasons why this is or is not true.

Reading Suggestions

(Keep these suggestions in mind as you read "Tips for Reducing Stress.")

1. In this article, the author names eight healthy strategies for managing stress. While reading, underline or highlight any strategies you find attractive. Identify at least one of the eight that you would like to learn more about, and think of two or three reasons why this strategy interests you or seems like a good idea.

2. While reading, you might remember or imagine yet other strategies for managing stress. Write these ideas down.

3. This article appeared in a magazine, *Health Journal*, published by a healthcare program. Of course these people want the people whose health they insure to stay healthy, but why might they present this information in this way? Think about what kind of person might read and benefit from reading this article.

Vocabulary Preview

aggravate: make worse, annoy. (Some medications <u>aggravate</u> rather than relieve stomach pains.)

induce: cause, encourage. (Nothing could <u>induce</u> me to start smoking cigarettes.)

B: Reading

"Tips for Reducing Stress"

Increased stress seems to arrive along with the end of summer and busy autumn schedules. While it's something we can't avoid altogether, we can learn to behave in ways that lessen the effect stress has on our lives and our health. There are many factors that affect our vulnerability to stress. Here are some tips that may increase your ability to deal with stress.

RELAX YOUR BODY AND MIND

Bringing about complete relaxation is important in managing stress. This can be done using one of the following techniques, preferably on a daily basis.

Muscle relaxation: The goal of this technique is to induce deep muscular relaxation by gradually flexing and releasing tension from various parts of the body, one part at a time. First, get comfortable, either lying or sitting down. Breathe deeply, and pay close attention to how your body feels. Starting with your toes, flex each muscle group for 10 seconds, then slowly relax the muscles.

Repeat this procedure three times before moving on to the next muscle group. After toes, continue with legs, abdomen, back, arms, hands, shoulders, neck, and forehead.

Meditation: This technique can also help release tension and bring about deep relaxation. Meditation should be done in a quiet environment where you won't be distracted. A sitting position is better than lying down (to avoid falling asleep). Breathe deeply throughout your meditation. It is important to remain passive and calm and let distracting thoughts float away. Use a mental focus to keep your concentration level high. Choose a focus that creates a feeling of peace and tranquility. Become aware of your breathing pattern as you meditate. Continue for 20 minutes or so.

Deep-breathing exercises: Deep breathing itself can help you deal with stressful situations. Breathe in until your lungs are full, hold for several seconds, and breathe out slowly.

TAKE GOOD CARE OF YOURSELF

Get involved in recreational activities. Increase your involvement in things that you enjoy. Get back into a favorite hobby. Plan something "just for fun" at least once a week.

Get enough sleep. Try to get seven to eight hours of sleep per night. Your mind and body will be rejuvenated and rested.

Reduce your intake of caffeine and alcohol. Caffeine can trigger or aggravate stress reactions. Drink fewer than three cups of coffee or other caffeine-rich drinks per day and fewer than five alcoholic drinks per week.

Get regular exercise. Exercise is an important coping mechanism for stress. Exercise at least three times a week for 20 minutes or more.

SUPPORTIVE RELATIONSHIPS

Friends and relatives can provide emotional support when it's needed. So keep a strong network of supportive relationships, and confide in people when it feels appropriate. Also, attend social activities on a regular basis.

You owe it to yourself and those around you to find ways to reduce stress in your daily life. Better physical, emotional, and behavioral health will be your reward. ■

"Tips for Reducing Stress." *Health Journal* (Sept. 1990): 4.

C: Post-Reading

Discussion Suggestions/Questions

Remembering

   1.   Why should a person meditate sitting up rather than lying down?

   2.   How much coffee per day does the article recommend to those who drink coffee?

Analyzing

   1.   Share with others the stress management option in the reading "Tips for Reducing Stress" that you find most attractive. Then share three reasons why you think this strategy would be or is beneficial or attractive.

   2.   Alone or with others, make an outline of the article "Tips for Reducing Stress." Then, using your outline in your discussion, talk with others about how this article is organized and why a reader might appreciate this clear organization pattern.

Discovering

1. Each adult in this stressful time and culture has strategies for relieving stress, techniques for helping him or her to relax. Share some of your strategies with others. Use details and examples to make clear to others what you actually <u>do</u> to reduce stress.

2. Can stress cause more stress? Do people worry because they worry too much? Are mental and physical stress different? Do they influence each other? Share your answers to these questions with others.

D: Vocabulary Building

1. Causative/noncausative verb pairs: *lay/lie; set/sit; raise/rise*

<u>Lying:</u> "A sitting position is better than **lying** down (to avoid falling asleep)."

Health Journal

The following three pairs of verbs are often confused: **lay/lie; set/sit; raise/rise**. Part of the reason for the confusion is that both verbs in each of these pairs of verbs are historically related to one another, but in a rather special and unusual way. Before discussing these three pairs, however, let us turn to another pair of verbs related in exactly the same way that is easier to work with: **fell/fall**. The verb *fell* means to "cause something to *fall*," as in the sentence "The loggers felled the trees," which means that the loggers caused the trees to fall. We will call *fell* a "causative" verb and *fall* a "noncausative" verb.

In an early stage of English there was a special ending that could be attached to nearly any verb. This ending had the meaning of "cause the action of the verb." So, for example, if this ending still existed today, we could attach it to the verb **sneeze** and create a new causative verb that would mean to "cause someone to sneeze." If we added this ending to the verb **stop**, the new causative verb would mean to "cause someone to stop."

The causative verb **fell** was created from the noncausative verb **fall** by adding this ending. In the same way, **lay** is the causative form of **lie**; **set** is the causative form of **sit**; and **raise** is the causative form of **rise**. The causative verb means to cause the action of the noncausative verb: to **lay** something means to cause it to **lie**; to **set** something means to cause it to **sit**; to **raise** something means to cause it to **rise**. Let's look at each pair in a little more detail.

lay/lie

The causative verb *lay* means to "put something down." *Lay* is a regular verb: its past tense is **laid**; its past participle form is (*have*) **laid**; and its *-ing* form is **laying**. Here are some sample sentences using the causative verb *lay*:

He **laid** the briefcase on the table.

I tried to **lay** my hands on some quick cash.

The builders were **laying** some pipes along the wall.

The noncausative **lie** means to "be spread out flat" or to "recline back in a horizontal position." *Lie* is an irregular verb: its past tense is **lay**; its past participle form is (*have*) **lain**; and its *-ing* form is **lying**. Here are some sample sentences using *lie*:

The briefcase is **lying** on the table.

Some coins **lay** on the table.

The pipes were **lying** along the wall.

Notice that the present tense of the causative verb *lay* looks the same as the past tense of *lie* (*lay*).

set/sit

The causative verb *set* means to "put something down." *Set* is irregular. Its past tense is **set**; its past participle is (*have*) **set**; and its *-ing* form is **setting**. Here are some sample sentences:

He **set** the briefcase on the table.

I **set** the baby back on her feet.

We were **setting** the table for dinner.

The noncausative *sit* means to "be seated" for people or to "be located" for objects. *Sit* is irregular. Its past tense is **sat**; its past participle is (*have*) **sat**; and its *-ing* form is **sitting**. Here are some sample sentences:

The briefcase is **sitting** on the table.

The children **sat** on the steps.

The house **sits** on a hill.

raise/rise

The causative verb *raise* means to "lift something up" or to "bring something up." *Raise* is a regular verb. Its past tense is **raised**; its past participle is (*have*) **raised**; and its *-ing* form is **raising**. Here are some sample sentences:

I **raised** my hand.

They **raised** the level of the water.

She was **raising** the children by herself.

The noncausative verb *rise* means to "go or move upward" or to "stick up in the air." *Rise* is an irregular verb. Its past tense is **rose**; its past participle is (*have*) **risen**; and its *-ing* form is **rising**. Here are some sample sentences:

The glider **rose** into the air.

The level of the water was **rising**.

The new office complex **rises** above all of the other buildings.

In distinguishing between the causative and noncausative verbs, remember that the causative verbs (*lay*, *set*, *raise*) have to have a noun phrase object that the verb causes to do something. The noncausative verbs (*lie*, *sit*, *rise*) do not have noun phrase objects.

Vocabulary Building Activity 1: Distinguishing the Causative and Noncausative Verb Pairs: *Lie/Lay; Set/Sit; Raise/Rise*

Following are sentences that use causative and noncausative verb pairs. Select the correct form, and write it in the space provided. The first question is done as an example.

1. I got sunburned from ___**lying**___ in the sun too long.
   laying/lying

2. I _____ the mat by the door.
   laid/lay

3. The mat _____ by the door for weeks.
   laid/lay

4. The baby was _____ quietly in the crib.
   laying/lying

5. _____ down, and be quiet.
   Lay/Lie

6. The cat is _____ in the window.
   setting/sitting

7. I _____ the cat in the window.
   set/sat

8. In winter, we all want to _____ next to the fireplace.
   set/sit

9. We _____ our chairs next to the fireplace.
   set/sat

10. We were _____ beside the pool.
    setting/sitting

11. The sun _____ in the east.
    raises/rises

12. She _____ an interesting point.
    raised/rose

13. The fog on the river was beginning to _____ .
    raise/rise

14. Please _____ your right hand.
    raise/rise

15. The committee is _____ several important issues.
    raising/rising

READING

E: Additional Reading

The following essay, "A View from the Plateau" by George Leonard, offers ideas and comments about stress. Read it if you like. Read it just for the joy of reading it.

"A View from the Plateau"[*]

BY GEORGE LEONARD

Early in life, we are urged to study hard so that we can get good grades. We are told to get good grades so that we can graduate from high school and get into college. We are pressured to graduate from high school and get into college so that we can get a good job. We are compelled to get a good job so that we can buy a house and a car. Again and again we are told to do one thing only so that we can get something else. We spend our lives stretched on an iron rack of contingencies.

No question, these contingencies are important. The achievement of goals is important. But the real juice of life, whether it be sweet or bitter, is found much less in the product of our efforts than in the process of living itself, in how it feels to be alive. We are taught in countless ways to value the product, the prize, the climactic moment. But if our life is a good one—a life of mastery—most of it will be spent on the plateau, that long stretch of diligent effort with no seeming progress. If not, a large part of it may well be spent in restless, distracted, ultimately self-destructive attempts to escape the plateau. The question remains: Where in our upbringing, our schooling, our career are we explicitly taught to value, to enjoy, even to love the plateau?

I was fortunate in my middle years to have aikido, a martial arts discipline so difficult and resistant to the quick fix that it showed me the plateau in sharp, bold relief. When I first started, I simply assumed that I would steadily improve. My first plateaus were relatively short and I could ignore them. After about a year and a half, however, I was forced to recognize that I was on a plateau of rather formidable proportions. This recognition brought a certain amount of shock and disappointment, but somehow I persevered and finally experienced an apparent spurt of learning. The next time my outward progress stopped, I said to myself, "Oh, damn.

Another plateau." After a few more months there was another spurt of progress and then, of course, the inevitable plateau. This time, something marvelous happened. I found myself thinking, "Oh boy. Another plateau. Good. I can just stay on it and keep practicing. Sooner or later, there'll be another spurt. And, actually, that doesn't even matter."

So there I was, an impatient, somewhat driven person who had always gone for the quickest, most direct route to any goal, practicing regularly and hard now for no particular goal at all. Months would pass with no break in the steady rhythm of my practice. It was something new in my life, a revelation. The endless succession of classes was rewarding precisely because it was, in the Zen sense, "nothing special."

I loved everything about it, this ritual that was always the same yet always new: bowing upon entering, pulling my membership card from the rack on the front desk, changing into my gi in the dressing room. I loved the comforting smell of sweat, the subdued talk. I loved coming out of the dressing room and checking to see which other students were already warming up. I loved bowing again as I stepped on the mat, feeling the cool firm surface on the soles of my feet. I loved taking my place in the long row of aikidoists all sitting in *seiza*, the Japanese mediation position. I loved the entry of our teacher, the ritual bows, the warmup techniques, and then my heart pounding, my breath rushing as the training increased in speed and power.

This joy, I repeat, had nothing at all to do with my progress or achievements of goals. I was taken totally by surprise, in fact, when one of my teachers called a fellow student and me into his office after a weekend of marathon training and handed us brown belts, the rank next to black belt.

One night, about a year later, the school's four most advanced brown belts talked casually about the possibility that we might achieve the rank of black belt ourselves someday. The idea was both exciting and troubling, and when I next came to class I was aware of something new: The worm of ambition was eating stealthily away at the center of my belly.

Maybe it was coincidence, but within three weeks of that conversation all four of us suffered serious injuries—a broken toe, torn ligaments in the elbow, a dislocated shoulder (mine), and an arm broken in three places. These injuries were effective teachers. After recovering, we settled back into steady, goalless practice. Another year and a half was to pass before the four of us got our black belts.

To be sure, goals and contingencies are important. But they exist in the future and the past, beyond the pate of the sensory realm. Practice, the path of mastery, exists only in the present. You can see it, hear it, smell it, feel it. To love the plateau is to love the eternal now, to enjoy the inevitable spurts of progress and the fruits of accomplishment, then serenely to accept the new plateau that waits just beyond them. To love the plateau is to love what is most essential and enduring in your life. ■

SECTION 2

Researching and Writing About a Stress Management Strategy

A: Pre-Writing

Reading is among the best kinds of pre-writing. Here you will be asked to locate, read, and think about three articles that you will find that discuss one kind of stress management. The best place to find these articles is a library, but first you need to choose one type of stress management as your focus.

In the article "Tips for Reducing Stress," the author names eight ways to reduce stress:

1. Muscle relaxation

2. Meditation

3. Deep-breathing exercises

4. Recreational activities

5. Getting enough sleep

6. Reducing your consumption of caffeine and alcohol

7. Regular exercise

8. Supportive relationships

You might choose to find additional articles on any one of these eight. For example, you might find and read three articles about meditation as a strategy for managing stress. You might also choose to find and read articles about a stress management strategy not mentioned in "Tips for Reducing Stress." Remember that the essay you will write will focus on one stress-management strategy, so the articles you find and read should be about that particular strategy.

Pre-Writing Activity 1: Finding Articles in the Library

1. First, of course, you need to choose which stress-reduction strategy you will investigate.

2. Next, make a short list of key words connected to the strategy you have chosen. For example, a person interested in researching caffeine consumption and stress might make the following list of key words.

    a. stress

    b. caffeine

    c. decaffeinated

    d. coffee

    You need such a list because libraries have indexes in which published articles are listed by subject. Many libraries also have computerized subject indexes. (You may choose to write about stress and a particular job or profession. If you do so, your key words list should include a few words concerning that job or profession.)

3. Next, take your list, a pencil, some paper to write on, and a few dollars in change for photocopying, and go to the library. It is customary to take a pencil rather than a pen. It is also customary <u>not</u> <u>to</u> <u>write</u> in any materials found in the library.

4. For this project, you need know where the indexes of periodicals and the periodicals are kept in the library. Periodicals are magazines, journals, and newspapers—things published at regular intervals or "periods," such as daily, weekly, monthly, or quarterly. *Newsweek*, for example, is a periodical. So is the *Washington Post*.

    Start with the indexes. Look in two or three subject indexes for your key words. A good index to start with is the *Reader's Guide to Periodical Literature*. This index lists articles from such popular publications as *U.S. News and World Report*, *Good Housekeeping*, and *Psychology Today*. When you find an article title in an index that looks like it may be useful, copy down the information included in the index. Normally this information will include the author's name, the article's title, the name, volume number, issue number, and date of the publication that contains the article, and the numbers of the pages in that publication on which the article appears. This information is called a *citation*.

5. Once you have three or four citations for articles written down, you need to find the publications that contain the articles. Most libraries have "serials' records." Serials' records list the periodicals in the library and indicate where the periodicals are kept. Some libraries have serials' records on computers. Whether in print or on a computer, the locations of periodicals are normally indicated by "call numbers." You need a call number for each periodical containing an article you hope to find.

6. With your citations and a call number for each written down, use the call numbers to track down your articles.

7. Once found, you should skim each article to see if it is really useful to you. Photocopy the articles you think will be useful. Remember to keep your list of citations—you will need it again later.

Using a library is one of the very best kinds of pre-writing. Librarians and instructors are usually eager to help individuals learn to use library resources.

In addition, articles in magazines, newspapers, and professional journals are often the best resource for writers because they are easily found, quickly read, and often contain the latest facts.

Pre-Writing Activity 2: Following Guidelines for Responsible Use of Sources

Gathering

1. Keep track of what you are reading so you can find the article again, use the facts you find, and document quotations and paraphrases correctly.

2. For any article you read, write down the following information:

   a. the author's name

   b. the title of the article

   c. the title of the magazine, newspaper, or journal that contains the article (for journals you also need volume and issue numbers)

   d. the publication date

   e. the page numbers on which the article appears

Reading

1. Take notes on articles that provide information you need:

   a. Quotations. When you copy the exact words of the author, you must use quotation marks (" "). Use quotations sparingly, choosing especially well-phrased sentences that address your subject directly.

   b. Paraphrases. When you write what the author is saying in your own words, you don't use quotation marks, but you need to document the source to give credit in your paper. (It is dishonest and illegal to use someone else's words or ideas and not give credit; this practice is called "plagiarism.")

✓ Note:

Student writers often commit plagiarism unintentionally—particularly when paraphrasing. Let's say that you have found a useful quotation from Dr. X, an expert on the subject of stress. Dr. X writes, "An often delitescent physical effect of prolonged stress is hypertension." You might be tempted to paraphrase Dr. X's words in this way: An often hidden physical effect of chronic stress is high blood pressure. However, this method of paraphrasing constitutes plagiarism because Dr. X's sentence structure has been copied if not his or her actual words. Correct paraphrasing means putting the ideas of others in your own sentence style as well as in your own words.

c. Your ideas. When you are reading an article and get your own ideas or thoughts, write them down, and then enclose them in square brackets ([ ]). Reading other people's ideas helps you develop more of your own insights and draw your own conclusions. These are often the most important notes that you make while reading outside sources.

B: Writing a First or Initial Draft

The topic for your essay is a single stress-reduction strategy. You are asked to promote or "sell" this strategy to your reader or readers. To do this, you need to have a fairly specific audience in mind (e.g., college students, law enforcement officers, business people). What you include in your essay should be based in part on the audience you choose.

You may organize your essay any way you like, but the following outline for an essay on this topic works pretty well. You may use this organization pattern if you like.

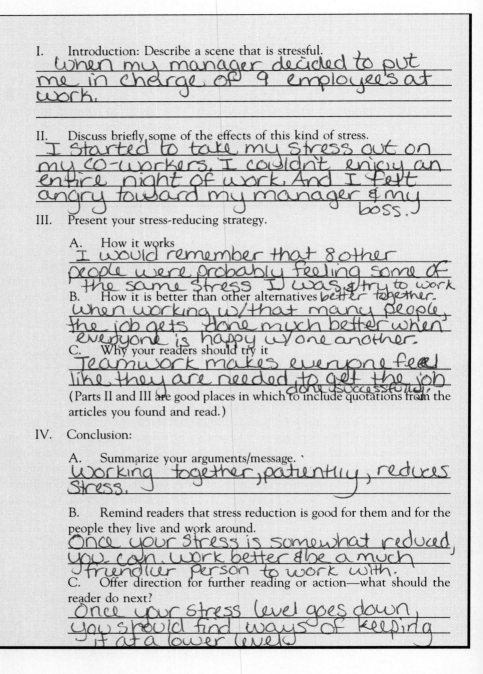

I.   Introduction: Describe a scene that is stressful.

When my manager decided to put me in charge of 9 employee's at work.

II.   Discuss briefly some of the effects of this kind of stress.

I started to take my stress out on my co-workers. I couldn't enjoy an entire night of work. And I felt angry toward my manager & my boss.

III.   Present your stress-reducing strategy.

A.   How it works

I would remember that 8 other people were probably feeling some of the same stress I was, & try to work

B.   How it is better than other alternatives   better together.

When working w/that many people, the job gets done much better when everyone is happy w/one another.

C.   Why your readers should try it

Teamwork makes everyone feel like they are needed to get the job done successfully.

(Parts II and III are good places in which to include quotations from the articles you found and read.)

IV.   Conclusion:

A.   Summarize your arguments/message.

Working together, patiently, reduces stress.

B.   Remind readers that stress reduction is good for them and for the people they live and work around.

Once your stress is somewhat reduced, you can work better & be a much friendlier person to work with.

C.   Offer direction for further reading or action—what should the reader do next?

Once your stress level goes down, you should find ways of keeping it at a lower level.

Now write your essay. The essay draft should be about eight hundred words—three typed, double-spaced pages or five hand-written pages. Try to include about three quotations or paraphrases from the articles you read in your essay.

Source Material in Your Essay

Include quotations or paraphrases in your essay to the best of your ability. Writers commonly break the flow of ideas that comes with drafting by worrying too much about integrating and crediting outside sources. If possible, give credit to the outside sources in your essay by putting the author's last name and page number on which the information was presented in parentheses after the quotation or paraphrase. If that is impossible, make a quick, informal notation—just enough to remind you where you got the material. You can revise your citations when you revise your essay.

SECTION

3

Revising to Make Responsible Use of Sources

REVISING

A: Responsible Use of Sources

Finding and reading published writing by experts helps people in several ways. Certainly reading other people's ideas helps people get more ideas of their own. Reading nourishes the mind like food nourishes the body. In addition, the facts, opinions of experts, and even the writing styles that other writers use are all resources for thought and for more writing.

The revision strategies in this chapter are about using these resources responsibly. You would not, for example, copy down another person's writing, word for word, and say you wrote it. That would be dishonest. It would be plagiarism. Plagiarism is against the law; it is intellectually dishonest.

On the other hand, using other people's published facts, opinions and ideas in your writing is an excellent strategy for developing and supporting your own ideas and arguments. You do this by quoting these other writers. You can also paraphrase other people's work—put their ideas in your own words—but even then you need to give credit to the writers from whom you are borrowing.

You give other writers credit by citing them, by including information in your papers that tells where these facts, opinions, and ideas are borrowed from. There are only a few ways to do this, and they are easy to learn:

1. Put the words written by others that you include in your writing in quotation marks.

2. Identify the source of the quotation in your essay. There are two ways to do this; one is optional, and the other is required.

    a. **Required**: At the end of a quotation, put the author's last name and the number of the page on which you found the quotation you are using. For example, "One benefit of fitness that is receiving attention is its ability to moderate the negative effects of stress" (Brown 555). Note that the period at the end of the quotation appears after the author's name and the page number in parentheses.

    b. **Optional**: You can also tell your reader who the author you are quoting is. This strategy adds weight to the quotation: Jonathan D. Brown of the University of Washington writes, "One benefit of fitness that is receiving attention is its ability to moderate the negative effects of stress" (555). Telling the reader something about the quoted author helps the reader to know what level of authority that other author has. In the example above, the reader would know that the quoted writer is associated with a university, that Jonathan D. Brown is probably a professor. Note also that using the quoted author's name within your essay makes it unnecessary to include his or her name within the parentheses.

These two ways of identifying the source are also used when paraphrasing, when you put another writer's ideas into your own words. The difference is the use of quotation marks. A paraphrase needs no quotation marks: Professor Jonathan D. Brown of the University of Washington notes that people are paying attention to how fitness can help ease the harmful effects of stress (555).

✓ Note:

Whenever you use a quotation or paraphrase, you need to <u>do</u> something with it. This means that a quotation or paraphrase does not stand alone. The writer needs to tell the reader how the quoted material is important or how it adds to the writer's ideas or argument. Basically, what a writer writes about a quoted source should be longer than the actual quotation or paraphrase.

After you have revised the quotations and paraphrases in your paper, type your bibliography. The bibliography, which appears at the end of your essay, includes a complete citation for each outside source used in the essay. The purpose of the bibliography is to give your reader the information he or she needs to find the source or sources you are using.

1. For an article, a complete citation includes the following:

   a. last name of author, first name with period after the first name;

   b. title of article in quotation marks with a period inside the quotation marks;

   c. title of magazine, newspaper, or journal, <u>underlined</u>;

   d. date of publication; and

   e. page numbers of entire article.

2. Sample bibliography citations:

   a. A complete citation for an article in a professional journal looks like this:
   Zastrow, Charles. "How to Manage Stress." <u>Indian Journal of Social Work</u> 44.4 (Jan. 1984): 365–375.
   Note the numbers "44.4" after the title of the journal. These numbers mean that this is the forty-fourth volume of this journal and the fourth issue in that volume. Note too that the date of publication following the volume issue number is in parentheses.

   b. A complete citation for a popular press (magazine) article looks this:
   Lang, Susan. "The Aerobic Antidote." <u>Vogue</u> Oct. 1988: 413, 490.
   Note that there is no volume/issue number in a citation for a popular press article. Sometimes there is no author named for these articles. When there is no author named, start with the title of the article: "Bathed in Splendor." <u>Harper's Bazaar</u>. Dec. 1988: 50.

   c. Sometimes useful quotations are found in books. To cite a book, use the parenthetical citation (author's last name and page number) in your essay, just as you would with an article. Then include a complete citation in your bibliography in the following form:
   White, Edward. <u>Teaching and Assessing Writing</u>. San Francisco: Jossey Bass, 1985.
   Here "San Francisco" is the place of publication, and "Jossey Bass" is the name of the business that published the book.

There are other kinds of sources, and for each kind there is a citation format. There are also different methods of documenting outside sources, but the one shown here (MLA) is widely accepted. The citation formats shown here, for professional journals, popular magazines, and books, are the most commonly used. For citing other kinds of sources, you might need to speak with your instructor or consult a citation style manual such as the *MLA Handbook for Writers of Research Papers*:

Gilbaldi, Joseph and Walter S. Achtert. <u>MLA Handbook for Writers of Research Papers</u>. New York: Modern Language Association, 1988.

REVISING

B: A Student Essay in Which the Writer Makes Responsible Use of Sources

Read the following essay written by Wei Y. This writer has made responsible use of her sources.

TAKE A BATH, TAKE A BREAK

Stress may occur to us in our daily lives from our work and our studies. As a college student, you may be familiar with the following experience.

You have to go to the library to do research for your paper on Friday afternoon while your friends are on their way downtown to shop. You spend three hours in the library but feel exhausted and frustrated because the periodicals you are anxiously looking for have been checked out by someone else, and the printer for the microfilm is out of order so you can't have a copy now until the next afternoon when the staff is on duty. It seems that you can't work on the paper that night. It gives you an excuse not to study.

Suddenly you remember that yesterday you invited your friend to come for lunch tomorrow, but your refrigerator is nearly empty. Also, you have another essay to write for this week, which means you will need to go to the computer lab to type it this weekend. What else? Oh, yes. You must also study for your anthropology test, which will be on Monday. You notice on your desk two letters from your friends, and you need to write them back. You feel your head aching after hours of looking through those microfilms. You even feel your neck and shoulders stiffen after five days of classes. Why do all these stressful things come together?

The possible effects of this stress will be that you feel a little bit angry with all those tasks and feel lost. Your physical pain seems to be getting even heavier. Sitting there, your thoughts are floating. You don't know for the time being what you should do. You can't concentrate on study because of your emotional and physiological responses to current stress.

You are not in form now, so in this case it is helpful to take a break and free yourself from stress for a while. A lot of de-stress strategies have been suggested by psychologists, doctors, and experts, such as deep-breathing exercises, recreational activities, meditation, regular exercise and reducing consumption of caffeine and alcohol. They all work in a way. However, there is another simple way which may "put you in touch with body and spirit" (Chazin 133) and treat stress instantly. Just go to the bathroom and take a warm bath.

It sounds easy enough. But how does it work? "When you are immersed in water, nearly 90 per cent of your weight is displaced; you feel lighter, slightly suspended, at ease" ("Bathed" 50). Just lying in the bathtub, surrounded by the hot water, you can feel like every capillary of your skin opens gradually, and those tensions built up in your body also gradually decrease. With the slow rise of water vapor from the bathtub, your whole body feels released, as well as your mind. You will also feel calm at this moment as the warm water lowers your blood pressure a little bit ("Bathed" 50). Either with your eyes open or closed, you can feel both your body and your mind are floating, freely floating in a world of purity and peace with no pain and no stress. You are purified and made whole again!

That is its advantage; it is simple but full of pleasure! You can take a bath whenever you feel stressful. It is no use to mention regular exercise and reducing consumption of caffeine and alcohol at this time as they are the preventive strategies that you should use. Doing recreational activities at the time of stress is probably not as easily accessible as just going into your bathroom, which may be only several steps away. Meditation needs attention and focus, but that is what you lack at this moment. Deep-breathing is also simple and effective, but the feeling after that is surely not as good as the satisfaction from bathing, which cleans both your body and your mind. So, next time, when you feel you are in stress, just turn on the tap, and step into your bathtub. Relax yourself!

REVISING

> When stress comes to you, don't just sit idle and do
> nothing. That will only increase your stress and make
> things even worse. There is a simple enough way to deal
> with it. Just go ahead and take a break. Take a warm and
> soothing bath, and take away tensions from your body and
> mind.
>
> Wei Y.
>
>
> Works Cited
>
>
> "Bathed in Splendor." Harper's Bazaar. Dec. 1988: 50.
> Chazin, Suzanne. "Of Time and Hot Water (the Benefits of
> a Hot Bath)". Reader's Digest March 1991: 133.

Wei Y.'s essay, "Take a Bath, Take a Break," is pretty good, partly because she makes responsible use of sources. She does all of the following:

1. She puts words written by others in quotation marks.

2. She identifies each quotation parenthetically with the author's name and the page number on which those words appeared. She also identifies the sources for her paraphrases in the same way.

3. She includes complete citations for all of her published sources at the end of her essay, using the proper form.

4. She uses the quotations and paraphrases to "build" her own ideas.

Wei Y. has made responsible use of her sources.

C: Revising Student Drafts for Responsible Use of Sources

Following are three drafts of student essays about stress management strategies. Working alone or with others, read the drafts, and check to see that these writers have used their published resources responsibly. Checking for responsible use of sources is normally done after a draft has been written a few times, after the draft has enough details and examples, after the draft is clearly organized, and after the draft communicates what the writer wants to communicate. Look for the four features of using sources responsibly already stated twice in this chapter: (1) quotation marks are used where they are needed, (2) parenthetical citations appear in the draft where appropriate and in the proper form, (3) complete citations for all sources are listed at the end of the draft, and (4) the quotations "fit" the writer's points and arguments, and the writer builds on the quotations rather than letting them stand alone.

REVISING

Student Draft: "Breathe to Relieve"

BREATHE TO RELIEVE

I crammed my key into the mail box lock and grabbed the letters. Two were for me, and one was to my roommate. I opened the first one and to my horror found that I owed the University $1350.00, which I did not have. I tried not thinking about it while I opened my second letter, but this one proved even more frightening. This letter told me that I was $192.00 in the hole in my bank account. I began to search frantically through my mind to try and find an answer to this problem.

About the only thing I could come up with was that I was in trouble. I had a very large fine to pay and was already in debt. What was I to do? My muscles began to tense up, which for me is a sure sign of stress. I knew that my GI Bill would be sent, but that would be too late. I started asking myself where I could come up with the money. I raced through my mind, lurching at any idea which would save me, but as soon as I grabbed one, it would suddenly disappear. I thought of calling my parents, but I knew that they would not have the funds to help.

About then the real stress hit. I had been backed into a corner and had no escape. I could not run from this dilemma nor joke about it because of its seriousness. My eyes began to water, telling me that this was one obstacle I could not avoid. A sudden pounding headache cropped up and began bellowing the price of school in my head. I turned to my Nintendo for some relief, but to no avail. Each time I tried to play, I saw those gold pieces Mario was running by. He didn't know what those gold pieces could do for a broke college student like me.

I tried to sit down and read a book, but it seemed like every time I did, I would start figuring how many books I have bought in my life and if that money would be enough to pay the fine. I tried to read a magazine, but the words were just that, words and nothing more. My mind was oblivious to everything but the obvious, which was my terrible circumstance.

I remembered my brother had told me that a sure way to rid yourself from stress was to listen to some old-fashioned country music. So I did and found myself even more stressed. The particular song I was listening to was about a young man who had just lost his wife, kids, pride and ego because the IRS had stripped him of all his money. Was this what was to become of me? I then thought of lifting weights to relieve my stress; needless to say, it did not work either. About the time I walked in the weight room and saw all those happy, rich, free-loading momma's boys was about the time I left, even more stressed than before.

Then I remembered an old stress reliever I learned while in Riyadh, Saudi Arabia, during the Gulf War. This technique does not ask the user to be a weight lifter or an awesome video game player, nor does it ask the user to be able to read a book with a million things on his mind. All this technique asks of you is to be able to breathe. Simple, isn't it?

The first step to reducing stress is to breathe deeply through your mouth and let it out nice and slowly through your nose. This mundane process has been studied by great doctors, and Dean Ornish, M.D., as quoted by Porter Shimer, says, "Deep breathing is one of the simplest yet most effective stress management techniques there is" (Shimer 100). The main reason that deep breathing is so useful is that "rapid breathing causes problems by ridding the blood of too much carbon dioxide." (Shimer, p. 101)

The next step is to imagine a warm place, a place that you would like to be more than any other place in the world. After each breath you are supposed to try and picture this place, and miraculously it works. With each breath the picture gets clearer. With each breath you begin to see the shapes which make up your imaginary world. With each breath you begin to hear the peaceful sounds which speak to you while you escape reality. With each breath your troubles are drowned out by the awesome power of tranquility.

REVISING

REVISING

The unique factor to this technique is it can be done any place, anytime and under any circumstances. The user of this method will learn that with practice this technique can reduce any extreme of stress. Again, this technique will reduce stress by doing what comes naturally, breathing. Stress is a very serious issue and should be dealt with in that way. Deep breathing "infuses the blood with extra oxygen, but also by causing the body to release endorphines, which are natural tranquilizing hormones." (Porter Shimer, page 99).

It is true that people like to work around happy people and vice versa, so do not think that having stress only concerns yourself. Stress, if not properly taken care of, may do real harm to a person and his or her close relations. So check out any health magazine, and look up "stress relief." There you will surely find the method that I like. Remember that we all have stress and must conjure up methods to reduce it. The advantage you have is that you now know the easiest way.

Matt K.

Works Cited

Shimer, Porter "Unwind and Destress." <u>Prevention</u> July 1990: 75-86.
Shimer, Porter "Unwind and Destress." <u>Prevention</u> Aug. 1990: 99-103.

Note

1. The Porter Shimer article was published in two parts—one in July and one in August of 1990.

2. Matt K. has quoted Dean Ornish as Dr. Ornish was quoted in Porter Shimer's article. This can be signaled in the text in two ways: (a) It can be noted by stating who the original source is in the essay, as Matt K. does in paragraph eight of this essay. (b) It can be signaled parenthetically in the text (qtd. in Shimer 101)—if the original source is not mentioned in the paragraph containing the quotation.

3. Hint: Matt K. needs a little help with form in his parenthetical citations within his essay and in his bibliography or works cited list.

Student Draft: "Working Out the Stress"

WORKING OUT THE STRESS

Finals week is finally here. This is the week that the whole campus dreads months before it even arrives. You have had a very busy schedule the whole quarter, and you are not sure if you can handle what this week is going to require from you. You go to your first class and find that you have a huge test over 50 chapters of reading that you never had time to do. Also there is going to be a 10- to 12-page paper due before you can even take the test. Your teacher has been a college professor for about 35 years, and he has seen every trick in the book. There is just no way you are going to be able to pull any strings with this guy. Your whole class is way ahead of you in the reading, so you ask your teacher for some extra time. He looks at you and gives you an evil scowl: "If I don't see that paper on my desk by three o'clock Thursday, prepare to see me again next quarter."

You decide that you had better go to your next class and find out what else you need to get done. You walk through the door and see the huge chalkboard in the front of the room full of subjects. The teacher explains to you that each student must pick out a subject and prepare an oral presentation. This presentation must be at least 20 minutes in length. You have been hoping all quarter that you would not have to give an oral presentation in front of the class. You were never very good at speaking in front of an audience.

One class to go--chemistry. Five labs. This should only take about three days. You ask your professor about the deadline date, 3 o'clock on Thursday. You are absolutely swamped with things to do. Your stress level has just gone to the moon. You have never been this stressed-out before. You have so many things to do and so little time to do them.

REVISING

Stress like this cannot be good for your body. You are very irritable. The slightest little thing makes you start yelling. You have never been this grouchy before. Your eyes are bloodshot, and you have a very short attention span. It is hard for you to sit down and really concentrate on anything. Your muscles feel tight and tense. You ache all over, and you are just plain miserable. I think stress like this can cause sickness. When I get stressed-out I tend to get sick or catch a cold. Stress can lower your immune system and cause you to be subject to illness.

When stress like this hits me, there is one thing that works for me to lower my stress level. I like to exercise when I get stressed out. "It has been suggested by Ismail and Trachtman (1973) that stress reduction benefits are the result of physiological and biological changes resulting directly from exercise" (as qtd. in Kieley and Hodgson 555). It causes me to forget about my problems. You can also release aggressions by exercising. Whatever is built up inside you tends to come out as you exercise. Exercise relaxes your muscles and takes away your tension. My mind is at ease when exercising. I do not have to think about all of the problems that have piled up. I just relax and do whatever form of exercise I choose to do. This is the only thing that I have to think about, and it is very stress relieving for me. "The review of literature on the physiological and psychological benefits of physical exercise as a means of offsetting occupational stress does indicate that exercise has positive benefits for the individual." (Kieley and Hodgson 568).

For me exercise seems to work better than anything because there are so many choices. Which type of exercise do I want to do? This depends on what type of stress I am feeling. For instance, if I need to release some aggression I might play racquetball or lift weights. I can take my anger and aggression out on the ball or the weights. Jogging, basketball, swimming, and volleyball all help me to relieve stress. These methods are all relaxing. They all require physical exertion, but this is good because it requires you to forget about what was troubling you. You have to concentrate on what you are doing, so your troubles leave you.

"Aerobic fitness drastically reduces one's physiological response to stress" (Holmes, 490). I agree with this statement. I would recommend exercise to anyone who has a high level of stress. It is a wonderful way to relieve stress. Ph.D. David Holmes also says, "Aerobic fitness not only lowers resting heart rate, blood pressure, and muscle tension; but the aerobically fit and well exercised person is more relaxed and less prone to illness under stress" (490). Exercise can keep you healthy. This is another reason that I encourage plenty of exercise.

Overall, I would recommend exercise as a great way to reduce stress. Stress management is very important in everyday life. Too much stress is unhealthy and can cause many problems that are very unnecessary. Stress may also cause problems for people around you. You may be too stressed out to do your job properly, and this can affect people other than yourself. This is another important reason to manage your stress, and exercise is a good way to do this. Some forms of stress management may cost you money. Exercise is free, and it really makes you focus. Focusing is the key to exercise. Focusing causes you to forget all of the things that have built up your stress. The plus about exercising is that you get to focus on something that is enjoyable. Exercise is very fun, and it is easy to focus upon. For this reason exercise is the stress-reducing strategy for me.

In order to find out more about the proper methods of exercise, I would contact your local gym or exercise facility. In particular, I recommend reading Muscle Fitness. This magazine provides important tips on reducing stress and using stress to properly train your body.

Tim H.

Works Cited

David Holmes. "The Aerobic Antidote." Vogue October, 1988: 413+.
Julia Kieley and George Hodgson. "Stress in the Prison Service: The Benefits of Exercise Programs." Human Relations November, 1990: 551-572.

REVISING

Note

1. The David Holmes article starts on page 413 but continues elsewhere in that issue of *Vogue*. This is signaled by adding "+" after the number of the starting page.

2. Tim H. needs a little help with putting his citations in the proper form.

Student Draft: "Escape to Magic Mountain"

ESCAPE TO MAGIC MOUNTAIN

Who says high school is all fun and games? In today's society parents underestimate the stress their teenagers encounter everyday. Teenagers are tired of listening to their parents' sob stories of how rough it was back in the old days. Every parent tells basically the same story about how "kids had to walk barefoot through ten feet of snow just to get to school." The truth of the matter is that high school students today would much rather walk the ten miles barefoot than deal with their difficult college applications, boyfriend or girlfriend problems, demanding sports, part-time jobs, and nagging parents. For many, high school is a time of complete confusion. Students ask themselves, "Aren't these supposed to be the best years of my life?" How do you plan the rest of your life in only a couple of months? How can you be sure you're making the right choices?

There are no right answers to these questions. The best option is to motivate yourself into becoming the person you want to be, and to start doing things for yourself instead of others. Ruth Daily wrote that "stress causes anxiety, and anxiety narrows perceptions. When stress is low, we are usually aware of our thoughts, our surroundings, what we are doing and plan to do. But when anxiety mounts, our perceptions narrow to focus on the threat" (15). Stress has been proven to soak up energy and motivation, making any closet an appealing place to hide. Richard L. Weaver II says that "all stressed out people who feel out of control need an electric charge to boost their spirits, and reinvigorate their emotions, and to reestablish balance in their life" (620). Professor Weaver also states that self-motivation is the key, but it can only come from the inside. Change must begin from within. "In order to free our spirits we must first recognize and work with our individuality" (620). I also strongly agree with professor Weaver's outlook on exercise: "Don't underestimate the importance of exercise to self-motivation. What happens to students is that many of them forget to exercise. Exercising the body keeps the mind sharp" (621).

High school should be the best years of your life. But with increasing stress levels in high school students, that important factor is rapidly fading. Once again the key is self-motivation. Every student has an image of the sort of person he or she wants to become. What's wrong with motivating yourself into becoming that person now? Students are so caught up in what everyone else is doing and their parents' expectations, they often forget what they want.

The question is how do you get exercise, build up motivation, relieve stress, and show your true individuality? The answer for me was snowboarding. After five days of hassles I hop in my Volkswagen and head for the mountains. The fresh air, "the mastering of a new and very different tool" (110), as Peter Shelton put it, and the motivating, beautiful view of snow-covered hilltops as far as the naked eye can see are enough to relieve my tense shoulders. Snowboarding is an exciting new way to escape all stress-related events; it's even becoming more and more popular among adults. A snowboard combines elements of skiing, skateboarding, and surfing into one exhilarating sport.

Snowboarding will give you the perfect chance to boost your spirits, restore your emotions, and organize balance in your life. Your individuality will shine through your own snowboarding techniques. Shelton observes that ''a real snowboarder strives for the essential beauty of it; it is in deep snow, the board carving and banking against an ethereal, giving substance very much like Mother Ocean." He says, "that's the sensual promise that I want to feel" (127). Personally I prefer his description of "descending a mountain transformed into one giant, powder-frosted wave." (127).

REVISING

```
    So if you're tired of being a huge stress ball, dig deep
within yourself, find that last ounce of motivation, and
put it to work. Maybe snowboarding isn't for you, but
you'll never know until you try it. Give it a chance. It's
a new sport that can free your spirit. Plan a mountain
journey, and bring along your willingness to practice.
It's your job to make these years the best and the most
memorable. No one else can do it for you. I can guarantee
that you won't forget it!

                                                Lisa W.


                        Works Cited


1. "Managing Stress." by Ruth Daily Grainger V91 Amer-
ican Journal of Nursing Sept 1991 p15-16
2. Self motivation: ten techniques for activating or
feeling the spirit. by Richard L. Weaver, II v57 Vital
Speeches August 1, 1991 p620-623
3. "Riding a new wave." (snowboarding) by Peter Shelton
il v40 Skiing Spring 1988 p108-111, 127
```

Note

1. All of the needed information concerning sources is included in this draft. Lisa W. does need your editorial help in putting her parenthetical citations and her works cited bibliography in the proper order.

2. This draft, "Escape to Magic Mountain," relies heavily on quotations. Are there places in the draft where the writer could add more of her own ideas and examples?

D: Revising Your Essay to Make Responsible Use of Sources

Working alone or with others, look at your own essay to make sure that you are making responsible use of sources. If you see other ways to improve your essay while doing this, make those improvements too.

REVISING

E: Optional Revision

You might also use the revision strategy—"Revising for Clarity and Completeness of Information"—presented in Chapter 7 to make your essay better.

SECTION
◄►
4
Final Editing for Apostrophe Errors

This section deals with three different uses of the apostrophe:

A. **Apostrophes in contractions**

B. **Possessive apostrophes**

C. **Apostrophes in time expressions**

We will cover these three uses of the apostrophe in turn.

A: Apostrophes in Contractions

The use of apostrophes to show missing letters in contractions goes back to sign painters in the Middle Ages who used apostrophes to show where they had deliberately left out letters. For example, if a painter had been asked to paint "Established 1407" on a small sign board, he might have fit it in this way: "Est'd 1407." Eventually, this use of the apostrophe to show missing letters became a part of the regular spelling system of English as a way of indicating contractions. The most commonly contracted word is *not*, which is spelled *n't* to show that the *o* has been left out. Examples and variations are *can't* for *cannot*; *shouldn't* for *should not*; and *didn't* for *did not*. The other common contractions are contractions of various combinations of personal pronouns with *be* and *will*, such as *I'm* for *I am*; *they're* for *they are*; *I'll* for *I will*; and *we'll* for *we will*.

A common mistake of beginning writers is to forget to add the apostrophe when using contractions. The person most likely to make this mistake is a person who writes by ear rather than by eye—a person who hears what he or she writes rather than seeing the words as they are actually written on the page. Especially difficult for persons who write by ear rather than by eye are contractions with *is* and *are* that happen to sound exactly like possessive pronouns. Here are some of these sound-alike words you are most likely to confuse:

Contracted word	Possessive pronoun
it's (it is)	its
they're (they are)	their
there're (there are)	their
you're (you are)	your
who's (who is)	whose

The most common mistake is confusing *it's* and *its*. Not only does the contraction *it's* sound exactly like the possessive pronoun *its*, the apostrophe in the contraction *it's* makes us think of the apostrophe used in possessive nouns (as, for example, the apostrophe in the possessive phrase *John's book*). Next in frequency of error is the three-way confusion of *they're/there're/their*.

Fortunately, there is a simple solution to the problem of all these sound alike words: **Just say "no" to contractions.** If you have any problems at all with these words, simply stop using the contracted forms. Contractions are really out of place in formal writing anyway. If nothing else, every time you use any of these easily confused words, stop and see if the word can be expanded into the uncontracted pronoun + *is* or *are* form. If this uncontracted form makes sense in your sentence, then use the apostrophe. If the uncontracted form does not make sense in your sentence, then use the possessive pronoun form. Here are some examples of this **expansion test** applied to *it's/its*, both spelled <u>*its:*</u>

1.   *Its my book.
2.   **Its** top came off.

When we apply the expansion test to sentences (1) and (2), we get the following results:

1a.   **It is** my book.
2a.   *It is top came off.

The uncontracted form *it is* is grammatical in sentence (1), so we know that we can use *it's*, the contracted form of *it* + *is*, if we wish:

1b.   **It's** my book.

However, the uncontracted form *it is* is ungrammatical in sentence (2), so we know that we must use the possessive pronoun *its*:

2b.   **Its** top came off.

Here is the expansion test applied to *they're/there're/their*, all spelled <u>there</u>:

3.   * **There** friends of mine. = **They are** friends of mine.

4.   * There some books here. = **There are** some books here.

5.   * The kids left **there** books. = * The kids left **there are** books.
                                      = * The kids left **they are** books.

The expansion test for sentence (3) tell us that <u>there</u> is a contraction of *they are*:

3a.   **They're** friends of mine.

The expansion test for sentence (4) tells us that <u>there</u> is a contraction of *there are*:

4a.   **There're** some books here.

The failure of the two expansion tests for sentence (5) tells us that <u>there</u> *is not a contraction of they are or of there are*. Therefore, <u>there</u> must be the possessive pronoun *their*:

5.   The kids left **their** books.

Editing Activity 1: Using the Expansion Tests to Identify Contractions and Possessive Pronouns

Each of the following questions has two short sentences. One sentence has a contraction with *is* or *are*, and the other sentence has the similar sounding possessive pronoun. On the second line of each question apply the expansion test. On the third line, write the correct form of the contraction or the possessive pronoun. The first two questions are done as examples.

1. a. **Your** the boss.
   You are the boss.
   You're the boss.

   b. **Your** boss called.
   You are boss called.
   Your boss called.

2. *a.* **Whose** turn is it?
   Who is turn is it?
   Whose turn is it?

   b. **Whose** that?
   Who is that?
   Who's that?

3. *a.* **Its** growing.

   b. **Its** growth is unusual.

4. a. **Theirs** a question.

   b. The question is **theirs.**

5. a. **There** questions.

   b. I answered **their** questions.

6. a. **Its** leg was broken.

   b. **Its** late.

7. a. **Their** waiting was over.

   b. **Their** waiting.

8. a. **Your** turn is next.

   b. **Your** ready to go.

9. a. **Its** time to go.

   b. **Its** time is up.

10. a **Their** anger is natural.

   b. **Their** angry.

B: Possessive Apostrophes

The two types of words use possessive apostrophes: possessive nouns and possessive indefinite pronouns. We will deal with these two types of possessive words separately.

Possessive Nouns

A possessive noun "possesses" or "owns" the noun that follows it, as in sentence (6):

6.   I found the **boy's** books.

The noun *boy* is in the possessive form *boy's* to show that *boy* owns or possesses the following noun *books*. A singular noun is made possessive by adding *'s*. When the noun is plural, we make it possessive by adding an apostrophe after the plural *s*, as in this example:

7.   I found the **boys'** books.

In sentence (7) the books are owned (individually or collectively) by more than one boy.

Irregular plural nouns—*men, women, children, oxen, mice, geese*—muddy the water slightly because they make their possessive in a little different way. Because these nouns have been made plural by a change in the form of the noun itself, there is no plural *s* to put the apostrophe after, the way we do with regular nouns. Instead, we add *'s* on the end of the plural nouns to show that these plural nouns are also possessive—*men's, women's, children's, oxen's, mice's, geese's.*

Everybody has heard all about how to use apostrophes with possessive nouns from the sixth grade on. But if everybody already knows how to use apostrophes with possessive nouns, why are some student essays filled with possessive apostrophe errors? The reason is that possessive nouns are hard to spot in our own writing because the possessive apostrophe—the marker of written possessive nouns—does not correspond directly to anything in the spoken language. For example, the plural *boys*, the possessive *boy's*, and the plural possessive *boys'* are all spelled differently, but they are pronounced exactly alike.

The big problem for all writers, experienced as well as beginning, is that we cannot trust our ears to tell us when to use an apostrophe. We can only use the apostrophe correctly when we consciously check each word that has an added *s* sound to see if that *s* sound means a possessive noun. Once we know that a noun is a possessive, it is (relatively) easy to add the apostrophe correctly. The goal of this part of the unit is to give you some simple and reliable ways for recognizing when a noun is possessive so that you can then add the apostrophe.

The first thing to do in checking for possessive nouns is to look for the "possessed" noun. Here are some examples of sentences with possessive nouns. The possessive noun is underlined, and the "possessed" noun is in bold:

8.   The <u>bird's</u> **leg** did not appear to be broken.

9.   We could hear the <u>truck's</u> **gears** a mile away.

10.   My <u>aunts'</u> big **kitchen** was always full of people.

11.   <u>Sam's</u> good **luck** had about run out.

Editing Activity 2: Identifying Possessive and "Possessed" Nouns

The following sentences all contain a possessive noun. Underline the possessive noun, and circle the "possessed" noun. The first question is done as an example.

1. I left the bone by the dog's dish.
   Answer: *I left the bone by the <u>dog's</u>* (dish.)

2. I left the package on my boss's desk.

3. The red wine ruined Carol's new tablecloth.

4. The teachers' difficult questions stumped all of us.

5. It was the answer to a mother's prayer.

6. Sam's complicated plan turned out to have some major problems.

7. The cats' dirty footprints were all over the table.

8. The robin's newly-hatched eggs were in the nest.

9. I picked up all of the children's toys.

10. The Civil War's outcome was determined largely by economic factors.

11. Nobody could figure out Jerry's strange directions.

A good way to identify possessive nouns is the ***whose* test**. Ask a *whose* question about the "possessed" noun. If the noun ending in s is actually a possessive noun, you will always get the possessive noun back as the answer to whose question. To see how this test works, let's apply it to the four example sentences from the beginning of this unit:

8. The **bird's** leg did not appear to be broken.
   Whose test: **Whose** leg?
   Answer: The **bird's** leg.

9. We could hear the **truck's** gears a mile away.
   Whose test: **Whose** gears?
   Answer: The **truck's** gears.

10. My **aunts'** big kitchen was always full of people.
    Whose test: **Whose** big kitchen?
    Answer: My **aunts'** big kitchen.

11.   **Sam's** good luck had about run out.
       Whose test: **Whose** good luck?
       Answer: **Sam's** good luck.

A great side benefit of the *whose* test is that it often makes it much easier to decide whether the possessive noun is singular or plural.

Editing Activity 3: Using the *Whose* Test to Find Possessive Nouns

The following sentences all contain possessive nouns, but the possessive apostrophes are missing.

1.   Use the *whose* question test to identify the possessive noun.

2.   Add the apostrophe correctly to the possessive noun in your answer to the *whose* question.

In some questions in which the possessive word could be either singular or plural, there will be two possible answers—either one is correct. The first question is done as an example.

1. The cats dish is in the sink.
   Whose question: **Whose dish?**
   Answer: *The cat's* dish.

2. Watsons story surprised Holmes.
   Whose question:_____
   Answer:_____

3. The council approved the budget committees request.
   Whose question:_____
   Answer:_____

4. The referees decision nearly caused a riot.
   Whose question:_____
   Answer:_____

5. The judges summary made a big impact on the jury.
   Whose question:_____
   Answer:_____

6. I put all my junk in my parents attic.
   Whose question:_____
   Answer:_____

7. The earths atmosphere contains a large amount of carbon dioxide.
   Whose question:_____
   Answer:_____

8. I bought it at Berthas Kitty Boutique.
   Whose question:_____
   Answer:_____

9. The workers repainted the buildings faded exterior.
   Whose question:_____
   Answer:_____

10. The banks reserve funds were dangerously low.
    Whose question:_____
    Answer:_____

Now you are ready to find and correct possessive apostrophe errors on your own. Remember to check every noun that ends in an *s* to see if it is followed by a second noun. If it is, use the *whose* test to confirm that the noun ending in an *s* is indeed a possessive noun that requires an apostrophe.

Editing Activity 4: Finding and Correcting Possessive Apostrophe Errors

The following student essay contains a number of possessive nouns that have not been correctly identified by the use of apostrophes. Check every noun ending in an *s* to see if it is possessive. Confirm that the noun is a possessive by the *whose* test. Underline each possessive noun, and add the apostrophe in the appropriate place. The number of apostrophe errors in each paragraph is given in parentheses at the end of the paragraph.

Kimberlee S.
English Writing, Sec 6
March 23, 1993

CHRISTMAS SHOPPING STRESS

For some people, going shopping at the mall is a chore. They know what they want, they get it, and then they go home without even glancing at Nordstrums sale merchandise. Then there are others like me who think that shopping is the best thing since pepperoni pizza was invented. Even though I have had my fun times at the mall, I have also experienced many irritating and stressful events. The biggest stress factor is the universal shoppers complaint--not enough money to buy the things I really want. (2)

I really like to go shopping during Christmas time because I like to look at all the stores decorations and watch the kids sitting in Santas lap. But even then the crowds can get on my nerves. I always seem to get jostled by impatient shoppers and banged by some ladys bags. After awhile I just want to sit down and smoke a cigarette, but there's no place to go. It is too cold to go outside, and if I go into a restaurant, I have to wait for a table and then order food that I don't want to eat. I end up sitting on the womens room couch, staring at a blank wall. (4)

Another stressful thing about shopping is having to deal with peoples frustrations. They are tired and impatient. Some are trying to shop with little children who are tired and fussy. Nothing puts you in the Christmas spirit like listening to a womans screaming kid running around the toy department. (2)

Christmas is already a stressful time because we have so many pressures from our families and our friends. We all try to do too much, and we have unreasonable expectations about the seasons activities. One danger is that we react to this pressure by going shopping. We shop to cheer ourselves up, and we shop to try to buy peoples happiness with gifts. We end up spending more money than we can really afford. (2)

> The only solution for stressed-out shopping is to be realistic about our expectations and to be aware of our emotions effects on us. Our familys presents should be things that they want, not things that we need to buy for our own reasons. We need to take control of our emotions and limit our shopping to the things we really do want to buy. (2)

Possessive Indefinite Pronouns

The most common indefinite pronouns (and the ones most likely to create problems) are *one* and the various combinations of *any-*, *every-*, *no-*, and *some-* followed by *-body*, or *-one*:

	-body	*-one*
any-	anybody	anyone
every-	everybody	everyone
no-	nobody	no one
some-	somebody	someone

The possessive form of these indefinite pronouns is made by adding the possessive apostrophe *'s*: *one's*, *anybody's*, *anyone's*, *everybody's*, *everyone's*, and so on. (Remember: all indefinite pronouns are singular, hence the *'s* rather than *s'*.) The problem is that many beginning writers tend to leave off this apostrophe. For example, note the following sentence taken from a student paper:

12.   * Going to college takes four years out of **ones** life.

This sentence is incorrect because the possessive form of the pronoun *one* must be used with an apostrophe:

12a. Going to college takes four years out of **one's** life.

One reason why this kind of error is so common is the fact that we treat the possessive form of indefinite pronouns as though they were like the much more common possessive forms of personal pronouns (*my*, *your*, *his*, *her*, *its*, *their*, and *our*) that do not use an *'s* to make the possessive form. However, indefinite pronouns are more like nouns: we add an *'s* to make the possessive form.

The *whose* test that we used to identify possessive nouns will work equally with possessive indefinite pronouns. For example, here is how we would apply the *whose* test to sentence (12):

12b. Going to college takes four years out of **one's** life.
        Whose test: **Whose** life?
        Answer: **One's** life

Editing Activity 5: Using the *Whose* Test to Find Possessive Indefinite Pronouns

The following sentences were taken from student essays.

1. Use the *whose* question test to identify the possessive indefinite pronouns (in bold).

2. Add the apostrophe correctly to the possessive indefinite pronoun in your answer to the *whose* question.

The first question is done as an example.

1. I feel that getting to know different people is an important part of **ones** college experience.
   Whose question: ***Whose college experience?***
   Answer: ***One's college experience***

2. Broadening **ones** knowledge for future use is very important.
   Whose question:_____
   Answer:_____

3. That would make college worth **anyones** time and effort.
   Whose question:_____
   Answer:_____

4. College is a time for learning to control **ones** actions.
   Whose question:_____
   Answer:_____

5. Education should be part of **everyones** life.
   Whose question:_____
   Answer:_____

6. The ability to manage **ones** finances is another benefit.
   Whose question:_____
   Answer:_____

7. Finding a job after college is probably **everyones** worry.
   Whose question:_____
   Answer:_____

8. While this will not only help **ones** grades, it will be invaluable in later life.
   Whose question:_____
   Answer:_____

9. Better support for schools is in **everybodys** best interest.
   Whose question:_____
   Answer:_____

10. Lack of money should not stand in **ones** way.
    Whose question:_____
    Answer:_____

EDITING

Now you are ready to deal with possessive apostrophe errors in both nouns and indefinite pronouns on your own. Possessive apostrophe errors are easy to correct once you see that a noun or indefinite pronoun is possessive. Check every noun and indefinite pronoun that ends in an *s*. Then use the *whose* test to confirm whether the noun or indefinite pronoun is really possessive.

Editing Activity 6: Final Editing for Possessive Apostrophe Errors

The following student essay is ready for final editing. It is error free except for a number of possessive apostrophe errors—both noun and indefinite pronoun errors. Correct the possessive apostrophe errors in the way that fits this essay best. The number of possessive apostrophe errors in each paragraph is given in parentheses at the end of the paragraph.

Joie T.
English Writing, Sec 6
May 17, 1993

GOOD AND BAD STRESS

Stress is a disease of the twentieth century. We have all heard the doctors warning that stress is harmful to ones health. However, we cannot break the habits that cause stress until we know what these habits are and how we can break them. First, we need to know what causes stress, what stress does to one, and why ones reaction to stress is so harmful. Second, we need to know ones symptoms of stress. Third, we need to know how to change ones behavior and attitude. And fourth, we need to learn simple techniques for managing ones stress. (6)

We respond to stress automatically. For example, when I walked into my secretarys office Monday morning, I saw a big stack of papers waiting for me to take care of. I started to stress out before I even started the project. If I had taken a deep breath and started the job at my normal rate, the job would have gone smoothly. What makes stress so difficult to cope with is that our bodys reaction to stress is automatic. Everyones body is different in the way that it reacts to stress, but the reaction is nonetheless real. (3)

After recognizing ones symptoms of stress, one is able to control ones reactions better. The problem is that one tends to blame stress on things unrelated to the actual causes of stress. For example, after a busy week at work, I noticed that I was having stomach pains. Instead of linking my stomachs pain to what was happening at work, I tried to blame it on the food I had had at a friends house. I was assuming that my pains were caused by food. I was ignoring my bodys cry for release from stress. (5)

The third step is learning how to change ones behavior and attitude. Stress is part of everyones life. You can make stress good or bad depending on how you perceive it. Some people work best under pressure and thrive in competitive situations. For them, stress is a positive thing. For most of us, however, stress results from situations that we have no control over. I couldn't control my jobs demands, so I needed to find a way to control negative stress. (3)

Finally, we can learn relaxation techniques that will help us cope with negative stress. Conscious relaxation is necessary to relieve our bodys stress. Sleep is one way to help one relax ones body. Another good technique is sitting down in a comfortable chair and listening to music. Meditation has also been used to help achieve deep relaxation and peace of mind. Deep breathing is a key ingredient in meditations success. There is a close relationship between our respiratory and nervous systems. We can use our breathing to control our nervous system. (3)

C: Apostrophes in Time Expressions

Historically, the s that we add to nouns and indefinite pronouns to indicate possession had several meanings in addition to "possession" or "ownership." Although most of these other uses of s have disappeared from English over the centuries, one of these uses of s has survived virtually intact: time expressions. Here are some example sentences with the time expression in bold:

13. **Monday's schedule** is posted on the bulletin board.

14. We must have **a ten years' supply** of paper clips.

15. **This semester's assignments** have been very hard.

16. Sunshine will replace **this morning's clouds**.

All of these time expressions require either an *'s* (if they are singular) or an *s'* (if they are plural). Not surprisingly, the *whose* test we can use to identify possessive apostrophes will not work with these expressions of time because time expressions do not mean possession or ownership. For example, compare the following sentences, the first containing a possessive apostrophe and the second containing a time expression:

17. Possessive: I saw the ad in **John's newspaper**.
    whose test: I saw the ad in **whose** newspaper?
    Answer: **John's** newspaper.

18. Time expression: I saw the ad in **today's newspaper**.
    whose test: *I saw the ad in **whose** newspaper?
    Answer: ***Today's** newspaper.

In sentence (17), John owns or possesses a newspaper, so the *whose* test correctly identifies *John* as a possessive noun. In sentence (18), however, the *whose* test fails because *today* does not own or possess a newspaper in the same sense that John does in sentence (17).

Fortunately, there is a simple test that will help us identify time expressions that require an apostrophe: paraphrase the time expression with *for* or *of*. Here is the ***for/of* test** applied to the time expressions we have seen so far:

13a. **Monday's schedule** is posted on the bulletin board.
    for/of test: **The schedule for Monday** is posted on the bulletin board.

14a. We must have **a ten years' supply** of paper clips.
    for/of test: We must have **a supply for ten years** of paper clips.

14a. **This semester's assignments** have been very hard.
    for/of test: **The assignments for this semester** have been very hard.

16a. Sunshine will replace **this morning's clouds**.
    for/of test: Sunshine will replace **the clouds of this morning**.

17a. I saw the ad in **today's newspaper**.
    for/of test: I saw the ad in **the newspaper for today**.

Editing Activity 7: Using the *For/Of* Test to Paraphrase Time Expressions

Each of the following sentences contains a time expression in bold. Use the *for/of* test to paraphrase the time expression. Write the revised sentence in the space provided. The first question is done as an example.

1. **Today's woman** is not satisfied with second-best.
   for/of test: __The woman of today__ *is not satisfied with second-best.*

2. **This year's sales** are down by 20%.
   for/of test:_____

3. There will be **a two weeks' delay** in delivery.
   for/of test:_____

4. Where is **tonight's TV guide?**
   for/of test:_____

5. The coach was upset at **Saturday's unexpected defeat.**
   for/of test:_____

6. **Tonight's concert** is being brought to you by Dain Bosworth.
   for/of test:_____

7. Nothing is less interesting than **yesterday's news.**
   for/of test:_____

8. I will get **two weeks' pay** in place of my vacation time.
   for/of test:_____

9. In **today's economic climate**, no business can ignore foreign competition.
   for/of test:_____

10. **Two seconds' thought** should have shown them their mistake.
    for/of test:_____

11. **This morning's lecture** is on gerunds.
    for/of test:_____

Now you are ready to find and correct all apostrophe errors on your own. The key to eliminating apostrophe errors from your papers is to check every noun and indefinite pronoun that ends in *s*. The *whose* test will help you identify possessive nouns and possessive indefinite pronouns that require an apostrophe. The *for/of* test will help you identify time expressions that require an apostrophe. Apostrophe errors are easy to correct once you have found them. The problem is that without carefully and systematically checking your paper, you will simply not see the possessive words and time expressions that require apostrophes.

Editing Activity 8: Final Editing for Apostrophe Errors

The following student essay is ready for final editing. It is free of errors except for a number of apostrophe errors. Underline the possessive apostrophe phrases and the time expressions, and then add the apostrophes in the correct positions. The number of apostrophe errors in each paragraph is given in parentheses at the end of the paragraph.

David D.
English Writing, Sec 6
February 12, 1993

BALANCING OUR PERSONAL AND
PROFESSIONAL LIVES

In todays society, stress is at such a high level that it affects every working persons life. Working people have to learn how to cope with stress in order to properly balance their personal and professional lives. The first step in dealing with ones stress is learning to work smarter and not harder. We must cut down on the inefficient meetings called on a moments notice, the endless games of telephone tag, and other time-consuming activities that don't really help get the job done. We suffer from too much crisis management that only responds to todays problems without looking ahead to how these problems could have been anticipated and avoided. The loss of so much time on the job causes us to work frantically in the little time that we do control, trying to do a whole days work in the last hour. (6)

Not only do we feel exhausted and frustrated at the days end, we are forced to take a lot of work home with us. Often we have to bring our paperwork home with us and try to fit it into our busy home lives. Even if we don't carry home a loaded briefcase, we bring home with us all of the jobs problems for us to worry about all night. (2)

We can keep this up for a few years time, but eventually it all catches up with us. We must protect our time at home. A few hours relaxation can make all the difference in the world. We need to spend time with our family, sit back and watch a little television, or even rent that movie we have been wanting to see. Tomorrows problems can take care of themselves. We can even deal with them better if we come back to work relieved of some of the tension our body has been experiencing. (3)

Weekends are especially important in coping with stress. It is important to plan our weekends activities to reflect the things that bring us real personal satisfaction. For example, my father enjoys doing yard work and other projects around the house, but his days activities are balanced. He doesn't put pressure on himself to get every job done in a certain amount of time. If he can't get the lawn mowed in two hours time, that's OK; he will finish it later. He gets up early and works in the yard for a couple of hours, but then he will take the next few hours off and just relax spending time with other members of the family or even watching a game on TV. This way he gets a lot done in a mornings work, but at the same time he feels he is in control, and he is doing what he wants to do when he wants to do it. (4)

Stress is very hard on everyones body. It causes us to be uptight with ourselves and with all of the people around us. It prevents us from doing a good job at work. The key to reducing stress is balancing our days activities so that we use the time available to us in an effective way. We must also learn to relax and enjoy our free time because a mind that is free of stress enables us to work more productively and efficiently. (2)

CHAPTER 11

BEING EDUCATED

SECTION
◀▶
1

Reading Opinions on What It Means to Be Educated

A: Pre-Reading

One of the goals of education is to increase critical thinking skills. "Critical thinking" does not mean being "critical" in the sense of criticizing or judging. It does not mean simply pointing out that people who do not agree with you are wrong. Instead, "critical thinking" means examining ideas and arguments to see if they are logical and balanced—looking closely at what you read and listening carefully to what you hear. Critical thinkers think for themselves. Critical thinkers read between the lines and listen for the ideas behind the words they hear.

One kind of critical thinking is considering both sides of an issue. Some issues are simple. For example, no one would seriously argue that we should legalize drunk driving. Drunk drivers kill other people and kill themselves. They cause millions of dollars' worth of damage to property each year. They damage individuals and families. On the other hand, most issues are not this simple; most problems do not have single, simple solutions or rules.

In fact, most issues about which people read and write are complex; people have a variety of beliefs, attitudes, experiences, and ideas concerning these issues. Most issues about which people write essays are complex.

The writer writing an essay about an issue that has no clear, generally accepted solution tries to convince his or her readers of the quality and usefulness of that writer's ideas and opinions. One important resource for making a convincing argument is for the writer to consider both sides of an issue.

For example, a writer might believe that high school students should not have jobs in addition to their school work. That writer would be wise to look closely (critically) at the other side of this issue—that some high school students really need the money that their jobs provide and that working at a convenience store, restaurant, or family business can be an important learning experience. A "critical thinker" would be aware of these other concerns and would know that the issue of working high school students is complex.

A writer's awareness of the complexity of an issue is one of his or her best resources for writing. Writers need to know what they think, but they should also know the opinions of people who disagree with them. By looking at opinions other than their own and the reasons behind them, writers can make their own thinking more complex and interesting.

In addition, a writer who can look at both sides of an issue and admit that some of the ideas held by his or her opponents are valid and important is often a better writer. That writer, by admitting the value of other people's ideas, actually makes his or her own ideas and arguments more convincing.

This chapter contains two readings. In them the authors wrestle with thoughts about what it means to be "educated." Neither author offers a perfect answer to this question. The issue itself—what it means to be "educated"—will always remain in doubt. Still, these two writers present their own ideas about this issue, and both look at and think critically about other people's ideas.

Pre-Reading Activities

Discussion

1. Some people believe that education is like a series of hoops a person has to jump through and that after that person has jumped through as many hoops as he or she can or wants to, then education stops. High school graduation, for example, might be one of these hoops. With others, discuss this idea of hoops. Try to see both sides of this issue—how education is like jumping through hoops and how it is not.

2. Another issue that is debated is whether people learn more in school or in the "real world": do they learn more by taking courses and studying or by going out, getting a job, and learning about that job by doing it? With others, discuss what kinds of things one learns in school and what kinds of things one learns from having and doing a job.

Reading Suggestions

(Keep these suggestions in mind as you read "Living Education" by Michele Cook and "Learning on the Farm" by Randall Trinkle.)

1. Watch for places in the two essays where the writers are being reasonable, where it looks like they are thinking "critically." Underline or highlight these places.

2. One of the best aspects of reading is the fact that it helps a reader come up with his or her own ideas on an issue. Write down a few of the ideas you get while reading "Living Education" and "Learning on the Farm."

3. What is each author's purpose? What point is each writer trying to make?

B.1: Reading

"Living Education"

BY MICHELE COOK

Last year in a classroom I was visiting, a teacher I know told her class that once they graduated from high school, they wouldn't have to read and write anymore. It's hard to believe that someone with a college education could say such a stupid thing, but enlightenment is not handed out with college degrees. This teacher has not been looking around, has not been reading about the changes in the world. She has stopped growing.

Education is a process of personal growth that continues throughout life. College degrees are helpful for getting a foot in various career doors, but once in the door whether you rise to the top or settle near the bottom of a profession depends upon your ability and willingness to continue learning and growing.

In times past, there were many high-paying jobs available that allowed a person to lead a comfortable life without education beyond high school, but these jobs are scarce now. Look around at the jobs available today. Without experience or training, you can probably get a job at a fast-food restaurant for minimum wage. That wouldn't be bad for awhile, but it is a no-frills lifestyle. I know a 42-year-old man, Jeff, who is working for $5 an hour at Toys R Us. As a young man, he made good money in an industry that has no place for him anymore. Now, he can't afford to buy a car. Jeff would love to find better paying work, but he is hoping that a nice state job will drop into his lap somehow. His education stopped years ago, and he has no idea how to get out of the hole he finds himself in. Jeff goes to work, goes home, watches television until bed, and starts over the next day. The point is not that Jeff has little money; many people never care about material possessions. What is important is that Jeff is not driving his own life. He just coasts.

Education can open doors to new opportunities, and it can open doors in your head. Education is about looking at something outside yourself, broadening your experience, and deciding if the new ideas fit into your life or not. Either way, your world is larger for having looked. Jeff may open a door now and then, but he is so rooted in his track that he just stands there and lets the wind blow through.

My friend Kathleen is on her third career. With a degree in chemistry, she worked for many years in a hospital examining human cells under a microscope. The work was fascinating for awhile, but she began to feel stifled, stuck. She wanted to own a restaurant, so Kathleen quit her well-paying job at the hospital and, for the next two years, she took jobs in several restaurants to learn the business. Her small cafe lasted less than a year; the restaurant business is tough to break into. What to do next? Kathleen looked outside herself, looked inside herself, and chose. She spent the next year at Gonzaga University, earning a Master's degree in Psychology. Kathleen was hired as the administrator of the Abused Women's program in Pullman/Moscow. Were the years she spent learning about the restaurant business wasted? No. The fact that she had once owned her own business was an important factor in getting the job with the Abused Women's program.

Kathleen is now perfectly happy, greeting each day with enthusiasm, wondering what her next adventure will be. And Jeff is now depressed, now raging against the universe because of his miserable existence. Kathleen and Jeff both held low-paying jobs; they both are of average intelligence. The difference between them is that Kathleen has an ongoing education; Jeff has stopped growing and cannot see beyond his own narrow existence. Kathleen has an expanding world, enriched by an incredible variety of friends and acquaintances. Jeff's world is walled with the things he knows that he can't do because he has chosen to stop growing, chosen to stop moving ahead, chosen to stop being educated.

Are you waiting for the day when you can close your textbooks for the last time? Looking forward to cruising along in life with no more demands on your brain? Well, think about this: if you stop learning right now, your personal world will begin to shrink. Eventually you may find yourself stuck on some small track like Jeff, unable to see a way out, believing that winning the lottery is your only real hope of improving your life. Scary, isn't it?

You don't have to be a chemist or a psychologist or a teacher to be educated. What you have to do is reach outside yourself to other people and ideas. Take classes when you can; any class—Chinese cooking, contract bridge—expands your life.

Not all of you will be in the position to allow your ignorance to sour a classroom like the teacher who ignorantly believes that education ends at high school graduation. Still, by making the choice to be an actively educated person, you will in some ways positively affect the lives of those around you as well as enrich your own. It's your choice. What will it be? ■

B.2: Reading

"Learning on the Farm"

BY RANDALL TRINKLE

For some reason, I have always been really hung up on the term, "educated," because, according to Webster, an educated person is one who has been trained or schooled. Well, this could really be talking about almost anyone, couldn't it? After all, is not everyone trained in something, even if that something is survival? Another reason that I have a real tough time with the term "educated" is because it is a highly relative term. In other words, is someone only educated if he/she has conformed to the formal training offered in a major university? I would have to say no; while this may be one type of education, it is not the *only* type of education. Mind you, I am not saying that formal education as we know it is bad; I am merely entertaining the thought that other types of education are just as important.

Growing up as a kid, for example, some things were learned relatively quickly, but then again after a few severe beatings anyone would get the hint. Sassing my mother was definitely a cardinal sin that was punishable by death. I remember one time sassing my mother and feeling the cold hard crack of a wooden spoon over my head; she broke it on my head. Well, I thought that she was mine; after all, she was weaponless. I quickly changed my mind when she brought out a large metal spoon. Likewise, tormenting and smarting off to my older, quite a bit larger brother was another resource for self-inflicted pain. Then there were times such as the one when a very large monster on the varsity baseball team looked at me and said, and I quote, "Trinkle, you are the ugliest thing that I've seen all day."

Well, without blinking an eye, I proceeded to enlighten him: "Gee Jim, you must not have looked in the mirror this morning, huh?"

Needless to say, I was promptly beaten without mercy, and I probably would not be here today if it weren't for my baseball coach stepping in and pulling this hairy galoot off me. From that day on I have walked with a limp.

Thanks to my little lessons in the *School of Hard Knocks*, it did not take much time to realize that in order to survive into my adolescence, I would have to tone down the smart mouth that God had so graciously given me. In a sense, then, a point could be argued that I was "educated." Mind you, not educated in the sense of formal education, but, nevertheless, educated.

Take another example. In my line of summer employment, wheat farming, education is a very important factor. No, I do not mean that all of the hired hands go to night class and study to be better farmers; rather, I mean that every single day some new experience comes up that can be added to the memory bank for future reference. I remember one afternoon while operating a cuber I happened to run across a leak in an irrigation pipe. I promptly proceeded to allow my cuber to sink up to the axles in an oozy patch of mud. Needless to say, I learned a valuable lesson that day about the correlation between boss happiness and cubers being stuck in the mud. Along the same lines, I remember all of the valuable times that I messed up, sometimes in grand proportions, while learning how to operate a Cat up in the fields. Without these experiences I would never have learned even half of what I know now about tractor operation. Mind you, these are only two examples of receiving education on the farm, and I could ramble on literally all night with more examples, but I want to point out one thing—I was "educated" on the farm.

I hope that in this short essay I am not coming across as being anti–formal education, for I believe that it is also very important. Obviously this is so because I am currently working toward my Bachelors of Arts in Education degree. To go a step further, in the not-too-distant future, I will be working toward achieving my master's degree. You see, society as a whole places high value on formal education. In fact, in the eyes of many people, unless a person has gone to a major university, he or she is not educated. I could even stick my neck out a tad bit further by asserting that many prospective employers view formal education as an indicator of a person's being educated. Therefore, I feel that it is very important to achieve a formal education because it fits nicely into the little formula for success in our society.

Now I ask you once again, what does it mean to be "educated"? Is the farmer who knows the optimal times to plant his crop educated? Is the person with a B.A. degree educated? Is the homeless person down on First Avenue educated? Are all of the above educated? I can honestly not answer these questions, although I tend to say that the answer to all of these questions is "yes." Now, how about a question that is *by far* easier to work with: What is the meaning of life? ■

C: Post-Reading

Discussion Suggestions/Questions

Remembering

1. Michele Cook writes about two people, Jeff and Kathleen. How are these two people different?

2. What is Randall Trinkle's attitude toward formal education—the kind of education offered in schools?

Analyzing

1. What is the focus or point of Michele Cook's essay?

2. What is the focus or point of Randall Trinkle's essay?

3. Identify places in Randall Trinkle's essay where he mentions ideas that are different from his own.

Discovering

1. What would Michele Cook, author of "Living Education," say to someone who thought education was simply jumping through a series of hoops?

2. Michele Cook writes that when a person stops learning, that person's world begins to shrink. What does she mean? Is she right?

3. Share and discuss with others some of the ideas you had and wrote down while reading these two essays.

D: Vocabulary Building

1. Building words with *en-* and *-ment*

Enlightenment: "It's hard to believe that someone with a college education could say such a stupid thing, but **enlightenment** is not handed out with college degrees."

Cook: "Living Education"

Roughly speaking, the noun *enlightenment* means something like "wisdom." To get a sense of *enlightenment's* full meaning, however, we need to see how the word is derived. The word *enlightenment* consists of four pieces: a prefix, **en-**, the stem or root, **light,** and two suffixes, **-en** and **-ment.** Here is how the four parts fit together to create the noun **enlightenment.**

First, the noun *light* is changed into *lighten* by adding *-en*, a suffix that changes adjectives into verbs. Next, the prefix *en-* is added to *lighten* (in its meaning of "to teach or give wisdom to someone") to produce *enlighten*. In addition to changing parts of speech, the prefix *en-* often adds the special meaning "to cause or to make." For example, **enslave** means "to make or cause someone to become a slave" and **enrich** means "to make or cause something to be rich." When *en-* is added to the verb *lighten*, the *en-* doesn't change the part of speech (because *lighten* is already a verb), but *en-* does add the meaning of "to cause or to make." For example, in the phrase "to enlighten someone," *enlighten* means "to cause or make that person understand something."

Finally, the suffix *-ment* is added to change the verb *enlighten* into the abstract noun *enlightenment*. When *-ment* is added to certain verbs, it creates a noun whose meaning is the "state" of the verb. For example, the noun *retirement* means the "state" of being **retired**. Likewise, *enlightenment* means the "state" of being **enlightened**.

Now we can see that the noun *enlightenment* is more than just a four-syllable word for "wisdom." The meaning of *enlightenment* carries with it all of its history of derivation from its root *light*. The various prefixes and suffixes add layers of meaning to the word so that as the word builds, it gets bigger, richer, and more complex. Good writers exploit the richness of complex words to convey ideas and attitudes that go far beyond the most literal meaning of a word.

Vocabulary Building Activity 1: Building Words with *En-* and *-Ment*

The abstract noun *enlightenment* is built with the prefix *en-* and the suffixes *-en* and *-ment*. The prefix *en-* (*em-* before words beginning with a *p* or *b*) is one of the few prefixes that changes nouns to verbs. The suffix *-ment* is one of several suffixes that changes verbs to abstract nouns. As is typical of prefixes and suffixes that change part of speech, both *en-* and *-ment* are rather unpredictable; they can be used with some words but not with others.

A list of nouns follows. See how many of them you can change to verbs by adding the prefix *en-*. Then see how many of these verbs you can further change into abstract nouns by adding the suffix *-ment*. Notice how the meaning of the word shifts when a prefix or suffix is added. The first question is done as an example.

Noun	Verb (en-)	Abstract Noun (ment-)
1. act	*enact*	*enactment*
2. body		
3. capsule		
4. chant		
5. circle		
6. code		
7. courage		
8. force		
9. list		
10. place		

2. Words related to *form*

> <u>Conform:</u> "In other words, is someone only educated if he/she has **conformed** to the formal training offered in a major university?"
>
> *Trinkle: "Learning on the Farm"*

The verb *conform* consists of a prefix **con-**, which comes from the Latin prefix *com-*, which means "same, together, with" plus **form**, which comes from the Latin noun *forma*, which means "shape." *Conform* usually means "to act in accordance with rules or customs." Sometimes it has a negative connotation of blindly following rules instead of thinking for oneself. In the essay "Learning on the Farm," *conform* is probably used with this negative meaning.

The word *form* appears in many English words. As a noun it can refer to the physical shape of something, or it can refer to the way in which something is organized. This second meaning of *form* is the basis for many related words.

The adjective **formal** refers to something that follows the rules or form. When we describe an event as being formal, we mean that it is done in a very traditional way (such as a **formal dance**) or that it follows some set of rules (such as a **formal hearing**). The opposite of *formal* is **informal**, which describes something that is done in a casual or unplanned way. Also related to *formal* is the noun **formality**, which means "something that is required by a rule" (often used in a negative sense of a mere technicality). The noun **formula** is a rule or a statement that follows certain rules. The verb to **formulate** means "to create something according to a formula or a set of rules."

Vocabulary Building Activity 2: Words Related to *Form*

Write in the word from the left column that best fits in each blank space in the sentences in the column on the right.

---

1. conform

2. formality

3. formula

4. formal

5. format

a. Something that has to be done, but which has no real meaning, is a mere _____ .

b. A _____ is a recipe for making something or a general rule stated in mathematical terms.

c. An outline or plan to be followed in doing something is a _____ .

d. Lawyers must _____ to the rules of evidence.

e. People always wear _____ clothing when attending religious services.

---

3. Different words derived from *specere*

Prospective: ". . . many **prospective** employers view formal education as an indicator of a person's being educated."

Trinkle: "Learning on the Farm"

Prospective is an adjective meaning "potential" or "possible." It is derived from the verb **prospect**, which means "to search for gold or other minerals." The **-ive** ending is used to change verbs into adjectives. Some other examples of **-ive** changing verbs to adjectives are **attract/attractive** and **possess/possessive.**

The verb *prospect* comes from a Latin word *prospectus*, which means "a distant view or a vista" (literally, something seen in front of you). The Latin word itself is derived from the prefix *pro-*, "in front of," and the verb *specere*, "to look." The Latin word *prospectus* also comes into English without change as the word **prospectus.** A *prospectus* is a formal proposal for an investment that allows a potential investor to see what he or she is getting into.

The word *prospect* comes from the Latin verb *specere*, "to look." This word appears in many English words borrowed from Latin. Among the nouns derived from *specere* are the following: a **specter** is a ghost that appears before our eyes. A **spectacle** is a performance for the public to look at. **Spectacles** is an old-fashioned word for glasses—something you look through. A **spectator** is someone who looks at a public event. The word **spectrum** originally meant the whole range of visible light.

An interesting verb derived from *specere* is **speculate**, which means "to think about or to make guesses about something." This verb is derived from a Latin word that meant "to observe from a watchtower." Related words are the noun **speculation**, which means "a theory or conclusion reached by **speculating**," and the adjective **speculative**, which describes an activity or idea of an unproved nature.

Vocabulary Building Activity 3: Different Words Derived from *Specere*

Write in the word from the left column that best fits in each blank space in the sentences in the column on the right.

---

1. spectacle	a. They invested in a _____ stock.
2. speculative	b. The defendant made a real _____ of himself.
3. spectrum	c. By law, companies offering stock are required to issue a _____ .
4. prospective	
5. prospectus	d. Her father looked carefully at the _____ son-in-law.
	e. The discussion group reflected a whole _____ of different views on the matter.

DRAFTING

Drafting to Present Your Opinion and Acknowledge Other Perspectives on the Issue

A: Pre-Writing

There are many ways people prepare themselves to write. Reading, thinking, and talking to others about what they have read and what they thought about it are all good ways to prepare to write. In very important ways, life itself prepares people to write. Michele Cook and Randall Trinkle, preparing to write the two essays presented earlier in this chapter, thought about things that had happened to them and about people they knew before they started to write. They used their life experiences as pre-writing.

In addition, both of these writers took time before writing to consider not just what they believed, but what people who did not agree with them might think. Again, this is a kind of critical thinking. Good communicators—and all good writers are good communicators—use this kind of thinking all the time. They consider how other people will respond to their ideas.

Pre-Writing Activity 1: Creating a Grid

One of the reading suggestions you were asked to use while reading "Living Education" and "Learning on the Farm" was to write down ideas <u>you</u> had while reading these two essays. You may use these ideas now. You need at least five of your own ideas about the issue for the essay you will soon write. That issue is "What does it mean to be 'educated'?"

You might not use all of your five ideas when you write your essay. Here we are practicing critical thinking for its own sake and because it is a good kind of pre-writing. The following grid is designed to encourage critical thinking.

The grid works like this. On the left side, write in your five ideas about the question, "What does it mean to be 'educated'?" Then, on the right, complete the three "but other people might say" clauses with ideas that oppose your own. One example is provided.

Writer's ideas	Possible responses from people who do not agree with those ideas
I think I can get a good job without a college degree,	but other people might say *there aren't many of those kinds of good jobs left.*
	but other people might say *yes, but you will have a tough time getting promoted.*
	but other people might say *college is about more than learning how to do a particular job.*

1. I think_____ but other people might say_____

_____

_____

_____

_____

but other people might say_____

_____

_____

_____

but other people might say_____

_____

_____

_____

_____

2. I think_____ but other people might say_____

_____

_____

_____

_____

_____

_____

but other people might say_____

_____

_____

_____

_____ .

but other people might say_____

_____

_____

_____

_____ .

3. I think_____   but other people might say_____

_____   _____

_____   _____

_____   _____

_____   _____ .

but other people might say_____

_____

_____

_____

_____ .

but other people might say_____

_____

_____

_____

_____ .

DRAFTING

DRAFTING

4. I think_____   but other people might say_____

_____   _____

_____   _____

_____   _____

_____   _____

_____   _____ .

but other people might say_____

_____

_____

_____

_____

_____ .

but other people might say_____

_____

_____

_____

_____

_____

_____ .

5. I think_____   but other people might say_____

_____   _____

_____   _____

_____   _____

_____   _____

_____   _____ .

_____

but other people might say_____

_____

_____

_____

_____ .

but other people might say_____

_____

_____

_____

_____

_____ .

DRAFTING

You do not need to limit your "but other people might say" responses to three for each of your ideas. If more occur to you, write them down.

B: Writing a First or Initial Draft

Once you have completed the pre-writing grid, write for thirty or forty minutes about one or more of <u>your</u> ideas. If one of your ideas has changed during the pre-writing process, consider the change a normal part of pre-writing. Writing helps people to write what they think, but it can also help people to reconsider what they think and change their minds. Write quickly once you start. Do not worry about spelling, punctuation, or grammar at this time. You will do more work on your draft after you have written it.

SECTION
3

Revising to Acknowledge Other Perspectives on the Issue

REVISING

A: Other Aspects of an Issue or Idea

Each person has ideas. Each person thinks. Resources for thinking include experience, training, reading, writing, and talking with others. We also use radio and TV programs and movies as resources for thinking. From all these resources we take facts and ideas and form our own opinions.

When we communicate our opinions, by speaking or writing them, it is normal to share some of the facts, experiences, and thinking that helped us to form those opinions. Often, we communicate our opinions hoping that the people we share them with will understand and share those opinions with us. We want others to see that our opinions are good ones. Usually, when we communicate, we are asking others *not to believe but to consider* our ideas and opinions.

Other people are more likely to consider our opinions when we ourselves appear to be willing to consider theirs. This is easy when talking to someone. We can say, "This is what I think. What's your opinion?" When communicating in writing, however, the person who reads what we write isn't sitting next to us and asking us questions and sharing his or her own opinions.

In writing, we can include language that tells the reader that we are willing to listen to and consider opinions that are different from our own. We do this by acknowledging, in writing, the other sides of an issue or idea. Doing this makes writers look reasonable and fair-minded. It encourages readers to read with open minds, to consider fairly the writer's ideas and opinions.

Look at the following examples.

Stating an opinion: *People learn to write by writing.*

Stating an opinion and acknowledging other aspects of the issue: *People learn to write by writing. Of course reading, talking, and listening are also important activities for people learning to write.*

The second example, for most people, seems more reasonable.

B: Revising Drafts of Student Essays

Presented here are three drafts of student essays written on the topic, "What does it mean to be educated?" Read the following student draft, "Educated Idiots." While reading, underline or highlight in the essay places where the writer could acknowledge other aspects of the issue and make herself look more fair or reasonable.

Student Draft: "Educated Idiots"

EDUCATED IDIOTS

What is an educated person? Well, some people think of an educated person as one who spends all his or her time in the library. Educated people are often seen as those who don't participate in anything of an unacademic nature, are considered by some to be nerds, and as complete nerds at that! Those who think of nothing but school and academics as the important things in life are IDIOTS! They don't know what they are missing.

After all, who needs to sit in the library reading books all day when there are places to go, people to see, and things to do? One sometimes wonders if these so-called "educated people" ever struggle through physical education classes. I mean, do they have any muscles in their bodies which are developed, other than the ones in their heads? We all know that everybody has a brain, but some of us find more to do with it than spend all our time with our noses in a book.

These nerds sometimes think the only way to learn anything is "by the book." This is fine, but what happens to this theory when the car dies and they don't have the slightest idea what's wrong? I'd like to see them check the points to see if they are opening or not! This is where experience best gained outside of the classroom comes in. After all, most people don't carry <u>Chilton</u> (an auto repair manual) around in their back pockets, and it definitely isn't one chosen for its reading enjoyment.

Car repair is a good example for me to use for showing a way of gaining a valuable education outside of the classroom. This is something learned most effectively through hands-on experience. Granted, <u>Chilton</u> does come in handy when you have to install new points and set them or check the firing order on your spark plugs, but let's be realistic. There usually needs to be a link somewhere between the book and the experience. This is knowledge gained hands-on. It is much easier to understand how to change a set of points when you look at the part and work from there. Just because the "nerds" walk around with their plastic pocket protectors and volumes of Shakespearean works doesn't mean, contrary to their belief, that they know everything. Maybe they figure they will make a lot of money and that they will hire someone to work on their cars? Don't count on it! Even if they want to continue with this attitude, they need to realize that pocket protectors aren't for everyone. If they were, who would work on their cars?

Some people gain their education outside of the formal classroom and are just as successful as those who do not. A degree from Harvard and an office on the eighth floor? BIG DEAL! This is not a desired image for everyone. What about the mechanic who opens up his or her own garage? This image may be just as powerful to some people. This is an important thing about education: a person has to enjoy what he or she is doing. For some reason I don't see Mr. or Ms. Mechanic sitting in an office eight hours a day, five days a week, nor do I see Mr. and Ms. Business Executive changing oil and spark plugs in a greasy shop for eight hours a day.

I know a person who dropped out of high school as a sophomore but used his knowledge and skills to his advantage. He used this skill and ability to work on cars; he can now do just about anything that might need doing. He is now a bus mechanic and transportation supervisor at a small school and enjoys his job as well as does it competently.

If one depends on a classroom education alone, how much knowledge can one actually gain? Sure, textual (yawn) knowledge, but how are you going to relate that to people or living? Once something is put into your head, you have to have the skills necessary to get this information and use it in an actual situation. If one cannot apply knowledge to a situation, one does not have a real grasp on the "educated" aspect of life.

So to those of you out there who may be pocket protector people, remember you are not the only educated persons around, and I may just be the one who changes your spark plugs! You don't have to sit in the classroom for fifteen to twenty years to be considered educated.

Shelly S.

REVISING

Now look again at the following revision of this essay. In this version, some of the writer's opinions have been underlined. Then language has been added to acknowledge other aspects of the issues addressed.

Revisions: "Educated Idiots"

```
                    EDUCATED IDIOTS

     What is an educated person? Well, some people think of
an educated person as one who spends all his or her time
in the library. Educated people are often seen as those
who don't participate in anything of an unacademic na-
ture, are considered by some to be nerds, and as complete
nerds at that! Those who think of nothing but school and
academics as the important things in life are IDIOTS! They
don't know what they are missing.
     After all, who needs to sit in the library reading books
all day when there are places to go, people to see, and
things to do? One sometimes wonders if these so-called
"educated people" ever struggle through physical edu-
cation classes. I mean, do they have any muscles in their
bodies which are developed, other than the ones in their
heads? We all know that everybody has a brain, but some
of us find more to do with it than spend all our time with
our noses in a book.
     These nerds sometimes think the only way to learn
anything is "by the book." This is fine, but what happens
to this theory when the car dies and they don't have the
slightest idea what's wrong? I'd like to see them check
the points to see if they are opening or not! This is where
experience best gained outside of the classroom comes in.
After all, most people don't carry Chilton (an auto
repair manual) around in their back pockets, and it
definitely isn't one chosen for its reading enjoyment.
```

Car repair is a good example for me to use for showing a way of gaining a valuable education outside of the classroom. This is something learned most effectively through hands-on experience. Granted, <u>Chilton</u> does come in handy when you have to install new points and set them or check the firing order on your spark plugs, but let's be realistic. There usually needs to be a link somewhere between the book and the experience. This is knowledge gained hands-on. It is much easier to understand how to change a set of points when you look at the part and work from there. Just because the "nerds" walk around with their plastic pocket protectors and volumes of Shakespearean works doesn't mean, contrary to their be-lief, that they know everything. Maybe they figure they will make a lot of money and that they will hire someone to work on their cars? Don't count on it! Even if they want to continue with this attitude, they need to realize that <u>pocket protectors aren't for everyone. If they were, who</u> <u>would work on their cars?</u> *On the other hand, not everybody* *needs a wrench in one hand and a screwdriver in the other.* *Some people go to school to be teachers, engineers, nurses* *and doctors. I say, ''Let 'em!''*

Some people gain their education outside of the formal classroom and are just as successful as those who do not. A degree from Harvard and an office on the eighth floor? BIG DEAL! This is not a desired image for everyone. What about the mechanic who opens up his or her own garage? This image may be just as powerful to some people. This is an important thing about education: a person has to enjoy what he or she is doing. For some reason I don't see Mr. or Ms. Mechanic sitting in an office eight hours a day, five days a week, nor do I see Mr. and Ms. Business Executive changing oil and spark plugs in a greasy shop for eight hours a day.

I know a person who dropped out of high school as a sophomore but used his knowledge and skills to his ad-vantage. He used this skill and ability to work on cars; he can now do just about anything that might need doing. He is now a bus mechanic and transportation supervisor at a small school and enjoys his job as well as does it competently.

If one depends on a classroom education alone, how much knowledge can one actually gain? Sure, textual (yawn) knowledge, but how are you going to relate that to people or living? Once something is put into your head, you have to have the skills necessary to get this information and use it in an actual situation. <u>If one cannot apply knowledge to a situation, one does not have a real grasp on the "educated" aspect of life.</u> *Some people think school teaches more than job skills, and they are right. Individuals learn thinking and social skills in the classroom, and these are valuable to everybody. The best classes actually help people to apply the knowledge they are learning. I just think education happens outside of school too.*

So to those of you out there who may be pocket protector people, remember you are not the only educated persons around, and I may just be the one who changes your spark plugs! You don't have to sit in the classroom for fifteen to twenty years to be considered educated.

Shelly S.

Practicing Revising to Acknowledge Other Aspects of the Issue

Following are two more student drafts on the same topic.

Revising Activity 1: "Fill in the Bubble"

Read the following student draft and look for places where the writer might add language to acknowledge other aspects of the issue. Then, working with others or alone, revise the second copy of the student draft "Fill in the Bubble" by adding language that acknowledges other aspects of the issue in the spaces provided. The goal is to help the writer appear to be more reasonable and fair.

REVISING

Student Draft: "Fill in the Bubble"

```
                    FILL IN THE BUBBLE

   I recall one early Saturday morning at around 7:00 a.m.
when I had to go down to my high school. I, along with
several other students, was directed into the large,
gloomy, cold-feeling atmosphere that was offered by the
school's auditorium. This cold, gloomy setting seemed
appropriate for the task each of us was about to encoun-
ter. For about three to four hours, we would have to turn
the pages of this thin booklet and keep our banana-
colored, number two pencils moving rapidly. After taking
this test, which was called the S.A.T. (Standardized
Aptitude Test), I was satisfied with just getting done. I
didn't feel like I had learned or accomplished anything
except turning booklet pages and breaking the leads of my
number two pencils. I wasn't allowed to express my
thoughts, feelings, or interests with my peers or use
resources to aid my understanding of the subject matter
covered.
   After reading an article entitled "Standardized Test,"
written by Charles Carroll, I discovered that these tests
are considered the ultimate traditional tests. They con-
sist of multiple choice questions, which I definitely
found out about, that are quickly scored by a computer
scan system. These tests are used to compare the perfor-
mances of groups, such as from one high school compared
with another.
   Usually, the items on these tests do not even reflect the
content being taught within the classroom. For example,
there was an item on the S.A.T.'s reading comprehension
section dealing with underwater fishing in some region in
Alaska, and I was supposed to answer the questions on this
section. I said to myself after reading this, "What in
the heck does this mean? I don't remember studying about
underwater fishing, and I can't relate to this subject
matter in any way."
```

REVISING

Another purpose of this test is to measure if an individual is able to enroll into a four-year university and certain programs within that university. I found out the hard way when I tried to enroll in a Teacher Education Program. The undergraduate advisor in the Education Department informed me that my S.A.T. scores were not meeting the minimum 800 point standard, so I had to take a Te-Tep test offered by the Education Program. This test consisted of the same three to four hour block, and I had to bring my famous banana-colored, number two pencils. After spending three to four hours in one of the classrooms on a hot, sunny afternoon, I was again satisfied to have just completed the task. Four weeks later, I discovered that I had received the score required by the state. However, I didn't successfully pass all parts of the test, so I couldn't enroll in the Education Program. I felt like I was in the same predicament I had been in five years ago. After three years of high school, I didn't have success on the S.A.T., and after going to college, I still could not totally pass a timed test.

I am seriously concerned about the usage of standardized tests. They are used for determiners in evaluating if an individual is knowledgeable or educated enough to go to college or to become a teacher. I do not see myself interacting with a stack of S.A.T. booklets within my classroom. I will be working with a group of young people with bright, intelligent minds who need to be able to express themselves. Self-expression is a very important concept within the school systems, and these standardized tests lack giving the students the opportunity for self-expression to surface.

I also can't stop thinking of all the young people who are living in low socio-economic situations, like the one I lived in, who will decide to attend college if given the opportunity through scholarships or financial aid. They will have to face the same difficult road as I, and I wonder if they will have the willpower and determination to strive forward. How many doors with opportunity on the other side of them will be sealed shut due to these people's lack of ability to relate to the content presented and pass these standardized tests, even after several attempts?

Until some modifications are done to these tests, they will continue to have the power to decide the futures of bright young men and women. Fortunately for me, I didn't lose sight of my goals and decide to discontinue my education after these two painful experiences. In a sense, I was educated enough to figure out the test taking strategies which helped fill in the bubbles of these limited and limiting standardized tests.

Ivan C.

Revisions: "Fill in the Bubble"

FILL IN THE BUBBLE

I recall one early Saturday morning at around 7:00 a.m. when I had to go down to my high school. I, along with several other students, was directed into the large, gloomy, cold-feeling atmosphere that was offered by the school's auditorium. This cold, gloomy setting seemed appropriate for the task each of us was about to encounter. For about three to four hours, we would have to turn the pages of this thin booklet and keep our banana-colored, number two pencils moving rapidly. After taking this test, which was called the S.A.T. (Standardized Aptitude Test), I was satisfied with just getting done. I didn't feel like I had learned or accomplished anything except turning booklet pages and breaking the leads of my number two pencils. I wasn't allowed to express my thoughts, feelings, or interests with my peers or use resources to aid my understanding of the subject matter covered.

After reading an article entitled "Standardized Test," written by Charles Carroll, I discovered that these tests are considered the ultimate traditional tests. They consist of multiple choice questions, which I definitely found out about, that are quickly scored by a computer scan system. These tests are used to compare the performances of groups, such as from one high school compared with another.

Usually, the items on these tests do not even reflect the content being taught within the classroom. For example, there was an item on the S.A.T.'s reading comprehension section dealing with underwater fishing in some region in Alaska, and I was supposed to answer the questions on this section. I said to myself after reading this, "What in the heck does this mean? I don't remember studying about underwater fishing, and I can't relate to this subject matter in any way."

Another purpose of this test is to measure if an individual is able to enroll into a four-year university and certain programs within that university. I found out the hard way when I tried to enroll in a Teacher Education Program. The undergraduate advisor in the Education Department informed me that my S.A.T. scores were not meeting the minimum 800 point standard, so I had to take a Te-Tep test offered by the Education Program. This test consisted of the same three to four hour block, and I had to bring my famous banana-colored, number two pencils. After spending three to four hours in one of the classrooms on a hot, sunny afternoon, I was again satisfied to have just completed the task. Four weeks later, I discovered that I had received the score required by the state. However, I didn't successfully pass all parts of the test, so I couldn't enroll in the Education Program. I felt like I was in the same predicament I had been in five years ago. After three years of high school, I didn't have success on the S.A.T., and after going to college, I still could not totally pass a timed test.

I am seriously concerned about the usage of standardized tests. They are used for determiners in evaluating if an individual is knowledgeable or educated enough to go to college or to become a teacher._____

_____

_____

_____

_____

I do not see myself interacting with a stack of S.A.T. booklets within my classroom. I will be working with a group of young people with bright, intelligent minds who need to be able to express themselves. Self-expression is a very important concept within the school systems, and these standardized tests lack giving the students the opportunity for self-expression to surface.

REVISING

I also can't stop thinking of all the young people who are living in low socio-economic situations, like the one I lived in, who will decide to attend college if given the opportunity through scholarships or financial aid. They will have to face the same difficult road as I, and I wonder if they will have the willpower and determination to strive forward. How many doors with opportunity on the other side of them will be sealed shut due to these people's lack of ability to relate to the content presented and pass these standardized tests, even after several attempts?

Until some modifications are done to these tests, they will continue to have the power to decide the futures of bright young men and women. Fortunately for me, I didn't lose sight of my goals and decide to discontinue my education after these two painful experiences. In a sense, I was educated enough to figure out the test taking strategies which helped fill in the bubbles of these limited and limiting standardized tests.

Ivan C.

Revising Activity 2: Learning to Be Different

Working with others or alone, revise the student draft "Learning to Be Different" in the following ways:

1. Underline or highlight places where the writer could add language to acknowledge other aspects of the issue.

2. In two or three sentences for each place you marked, add language that makes the writer seem more fair or reasonable.

REVISING

Student Draft: "Learning to Be Different"

LEARNING TO BE DIFFERENT

When I began college, my ideal of an "educated" person was the professor who dressed very conservative, spoke in a very clear dialect, and displayed a great deal of self-confidence. I developed an almost instant respect for these "all-knowing" professors who were such a contrast to the people I had known in my previous occupation. I guess I found it refreshing to see someone with what appeared to be "logical" solutions to many of society's problems.

As my education progressed, I became aware of a certain characteristic in many of my professors. I noticed that while they all preached objectivity, few of them even came close to being objective. Most of them had as much a mind set as a union steel worker; the only difference was that the professor could use academic language and "research" methods to "prove" what he or she already believed. I soon learned that I could write a really silly paper with a professor's viewpoint and get a better grade than if I wrote a well-planned paper with a different view than the professor had.

I soon began questioning the value of being "educated." The only thing that really stopped me from becoming disillusioned were the changes I saw taking place within myself. When I entered college, I had just come from an environment where everything was black and white and where every problem had a simple solution. I had very negative opinions toward all individuals who did not share my values. For example, I believed that all individuals who dressed in a unique manner were burdens on society because I had been taught that individuality was counterproductive to a society.

It was during my first quarter in higher education that I saw these values of mine begin to slowly change. I began to understand that it was necessary for me to examine both sides of an issue if I wanted to have an objective opinion on that issue. This is to say that when one group opposes new taxes and another group of residents is in favor of them, one should listen to both of their opinions before drawing a conclusion. I also began to understand a concept often called "cultural relativity," which basically means "accept people for what they are because they are products of their environments." An example of this is the tendency of some international students to cut in the middle of a dining hall line. To the average observer, it would appear that these students are rude, while an individual who understands "cultural relativity" will ask him or herself if this behavior is a result of not knowing local customs.

Now, after some higher education, I believe that there are two factors that must be present for an individual to fit my definition of an "educated" person. The first factor is "cultural relativity." I believe an individual is only truly educated if he or she can accept the cultures of those who are different. A second factor of an educated person is to be able to examine all sides of an issue before arriving at a conclusion.

These are my ideas of what an educated person should be. They are what I strive for.

Jack M.

REVISING

C: Revising Your Draft

Working alone or with others, revise the draft of a paper you wrote on the topic of what it means to be "educated." For this revision, use the strategies you have learned and practiced in this chapter.

D: Helping Others to Revise Their Drafts

It is often easier to see in someone else's writing where an idea or opinion needs to be revised to acknowledge other aspects of an issue. Exchange drafts with another writer and identify places in each other's papers where revisions are needed.

E: Optional Revision

Use the revision strategy—"Revising to Add Transitions"—from Chapter 8 to make your essay even better.

SECTION

4

Final Editing for Faulty Parallelism

Parallelism refers to a series of two or more elements of the same type joined by a coordinating conjunction—usually *and* but sometimes *or* or *but*. For example, in the essay "Living Education," the first of the two readings, the author uses three parallel noun phrases:

1.   You don't have to be <u>a chemist</u> or <u>a psychologist</u> or <u>a teacher</u> to be educated.

In sentence (1) the three parallel elements are noun phrases.

Faulty parallelism is a series that contains elements that are not of the same type. A common kind of faulty parallelism occurs when the elements that are supposed to be parallel are not the same part of speech, as in this example:

2.   * Senator Blather is <u>vain</u>, <u>pompous</u>, and **a bore.**

EDITING

The first two elements in the series are the adjectives *vain* and *pompous*. However, the third element in the series is not an adjective; it is the noun phrase *a bore*. Mixing different parts of speech in a series is faulty parallelism—sort of like mixing apples and oranges.

Once we have seen that a series contains faulty parallelism, it is usually easy to fix the problem. For example, we can correct sentence (2) by changing the noun phrase *a bore* into the corresponding adjective *boring* so that all three elements in the series are now adjectives:

2a.   Senator Blather is <u>vain</u>, <u>pompous</u>, and **boring**.

As is often the case, the problem is not fixing the error after it has been found; the problem is finding the error to begin with. Accordingly, we will begin this section by developing some ways to test elements in a series to see if they are parallel.

A useful way to visualize parallelism is to stack up the parallel elements in the same place in the sentence. For example, we could visualize the parallelism in sentences (1) and (2a) this way:

1a.   You don't have to be   **a chemist,**
                          or   **a psychologist,**
                          or   **a teacher**   to be educated.

2b.   Senator Blather is   **vain,**
                              pompous,
                  and   **boring**.

The advantage of stacking the elements in a series is that we can see if the elements in the stack are all of the same kind. For example, it is easy to see that each of the elements stacked in the two example sentences are the same type as the other elements in the same stack. We will call this way of representing parallel elements a **parallelism stack**. Now you try your hand at representing parallel elements in a parallelism stack.

Editing Activity 1: Parallelism Stacks

The following sentences are taken from the two essays in the reading. Each of the sentences contains a series of parallel elements.

1.   Underline the parallel elements in the sentence.

2.   Rewrite the sentence in the form of a parallelism stack in the space provided.

The first two questions are done as examples.

EDITING

1. Jeff goes to work, goes home, watches television until bed, and starts over the next day.
   Answer:
   Jeff **goes to work**, **goes home**, **watches television until bed**, and **starts over the next day**.
   Jeff **goes to work,**
       goes home,
       watches television until bed,
   and **starts over the next day.**

2. . . . enriched by an incredible variety of friends and acquaintances.
   Answer:
   . . . enriched by an incredible variety of **friends** and **acquaintances.**
   . . . enriched by an incredible variety of **friends**
                               and acquaintances.

3. This teacher has not been looking around, has not been reading about the changes in the world.

   _____

   _____

4. No, I do not mean that all of the hired hands go to night class and study to be better farmers.

   _____

   _____

5. I remember one time sassing my mother and feeling the cold hard crack of a wooden spoon over my head.

   _____

   _____

6. He is so rooted in his track that he just stands there and lets the wind blow through.

   _____

   _____

7. . . . if it weren't for my baseball coach's stepping in and pulling this hairy galoot off me.

   _____

   _____

8. Education is about looking at something outside yourself, broadening your experience, and deciding if the new ideas fit into your life or not.

   _____

   _____

   _____

9. . . . whether you rise to the top or settle near the bottom of a profession depends on your ability.

10. (It) depends upon your ability and willingness to continue learning and growing.

11. Kathleen looked outside herself, looked inside herself, and chose.

In order to be sure that your writing is free from parallelism errors, you need to develop the habit of checking every coordinating conjunction to see what kind of elements are being joined. The best way to make sure that the elements are parallel is to do a quick mental parallelism stack to ensure that the elements are all the same part of speech.

Editing Activity 2: Checking Coordinating Conjunctions for Parallel Elements

In the following student essay, all the coordinating conjunctions appear in bold.

1.   Underline all of the elements that are joined by the coordinating conjunction.

2.   Write out a parallelism stack on a separate piece of paper to see exactly what elements are parallel.

All of the elements in this essay are correctly parallel; there is no faulty parallelism.

EDITING

Christine C
English Writing, Sec 6
May 24, 1993

ACADEMIC EDUCATION VS. REAL-LIFE
EDUCATION

There are several different types of education. Education is an on-going process **and** a constant renewal. We never stop learning **and** evolving. Many people think that education applies only to high school **and** college, **but** this is not true. Another type of education is the general education of life.

While it is important to be educated in history, math **and** English, it is equally important to know how to deal with real situations **and** how to cope with life's challenges. Some of the people I went to high school with were good students who got high grades **and** went on to prestigious colleges. They knew a lot about academics, **but** they didn't necessarily know about dealing with people **or** solving everyday problems. Getting a formal education doesn't help a person keep the apartment clean, get to work on time, eat a proper diet, **and** deal with personal relationships. Many people with good academic education have very poor communication skills **and** have a hard time getting along with the people they come into contact with.

The general education of life doesn't come out of books **or** from college lectures. It only comes through experience, such as dealing with all sorts of people **and** handling the frictions of daily living. Life education is self-taught **and** never-ending. It is a course that has daily quizzes **but** no final grade. Without a real-life education, an academic education will not allow an individual to be well-rounded **or** truly successful in the important things in life.

Types of Faulty Parallelism

Faulty parallelism is the result of joining elements with a coordinating conjunction when those elements are not of the same type. Two kinds of faulty parallelism are especially common: elements that are not the same part of speech and verbs that do not have parallel forms. We will look at each type separately because we need to correct these two different kinds of error in different ways.

A: Elements That Are Different Parts of Speech

Faulty parallelism that is caused by joining two different parts of speech is often the result of poor sentence planning. The writer produced a complete sentence and then thought of another, closely related idea and tacked the idea on with a coordinating conjunction. Sometimes the two ideas are parallel, so correction is merely a matter of putting the two ideas into the same part of speech. Here is an example of this kind of faulty parallelism:

3.   *You can acquire <u>job skills</u>, <u>basic knowledge</u>, <u>responsibility</u>, and <u>to respect others</u>.

Here is the parallelism stack for sentence (3):

3a.   *You can acquire   **<u>job skills</u>,**
                           <u>basic knowledge</u>,
                           <u>responsibility</u>,
                 and   **<u>to respect others</u>.**

In sentence (3) the first three elements in the series—*job skills, basic knowledge,* and *responsibility*—are noun phrases, but the last element, *to respect others,* is not. (The technical term for *to respect others* is an infinitive phrase, but it is not necessary that you know the technical grammatical terms for the elements in a parallel structure, only that you recognize when one element is not the same as the others.) A good solution for this sentence is to make the final element, *to respect others,* into a noun phrase like the other three elements:

3b.   You can acquire   <u>job skills</u>,
                          <u>basic knowledge</u>,
                          <u>responsibility</u>,
                 and   **<u>respect for others</u>.**

Often, however, there is no way that you can make the parallel ideas into the same part of speech. If you still want to keep the ideas parallel, a good solution may be to change the sentence, so that now there will be two parallel verbs. Here is an example of a sentence with this kind of faulty parallelism followed by its parallelism stack:

4.   * The skills learned in college are <u>an asset</u> and <u>important in any career.</u>

4a.   * The skills learned in college are **an asset**
                            and **important** in any career.

The problem is that *an asset* is a noun phrase and *important* is an adjective. The only way we can keep these two ideas parallel is to add a second verb and make two parallel verbs or verb phrases:

4b.   The skills learned in college   <u>**are** an asset</u>
                        and   <u>**will be** important in any career.</u>

Finally, there will be many cases of faulty parallelism that shouldn't be corrected by trying to keep the ideas parallel. In other words, the ideas would be clearer if the sentence were completely rewritten so that the ideas were no longer parallel, as in these examples:

5.   * The cost of college may be <u>high</u> and <u>an impossible barrier for some.</u>

5b.   * The cost of college may be   <u>**high**</u>
                        and   <u>**an impossible barrier for some.**</u>

The problem in sentence (5) is not just that the adjective *high* is not parallel with the noun phrase *an impossible barrier for some*; the real problem is that these two ideas these words reflect are not parallel ideas. What is an impossible barrier for some is the fact that the cost of college is high. Completely rewriting the sentence to eliminate the parallelism is the best way to show the relationship of the ideas:

5c.   The **high** cost of college may be **an impossible barrier for some.**

Another way to treat cases of faulty parallelism where the ideas are not truly parallel is to rewrite the original sentence as two sentences. Remember, if you choose to join the new sentences with a coordinating conjunction, be sure to use a comma. Here is an example:

6.   * We are happy <u>to fill your order</u> and <u>about your interest in our company.</u>

6a.   * We are happy **<u>to fill your order</u>**
                        and **<u>about your interest in our company.</u>**

The author of sentence (6) wants to say two very different things. Trying to put these two different ideas into the same sentence is both grammatically and logically impossible. The best solution is to put the ideas into separate sentences that may be joined by a comma and a coordinating conjunction:

6b. **We are happy to fill your order,** and **we are grateful for your interest in our company.**

Editing Activity 3: Rewriting Faulty Parallelism Caused by Different Parts of Speech

Most of the following sentences were taken from student essays. All of them contain faulty parallelisms caused by joining elements that are not the same part of speech.

1. In the space provided in part (a), rewrite each sentence as a parallelism stack.

2. In the space provided in part (b), redo the sentence, correcting it in whatever way you think best captures the ideas of the original sentence. Part (b) will have many possible correct answers.

The first two questions are done as examples.

1. A good movie has to be honest and a mirror of society.

   a. *A good movie has to be **honest***
         *and **a mirror of society.***

   b. *A good movie has to **be honest** and **act as a mirror of society**.*

2. The horse was tall, rangy, and a purebred.

   a. *The horse was **tall***
            rangy
      *and **a purebred**.*

   b. *The **tall, rangy** horse was **a purebred**.*

3. The reasons for going to college are friends, an education, and significant.

   a. _____
      _____

   b. _____
      _____

4. You have got to believe in yourself and that something will come up.

   a. _____
      _____

   b. _____
      _____

5. I was angry, upset, and a fool to put up with it any longer.

   a. _____
      _____

   b. _____
      _____

6. One learns to buckle down and study and that the rewards for studying usually will result in good grades.

   a. _____
      _____

   b. _____
      _____

7. An individual can benefit not only by getting a job but also benefit intellectually.

     a. _____

         _____

     b. _____

         _____

8. Education is a great investment for the future—not only as a student but also the individual.

     a. _____

         _____

     b. _____

         _____

9. It is the only job that you would like and will consider no alternatives.

     a. _____

         _____

     b. _____

         _____

10. Make sure you have plenty to eat, enough sleep, a clean surrounding, and are doing your very best.

     a. _____

         _____

     b. _____

         _____

11. College students are better prepared for their careers and the skills needed for daily life.

     a. _____

         _____

     b. _____

         _____

EDITING

B: Faulty Verb Form Parallelism

So far we have looked at a number of examples of faulty parallelism resulting from mistakenly joining elements that are not the same part of speech. We will now look at a type of faulty parallelism in which the parts of speech are the same: they are all verbs of one kind or another. The problem is that the **forms** of the verbs are not parallel. Since the same parts of speech are involved in this type of parallelism error, correcting this kind of parallelism error is relatively easy. The problem, again, is seeing the error to begin with. There are two common parallel problems with verb forms:

1. Using *to* inconsistently with parallel infinitives

2. Confusing infinitives and gerunds

We will deal with these two types of verb form problems separately.

Using *To* Inconsistently with Parallel Infinitives

An **infinitive** is a verb preceded by *to*, such as *to go*, *to be*, *to decide*. A common mistake with parallel infinitives is forgetting whether you have chosen to keep the *to* with the second and third verbs. Here is an example:

7. * You'll have the freedom <u>to grow</u>, <u>develop</u>, and furthermore, <u>to express your feeling toward college</u>.

The faulty parallelism may be more obvious if we make a parallelism stack:

7a. * You'll have the freedom **to grow,**
develop,
and furthermore **to express** your feeling toward college.

In sentence (7) the writer dropped the *to* from the second infinitive (*develop*), but put the *to* back in with the third infinitive (*to express*), creating faulty parallelism. When we have parallel infinitives, we can either repeat the *to* with each of the following verbs like this:

7b. You'll have the freedom **to grow,**
to develop,
and furthermore <u>**to express** your feeling toward college</u>.

or use the *to* only with the first verb and make the verbs parallel like this:

7c.   You'll have the freedom to **grow,**
   develop,
   and furthermore **express** your feeling toward college.

The one thing we cannot do is inconsistently repeat the *to* with some of the verbs following the first verb in the series but not with others, as we did in sentence (7).

Confusing Infinitives and Gerunds

A **gerund** is a verb form ending in *-ing.* Often infinitives and gerunds mean the same thing and can be used interchangeably, as shown here:

8.   I like **to ski.** (infinitive)

9.   I like **skiing.** (gerund)

The very fact that infinitive and gerunds are so interchangeable makes it easy to create a parallelism error in which one part of a sentence has a gerund and another part of the same sentence has an infinitive:

10.   * It is easier asking for forgiveness than to ask for permission.

Here is the parallelism stack for sentence (10) with the two verbs in bold:

10a.   * It is easier **asking** for forgiveness
   than **to ask** for permission.

We can correct this problem by using parallel infinitives:

10b.   Infinitive: It is easier **to ask** for forgiveness than **to ask** for permission.

We can also correct this problem by using parallel gerunds:

10c.   Gerund: It is easier **asking** for forgiveness than **asking** for permission.

However, we cannot mix the two forms in the same sentence as we did in sentence (10) with one infinitive and one gerund. Mixing infinitives and gerunds in the same sentence is like wearing one blue sock and one brown sock. Either kind is fine, but we have to have a matched set.
   Sometimes both alternatives are not equally good; sometimes one alternative is better:

11.   * College is a chance for them to be away from home and becoming dependent on themselves.

The parallelism stack shows us that the verbs are not parallel:

11a.   * College is a chance for them **to be** away from home
                                     and **becoming** dependent on themselves.

Making both verbs into gerunds produces a sentence that is awkward sounding at best:

11b.   College is a chance for them **being** away from home
                                     and **becoming** dependent on themselves.

Making both verbs into infinitives is a much better sounding alternative:

11c.   College is a chance for them **to be** away from home
                                     and **to become** dependent on themselves.

We can see from the various versions of sentence (11) that it is probably a good idea to try out both alternatives (parallel infinitives and parallel gerunds) before deciding which alternative to pick.

Editing Activity 4: Correcting Errors Caused by Faulty Verb Form Parallelism

All of the following questions contain sentences that have faulty verb form parallelism: either parallel infinitives that inconsistently use *to* or an inconsistent use of infinitives and gerunds.

1.   In the space provided in (a), rewrite each sentence as a parallelism stack.

2.   In the space provided in (b), rewrite the sentence, correcting it in whatever way you think best captures the ideas of the original sentence. Part (b) will have many possible correct answers.

The first two questions are done as examples.

---

1. It is just as enjoyable to watch *Gone with the Wind* as it is reading the book.

   a. *It is just as enjoyable **to watch** Gone with the Wind*
                    *as it is **reading** the book.*

   b. *It is just as enjoyable **watching** Gone with the Wind as it is **reading** the book.*

---

2. During the summer, I like to swim, hike, and to go fishing with my family.

    a. *During the summer, I like **to swim,***
                         hike
        *and **to go** fishing with my family.*

    b. *During the summer, I like to **swim, hike,** and **go** fishing with my family.*

3. College will enable an easier transition for living on your own and to develop your own goals.

    a. _____

    _____

    b. _____

    _____

4. It is very hard going to school and to make a living at the same time.

    a. _____

    _____

    b. _____

    _____

5. We want the freedom to do whatever we want, to go wherever we want, and be whatever we are capable of.

    a. _____

    _____

    _____

    b. _____

    _____

6. I want to improve my decision-making skills as well as gaining access to modern technology.

    a. _____

    _____

    b. _____

    _____

EDITING

7. It is necessary for the secretary to attend all meetings, call the roll, and to report the voting.

   a. _____
   _____
   _____
   _____

   b. _____
   _____

8. Most students like having a major that will lead to a good job and to have time to also take some liberal arts courses.

   a. _____
   _____

   b. _____
   _____

9. The biology teacher prefers showing movies about dissections and to give demonstrations.

   a. _____
   _____

   b. _____
   _____

10. The book will teach you how to plant a garden, fertilize the plants, and to get rid of garden pests.

   a. _____
   _____
   _____

   b. _____
   _____

11. It is wise beginning your presentation with a joke and to conclude with a summary of what you said.

   a. _____
   _____

   b. _____
   _____

Now you are ready to identify and correct faulty parallelism. As part of the final step in editing your own writing, be sure to check every coordinating conjunction to see that the elements being joined are actually parallel. Remember that the two most likely sources of faulty parallelism are (a) coordinating conjunctions linking different parts of speech, and (b) coordinating conjunctions linking different forms of verbs.

Editing Activity 5: Final Editing a Paper for Parallelism Errors

The following student essay is ready for final editing. It is free of errors except for a number of faulty parallelism errors. Underline the errors and correct them in the way that you think fits the essay best. The number of errors in each paragraph is given in parentheses at the end of the paragraph.

Todd B.
English Writing, Sec 6
April 12, 1993

EDUCATION NEVER STOPS

I believe that it is nearly impossible to stop learning and educating oneself. Although one might try to stop learning, this cannot be truly achieved or a real outcome. Conscientious individuals will always try to learn new things, search for new knowledge, and to adapt to change in their lives. For this reason I believe that no individual is ever completely educated. The only way to stop the procedure is giving up on life. (3)

Education is the process of gaining more knowledge and to experience new things. This can be done by going to school, working, watching television, and even sleep. Just about anything individuals do in their lives is a unique experience, and each new experience causes us to learn new things, to deal with new circumstances, and find new ways to solve problems. (3)

School is one of the most important and valuable forms of education. Since school allows teaching in an environment specifically designed for learning, it offers knowledge that would be unobtainable and an impossibility anywhere else. School is the main source of our formal education and very important in our future. Finally, most employers will look at our school records to evaluate our background, judge our abilities, and to decide whether or not to hire us. (3)

Every day at work is not the same because new things happen all the time. Every customer is different and a challenge. Even the most routine tasks can be done in new and possibly more efficient ways. Even when we try something new and it fails, we have learned something from the experience. (1)

Watching television can be a great teacher because of all the information and entertaining that is available to us. A game show like <u>Jeopardy</u> is there to not only to amuse us, but also challenging us to think. There are also a number of programs that provide a highly stimulating educational content: <u>National Geographic</u> for adults and teenagers and <u>Sesame Street</u> for children. (2)

I believe that even when people are doing a simple task like sleeping,they can educate themselves. We can gain some insight into our own fears and concerns by interpreting our dreams and to cope with our unconscious feelings. If nothing else we can learn how much sleep we need in order to be mentally alert and staying in good physical shape. (2)

Everything we do educates us in some way, and this procedure does not stop as long as we are alive and students at heart. Of course some things do more to educate us than other things, but the limitation is only in us, not in our experiences. (1)

CHAPTER 12

USING COLLEGE LANGUAGE SKILLS

Revising Your Best Paper

This chapter is unlike any of the others in this book. It assumes that you have done the reading, pre-writing, writing, talking, revising, and grammar and vocabulary activities and exercises in most of the other chapters. It assumes that you have survived this course. Congratulations! There are three more tasks you will be asked to do. In a way, this final chapter becomes the measure of what you have learned.

The first task is to choose the best paper you have written during this course, do even more work on it, and make it even better. The second task is to demonstrate your present knowledge of grammar and punctuation. You will be asked to edit one or more student essays—to find and correct grammar and punctuation errors in them. The third task is to edit your own recently revised paper.

Task 1: Choosing Your Best Paper

1. Read all of the papers you have written for this course. Choose the one you think is best. It may be best because it is the most interesting to read or because it addresses an issue or topic you think is very important. It may be the best because it is already so well written.

2. Review all of the revision portions of all the chapters you have completed. Nine chapters include revision strategies:

Chapter 2: Revising for Details of Place

Chapter 3: Revising for Specificity, Clarity, and Form

Chapter 4: Revising for Details of Emotion

Chapter 5: Revising by Adding Qualifiers

Chapter 6: Revising by Adding Supporting Examples

Chapter 7: Revising for Clarity and Completeness of Information

Chapter 8: Revising by Adding Transitions

Chapter 10: Revising by Using Published Resources Effectively

Chapter 11: Revising by Acknowledging Other Aspects of an Issue or an Idea

3. Now, thinking about the paper you have chosen and all nine revision strategies, choose two or three revision strategies you will use to make your paper even better. For example, your "Service Industry Job" paper from Chapter 6 might be improved by (1) adding details of place (Chapter 2), (2) adding transitions (Chapter 8), and (3) using published resources effectively (Chapter 10).

Sometimes it is difficult to read your own essay and see which kinds of revision would make it better. When this happens, exchange papers with someone you trust, read each other's papers, and then talk about which revision strategies you might use.

4. Once you have chosen the two or three revision strategies you will use, review those strategies by rereading the relevant sections of this book. Remember that the pre-writing sections in most chapters are connected to the revision sections, so look at these too.

5. Then, using the strategies you have chosen, revise your paper to make it even better.

6. Optional: For practice, revise one or both of the following student drafts <u>before</u> you do work on your own draft.

Student Draft: "Service Jobs"

SERVICE JOBS

Working with elderly people has many advantages. Although it is not always easy to understand these people, it's lots of fun, very rewarding, and ever so interesting.

I work at Northcrest Convalescent Center, and on one of the shifts I work I get the opportunity to work in the dining room. The dining room is where the residents at Northcrest gather to eat their meals. The residents that are in good enough shape also gather here when they have activities. Bingo, exercise and tea socials are examples of the things that go on in the dining room. Working with these people helps me to get a better understanding of what it feels like to get old, but it also makes me look at every birthday as if I were having a root canal. It just shows how people act when they get elderly, although most of the time it is not their choice.

Most of these elderly people are very loving and caring. They are always happy to have someone say hello to them or ask them how they are doing. It is very neat to see their eyes light up as you come to them and show them that someone really cares.

Working in the dining room, I set up the square tables with peach colored polyester tablecloths. We also use the same peach color for the napkins that we set for every resident. At every place setting, I also place a water glass, a coffee cup if they drink coffee or tea, and all their utensils. This makes the tables look very nice. But the icing on the cake, the grand finale, the final episode, is when I place the pale, plastic, pink, gray, and white flowers in the small stout pink vase in the middle of the table. The sparkle in their eyes when I place this there is enough to nearly blind a person, but it's the brave step that a dietary aide must take to please these residents.

These lonely people have nothing better to look forward to than their next meal. The only meal we set the dining room up so nicely for is dinner. So I believe that dinner is the meal that they look forward to so much, or at least it's the meal that they always say looks so pretty.

Because they are lonely, they love to come down and interact or mingle with their friends and neighbors in the facility. Their conversations are very humorous but can cause conflicts. Some of them are in very good shape and could carry on a conversation with you for hours, and they probably would like to do so. The problems, or the conflicts, start when one person tries to talk to another person who cannot hear very well. Sometimes these people have trouble talking because of a stroke, and when your voice goes, it is also harder to understand people. Some of these elderly people get very frustrated and mad when either they cannot understand someone or the other person cannot understand them.

As an employee of the dietary department, I am supposed to make sure that the residents receive all the food they want and are allowed to have. It is hard for me to understand them many times, and I know it is not only frustrating for them to have to repeat what they have just said, but for me to ask them to repeat what they have just said becomes very repetitious. Talking to some of them is even worse than listening to them. With some of them, you must shout as if yelling to a crowd of over three hundred people, but you must direct this into the ear of an eighty-year-old.

As you can see, it is not always an easy job understanding these elderly people, but it helps you to respect them and try to help them if they are handicapped in one way or another. Elderly people are lots of fun to work with.

Shawn C.

The following is another student draft which would benefit from additional revisions.

Student Draft: "The Good New Days"

THE GOOD NEW DAYS

As we discussed in class the positive differences between family "cultures," I noticed that the majority of
the conversation led back to "the good old days." I
enjoyed hearing about the many family traditions that
have survived. However, there are new traditions being
forged by today's single-parent homes. These traditions
may have been developed out of necessity, but they do have
a positive side. There is a tradition being forged of both
girls and boys learning car maintenance and yard upkeep.
There is a "team spirit" being forged, which is replacing
the old "team spirit." Traditional meals have changed,
too; no more days are spent in the kitchen preparing a
meal that will take twenty minutes at the most to consume.

Because many youngsters come home to an empty house,
they are learning at an early age how to care for themselves, including the preparation of meals. Both boys and
girls are learning at an early age how to cook simple
meals. My brothers have been cooking macaroni and cheese
since they were old enough to operate the stove safely.
My eleven-year-old brother has developed an incredible
recipe for omelets in the microwave. My seventeen-year-
old brother can make a mean plate of spaghetti!

Because my father didn't live with us, he taught me to
do maintenance and repair on my own car, repair horse
corrals, and many other "handy-PERSON" tasks so that I
could take care of myself and teach my mother to do the
same. One winter, my mother and I had to repair a section
of corral fence almost daily. We kept doing it the way Dad
had showed me, but the horses, or maybe the wind, kept
knocking it down. Finally we did it Mom's way, which is
"more is better." We took a bucket full of nails and two
hammers, and we put so many nails in that section of fence
that I swear it changed the earth's magnetic field. It
still stands.

The old family spirit of "All for one, and one for all . . . but, Dear, you stay in the kitchen, and I'll work on the car" is gone. In my family, as well as many other single-parent homes, there are many things to get done and only half of the adult power to do them. My mom organizes parties that all of her children are expected to attend. We have a couple of "Leaf Raking Parties" per year, and a couple of "Barn/Corral Cleaning Parties" per year. Last summer, we had a "House Painting Party." My mom, she really knows how to have a good time! This fall, I extended invitations to family members to my "Apartment Painting Party," and everyone showed up, even two friends of my brother!

Last but not least the microwave, prepackaged meals and fast food places are rapidly replacing home-cooked, sit-down meals. I have often heard this lamented. However, such meals are convenient, allowing us more time to be involved in other activities. Our family does make it a point to attend most Little League games, ballet recitals, Jazz Band concerts, etc. These quick meals enable us to have our own activities as well as to support the activities of each other.

All in all, these new "traditions in the making" may be different, but some of them are good. Time marches on, and often times our way of life changes. In order to be happy, one must adapt and develop the good in the changes.

Veronica P.

Task 2: Editing Your Own Recently Revised Essay

Now, use your editing skills on the paper you have just revised. Once again, since you might find it difficult to find grammar and punctuation errors in your own writing, you might exchange papers with someone and help each other find these errors. Then make any corrections to your paper that you think are needed.

Final Editing Strategies

We have used the term *final editing* in this book to mean editing for certain errors of punctuation (sentence fragments, run-on sentences, various types of comma errors, and apostrophe errors) and grammar (wrong choice of verb tense, incorrect subject-verb agreement, faulty pronoun reference, and faulty parallelism). We will refer to these kinds of errors collectively as **surface errors**. This chapter deals with strategies that will help you do the final editing of your papers accurately and quickly. In order to do this, you need to have a set of final editing strategies that you employ in a systematic way. In this chapter we will deal with four final editing strategies that you may find helpful in eliminating surface errors from your essays.

Strategy 1: Setting Aside Sufficient Time to Do Final Editing

The biggest single obstacle to doing an adequate job of final editing is not allowing enough time. Virtually all writing that we do—whether as students or as professionals—is done under time pressure. It is human nature to postpone the task of final editing until the last possible moment. If nothing else, we always want more time to improve the content and expression of what we are writing. Moreover, less experienced writers tend to underestimate the importance of final editing and are thus even less likely to allow sufficient time for final editing.

Here are some reasons why final editing is so important. While sometimes surface errors cause the reader to misunderstand what the writer is trying to say, more often surface errors distract and annoy the reader. Punctuation marks and rules of grammar serve as signposts and traffic signals that direct the flow of the reader's movement though the sentence. Surface errors are incorrect signposts and broken traffic signals that bring the reader to a halt. The reader is forced to back up and reread in order to get back on the right track. At the very least, the reader is forced to concentrate not on **what** the writer is trying to say, but on **how** the writer is trying to say it. If there are very many surface errors, the reader simply gives up. After all, if the writer does not care enough about the paper to present it in a professional manner, then why should the reader care about it either?

How much time should we set aside to do final editing? Obviously the answer depends on how many surface errors there are and how efficient we are at finding them. A large number of surface errors in the final editing draft is not necessarily a sign of bad writing. Some experienced writers focus exclusively on content in the various revision drafts; other experienced writers edit for surface errors all throughout the revision process. The first type of writer must do a time-consuming final editing since the entire burden for surface correctness is placed on this final step in the writing process. The second type of writer will need to spend relatively little time in final editing since the final revision draft is nearly free of surface errors.

You need to be aware of the type of writer you are and budget your time accordingly. If you are the first type, you need to budget a relatively large amount of time for final editing. If you are the second type, you only need to budget a couple of minutes per page for final editing. Even in the worst-case scenario, the first type of writer will probably spend less than one percent of the total time in writing a paper in doing final editing. Given the time and effort that goes into producing a good essay, don't you think that an additional one percent contribution of your time is a good way to protect your investment?

Strategy 2: Focusing on Surface Errors, Not Meaning

All writers—experienced as well as beginning—have trouble staying on task when doing final editing. The problem is that we all get distracted by the content of what we read and neglect to pay attention to errors in the way we say it. The language that we write is a vehicle for conveying meaning. Final editing requires that we focus our attention entirely on the vehicle and not on the content that the vehicle conveys—an unnatural process. Ideally, we would all write our papers days before they are due. Then when we did the final editing, we would see the paper with the fresh eyes of a reader who sees the surface language for the first time. Few of us, however, live in this ideal world. It is not unrealistic, though, to budget enough time to allow a final revision draft to sit overnight before we do a final editing so that we have at least a little distance from what we have written.

In any case, the one tried-and-true final editing technique we should all follow is to read our papers backwards sentence by sentence. That is, start with the last sentence in the paper. Read the sentence in the normal way from front to back, running through a checklist of likely errors. The purpose of reading backwards sentence by sentence is to help keep our attention focused on the surface form of the sentence, not on the meaning of the sentence. This technique requires a good deal of self-discipline. There is always a temptation to jump to the beginning of the paragraph and read through the paragraph in the normal left-to-right order. But almost always, when we do that, we slip back into reading for content without being aware of it. The result is that we read right over all but the most extreme surface errors without consciously noticing them. Unfortunately, we do not correct surface errors that we do not consciously notice.

If you are writing on a computer, do final editing on a hard copy—not on the screen— if at all possible. A good technique for working with hard copy is to put a pencil mark at the beginning of each sentence as you finish checking it. If you must do final editing from the computer screen, select (darken) the sentence you are working on in order to keep yourself focused on it. If you are working on a typewritten copy, put your finger below the sentence you are editing and don't move it until you have finished that sentence. All of these techniques are merely ways of forcing yourself to stay focused on the surface form of one sentence at a time and keeping you from jumping ahead and beginning to read for content instead of surface form.

Strategy 3: Editing by Eye, Not by Ear

There is a profound difference between writing and speaking. We are all experts at talking. In talking, since we cannot plan what we are going to say very much in advance, we develop our ideas as we speak them. We give examples to show what we mean, we repeat for emphasis, and we loop back for clarification—all according to the feedback we receive from our listeners. We also rely on the intonation of our voices for emphasis and to show which ideas are related and which are contrasted.

Many of the communication skills that we have developed for talking are irrelevant to writing. When we write, we lose the opportunity to modify what we say on the basis of listener feedback, and we cannot use intonation and stress for clarification and emphasis. However, what writers gain in exchange is the opportunity to revise and correct their message before communicating it to the reader. As a result, writing is much more carefully planned than talking.

Eventually, of course, beginning writers develop a new set of communication skills for the written language. In the meantime, however, beginning writers are stranded between the two forms of communication. The transition strategy that many beginning writers adopt is to write down their own spoken language. The essays of many beginning writers look like transcripts of a spoken monologue. The problem with such self-dictated language is that while the writer can hear the features of intonation and stress that are so effective in the spoken language, the reader cannot. The reader only sees the script; the reader cannot hear the spoken language underlying it. The signals of stress and intonation that convey meaning in the spoken language are lost in the translation to the written language.

Some surface errors in the written language are direct results of this mismatch between the spoken and written languages. For example, sentence fragments are an easily understood form of mid-course correction in the spoken language. Sentence fragments allow us to explain or qualify the sentence we have just uttered without having to start the sentence over again. In the written language, however, sentence fragments are inappropriate because we have the opportunity to revise a sentence to make it clear to begin with so that it doesn't need mid-course correction. When we do final editing by ear rather than by eye, normal features of the spoken language that have been inappropriately carried over into writing—such as sentence fragments—are not noticed and corrected because they seem perfectly normal by the standards of the spoken language.

Certain kinds of punctuation errors are also the result of the difference between the spoken and written languages. These errors are likely to be overlooked if the writer does final editing by ear because the spoken language provides no guidance in correcting the error. An example of such an error is the use of the apostrophe to mark the possessive -s. This apostrophe does not correspond to any feature in the spoken language—plural -s and possessive -s are pronounced exactly alike. Since we are not used to making a difference between a plural -s and a possessive -s in the spoken language, writers who do final editing by ear are very unlikely to notice the missing apostrophe in the written form of the possessive.

The moral of all this is quite simple: we must learn to apply the standards of the written language when we do the final editing of our papers. When we do final editing by ear, we are likely to fall into the trap of translating our papers back into the much more familiar and comfortable standards of the spoken language. If we hear our papers rather than see them, we run the risk of missing the places where we have used inappropriate features of spoken communication—such as sentence fragments—and places where the conventions of the written language—such as using apostrophes for possession—do not correspond to anything in the spoken language.

Strategy 4: Knowing What Surface Errors to Look for in Your Writing

The keys to effective final editing are (a) knowing what surface errors you are most likely to make, and (b) knowing how to spot these errors and correct them. This book has given you a number of tools for doing the latter—spotting and correcting surface errors. However, only you can tell what surface errors you are most likely to make. In order to become proficient at final editing, you need to be aware of the mistakes you make most often. If you are making the same mistake over and over again, you must take special pains consciously to monitor for that particular error. A critical first step is to keep a log or list of the mistakes you have made in previous papers. If you are consciously aware of what your high-frequency surface errors are, you can create your own checklist of procedures for spotting these errors.

Finally, a word about grammar checkers for computers—a number of grammar-checking programs are now on the market. For example, the newest version of Microsoft Word for the Macintosh even has a grammar checker built in. Eventually grammar checkers may be as useful and reliable as spelling checkers, but that day is still far in the future. In a test conducted at Eastern Washington University, a state-of-the-art grammar-checking program found fewer than 10% of the surface errors in 100 essays written by students in the freshman writing program. However, that overall figure of 10% is some-what misleading because the grammar program was able to find most of certain types of errors and none of other types of errors.

There are two areas where grammar checkers are accurate enough to be helpful in final editing: (1) identifying apostrophe errors and (2) identifying subject-verb agreement errors, especially the *there is/there was* type of error. On the whole, it is probably worth your while to use a grammar checker if it is available, as long as you realize its limitations.

Final Editing Activity: Finding All Types of Surface Errors

The following essay contains a single, typical example of each of the ten types of errors covered in this book:

sentence fragments (Chapter 2)

run-on sentences (Chapter 3)

commas omitted with coordinating conjunctions that join independent clauses (Chapter 4)

error in subordinating conjunctions and conjunctive adverbs (Chapter 5)

wrong choice of verb tense (Chapter 6)

subject-verb agreement error (Chapter 7)

faulty pronoun reference (Chapter 8)

error in restrictive and nonrestrictive relative clause punctuation (Chapter 9)

apostrophe error (Chapter 10)

faulty parallelism (Chapter 11)

Demonstrate your final editing skills by finding and correcting all ten types of surface errors in the following essay. Remember, there is one example of each type. The number of errors in each paragraph is given in parentheses at the end of the paragraph. Correct the errors in the way that you think works best for this essay.

[P.S. The grammar checker included in Microsoft Word found only two of the ten errors.]

```
                                        Robert S.
                           English Writing, Sec 6
                                    June 3, 1993

          THE BENEFITS OF GOING TO COLLEGE

   College is an expensive investment and some people can
only justify that investment because they think it will
automatically give them a great job. However, it doesn't
really work that way for most people. Most students who
have taken four years of their lives working toward a
degree do not automatically have a job to look forward to
upon graduation. However, the experience of going to
college has given them three main benefits: fellowship,
independence, and knowledge. (1)
```

Going to college affects not only a students academic life but also their social life. There is many more opportunities to meet people in college than at any other time or place. Classes, dorm life and all the special activities are places to meet people from very different backgrounds. Students from little towns get to see how people from big cities like Seattle and Los Angeles look at the world, and vice-versa. It is a time to observe people in a new environment, see how they adapt, and to learn to respect them for what they are. Dorm life teaches people how to live with a person, whom they have never even met before. (5)

College is a transition period for students. College enables a person to break the ties that hold him to his parents and the community that he or she grows up in. Probably for the first time the student lives away from home and learns to do everything for him or herself. While the student is still tied to his parents financially the student is becoming responsible for his or her own life. Especially for managing his or her own finances. (3)

The final benefit of going to college is the main one of getting an education. College graduates may or may not acquire specific skills that will get them jobs right away, but they have learned how to learn. They can get information from books, they can deal with contradictory sources of information. They have learned how to distance themselves from problems so that they can look at the issues unemotionally. (1)

While it would be great if a college degree would guarantee all of us a job, we should not lose sight of the things that the experience of going to college does give us: a totally new circle of friends, a new sense of independence from our family, and the ability to acquire whatever new knowledge our careers will demand of us.

Afterword

If after all the reading and writing you have done in this course, you read and write only when somebody else tells you to, then we, the authors, and you, the student, have failed.

On the other hand, if you are someone who reads and writes not just at school or at work—if you choose to read and write to help you to find, remember, organize, and discover facts, ideas, and opinions—then everyone has won. Most importantly, you have won.

The learning you have done while working with this book, your peers, and your instructors, is only the beginning. Unless you continue to use, practice, and develop your language skills, you will lose them. This is called "atrophy." The aphorism "Use it or lose it" applies. Just as a good musician or ice skater continues to make progress only with practice, your language skills will continue to improve only if you use them.

Please make reading, writing, and learning normal parts of your whole life. You will not regret it.

APPENDIX I

Glossary of Grammar Terms

Note: Examples appear in *italics*. Especially important references to related terms are <u>underlined</u>.

Adjective There are two kinds of adjectives: (a) adjectives that modify nouns (*an ugly building*) or (b) <u>predicate adjectives</u>, adjectives that follow the verb *be* or similar verbs such as *seem, become,* and *sound.* (*The music is* **loud**. *The music sounded* **terrible.**)

Adjective clause This is another name for <u>relative clause</u>. Adjective clauses always modify nouns. *The students* **whom you met** *were friends of mine.*

Adverb An adverb is a word that modifies a verb, an adjective, another adverb, or the whole sentence. Adverbs typically answer questions like *when, where, why,* and *how.* Adverbs that modify the verb are easily moved to the front of the sentence. *We had a lot of rain* **yesterday.** / **Yesterday** *we had a lot of rain.*

Agreement (a) <u>Subject-verb agreement</u> in clauses or (b) in pronoun <u>antecedent</u>, agreement refers to the relationship between a pronoun and the person or thing it refers to. In *John lost his cap,* the pronoun *his* agrees with its antecedent *John.*

Ambiguous pronoun reference Ambiguous pronoun reference refers to a pronoun that has more than one possible <u>antecedent</u>. In *John went to see his father because* **he** *wasn't well,* the *he* has ambiguous pronoun reference because the pronoun *he* could refer to either *John* or *his father.*

Antecedent Many pronouns refer to some person or thing mentioned earlier in the same sentence or in a previous sentence. In **Aunt Sally** *lives next door.* **She** *is my mother's sister,* the antecedent of *she* is *Aunt Sally.*

Appositive An appositive is a noun that renames a preceding noun. In *My English teacher,* **Mr. Smith,** *also teaches Latin,* the noun *Mr. Smith* is an appositive that renames *teacher*. In this book we have used the term "noun renamer" in place of the term "appositive."

Apostrophe An apostrophe is a mark of punctuation (') used for two quite different purposes: (a) to indicate the missing letters in a <u>contraction</u> (for example, the apostrophe in **don't** indicates where there is a missing letter) and (b) to identify a possessive *s* in a <u>possessive noun</u> (for example, the *'s* in **Barbara's** *book*) or the possessive *s* in a <u>possessive indefinite pronoun</u> (for example, the *'s* in **somebody's** *book*).

Auxiliary verb See <u>helping verb</u>.

Clause A clause contains a <u>subject noun phrase</u> and a <u>verb phrase</u> in <u>subject-verb agreement</u>. There are two kinds of clauses: (a) an <u>independent clause</u>, which can stand alone as a complete sentence, and (b) a <u>dependent clause</u>, which must always be attached to an independent clause.

Comma splice A comma splice is two <u>independent clauses</u> incorrectly joined together inside a sentence with only a comma. The following is a comma splice: * *Alice answered the question, she won the prize.* A comma splice is a type of <u>run-on sentence</u>.

Common noun A common noun refers to categories of people, places, things and ideas as opposed to <u>proper nouns</u>, which name actual individuals. *Woman* is a common noun, but *Ms. Richards* is a proper noun. Most common nouns can be used with *the*, as in *the woman*.

Complement A complement is a phrase that a <u>verb</u> requires to make a complete sentence. For example, the verb *see* requires a <u>noun phrase</u> as its <u>object</u>: *Mary saw* **the bird.**

Compound A compound refers to two or more grammatical units of the same type joined by a coordinating conjunction. **A man** *and* **a woman** is an example of a compound <u>noun phrase</u>.

Compound object A compound <u>object</u> is two or more object <u>noun phrases</u> joined by a coordinating conjunction: *Sally saw* **Sam** *and* **his cousin Susan.**

Compound sentence A compound sentence is a <u>sentence</u> consisting of two or more <u>independent clauses</u> joined by a coordinating conjunction (for example, **Sally saw Sam,** *and* **Sarah saw Slim.**). In compound sentences, the independent clauses must be joined either by both a comma and a coordinating conjunction (as in the example) or by a semicolon (for example *I came; I saw; I conquered.*).

Compound subject A compound <u>subject</u> is two or more <u>subject noun phrases</u> joined by a coordinating conjunction. *The* **girl next door** *and* **her little brother** *are always fighting.*

Compound verb phrase   A compound <u>verb phrase</u> is two or more verb phrases joined by a coordinating conjunction. *Ralph **borrowed some money** and **bet it on the horses.***

Conjunction   A conjunction is a word used to join grammatical elements together. There are two completely different types of conjunctions: (a) <u>coordinating conjunctions</u>, such words as *and, or, but*; and (b) <u>subordinating conjunctions</u>, such words as *because, if, whenever*, which are words that begin <u>subordinate clauses</u>.

Conjunctive adverb   A conjunctive adverb relates the meaning of the second of two <u>independent clauses</u> to the meaning of the first independent clause: *I answered all the questions.* ***However**, I didn't get a perfect score.* In this example, the conjunctive adverb is *however*. Conjunctive adverbs, unlike <u>subordinating conjunctions</u>, can be moved to the middle or end of their independent clause: *I answered all the questions. I didn't get a perfect score, **however**.*

Contraction   A contraction is a shortened version of a word created by dropping out a sound. In writing, a contraction is indicated by an apostrophe (') to show where letters have been dropped: *I'll* is a contraction of *I will*. Be careful not to confuse an apostrophe to mark a contraction with a <u>possessive apostrophe</u>, which is used to mark a possessive noun or pronoun. A contraction apostrophe (unlike a possessive apostrophe) can always be eliminated by expanding the contraction back to the full uncontracted form of the word. For example, we can expand the contraction *I'll* back to *I will*.

Coordinating conjunction   Coordinating conjunctions join grammatical units of the same type (see <u>compound</u>). The coordinating conjunctions are *and, but, or, nor, so, for, yet*.

Demonstrative pronoun   The demonstrative pronouns are *this, that, these,* and *those*. When these same words are used to modify a noun, they are adjectives: ***these** books*. When these words are used by themselves, they are pronouns: *I want **these**.*

Dependent clause   A dependent clause is a <u>clause</u> that cannot stand alone as a complete sentence. All dependent clauses must be attached to an <u>independent clause</u>. This book deals with two types of dependent clauses: <u>relative clauses</u> (adjective clauses) and <u>subordinate clauses</u> (adverb clauses).

Direct quotation   A direct quotation uses quotation marks to show the reader that the words quoted are exactly what the speaker or writer said: *Mary said, "I know what you mean."* Notice the use of the comma before the quoted words. Compare with <u>indirect quotation</u>.

Faulty parallelism   Faulty <u>parallelism</u> is a series of supposedly parallel grammatical units that actually contains elements that are not of the same type. A common kind of faulty parallelism occurs when the elements that are supposed to be parallel are not the same part of speech: * *Senator Blather is **vain, pompous,** and **a bore,*** where *vain* and *pompous* are adjectives, but *a bore* is a noun phrase.

Fused sentence A fused sentence is two independent clauses joined together in the same sentence without any mark of punctuation. In * *We went to the movies we had a good time*, the independent clause *We went to the movies* is joined to a second independent clause *we had a good time* without the necessary semicolon or comma and coordinating conjunction. A fused sentence is a type of run-on sentence.

Future perfect tense The future perfect tense construction consists of *will* (future) + *have* (perfect tense) + a past participle verb form. *They **will have gone** home by now.* The future perfect indicates by which time in the future an action will be finished. See also perfect tense.

Future tense The future tense consists of *will* (a helping verb that signals future time) followed by an infinitive (the dictionary form of a verb). *I **will return** it tomorrow.*

Gerund A gerund is the *-ing* form of a verb used as a noun. ***Skiing** is my favorite sport.* See also gerund phrase.

Gerund phrase A gerund phrase consists of a gerund (the head of the phrase) together with the gerund's modifiers and required words: ***Answering my phone calls** took all afternoon.* Gerunds and gerund phrases can always be replaced by *it*: ***It** took all afternoon.*

Helping verb Helping verbs are verbs used in front of the head or main verb in a verb phrase. There are four groups of helping verbs: *be*, used in forming the progressive (for example, *He **is** washing the car now*) and the passive, (for example, *The accident **was** reported by Fred*); *have*, used in forming the perfect tenses (for example, *We **have** lived here for three years*); *do*, used in forming questions (for example, ***Do** you know the answer?*) and negative sentences (for example, *I **do** not know the answer*); and the "modal" verbs *can, may, must, will, shall* (for example *I **may** go back*).

Indefinite pronoun Indefinite pronouns are "generic" pronouns that do not refer to a specific individual. There are two groups of indefinite pronouns. One group consists of compounds ending in *-one* (*someone*); *-body* (*anybody*); *-thing* (*everything*). The second group includes such words as *all, most, few, several*. Words in the second group can also be used as adjectives. In *I would like a **few** apples, few* is an adjective modifying the noun *apples*. In *I would like a **few,** few* is an indefinite pronoun.

Independent clause An independent clause is a clause that can stand alone as a complete sentence. Every sentence must contain at least one independent clause. Both of the preceding sentences contain a single independent clause. Only independent clauses can be turned into questions answered by "yes" or "no." For example, the "yes/no" question form of the independent clause *Tomorrow will be a holiday* is *Will tomorrow be a holiday?*

Indirect quotation An indirect quotation is a paraphrase of what somebody said or wrote. An indirect quotation does not use quotation marks. Compare the following. Indirect quotation: *Mary said **that** she wanted to go.* Direct quotation: *Mary said, "I want to go."* Notice that indirect quotation uses *that* before the paraphrased words. Compare with <u>direct quotation</u>.

Infinitive An infinitive is the form of a <u>verb</u> that appears in the dictionary. For example, we would look up *is, am, are, was,* and *were* under the infinitive form *be*. In <u>verb phrases</u>, the infinitive is used without *to: I will **win.*** When an infinitive is used as another part of speech, the infinitive is used with *to.* In the following sentence the infinitive *to win* is used as a noun: ***To win** was our only goal.*

Infinitive phrase An infinitive phrase is an <u>infinitive</u> together with modifiers and any other required words. Infinitive phrases are commonly used as nouns (for example, ***To win the game** was our only goal*) or adverbs (for example, *You must practice hard **to win at basketball***).

Irregular verb An irregular verb is a verb whose <u>past tense</u> form and/or <u>past participle</u> form is irregular—that is, formed in some way other than adding *-ed.* For example, the past tense of *go* is *went,* and its past participle form is *gone* (rather than the nonexistent regular form *goed*). A list of irregular verbs is given at the end of Chapter 6.

Main verb A main verb is the head of a <u>verb phrase</u>. If there is only one verb in a verb phrase, it is automatically the main verb. If there is a string of multiple verbs in a verb phrase, then the main verb is the last (or right-most) verb in the string (*has **been**; might have **gone**; will **go***). The verbs preceding the main verb are <u>helping verbs</u>.

Nonrestrictive clause A nonrestrictive clause is a kind of <u>relative clause</u>. Relative clauses modify nouns in two different ways. A nonrestrictive relative clause (as opposed to a <u>restrictive clause</u>) does not change the meaning of the noun it modifies. In *My mother, **who is a graduate of Berkeley,** relishes diagramming,* the relative clause *who is a graduate of Berkeley* is nonrestrictive because it does not change the meaning of the noun it modifies: my mother is still my mother whether she is a graduate of Berkeley or not. Notice that nonrestrictive clauses are always separated from the nouns they modify by commas. See also <u>restrictive clause</u>.

Noun Nouns are names of people, places, things, and ideas. There are two types of nouns: <u>common nouns</u> and <u>proper nouns</u> (names of actual individuals). Most nouns are common nouns. Common nouns can be identified by *the.* For example, *destroy* and *destruction* are related words. We can tell that *destroy* is not a noun because we cannot say ** **the** destroy.* We can tell that *destruction* is a noun because we can say ***the** destruction.* See also <u>noun phrase</u>.

Noun phrase A noun phrase consists of a head <u>noun</u> together with its modifiers (if any). For example, *a city on a hill* is a noun phrase consisting of the head noun *city* together with its modifiers *a* and *on a hill.* All noun phrases can be identified by replacing them with the appropriate personal pronouns. *We saw **a city on a hill** = We saw **it**.*

Object (of verb or preposition) An object is a <u>noun phrase</u> that is required by a verb as part of a <u>verb phrase</u> or by a preposition as part of a <u>prepositional phrase</u>. For example, the verb *fix* requires an object noun phrase in order to make a grammatical verb phrase (*I fixed **the sink***). All prepositions require an object noun phrase to make a grammatical prepositional phrase, for example, *on **the table**; by **the river**; in **the future**.*

Object forms of pronouns Many personal pronouns have a special form when they are used as an <u>object</u> of a verb or preposition. Here are all of the object pronoun forms that are different from their corresponding subject forms: *me, him, her, us, them.* The question word and relative pronoun *who* also has a different form: *whom.*

Parallelism Parallelism refers to a series of two or more elements of the same type joined by a coordinating conjunction—usually *and* but sometimes *or* or *but*; for example, in *You don't have to be **a chemist** or **a psychologist** or **a teacher** to be educated,* there are three parallel <u>noun phrases</u>. Failure to keep parallel elements in the same grammatical form is called <u>faulty parallelism</u>.

Passive The passive is a form of paraphrase that shifts the focus of the <u>sentence</u> away from the <u>subject</u> and onto what was done in the <u>verb phrase</u>. For example, the passive paraphrase of the sentence *John saw Mary* is *Mary **was seen** by John.* The distinctive feature of the passive is the use of some form of *be* as a <u>helping verb</u> (*was* in the example) followed by a verb in the <u>past participle</u> form (*seen* in the example).

Past perfect tense The past perfect tense form consists of *had* (the past tense form of *have*) + a <u>past participle</u> verb form: *They **had gone** home before the sitter called.* The past perfect is used to describe a past action that was completed by the time of a more recent past action. See also <u>perfect tense</u>.

Past tense The past tense form of <u>regular verbs</u> is made by adding *-ed* to the form of the <u>infinitive</u>: *laughed, cried, smiled.* See pages 264–265 for a list of the past tense forms of <u>irregular verbs</u>. The past tense is used to refer to a single action (as opposed to repeated or continual actions) begun and completed in the past. *The Yankees **lost** again last night.*

Perfect tense The perfect tense is formed by a combination of two verbs: the <u>helping verb</u> *have* (in some form) followed by a verb in the <u>past participle</u> form. If *have* is in the <u>past tense</u> form, the combination is called a <u>past perfect</u>. If *have* is in the <u>future tense</u> form, the combination is called a <u>future perfect</u>. If *have* is used in the present tense form, the combination is called a <u>present perfect</u>. The basic meaning of the perfect tense is that the action described by the verb is finished or completed with reference to some later time.

Personal Pronoun There are three types of personal pronouns: (a) a set of first person pronouns that refer to the speaker (*I*, *me*, *mine*; *we*, *us*, *ours*); (b) a set of second person pronouns that refer to the hearer (*you*, *yours*); and (c) a set of third person pronouns that refer to a person or thing that is neither the speaker nor the hearer (*he*, *him*, *his*; *she*, *her*, *hers*; *it*, *its*; *they*, *them*, *theirs*). Third person pronouns can substitute for entire <u>noun phrases</u>. For example, we can replace the subject noun phrase *five friendly firebugs* in the sentence **Five friendly firebugs** *lit up the room* with the third person pronoun *they*; **They** *lit up the room*. Possessive pronouns that modify nouns (*my*, *your*, *his*, *her*, *its*, *their*) are considered <u>possessive adjectives</u>.

Possessive Nouns and pronouns (both personal pronouns and indefinite pronouns) have special possessive forms that are used to modify nouns. The basic meaning of these forms is "possession" or "ownership." For example, in **John's** *book*, the possessive noun *John's* modifies the noun *book* and expresses the idea that the book is owned or possessed by John. See also <u>possessive adjective</u>, <u>possessive indefinite pronoun</u>, and <u>possessive noun</u>.

Possessive adjective When a noun or pronoun is used in its possessive form, the possessive noun or pronoun must "possess" or "own" something. In other words, possessive nouns and pronouns function as adjectives that modify the following noun. For example, in the expressions **John's** *book*, **his** *book*, *and* **someone's** *book*, the possessive noun (*John's*) and pronouns (*his* and *someone's*) all modify the following noun *book*.

Possessive apostrophe <u>Possessive nouns</u> (*John's*) and <u>possessive indefinite pronouns</u> (*someone's*) form their possessive forms by adding an *s* sound. In writing, this "possessive" *s* is spelled with an <u>apostrophe</u> (') in order to distinguish the "possessive" *s* from the plural *s*. Possessive nouns use the possessive apostrophe in two different ways. If the possessive noun is singular, the apostrophe goes inside the *s* (*girl's*), but if the possessive noun is plural, the apostrophe goes outside the *s* (*girls'*). Be sure to distinguish possessive apostrophes from apostrophes used to mark <u>contractions</u>.

Possessive indefinite pronoun The indefinite pronouns ending in *-one* (*anyone*, *everyone*, *no one*, *someone*) and *-body* (*anybody*, *everybody*, *nobody*, *somebody*) have possessive forms spelled *'s*. **Everyone's** *concern*, **someone's** *book*, **anybody's** *locker*, **everybody's** *problem*.

Possessive noun Possessive nouns have two forms: *'s* for singular possessive nouns (*boy's*, *girl's*, *cat's*) and *s'* for plural possessive nouns (*boys'*, *girls'*, *cats'*). Irregular nouns mark possession (whether singular or plural) by adding *'s*: *man's/men's*; *woman's/women's*; *child's/children's*.

Possessive pronoun Possessive pronouns function as adjectives that modify nouns. Possessive pronouns indicate "possession" or "ownership." For example, in **my** *book*, the possessive personal pronoun *my* modifies the noun *book* and indicates that the speaker "owns" or "possesses" the book. There are two kinds of possessive pronouns: <u>possessive personal pronouns</u> and <u>possessive indefinite pronouns</u>.

Possessive personal pronouns   The possessive personal pronouns are *my, your, his, her, its,* and *their.* Possessive personal pronouns differ from possessive nouns and possessive indefinite pronouns in that possessive personal pronouns do not show possession by adding *'s.* See also <u>possessive pronoun</u>.

Predicate   See <u>verb phrase</u>.

Predicate adjective   Predicate adjectives are adjectives that follow the verb *be* (and verbs such as *seem* and *become* that can be paraphrased with *be*): *John is **tall/angry/ upset/interested/interesting.*** A good way to tell predicate adjectives from verbs is to use *very. Very* can be used with most predicate adjectives, but *very* can never be used with verbs. For example in *The doctor is **encouraging,*** *encouraging* is a predicate adjective because we can say *The doctor is **very** encouraging.* However, in *The doctor is **working,*** *working* is not a predicate adjective because we cannot say ** The doctor is **very** working.*

Preposition   Prepositions are words such as *on, by, with, under, of,* and *during.* Prepositions exist only as the heads of <u>prepositional phrases</u>.

Prepositional phrase   Prepositional phrases are phrases consisting of a preposition head + a <u>noun phrase object</u>: *down the street, by Shakespeare, during the night.* Prepositional phrases function either as adverbs (*I got a call **during the night***) or as adjectives (*A man **in my office** called me*).

Present perfect tense   The present perfect tense form consists of *has* or *have* (the present tense forms of *have*) + a <u>past participle</u> verb form: *They **have lived** there for three years.* The present perfect is used to describe actions that began in the past and which continue up to the present time. See also <u>perfect tense</u>.

Present tense   There are two forms of present tense verbs. One form ending in *-s* agrees with singular subjects (for example, *Popeye **loves** spinach*) and third person singular pronouns (for example, *He **loves** spinach*). Another form without the *-s* agrees with plural subjects (for example, *Popeye and Olive Oyl both **love** spinach*) and the third person plural pronoun *they* and with the pronouns *I* and *you.* The meaning of the present tense form is not present time. We use the present tense form for "timeless" events: for habitual actions (*I always **shop** at Safeway*); for repeated actions (*We **go** there every weekend*); or for generalizations (*Life **is** unfair*). If we want to talk about a single, specific action, we almost always use the <u>past tense</u> verb form.

Progressive   The progressive is the name for a verb construction that employs *be* (in some tense form) as a helping verb followed by a verb in the *-ing* form. If *be* is in the present tense form, the construction is called a present progressive (*I **am starting** a new job today*). If *be* is in the past tense form, the construction is called a past progressive (*I **was working** in Chicago then*). If *be* is in the future tense form, the construction is called a future progressive (*I **will be working** late tonight*). The progressive is used to refer to actions that are ongoing at the time the sentence refers to. For example, the present progressive refers to action that is taking place now. Compare with the present tense, which almost never means "now."

Pronoun Pronouns (along with nouns) are the head words of noun phrases. Pronouns play the normal noun phrase roles: subjects (for example, **You** look great), objects of verbs (for example, Ralph heard **me**), and objects of prepositions (for example, The book is on **it**). The two main types of pronouns discussed in this book are personal pronouns (for example, I, you, him) and indefinite pronouns (for example, somebody, most, all).

Proper noun Proper nouns are the names of individual people (Ms. Rudolph, Santa Claus, George Washington) and places (New York, Canada, Oregon). Proper nouns are spelled with a capital letter. See also common noun.

Quotation See indirect quotation and direct quotation.

Regular verb Regular verbs form both their past tense and past participle tense by adding -ed to the infinitive (or dictionary) form, as in smiled, worked, wished.

Relative clause A relative clause is a dependent clause used as a noun modifier. For example, in The woman **who lives next door** called about the cat, the relative clause is who lives next door. This relative clause modifies the noun woman. Relative clauses begin with relative pronouns (who in this example). The two types of relative clauses differ in the way that they affect the meaning of the noun they modify: restrictive clauses and nonrestrictive clauses. Relative clauses are also called adjective clauses.

Relative pronoun Relative pronouns begin relative clauses. The relative pronouns are who, whom, whose, which, and that. Relative pronouns must refer to the noun in the independent clause that the relative clause modifies. For example, in I sprayed the weeds **that** are growing along the driveway, the relative pronoun that refers to weeds.

Restrictive clause A restrictive clause is a kind of relative clause. Relative clauses modify nouns in two different ways. A restrictive relative clause (as opposed to a nonrestrictive clause) changes the meaning of the noun it modifies. For example, in Students **who are not registered** may not attend the class, the relative clause who are not registered restricts (and thereby changes) the meaning of the noun students to "just those students who are not registered." The implication is that only students who are registered may attend the class. Notice that restrictive clauses are not separated from the nouns they modify by commas. Compare with nonrestrictive clause.

Run-on sentence Here this term refers to various kinds of incorrectly punctuated combinations of two (or more) independent clauses within a single sentence. Two independent clauses can be used in the same sentence if they are joined by (a) a comma and a coordinating conjunction (I laughed, **and** I cried), or (b) a semicolon (I laughed; I cried). However, if the two independent clauses are joined together without adequate punctuation, the result is called a run-on sentence. There are two types of run-on sentences. (a) If the two independent clauses are joined with no punctuation at all, the result is called a <u>fused sentence</u> (for example, *I laughed I cried*). (b) If the two independent clauses are joined with a comma (without a coordinating conjunction), the result is called a <u>comma splice</u> (for example, *I laughed, I cried*).

Sentence   A sentence is an <u>independent clause</u> punctuated with a period, exclamation mark, or question mark. Every sentence must contain at least one independent clause.

Sentence fragment   A sentence fragment is any group of words or phrases punctuated with a period or question mark that is not an <u>independent clause</u>. A good test for identifying sentence fragments is to see if you can turn them into a question that can be answered by "yes" or "no." Only independent clauses can be turned into a question that can be answered "yes" or "no." For example, we can tell that * *No matter what you think* is a sentence fragment because it cannot be turned into a question that we can answer "yes" or "no."

Sexist pronoun use   Using a masculine pronoun (*he/him/his*) to refer to a person whose gender is unknown or whose gender is irrelevant can constitute a sexist pronoun use. For example, *Find a doctor and ask **him** to come quickly!* is sexist because the use of the masculine pronoun *he* implies that doctors are naturally men and that women are not doctors.

Subject   The subject of a sentence is the head of the <u>subject noun phrase</u>. Within the subject noun phrase, the head noun or pronoun is the first (or left-most) noun or pronoun. For example, in **One** *of the elderly alligators just* **loves** *Captain Hook*, the subject is the indefinite pronoun *one*. The verb *loves* agrees with the subject *one*, not with the nearer noun *alligators*, which is part of a prepositional phrase that modifies the subject. The subject is sometimes called the simple subject to distinguish the subject noun or pronoun from the entire subject noun phrase.

Subject noun phrase   The subject noun phrase can be identified by asking a "who" or "what" question. For example, the "who/what" question for the sentence *One of the elderly alligators just loves Captain Hook* is **Who** *just loves Captain Hook?* The answer, *one of the elderly alligators*, is the subject noun phrase. The subject noun phrase is sometimes called the complete subject to distinguish the entire subject noun phrase from the head noun or pronoun.

Subject-verb agreement   In a <u>clause</u>, the subject noun and the verb must agree with each other in form. For example, compare the following independent clauses: *This* **bird looks** *yellow. These* **birds look** *brown.* In the first sentence, the verb *looks* agrees with the singular subject *bird*. In the second sentence, *look* agrees with the plural subject *birds*.

Subordinate clause   In this book, this term refers only to a <u>dependent clause</u> beginning with a <u>subordinating conjunction</u>. (The term subordinate clause can be used more generally to refer to any kind of dependent clause.) For example, in *We* *opened the windows **because it was getting stuffy,*** the subordinate clause is **because it was getting stuffy.** Subordinate clauses function as adverbs that answer adverb questions such as *when, where,* and *why.* For example, we could ask of the example sentence, *Why did you open the windows?* and get back the subordinate clause *Because it was getting stuffy* as the answer.

Subordinating conjunction Subordinating conjunctions begin subordinate clauses. Some typical subordinating conjunctions are *before, when, where, as, because, if,* and *although.* Unlike conjunctive adverbs, subordinating conjunctions cannot move around inside their clause. However, clauses beginning with subordinating conjunctions can be moved in front of the independent clause. That is, we can change *We opened the windows **because it was getting stuffy*** to ***Because it was getting stuffy,*** *we opened the windows.* (Notice the comma.)

Tense This term has two different meanings. In this book, the main use of *tense* is to refer to the form of a verb (as opposed to its meaning). For example, *the present **tense** of verbs can end in -s; or the regular past **tense** ends in -ed.* The other meaning of "tense" is time: past time; present time; future time. A problem of the two meanings of "tense" is that sometimes they conflict with each other. The basic meaning of the present tense is "timeless" generalizations; for example, the verb *be* in *Two plus two **is** four* is in the present tense form *is,* but the meaning of the present tense form has nothing to do with the meaning of present time: two plus two is always four, not just at the present time.

Verb A verb is a word that changes form to show tense. Verbs have a past tense form (ending in -ed if the verb is regular), and verbs can be used to show future time by being used in combination with *will* (for example, *will go; will start; will stop*). There are two kinds of verbs: main verbs and helping verbs. The main verb is the head of a verb phrase. If a verb phrase contains only one verb, then that verb is automatically the head or main verb. Main verbs can be preceded by one or more helping verbs (for example, ***can be*** *going;* ***might have been*** *working;* ***had*** *seen*). In a string of verbs, the main verb is always the last (or right-most) verb in the string.

A simple test to see if a word is a verb is to see if you can change the word into a past tense by adding -ed to it or change it into a future tense by putting *will* in front of it. For example, *fail* and *failure* are related words. We can tell that *fail* is a verb by changing it into the past tense form *failed* or into a future by adding *will—will fail.* When we try these two tests on *failure,* the results are ungrammatical: * *failured/will failure,* proving that *failure* is not a verb. See also verb phrase.

Verb phrase A verb phrase consists of a main verb (which functions as the head of the verb phrase) together with helping verbs (if any), the complement of the verb (if any), and adverb modifiers (if any). For example, in *The plumber **will fix the sink tomorrow,*** the verb phrase is *will fix the sink tomorrow.* The main verb is *fix.* *Will* is a helping verb. *The sink* is a noun phrase that is required by the verb *fix* as its complement. *Tomorrow* is an optional adverb modifier.

Verb tense See tense.

APPENDIX II

Using a Dictionary

BY LYNN HARTY

The great-great-grandparent of our modern English language dictionaries, entitled *A Table Alphabeticall*, was compiled by Robert Cawdrey in 1604. Since that time, generations of dictionary users have puzzled over such questions as, "What does 'ə' stand for?" and "Why can't I find the word I'm looking for in this dictionary?" If you have ever had difficulty using a dictionary, recognizing the following statements as myths may prove helpful.

Myth 1: Each Word in the Dictionary Has Only One Meaning

Words tend to be very flexible units of meaning; any given word might have several definitions. Often, a word's definitions are similar; occasionally, its definitions are quite different. Consider the definitions of the word *myth*:

1.   a traditional story serving to explain some phenomenon, custom;

2.   mythology (the study of myths);

3.   any fictitious (untrue or "made up") story, person, or thing.

In the dictionary, any word with more than one meaning will have its various meanings displayed in a numbered sequence, starting with the most common definition. When you saw the word "myth" in the first paragraph, perhaps you thought of the early American myth of Johnny Appleseed—the person who wore a pot upside down on his head and wandered across America, planting apple seeds as he went. The Johnny Appleseed myth provides one explanation of how apple trees first appeared throughout the country. However, the definition that goes with the word *myth* in this piece of writing is the third: any fictitious story, person, or *thing* . . . in this instance, untrue statements about dictionaries and using dictionaries. Another feature of definitions is the fact that they may vary from dictionary to dictionary. Also, words undergo changes in meaning over the course of time. For many years, "hardware" was a widely used expression for the nails, screws, hammers, etc., that could be purchased at—where else? The local hardware store. Although hardware is still used when referring to home repair items, the word has gradually become an expression for the mechanical components—printers, keyboards, circuitry—of computers.

Myth 2: Everybody Knows How to Use a Dictionary

People often assume that everybody just *knows* how to do certain tasks—studying well for a test, for example, or writing the perfect essay in a single try. However, just like studying, writing, and many other activities, using the dictionary effectively takes practice. The following analysis of a typical dictionary entry should help you to use your dictionary more efficiently.

> **xe•rog•ra•phy** (zir äg´ rə *fee*) **n.** [<Gr *xeros*, dry + GRAPHY] a process for copying printed material, etc., by the action of light on an electrically charged surface—xe•ro•graph•ic [zir o graf´ ik] *adj.*

Pronunciations

The first part of this sample entry is the word itself, *xerography*, broken into syllables (separate units of sound). The pronunciation (or phonetics) of the word comes next. As you can see, special symbols such as the schwa (ə, which is pronounced "uh") are used to help you pronounce the word correctly. The pronunciation entry also includes an accent mark (´) that tells you which syllable to stress. Thus, xerography is pronounced zir-**ah**-gruh-fee instead of zer-o-**graf**-ee. Dictionaries always include usage guides that explain pronunciation symbols and abbreviations. Look for this guide in the front or the back of your dictionary.

Parts of Speech

The part of speech label follows the pronunciation of xerography. In this case, it's **n.**, which stands for "noun." This is logical because xerography is a process or activity—a *thing*, in other words—and a noun is a word for a person, place, or thing. Words can often be used as various parts of speech with little or no change. Think about the many ways to use the word **run,** for example. "Run" might be a noun that means race, as in a ten-kilometer **run**, or it could just as easily be an action verb, as in "Olympic athletes usually **run** five miles every day to improve their strength and stamina." Note that *xerographic*, an adjective (*adj.*), is listed at the end of the sample dictionary entry.

Word Origins

The etymology, or specific history of the word *xerography*, is contained in the square brackets. In this sample, *xerography* comes from the Greek word *xeros*, which means "dry," combined with *graphy*, which means "a process or method of writing or representing graphically" as an ending or suffix. Once again, check your dictionary's usage guide for any abbreviations that are unfamiliar to you. Here, for example, **Gr.** means "Greek."

Other Information

The etymology of xerography is followed by its single definition. A typical dictionary entry might also include additional information such as various spellings of a word (as in *theater* and *theatre*); inflected forms, which are unusual versions of a word (as in *index* and its plural, *indices*); or usage lables for nonstandard words (as in *dude*, which is slang for "man" or "boy").

Myth 3: If I Can't Find the Word I'm Looking for, It's Not in the Dictionary

Virtually all of us have at some time concluded, when looking for a word in a dictionary, that "It's not in there," because we can't find the word we seek. Consider the possibility that you are unable to find "your" word because you are spelling it incorrectly. This idea may remind you of a common lament: "How can I look up the word to see how it's spelled when I can't spell it in the first place?" Don't give up; the following strategies might help you to find that elusive word.

1.   Begin with the idea that you are probably spelling the first few letters of the word incorrectly. Here's why: let's say that you are trying to spell the word *hygiene*, which you are spelling *hijean*. Naturally, you would look under the "hi's," which are pages away from the "hy's" in your dictionary. If you can spell the first part of your word correctly, you stand a good chance of finding it.

2. In order to spell the first part of *hygiene* (or any other word) correctly, try substituting vowels. For example, if you think that *hygiene* begins with *hi* and you try *hy* instead, you will find the word you want. Vowels and vowel combinations are very unpredictable in written English: the sound "ee," for example, might be spelled with an *e*, an *i*, *ee*, *ea*, *ae*, *ei*, or *ie*. Often, the key to correct spelling is figuring out the vowels—*a, e, i, o, u, y*—and combinations of vowels.

3. If substituting vowels fails to produce the word you want, try substituting consonants. An "f" sound might be spelled with *v* or *ph*; a "t" sound might be spelled with a *d*. Think about the words *farm, pharmacy,* and *varmint* (an objectionable person or animal). Although they are spelled with different consonants, each begins with a nearly identical "f" sound. Another strategy to use is doubling consonants that you think are singular or looking for single consonants in place of ones that you think should be doubled. Let's look at the word *recommendation*. How is this word actually spelled? Recomendation? Recommendation? Reccomendation? Reccommendation? Using the single/double consonant strategy will enable you to find this word (which really is spelled with one *c* and two *m*'s) in your dictionary.

✔ Note:

Occasionally, you won't be able to find a particular word in the dictionary because it truly isn't there. There are two main reasons for a word's exclusion:

1. The dictionary is too small.

2. The dictionary is too old.

Pocket dictionaries have become popular with students, and rightly so, because of their compact size and usefulness as quick reference tools. Because they are so compact, however, pocket dictionaries have room only for the most frequently used words in the English language. You would be able to find the everyday word *arthritis* (an inflammation of the joints) in a pocket dictionary; however, an unusual word such as *spondylitis* (an inflammation of the vertebrae) would not be included.

A common assumption about language—any language—is that it always stays the same. In fact, language is a very dynamic method of communication: words become more or less popular; new words are coined or created as needed; old words become obsolete and disappear or change meanings. For example, the traditional definitions of the word *feedback* are:

1. the transfer of part of the output back to the input, as of electricity or information (for example, static coming out of a public address system);

2. a response.

As you know, however, feedback has also come to mean making suggestions about how a piece of writing might be changed and strengthened. Dictionaries are constantly revised and updated to reflect language's changing nature. If your dictionary is more than ten years old, you might consult a newer dictionary for the word you are seeking; you will find your dictionary's date of publication on the back of its title page.

Myth 4: I'll Understand What a Word Means after I Read Its Definition

Not necessarily. Let's go back to the word xerography. Having read the word's definition, you might think, "Oh! Xerography is the formal term for photocopying." Consider, however, the following word and its definition.:

mag•nan•i•mous (mag nan' ə məs) **adj.** [< L *magnus*, great + *animus*, soul] rising above pettiness

As you can see, the key word in the definition of magnanimous is "pettiness." If you are unsure of the meaning of "pettiness," look it up next.

pet•ti•ness (pet' ē nəs) **n.** [< OFr *petit*] the quality of small mindedness or meanness

If you put the two definitions together, you can see that *magnanimous* might describe someone (or something, as in a magnanimous gesture) who is noble, not small-minded. Sometimes a dictionary user must look up several words in order to get a clear understanding of the word that he or she first looked up.

If you remember these common myths when you use your dictionary, you should find the process much easier. Some people even enjoy browsing through their favorite dictionary in search of new or unusual words. With practice you will become an expert at using the dictionary.

Dictionary definitions in this appendix were provided by *Webster's Vest Pocket Dictionary*, *Webster's New World Dictionary*, and *Webster's Third New International Dictionary*.

APPENDIX III

Easily Confused Words

accept (verb: *to receive*); **except** (preposition: *not including*)

Please **accept** my apologies.
Everybody finished the test **except** Fred.

adapt (verb: *to modify*); **adopt** (verb: *to take*)

We **adapted** the suggestion to fit our requirements.
We **adopted** a new baby.

advice (noun: *a suggestion*); **advise** (verb: *to give suggestions to someone*)

Scrooge gave Tiny Tim some good **advice.**
Scrooge **advised** him to look both ways before crossing the street.

affect (verb: *to influence someone or something*); **effect** (noun: *the result of something*)

The results of the election will **affect** everyone.
The news produced a visible **effect** on Scrooge.

all ready (adjective: *completely ready*); **already** (adverb: *just now*)

We are **all ready** to go.
They have left **already.**

all together (adverb: *in unison*); **altogether** (adverb: *completely*)

Let's get it **all together** now.
They were not **altogether** wrong.

allusion (noun: *a reference to something*); **illusion** (noun: *a false appearance or hoax*)

He made an **allusion** to what happened last year.
The promised benefits turned out to be an **illusion.**

altar (noun: *a part of a church*); **alter** (verb: *to change something*)

The priest stands in front of the **altar.**
He decided to **alter** his position on the issue.

ante- (prefix: *before*); **anti-** (prefix: *against*)

The **ante-bellum** South is the South before the Civil War.
They supported the **antipoverty** program.

any way (noun: *some way to do something*); **anyway** (adverb: *even so*)

We will try **any way** that we think might work.
We still wanted to do it **anyway.**

capital (noun: *the seat of government; money*); **capitol** (noun: *a statehouse building*)

The **capital** of California is Sacramento. We raised the **capital** through a bond issue.
We took their pictures on the steps of the **capitol.**

cite (verb: *to refer to a reference or authority*); **site** (noun: *the location of something*)

He **cited** all the important facts in his paper.
The **site** of the new campus will be decided by the legislature.

complement (noun: *something that accompanies something else*; verb: *complete or to go together with*); **compliment** (noun: *praise*)

The object is the **complement** of a transitive verb; The pearls **complement** her dress.
Everyone likes to receive a **compliment** on his or her work.

conscience (noun: *the feeling of right or wrong*); **conscious** (adjective: *aware*)

He had a guilty **conscience** about what he did.
He was very **conscious** of his responsibilities.

council (noun: *a committee*); **counsel** (verb: *to give advice*; noun: *an attorney or adviser*)

The **council** will vote on the matter after the election.
Bugsy's lawyers **counseled** him to plead guilty. He wanted to see his **counsel.**

credible (adjective: *believable*); **creditable** (adjective: *worthy of praise*)

His testimony impressed the jury as being quite **credible.**
The president's firm action during a time of crisis is **creditable.**

desert (noun: *barren area*; verb: *to abandon someone or something*); **dessert** (noun: *last course in a meal*)

We hiked into the **desert.** John's date **deserted** him at the party.
For **dessert,** we have cake and ice cream.

discreet (adjective: *prudent*); **discrete** (adjective: *easy to tell apart*)

Diplomats must be very **discreet** about what they say.
Each layer of sandstone was marked by **discrete** bands of color.

disinterested (adjective: *impartial*); **uninterested** (adjective: *having no interest in*)

The dispute was referred to a **disinterested** third party to judge.
The children were **uninterested** in the movie.

eminent (adjective: *prominent*); **imminent** (adjective: *about to happen*)

She is an **eminent** expert in her field.
The reporters were all waiting for the **imminent** announcement.

every day (adverb phrase: *each day*); **everyday** (adjective: *normal*)

They come here **every day** for lunch.
It is an **everyday** occurrence.

every one (pronoun: *each one of a group*); **everyone** (pronoun: *everybody*)

We had to pick out **every one** of the spoiled apples.
Everyone can come.

foreword (noun: *preface of a book*); **forward** (adverb: *ahead*)

Read the **foreword** and the first chapter for Monday's class.
During the night, the soldiers had moved **forward.**

it's (contraction of *it is*); **its** (possessive pronoun)

It's a nice day.
The company is rethinking **its** marketing strategies.

later (adverb: *at a later time*); **latter** (adjective: *last one mentioned*)

I'll come back **later.**
We picked the **latter** alternative.

lay (transitive verb: *to place an object somewhere*); **lie** (intransitive verb: *to recline*); **lie** (verb: *to tell a lie*) (See the vocabulary exercise in Chapter 10 on page 414–415 for a detailed discussion of the difference between **lay** and **lie.**)

He **laid** his cards on the table. (principle parts: **lay, laid, have laid**)
The cats **lay** in the sun this morning. (principal parts: **lie, lay, have lain**)
The salesman **lied** about the car's mileage. (principal parts: **lie, lied, have lied**)

loose (adjective: *slack*); **lose** (verb: *to mislay*)

The boards on the deck are getting **loose.**
Don't **lose** the map!

may be (verb phrase); **maybe** (adverb: *perhaps*)

I **may be** late tonight.
Maybe we can stop for something to eat.

passed (past tense verb: *went by*); **past** (adjective; *previous*)

We just **passed** our exit.
Shirley thought she had been a female wrestler in a **past** life.

peace (noun: *tranquility*); **piece** (noun: *a part of something*)

A great feeling of **peace** came over me.
The FBI agent ordered another **piece** of cherry pie.

persecute (verb: *to pick on someone*); **prosecute** (verb: *to bring someone to trial*)

They always **persecuted** anyone who wasn't a member of their group.
The District Attorney decided to **prosecute** Bugsy.

precede (verb: *to go in front of someone or something*); **proceed** (verb: *to advance*)

A rapid drop in air pressure **preceded** the storm front.
The storm **proceeded** up the coast.

principal (noun: *main thing, head person, or money*; adjective: *most important*); **principle** (noun: *a rule or law*)

The **princip<u>al</u>** is your <u>pal</u>. We listed the **principal** reasons for the conflict.
Even politicians have their **principles.**

raise (transitive verb: *to lift up something*); **rise** (intransitive verb: *to go upward*) (See the vocabulary exercise in Chapter 10 on pages 415–416 for a detailed discussion of the difference between **raise** and **rise.**)

We **raised** the beam to the ceiling. (principal parts: **raise, raised, have raised**)
Smoke **rose** from the chimney. (principal parts: **rise, rose, have risen**)

set (transitive verb: *to place an object somewhere*); **sit** (intransitive verb: *to be seated*) (See the vocabulary exercise in Chapter 10 on page 415 for a detailed discussion of the difference between **set** and **sit.**)

Just **set** the books on the floor. (principal parts: **set, set, have set**)
Please **sit** down. (principal parts: **sit, sat, have sat**)

stationary (adjective: *still, unmoving*); **stationery** (noun: *paper*)

His car struck several **stationary** objects.
We bought our office supplies at a **stationery** store.

than (comparison); **then** (adverb: *next*)

He is taller **than** his father.
I had dinner, and **then** I did my homework.

their (possessive pronoun); **there** (adverb: *that place* or *something exists*); **they're** (contraction of *they are*)

They wanted me to return **their** books.
There are several problems with this answer.
They're in the back.

to (preposition: *toward*); **too** (adverb: *also, excessively*)

I went back **to** the coffee shop.
I got there **too** late.

use (verb: *to utilize*); **used** (adjective: *accustomed to*)

Please **use** the computer if you want to.
I am not **used** to this kind of keyboard.

weather (noun: *the state of the atmosphere*); **whether** (conjunction: *if*)

What will the **weather** be like tomorrow?
I don't know **whether** I should go.

who's (contraction of *who is*); **whose** (possessive relative pronoun)

Who's going to be there?
Whose gloves are on the table?

you're (contraction of *you are*); **your** (possessive pronoun)

You're next.
Your coat is in the closet.

INDEX

Accept, 543
Acknowledging other perspectives
  drafting to acknowledge other perspectives, 472–478
  revising to acknowledge other perspectives, 478–494
Adapt, 543
Adjective, 21–22
Adopt, 543
Adverb, 22–23
Advice, 543
Advise, 543
Affect, 543
All ready, 543
All together, 543
Allen, Rebecca, 164
Allusion, 543
Already, 543
Altar, 544
Alter, 544
Altogether, 543
Anderson, T. H., 377
Ante-, 544
Anti-, 544
Any way, 544
Anyway, 544
Aphorisms, 124
Apostrophe errors
  apostrophes in contractions, 441–444
  apostrophes in time expressions, 455–457
  possessive apostrophes
    possessive indefinite pronouns, 451–453
    possessive nouns, 444–451
Applebee, A. N., 377
Armbruster, B. B., 377
Aronson, Elliot, 385

Articles in the library, 420–422
Atrophy, 526
Audience. *See* Essay form
Axsom, D., 391

Baxter, Neale, 270
Bergen County Technical Schools District, 276
Bibliography, 425–427. *See also* Published sources
Breckler, S. J., 391
Breland, H. M., 377

Cacioppo, J. T., 391
Capital, 544
Capitol, 544
"Careers 101: Occupational Education in Community Colleges," 270–278
Categorical statements and qualifiers, 184–185
Cawdrey, Robert, 538
Chaiken, S., 391
Citation. *See* Published sources
Cite, 544
Clarity and completeness of information
  drafting for clarity and completeness of information, 283–288
  revising for clarity and completeness of information, 288–295
Clause
  defined, 27
  dependent clause, 29
  independent clause, 28–29
College language skills, 4
"Collision on a Country Road," 42–46
Communication situation, 88

Compare and contrast, 333–335
Complement, 544
Compliment, 544
Compound, 30
Conscience, 544
Conscious, 544
"Consumer Communication," 87–90
Consumer letters
    consumer complaint, 82–83
    consumer praise, 83
    consumer request, 83
    consumer suggestion, 83
Cook, Michele, 464
Coordinating conjunction, 30
Council, 544
Counsel, 544
Credible, 544
Creditable, 544
Critical thinking, 462
Crowfoot, 320
Cultural differences
    drafting with details and examples of posi-
        tive cultural or familiar differences,
        328–335
    reading about, 316–317

Desert, 544
Dessert, 544
Details of emotion
    drafting for details of emotion, 134–138
    reading for details of emotion, 124–130
    revising for details of emotion, 138–148
Details of place
    drafting with specific details, 50–56
    reading about details of place, 38–47
    revising for details of place, 57–65
Dictionary, using a, 538–542
Discreet, 545
Discrete, 545
Disinterested, 545

Easily confused words, 543–547
East San Gabriel Valley Regional Occupa-
    tional Program, 278
Effect, 543
Elder, D. C., 87
Eminent, 545
Essay exams
    essay-exam writing process

analyzing the exam question, 374–375
dealing with constraints, 375–377
facing future exams, 377
learning and recalling course informa-
    tion, 372–373
reading about, 368–379
strategy, 370
studying for and writing an essay exam,
    384–392
understanding essay exam prompts and
    organizing your response, 382–384
Essay form, 223–224
Every day, 545
Every one, 545
Everyday, 545
Everyone, 545
Except, 543

Faulty parallelism
    defined, 494–495
    elements that are different parts of speech,
        499–503
    faulty verb form parallelism
        confusing infinitives and gerunds, 505–
            508
        using *to* inconsistently with parallel in-
            finitives, 504–505
    parallelism stack, 495–497
Fierman, J., 391
Final editing strategies, 520–523
Five-paragraph essay form, 228–230
Focus. *See* Essay form
Foreword, 545
Forward, 545
Four Guns, 318
"Four Guns' Speech," 318–319
Fragment. *See* Sentence fragment
Friend, Christy, 370

Glossary of grammar terms, 527–537
Grammar terms. *See* Glossary of grammar
    terms
Greater Lowell Regional Vocational Techni-
    cal School, 276
Greenwald, A. G., 391

Harty, Lynn, 538
Hayes, J. R., 377
Health Journal, 413

Hochschild, Arlie, 167
Hume, S., 391

"I Want a Wife," 171–173
Illusion, 543
Imminent, 545
"Inside the Golden Arches," 214–216
"Invest in Your Children's Future," 173–174
Irving, Virginia, 319
Issue. *See* Essay form.
It's, 545
Its, 545

Jones, R. J., 377

Kiamichi Area Vocational-Technical
    School, 277

Laid. *See* Lay
Lain. *See* Lie
Language skills self-assessment
    other, 12
    reading, 8
    revising and editing, 11
    writing, 10
Later, 545
Latter, 545
Lay, 545
"Learning on the Farm," 466–467
"Learning to Succeed Under Pressure: Essay
    Exam Strategies," 370–377
Leonard, George, 418
Letter format, 102
Libel, 316
Library, 420–422
Lie, 545
"Living Education," 464–465
Longview Community College, 277
Loose, 545
Lose, 545
Louie, Debbie, 320

Mabry, Marcus, 214
Machung, Anne, 167
May be, 545
Maybe, 545
McLuhan, T. C., 320
Meiser, M., 377

MLA Handbook for Writers of Research Papers, 427

Noun, 19–20
Noun phrase, 23–25

Occupational Outlook Quarterly, 269
Oklahoma, University of, 370
Opinion, 472–478. *See also* Essay form

"Packages," 385–390
Parallelism, defined, 494. *See also* Faulty parallelism
Parts of speech. *See* Adjective; Adverb;
    Noun; Prepositional phrase; Pronoun;
    Verb
Passed, 546
Past, 546
Peace, 546
Pearson, P. David, 377
Persecute, 546
Petty, R. E., 391
Phrase, defined, 23. *See also* Noun phrase;
    Prepositional phrase; Verb phrase
Piece, 546
Plagiarism, 423
Popken, R., 377
Positive difference compare and contrast
    grid, 334
Prakanis, Anthony, 385
Pratkanis, A. R., 391
Precede, 546
Prejudice, 316
Preposition. *See* Prepositional phrase
Prepositional phrase, 27
Presenting your opinion, 472–478
Prince Georges Community College, 277
Principal, 546
Principle, 546
Problem and solution essays, 174–183
Proceed, 546
Prompt, 6
Pronoun, 24
Pronoun problems
    indefinite *you*, 357–359
    they with a singular antecedent, 359–363
    unclear pronoun reference
        ambiguous pronoun reference, 351–353
        vague pronoun reference, 353–357

wrong pronoun form in noun compounds, 346–350
Prosecute, 546
Published sources
  guidelines for responsible use of
    paraphrases, 422
    plagiarism, 423
    quotations, 422
  revising to make responsible use of, 425–441
  sample bibliography citations
    complete citation for a book, 427
    complete citation for a popular press (magazine) article, 427
    complete citation for an article, 427
  See also MLA Handbook for Writers of Research Papers

Qualifiers, 184–185

Raise, 546
Raised. See Raise
Relative clause
  choosing between *that* and *which*, 398–400
  choosing between *who* and *whom*, 400–402
  punctuating restrictive and nonrestrictive clauses, 393–398
Research paper, 420–425
Revising for specificity, clarity of purpose, and form, 103–106
Rhetoric, 90
Rose. See Rise

Sat. See sit
"Second Shift: A Candid Look at the Revolution at Home, The," 164–167
Sentence fragment
  defined, 66–67
  types of
    emphatic adverb, 71–73
    -ing word, 74–76
    noun renamers, 76–77
  ways to correct, 67–71
Set, 546
Sexist pronouns, avoiding, 360–361
Simon, H. A., 377
Sit, 546
Site, 544

Slander, 316
Southwestern University, 370
Spokane Community College, 278
Stationary, 546
Stationery, 546
Strategies for final editing. *See* Final editing strategies
Stress management strategies
  reading for stress management strategies, 410–414
  researching and writing about a stress management strategy, 420–425
Subject-verb agreement
  defined, 295–297
  types of subject-verb errors
    "all of the above" error, 303–308
    "lost subject" error, 297–302
    there is/there are error, 309–310
Supporting examples
  drafting with supporting examples, 220–223
  reading for examples that support generalizations, 212–217
  revising for supporting examples, 230–240
Syfers, Judy, 171

Tests and helpful hints for grammar and punctuation
  expansion test to identify contractions, 442–443
  for/of test to identify time expressions, 456–457
  movement test for identifying adverbs that modify verbs, 22–23
  movement tests for distinguishing subordinating conjunctions and conjunctive adverbs, 204–207
  parallelism stack to identify parallel elements, 495–498
  personal pronoun test to distinguish *who* and *whom*, 401–402
  plural pronoun substitution test for pronouns in compound noun phrases, 348–350
  pronoun substitution test for identifying noun phrases, 24–25
  strip search test for "lost subject", 298–302
  the test for identifying common nouns, 20

Tests and helpful hints for grammar and
punctuation (*continued*)
very test for identifying predicate adjectives, 21–22
what do test for identifying verb phrases,
26
who/what question test to identify restrictive and nonrestrictive relative clauses,
395–397
who/what test for identifying subject noun
phrases, 27–28
whose test to identify possessive nouns and
indefinite pronouns, 446–453
will test for identifying verbs, 20–21
yes/no test:
for identifying complete sentences,
149–151
for identifying independent clauses, 29
for identifying run-on sentences, 108–
111
for identifying sentence fragments, 67
Than, 546
Their, 547
Then, 546
There, 547
They're, 547
Thief River Falls Technical College, 277
"Time Peace," 320–323
"Tips for Reducing Stress," 412–413
To, 547
Too, 547
Transitions, revising by adding, 336–346
Trinkle, Randall, 466
Two-income families, 162–168

U.S. Department of Health and Human Ser-
vices, 391
U.S. Department of Labor, Bureau of Labor
Statistics, 269
Uninterested, 545
Use, 547
Used, 547

Valencia Community College, 277
Verb phrase, 25–26
Verb, 20–21
"View from the Plateau, The," 418–419
Vocabulary building
-*ee* and -*or* pairs, 279–280

-*ic*, 380–382
-*ify* and -*ication*, 169–170
-*ive* , 92–93
causative/noncausative verb pairs: *lay/lie*;
set/sit; raise/rise, 414–415
changing *d* in verbs to *s* in nouns, 282
cross, 131–132
dis-, 325–326
domus, 324–325
en- and -*ment*, 468–469
faith, 130–131
form, 470
in-, 93
Latin numbers, 169
Latin phrases, 217–218
note, 91
noun/verb stress shifts, 280–281
occupational terms ending in -*er*, -*ist*, and
-*ian*
post- , 47
prior/primus, 326–327
re-, 379
specere, 471
traction, 132–133
trans-, 48
tri-, 168
word connotations, 49

Walton, Anthony, 126
Washington Water Power Gazette, The, 173
Weather, 547
Weber State College, 278
Whether, 547
Who's, 547
Whose, 547
Wissler, Clark, 319
Words
defining, 538
easily confused words, 543–547
origins, 540
"World According to Claude, The," 126–
129

Yates, S., 391
You're, 547
Your, 547

Ziegler, Edward, 42